AN INTRODUCTION TO
ASTRO▲PSYCHOLOGY

A Synthesis of Modern Astrology & Depth Psychology

Other books by Glenn Perry

The Shadow in the Horoscope
Five Essays on Jung's Concept of the Shadow

Mapping the Landscape of the Soul
Inside Psychological Astrology

Depth Analysis of the Natal Chart
Advanced Therapeutic Astrology

From Royalty to Revolution
The Sun Uranus Relationship

Stealing Fire from the Gods
New Directions in Astrological Research

Issues & Ethics
In the Profession of Astrology

From Ancient to Postmodern Astrology
An Evolution of Ideas, Techniques & Perspectives

An Introduction to
Astro▲Psychology

A Synthesis of Modern Astrology & Depth Psychology

Glenn Perry

AAP Press

East Hampton, CT • www.aaperry.com

ISBN 10: 061561602X
ISBN-13: 9780615616025

For my father

CONTENTS

TABLE OF FIGURES

Preface

It is perhaps fitting that a book on growth oriented astrology should reflect the evolution of my thinking about astrology itself. Like strata in an archaeological dig, the very first version of this book served as my Master's Thesis at Lone Mountain College in San Francisco, which I attended from 1976 through 1978. I subsequently developed it into a manual for my students. From there, it gradually expanded and was refined in accordance with my thinking about the subject. It would not be inaccurate to say that *Introduction to AstroPsychology* has been thirty years in the making.

The central ideas of the text had their genesis in classes with my mentor, Richard Idemon, who was a brilliant, world renowned astrologer teaching in the San Francisco Bay Area from the late sixties until his death in 1987. During the entire twelve year period that I knew Richard, I was also attending various schools and training programs to earn my Masters and Doctoral degrees in psychology. To gain licensure as a psychotherapist necessitated that I graduate from an appropriate program with all the requisite courses in personality theory, development, psychopathology, counseling techniques, ethics, and the like. But, all the while, astrology remained my first love.

I received my license in 1979 and started private practice at that time; however, I continued my education at Saybrook Institute throughout the 1980's where I majored in consciousness studies and general systems theory under the tutelage of Stanley Krippner. I also continued taking classes with Richard outside the framework of my doctoral program. As I moved back and forth between two worlds—astrology and psychology—I felt like a secret agent infiltrating the academic sphere to gather information that I could use to empower astrology in its efforts to gain legitimacy.

My passion for study was not merely about enhancing astrology's legitimacy, of course; it was also about cross-fertilization of the two fields. To my delight, I discovered that astrology was sufficiently broad that it could be integrated in one form or another with all my college courses. I am especially grateful to Lone Mountain College and Saybrook Institute that they both allowed me to do so.

Very often I would learn something in astrology that clarified and deepened a corollary psychological concept. For example, Richard might be discussing the chart of a famous person with a known propensity for depression, explaining how for *that* individual it correlated to a specific configuration involving multiple planetary functions in conflict. Whereas psychology could describe the generic symptoms of depression and speculate that it was caused by environmental deficits or a genetic predisposition, astrology revealed the intrapsychic dynamics of depression at an individual level with a startling clarity.

The situation also applied in reverse; a theory from one of my psych courses would clarify a comparatively fuzzy astrological idea and thereby catapult my thinking in entirely new directions. This was especially true in developmental psychology, which substantiated transits and progressions while extending their meanings in ways that went far beyond interpretations I might find in astrological texts. It gradually dawned on me that both fields were constrained by certain limitations of view and could benefit immeasurably from one another.

As a psychotherapist, I had the good fortune of being able to test what I was learning by observing individuals, couples, and families that struggled with real problems over significant durations of time. One of the limitations that afflict the world of astrology is that most of us work with clients on a very limited basis, seeing them only once or sporadically as they come in for periodic updates. The very nature of the relationship makes it difficult for astrologers to know their clients on a deeper level, test whether presuppositions derived from the chart are truly accurate and useful, or witness how people change and grow over time.

Accordingly, it is to my clients that I owe the deepest debt of gratitude. This book is largely the result of what I learned from Richard combined with my courses in graduate school, but it was work with clients over the last thirty years that melded what was purely theoretical into a practical tool forged, tested and refined in the furnace of psychotherapy.

Introduction to AstroPsychology, as the title attests, is an introduction to the topic. While the book is entirely suitable for beginners, it is also guaranteed to stretch and sharpen the thinking of experienced astrologers. You will find no prefabricated, ready-made interpretations pertaining to planets in sign, house, or aspect in these pages. Rather, readers are instructed how to understand the implicit syntax of astrology so that they can confidently construct accurate, precise, and useful interpretations on their own. Not only does the book define in crisp, psychologically relevant terms the underlying meanings of signs, planets, houses, aspects, and dispositorships, it provides clear rules for combining these factors in progressively more sophisticated ways.

One cannot rely upon astrological cookbooks when working with actual clients. This makes knowing rules of chart synthesis especially important. Rules also help strengthen the astrologer's capacity to think more critically about interpretations that are offered in textbooks. Like any other field, astrology evolves; yet, because the divine art has been shut out of academia for the past four centuries, practitioners have not had the benefit of learning research and critical thinking skills applied specifically to astrology. Accordingly, due to a general lack of academic rigor, a significant amount of sloppiness and archaic thinking permeates the field. With no means for separating the proverbial wheat from the chaff, questionable ideas that have accumulated from past centuries are being passed on to succeeding generations.

This book in part seeks to remedy that deficiency. Its primary strengths can be summarized in three words: clarity, structure, and precision. My fervent hope is that explication of the formal structure of astrology as a language can restrain the temptation, to which our scientifically still-immature field is so susceptible, to find causes that are too simple for complicated conditions. While the approach is conservative in that I stick to fundamentals, it is also progressive in that I am willing to question archaic concepts and offer new ideas in their stead.

~Glenn Perry
Haddam Neck, CT
May 9, 2012

Chapter One

Introduction

OVERVIEW OF MAIN THESIS

A book on AstroPsychology should begin with a brief history of the term. AstroPsychology is a branch of psychological astrology, which began at the turn of the 20th century with the work of Alan Leo, Marc Edmund Jones, and Dane Rudhyar. The term *Astro-Psychology* was in use as far back as the 1970's by my own mentor, Richard Idemon, who was practicing at the same time as the Swiss astrologer, Bruno Huber, who popularized the term in Europe. My work can be seen as an offshoot of Richard's, though I have little in common with Huber.

AstroPsychology can be distinguished from psychological astrology by virtue of several unique features. Before detailing these, it might be useful to review its more generic parent, which itself is a sub-discipline within the more encompassing field of astrology. On the face of it, psychological astrology can simply be defined as a synthesis of psychology and astrology. But it is much more than that. Each discipline—astrology and psychology—is radically transformed and empowered by its marriage to the other. Indeed, there are so many correlations and possibilities for cross-fertilization that one could easily spend an entire lifetime exploring the connection.

In many ways, astrology was the first psychology in that it constituted an early means for understanding human nature. Rooted in the observation that cosmos mirrors the earthly realm, the ancients systematically observed how the nature and cycles of the planets corresponded to the nature and experiences of human beings. Prior to the 20th century, however, there was little understanding of the human psyche as such. Our subjective interior was more of a black box—a dark, impenetrable container of impulses, thoughts and feelings that had yet to be mapped in any realistic way.

For all their brilliance, our progenitors practiced an exceedingly simplistic form of astrology in comparison to what we are capable of today. Here, emphasis should be on the word *capable*, for much of modern astrology is still mired in the dogma of the past. Ancient and medieval astrologers were preoccupied with so-called "good" and "bad" planetary positions—malefic planets, evil aspects, debilitations, falls, afflictions, and other such ominous categories of meaning. While they were obviously aware that people were subject to a process of ageing that culminated in death, there was little or no concept of *evolution*, that is, of the psycho-spiritual growth of the individual. Accordingly, astrology was largely limited to superficial trait descriptions, fated events, and dubious predictions of good and bad times for various enterprises.

While some scholars might argue that ancient astrology was actually more complex and technique-rich than its contemporary offshoots, this should not obviate the fact that our ancient forebears were wedded to a fatalistic and deterministic model of the cosmos that precluded them from appreciating how lived experience, i.e., fate, can serve as a catalyst for learning and change, and how learning and change can, in turn, alter fate.

Astrology was largely discredited following the scientific revolution of the 17th and 18th centuries because it was not intelligible within the mechanistic paradigm that constituted the zeitgeist of the new, modern era. Out of this renaissance of scientific thought, psychology was born, and eventually came to replace astrology as our primary means for understanding behavior.

It was not until the first half of the 20th century, following Darwin and then Freud, that the concept of psychological growth and evolution actually entered public awareness. Unencumbered by presuppositions of a fixed character and unalterable fate, early psychologists grounded their theories in that which was observable—human physiology and outward behavior. From these early observations, psychologists developed theories of the human personality.

Psychology was not limited to merely describing types of personality. It was also capable of explaining how people change and develop over time. Developmental psychology evolved in parallel with theories of psychopathology and psychotherapy, the former being concerned with how normal development can be derailed, and the latter with how best to facilitate a process of healing and recovery. In this regard, psychology began to carve out territory that had not previously been explored in the field of astrology.

Starting in the 20th century, astrologers began incorporating concepts from humanistic psychology and Carl Jung's analytical psychology. Following the lead of Dane Rudhyar, the field of humanistic astrology was born, which triggered a resurrection of astrology in the late 60's and 70's. Throughout the latter half of the 20th century, innovators were exploring how psychology and astrology might fruitfully be integrated to form a new hybrid.

While most of psychological astrology can be characterized as a mish-mash of humanistic and Jungian ideas, to date no one has attempted to develop psychological astrology into a full blown personality theory. A number of different authors—including but not limited to Liz Green, Howard Sasportas, Richard Idemon, Tracy Marks, Donna Cunningham, Richard Tarnas, and Stephen Arroyo—have made noteworthy contributions to the field. However, none of these contributions reached the level of a comprehensive theory of personality in the tradition of a formal, psychological model. According to Hall and Lindzey's classic tome, *Theories of Personality*, any adequate theory of personality must accomplish the following minimal objectives:[1]

1. It must be comprehensive, or integrative, in that it deals with the total, functioning person.
2. It must account for what motivates the human being.
3. It must contain a set of empirical definitions concerning the various parts of the personality, thus permitting observation.
4. It must consist of a network of assumptions about behavior that are systematically related in accordance with certain rules.
5. It must be useful in that it is capable of generating predictions

about behavior that are testable and verifiable, thus expanding knowledge.

Again, there has been little if any attempt to meet the foregoing objectives in an explicit, systematic way. Yet, anyone familiar with astrology knows that it implicitly meets all these requirements. Astrology is comprehensive in that it is concerned with all the parts and processes that make up the human psyche. The signs of the zodiac symbolize the basic drives that motivate human conduct, and their planetary rulers constitute parts of psychic structure that can be empirically defined, thus permitting observation. Rules of chart interpretation—chart synthesis—represent a network of assumptions about behavior that are systematically related. Finally, astrology is useful in that it is capable of generating predictions that are verifiable, thus promoting research and expanding knowledge.

The present work represents an effort to develop astrology into a comprehensive model of the psyche—an astrological theory of personality, if you will—that explicitly meets all of Hall and Lindzey's criteria. This is what distinguishes AstroPsychology from psychological astrology in general: its broad, inclusive structure, depth of focus, and systematic precision. Jungian (archetypal) concepts are central, but other models contribute relevant and useful ideas, too, including psychodynamic, developmental, cognitive-behavioral, transpersonal, and general systems theories. Accordingly, AstroPsychology is cross-theoretical in that it integrates and subsumes relevant concepts from a number of different traditions.

While ancient astrology roughly described how human behavior correlated to planetary positions, these descriptions were limited to surface features of the personality. In contrast, AstroPsychology plumbs the depths of the psyche, and does so in terms that are significantly more detailed than its predecessors. It depicts how astrology symbolizes basic needs, developmental stages, psychological functions, cognitive structures, internal dialogues, intrapsychic conflict, unconscious complexes, defense mechanisms, and personality disorders—concepts that did not even exist prior to the 20th century. The reader does not need to have any background in psychology to understand these concepts, for they are seamlessly interwoven with astrology throughout the text.

Essentially, AstroPsychology is a systematic reformulation of astrology in terms of psychological concepts and practices. Perhaps the single most defining attribute is its focus on integrating the birth chart and, thus, supporting the human potential for growth and change. This emphasis is grounded in research that suggests the very purpose of human life—if not *all* life—is to evolve into more complex states until individuals recognize their at-one-ment with source. As the philosopher Manly Hall put it, "Man can think of his own life either as the fulfillment of himself, or as the gradual completion of a greater existence of which he is a part and with which he is indissolvably associated."[2]

AstroPsychology's focus on psycho-spiritual evolution qualifies it as a transpersonally oriented theory, for transpersonal psychology is that branch of psychology that incorporates spiritual notions into its framework. As such, it is a more inclusive school of psychology—a "fourth wave," as Abraham Maslow cal choanalysis, behaviorism, and humanistic psychology. One should not, therefore, equate AstroPsychology with conventional notions of psychology and thereby strip it of its transpersonal dimension.

As a transpersonal theory, AstroPsychology adds significant breadth and depth to psychology, transforming it into a more spiritualized model that links psyche to cosmos and reconnects humanity with its divine heritage. In so doing, it challenges the deterministic presumption of psychology that consciousness is merely an epiphenomenon of its biological substrate and social milieu. Biological determinism and social determinism are but modern versions of the celestial determinism that characterized ancient astrology. Determinism is determinism, no matter what you presume the determining factor to be.

The point is that AstroPsychology is decidedly not deterministic; rather, it regards the psyche as its own cause, an eternal, irreducible essence that is self-generating and capable of manifesting in biological and social conditions. This, in effect, is what the chart symbolizes—an exteriorization of the soul's pattern in terms of physiology, personality, and environment. Material reality is conceptualized as a synchronistic reflection of an innate, pre-existent psychic structure that evolves over time (possibly lifetimes). From this perspective, the psyche is reflected in, but not caused by, the positions of the planets at the moment of birth.

Given that AstroPsychology is non-deterministic, its approach to forecasting warrants comment. Over the last several decades, psychological astrology has been characterized as lacking sufficient focus on concrete, external events. Its seeming indifference to prediction rendered it vulnerable to criticism and even rejection by practitioners who believed astrology's primary function is (or should be) foreknowledge of the future. Also, if psychological astrologers do not have to predict empirical events, they are insulated from any kind of disproof mechanism; statements about the inner world cannot be evaluated for accuracy with the same rigor as statements about the outer world. As a result, much of psychological astrology drifted into a fuzzy, vague, shoot-from-the-hip approach that made it suspect in the eyes of serious scholars. AstroPsychology strives to remedy this problem. While its primary focus *is* the psyche, there is also a keen interest in external events—not merely to predict them for their own sake, but to discern their significance as evolutionary drivers.

An evolutionary driver is an event that serves as a catalyst and vehicle for a developmental process. As a catalyst, it triggers a shift in the native's thinking and behavior that empowers him or her to meet a situation more effectively. And as a vehicle, it provides exactly the right type of situation—whether in marriage, career, health, or otherwise—to serve a corrective or educative purpose. Understanding the significance of outer events enables astrologers to discuss them with clients in ways that support a natural, evolutionary process, for the event in question will always reflect a key configuration in the birthchart, whether natally or by transit/progression. When clients gain insight into what a situation means and requires from a growth perspective, they are better able to consciously evolve—i.e., intentionally collaborate with the cosmos toward realization of their higher potential.

Another reason that events are important is that they provide a barometer for measuring the native's level of functionality in a particular area of life. In other words, they serve a diagnostic function. If, for example, a woman with Neptune conjunct Mars in Scorpio in the 7th house consistently marries alcoholic, abusive men who exploit her financially, this is an important indication that she has significant work to do in the area of partnerships. On the other hand, if she enjoys a stable marriage with a man with whom she sets up a joint therapy practice that specializes in helping undifferentiated, low functioning couples in crisis, then this is an indicator that she is expressing that same configuration at a higher, more integrated level.

The question arises as to whether either outcome could be predicted. From the perspective of AstroPsychology, predicting specific outcomes is a guessing game of dubious merit even when the guess turns out to be correct. First, a given configuration can be expressed at different levels of integration; thus, predicting outcomes is problematic—especially in the absence of knowledge about the person. Second, and more importantly, foreknowledge of an event is unhelpful if there is no understanding of the event's significance as a vehicle for a specific kind of developmental process. What can be predicted, however, is the process that underlies the particulars of the event, i.e., the psychological and developmental significance of the configuration in question.

Any number of events can serve the process just as well. Accordingly, predicting concrete events is secondary to knowing the abstract function they serve. Prediction is important, but not as an early warning system to advise clients in taking evasive or exploitive action; rather, prediction can be utilized as a means of supporting the client in meeting life's opportunities and challenges with the proper attitude. By understanding the underlying purpose of a given period, clients are better able to maximize the growth potential inherent in the time.

AstroPsychology's de-emphasis on predicting concrete events is also in keeping with the multidimensionality, intra-dimensional variability, and polyvalence of astrological archetypes. An astrological variable is multidimensional in the sense that a planet, for instance, can symbolize a psychological function, a state of mind (attitude, affect), and a behavioral trait, while also representing an external character, place, thing, or event. Within any of these dimensions there is considerable variability, e.g., as an event Mars could be an argument, a new beginning, a competition, or simply an adventure.

Finally, astrological archetypes are polyvalent in that they combine with other variables—signs, houses, and aspects—which shape and modify their expression in countless ways. For example, a larger configuration such as a planetary aspect, which can involve multiple signs, planets, and houses, constitutes a higher level system that exerts regulative control over its component parts. The aspect constrains, shapes, and modifies the functioning of the parts so that they comply with the objectives of the higher level system. Although every component has multiple possible expressions, each is swept up in the structure of the thought form it helps to comprise; thus, from the myriad potential expressions of each part, each particular expression is selected and coordinated to form a single, coherent, relatively integrated holistic pattern, much like a family exerts regulative control upon its members to comply with the beliefs, values, and objectives of the family as a whole. Without such downward causation, the internal world of the psyche would be a teeming, buzzing chaos.

Astrology's enormous flexibility as a language means there is an inescapable ambiguity and indeterminacy to birthcharts. One cannot reliably determine concrete particulars from a system that is inherently indeterminate. This underscores why predicting process—the purpose and meaning of a time period—is not only of greater value than guessing outcomes, it is also more in alignment with what is actually possible. Purpose and meaning occurs at a higher level of abstraction than concrete particulars—or, stated in the reverse, different manifestations of a configuration can have the same or similar meaning.

For example, imagine two individuals, both of whom have transiting Jupiter conjuncting Pluto in Scorpio in the 9th opposing Mars in Taurus in the 3rd. Separate events occur that are personally relevant to each person. In the first, a Catholic priest sexually molests a young boy in his congregation; in the second, a prejudiced Alabama court exonerates a white supremacist being tried for blowing up a black church and killing a little girl. Concretely, the events seem different; yet, at a higher level of abstraction, each incident constitutes an injustice in which a powerful but corrupt moral authority violates the life/body of a victim. Although the particular outcome in each case is not predictable, astrology allows one to surmise the likely meaning of the period independent of the events that occur. Moreover, one can infer from the variables involved that the purpose of such a transit is to reflect deeply upon the moral implications of flagrant abuse of power, to put it simply.*

---

* Certainly other outcomes could occur at a higher level of integration, e.g., an individual wins a court battle and experiences justice with regard to a violent crime committed against his person. It follows that there are other ways the transit could be interpreted with regard to the purpose it serves. Interpretations should ideally be customized to the life and concerns of the individual client.

In sum, AstroPsychology is both a personality theory and a diagnostic tool. As a personality theory, it reveals how the structure and dynamics of the psyche are mirrored in external conditions that provide a stimulus to psycho-spiritual growth. And as a diagnostic tool, it provides unparalleled insight into the underlying, characterological issues that cause distress and impairment. Perhaps the horoscope is best understood as an unfolding story in which fate is altered by the development and unfoldment of character.

THE HOROSCOPE AS PERSONAL NARRATIVE

A unifying theme throughout the text is that the horoscope symbolizes an unfolding story. In effect, we all have—or, more accurately *are* a story that we self-construct, amend, and revise over the course of our lives. While the story invariably conforms to the range of parameters indicated by the astrological chart, there is more than one possible version depending upon the level of integration at which the chart is expressed.

The situation is not unlike the Bill Murray film, *Groundhog Day*, in which Murray's character, Phil Collins, a narcissistic weatherman with sardonic contempt for everyone around him, finds himself trapped within the confines of a particular day in a specific locale—Punxsutawney Pennsylvania—and is forced to relive the same day, over and over again. Once he realizes and accepts his plight, Collins uses his foreknowledge to advantage, exploiting the townspeople for his own self-aggrandizement. Soon, however, he realizes the utter emptiness of this strategy and collapses into suicidal despair. Eventually he begins to experiment with other possibilities the day offers, seizing available opportunities to develop creative talents and engage in altruistic acts. As the days roll by, Collins evolves, and appears happier. Moreover, he becomes increasingly integrated into the fabric of the community until; finally, he is the most beloved person in town.

I am particularly fond of this film because I think it metaphorically encapsulates the human predicament. The astrological chart defines the parameters of an individual's life, much like Phil Collin's Groundhog Day defined his. Each planet corresponds to an outer character; houses establish settings for the actions of the characters; planetary sign positions determine character styles; angles (aspects) establish the nature of their relationships; and, finally, dispositorships reveal the overall plot structure and sequence of action, which is repeated over and over. While the entire chart manifests externally in the guise of the people and circumstances we attract, astrology reveals that these are simply mirrors of internal correlates, providing appropriate vehicles for the further evolution of the soul.

Like Phil Collins predicament in Punxsutawney, every person is constrained by the fate that their chart decrees; yet, they are also free to experiment with new attitudes and behaviors within the framework of that fate. As they learn from the consequences of their own choices, and as they utilize opportunities to develop innate capacities more fully, their life pattern is gradually modified, allowing for more rewarding experiences, increasing degrees of satisfaction, and deeper connections with others. In effect, an astrological chart and the life it reflects is characterized by fixed rules and flexible strategies. One can never escape the fixed positions of the natal planets and the requirements they impose; yet, one's strategies and capacities for meeting those requirements can forever evolve.

In a very real sense, every birthchart is a kind of allegory, a didactic narrative that uses an interdependent set of personified abstractions to convey a message, usually moralistic. Characters, objects and events in an allegory are to be taken, not as merely real but as standing for some set of ideas; that is, each item in the narrative is equated with some item amongst the ideas. George Orwell's *Animal Farm*, for example, is an allegory about the communist revolution in Russian in which pigs represent the Bolsheviks. The pigs are real characters in his story, but they also symbolize communist beliefs and practices. Likewise with the natal chart, the actual people one engages are not merely real, but also representative of psychological variables as symbolized by corollary signs, planets, and houses associated with those figures.

As an allegory, the astrological chart has a systematic and complicated structure of equivalents. One's father is one's father, of course, but he also embodies a specific archetype that has a corresponding meaning on an internal level. Actual experiences with the father both foreshadow and signify the individual's capacity for discipline, responsibility, and achievement, as symbolized by Saturn. Taken as a whole, the concrete elements of a person's life are both real and representative of underlying needs, functions, values, ideas, and conflicts, all of which are symbolized by the astrological chart.

An allegory always has a message, or moral, which summarizes the lesson that the main character has to learn. This takes place through a reoccurring sequence of events that constitute plot structure. As incidents accumulate that have a similar meaning, there is a gradual elevation of awareness that reaches a critical pitch, a tipping point; suddenly, the protagonist has a clear, conscious revelation that propels the story towards resolution of the main conflict.

It is the same with the astrological chart. The arrangement of planets constitutes a pattern, a plot structure of sorts, which invariably includes certain conflicts and tensions. Internally, these tensions are experienced as painful memories, attendant defenses, and self-limiting ideas that accrue over time as the pattern repeats. Externally, these psychological conflicts are compulsively reenacted in adult experiences that mirror the internal conflict and provide a vehicle for its eventual resolution. To resolve the conflict is to learn the lesson; this is the moral of the story implicit in every birthchart.

Introduction to AstroPsychology is rooted in the conviction that human beings and horoscopes are better explained by the concept of story than of thing. By 'thing' I mean the current tendency in psychiatry to reduce people to biological machines that need to be medicated to function properly. Likewise, people are made into things when they are diagnosed as obsessives, schizophrenics, borderlines, narcissists, or any other category of mental disorder that implies individuals have or *are* a disease. Conversely, stories have movement built into them; characters evolve, conflicts resolve, and the entire narrative potentially moves in the direction of a satisfying ending.

It is precisely astrology's potential to objectify the internal story that makes it such a useful tool for conscious evolution. Once a person recognizes that he or she is an embodied, self-created story with a specific evolutionary trajectory, there is freedom to improvise and move the story forward toward all that one can be.

In the present work, each chapter introduces a component of the life story and leads incrementally toward a more comprehensive understanding. The remainder of this introduction provides a brief summary of each chapter. While some chapter summaries may contain examples that exceed the understanding of the beginning astrologer, they are merely intended to illustrate the general idea being discussed. The reader is assured that all relevant concepts will be thoroughly defined and explained in the chapters to follow.

THE ZODIAC AND THE PSYCHE

Chapter Two provides an overview of astrological archetypes. It goes on to deconstruct the zodiac into 14 separate categories, which are further organized into five subgroups—individual and collective signs, four elements, three modalities, two polarities, and three perspectives. The latter pertains to how the zodiac can be organized into personal, social, and universal signs, each perspective constituting a different stage of life and a distinct way of experiencing time and space. In addition, the essential angles between the signs are previewed in terms of seven primary relationship themes—conjunction, semi-sextile, sextile, square, trine, quincunx, and opposition. Since the zodiac is the foundation of the birthchart, this chapter constitutes an introduction to the generic structure of the collective psyche.*

UNDERSTANDING THE LEGEND

Chapter Three extends this concept further, showing how the various zodiac categories—elements, modalities, and so on—can be quantified to reveal their relative strength or weakness at an individual level. By assigning a numerical value to each planet, one can readily see how psychic energy is distributed via planetary positions for that person.

This snapshot of the total, archetypal field is called *The Legend*, so named because it provides a brief description of the chart as a whole. For example, if there is a preponderance of planets in fire signs, no planets in earth, and a relative absence in fixed signs, one might hypothesize that such a person would see life as a field of adventure but perhaps lack constancy, practicality, and the ability to produce something of tangible, enduring value. The Legend, in short, offers a quick overview of general psychological tendencies.

---

*By 'collective psyche' I mean the Jungian concept of an objective psyche that includes but also transcends the lesser psyches of its component parts. Often Jung spoke of this as 'the collective unconscious', which was thought to be a repository of all the accumulated thoughts, feelings, and habits of humankind over eons. For our purposes, the collective psyche is best conceived as a kind of generic template—the zodiac—that constitutes the root structure of the human psyche.

In terms of a story metaphor, the Legend is analogous to a preview that gives us a foretaste of what is likely to occur. It not only describes the inner landscape of the soul, but also the contours and characteristics of the outer world. And since the distribution of psychic energy can be measured in over a dozen categories, the Legend mitigates against the tendency to type people as a 'this' or 'that'. It reminds us that real people are unique, complex, multidimensional beings, not one-dimensional stereotypes that can be slotted into simplistic groups.

SIGNS AS ASTROLOGICAL ARCHETYPES

Chapter Four explores the myriad functions of zodiacal signs. Starting with the premise that astrological archetypes can manifest in a multiplicity of ways, signs are subsequently described as: 1) core motivational principles, drives, or needs; 2) behavioral traits, attributes, and values that are self-consistent within each sign; and 3) sets of empirical phenomena—things, people, places, and events that are mutually consistent in their meanings.

The need of a sign can be inferred from behavior that is characteristic of that sign. Likewise, a behavioral trait can be understood in the context of the need that behavior serves. With regard to signs as sets of empirical phenomena, each member of a sign-set is the derivative of an underlying archetype and provides a vehicle for its outward expression. Exemplifying this category are signs as archetypal characters that manifest as subpersonalities with distinct behavioral styles as well as character-types encountered in the event world. Someone with a strong Scorpio streak, for instance, might occasionally act the part of a healer with a tendency to attract wounded souls—or, equally likely, a wounded soul with a penchant for attracting healers.

Zodiacal signs are sharply differentiated from Sun signs. The latter, of course, are actually a combination of the Sun *and* sign, but have regrettably become conflated with the meanings of signs themselves. The popularization of Sun signs via trite books and mindless newspaper columns has inadvertently debased astrology into yet another typology that reduces the complexity of the human being to one or another cardboard stereotype.

Also included in Chapter Four is the notion that zodiacal signs can function as parts of speech within an implicit astrological grammar.

When qualifying the expression of a planetary action, for example, signs perform the function of adverbs. Mercury in Aries can be translated as, "She spoke freely," with Mercury the verb *spoke* and Aries the adverb, *freely*. As a motivational factor, signs can also signify nouns, e.g., the need for *freedom* denotes Aries as a noun.

Last but not least in Chapter Four is the linkage of signs with developmental stages. While this idea is not explicated in detail, it is introduced to the reader as food for thought.* A zodiacal sign is actually a phase relationship of the earth's orbit about the Sun; as such, every sign corresponds to a segment of the yearly cycle as expressed in seasonal phenomena. Like all earthly organisms, human beings are biological clocks, embodying annual, monthly, diurnal, and presumably a host of other cycles as represented by the varying orbital periods of planets in our solar system. The unifying factor in all these cycles, however, is the transcendent notion of *cycle* itself, which can be subdivided into twelve angular phases that retain the same meanings regardless of the planetary cycle being delineated. Just so, the human life cycle can be subdivided into twelve stages, with each zodiacal sign signifying a distinct phase of development with its own tasks and requirements.

PLANETS AS ARCHETYPAL PROCESSES

Planets in all their variegated forms are the focus of Chapter Five. First, a distinction is made between *process* and *content*, with the former described as the internal, psychological meaning of planets and the latter their outward manifestation as people, places, things, and events. The basic rule here is that content mirrors process; events in the outer world invariably reflect the structure and dynamics of the inner world.

A theory of intrinsic motivation is presented that defines planets as active agents of sign-needs. Every planet constitutes a set of interrelated psychological *functions* that are motivated to perform specific actions designed to fulfill the need(s) of the sign it rules. Sign-needs are conveyed by feelings that, in turn, trigger planetary processes (actions). If a planet fulfills its motivating need, it attains a target state—an experience of satiation—that allows it to recede into the background only to be replaced by a new dominant motive. In this way, sign-needs

---

* For more information on signs as developmental stages, see G. Perry's Mapping the Landscape of the Soul, and Depth Analysis of the Natal Chart. The latter book goes into greater detail.

and their associated affects provide a means of identifying moment-to-moment shifts in motivational dominance and accompanying changes in behavior. The relationship of feelings, actions, and states is particularly important for understanding how internal conflicts are subjectively experienced and managed, which is a topic that will be explored in later chapters.

The *content* of planetary processes is analyzed in a manner consistent with Jung's concept of synchronicity. According to Jung, synchronicity is the meaningful coincidence of a momentary subjective state with an external situation that parallels the subjective state. Such meaningful coincidences cannot be explained by physical laws of cause and effect because a non-physical internal state is thought to be lacking causal power, i.e., a wish, fantasy, or idea, no matter how fervently felt or believed, is unable to influence the physical (event) world in a linear cause-effect manner, or so it is presumed. Consciousness may attract or influence events through some other (paranormal) medium, but we are uncertain how exactly this might work. Suffice to say that synchronicity groups internal and external events by *meaning* rather than cause.

This has enormous implications for astrology because the very nature of the discipline assumes that the same variables which symbolize the inner world also symbolize the outer one. Every astrological glyph signifies both an internal, psychological factor, such as a need, function, or belief, and an outer, environmental factor such as a person, place, or thing. From an astrological perspective, synchronicity is chronic in the sense of being constant and protracted; it does not occur only momentarily, but stretches out to encompass virtually every aspect of our lives, from the immediate present to the distant future. This core conviction is encapsulated in standard aphorisms: as within, so without; character is destiny; plot is the unfoldment of character.

HOUSES AS PSYCHOLOGICAL ENVIRONMENTS

If planets are the characters that populate our inner and outer realms, and signs represent their underlying motives, Chapter Six extends our narrative metaphor to houses as *settings* for planetary action. Like signs, houses are based on the standard division of a 360° cycle into twelve phases. Whereas the zodiac is based on the annual cycle of the earth's orbit about the Sun, houses are based on the earth's diurnal rotation on its axis. It follows, therefore, that houses have analogous meanings as signs; each house is the situational, experiential or mundane derivative of the sign to which it corresponds.

In literature, settings not only provide a context for action, they also help to motivate that action. Signs, as stated, are the primary motivators of planetary actions, but houses impose a set of conditions to which planetary action(s) must adjust. Every situation that a house symbolizes is best met by the nature of the planets and signs that rule that house, e.g., the 7th house of partnership requires tact, diplomacy, and cooperation—traits that correspond to Libra and Venus, which rule the 7th. Knowing rulerships helps to determine the compatibility of signs and planets that actually tenant a house, for their natures may not be well suited to the requirements that apply in that locale.

For example, if Mars tenants the 7th house, it is motivated to accommodate itself to the requirements of partnership, but how readily can it do so? The answer is found in the natural relationship of the sign Mars' rules, Aries, to the sign that corresponds to the 7th, Libra. Since those two signs are opposed in the natural zodiac, this implies that Mars in the 7th has the quality of an opposition; its very nature is inherently opposed to the requirements of collaboration and compromise that apply in the locale it occupies. This is the equivalent of capturing the gladiator Spartacus and requiring him to be a diplomat on behalf of Rome. It is precisely these sorts of odd pairings that provide a story with essential conflict, without which the story has nowhere to go.

INTERPRETIVE RULES FOR PLANETS IN SIGNS

The remaining chapters deal with chart synthesis. Chapter Seven introduces the topic of grammar and argues that grammatical rules are not only implicit in astrological interpretations; their explication empowers practitioners to master the language more quickly. As stated, signs can function as nouns when defining basic needs and as adverbs when qualifying the expression of planets in signs. Planets, likewise, represent their own parts of speech, being nouns when they signify a person, place, thing, or function—e.g., Jupiter can be a professor, a university, a college text, or the function of expansion—and verbs when connoting planetary actions, e.g., Jupiter is the action to *expand*, to *teach*, to *travel*, and so forth.

When a planet is in a sign, astrological grammar can be utilized creatively. There are essentially five different ways a sign can qualify the expression of a planet. These include making a statement about a planetary function; describing a planetary character; qualifying a planetary action; associating a planetary state with a particular field of activity; and citing the intention or outcome of a planetary action.

From a narrative perspective, a planet is like an archetypal character, both within and without, which has the potential for certain types of action. Just as actors can perform different roles, so planets perform differently depending upon their sign position. The sign, in other words, is analogous to the role the planet is playing. Mercury in Sagittarius is playing the part of an upbeat, optimistic herald with a positive message about the future. He might not have his facts quite right, but can be quite persuasive none-the-less!

This chapter discusses the archetypal relationship of planets in signs, showing how quality of fit can be evaluated by noting the natural relationship between the sign the planet *occupies* and the sign it *rules*, e.g.,. Mars in Cancer is a square-like relationship because Aries (which Mars rules) naturally squares Cancer, the sign Mars occupies. An argument is made that this way of evaluating planetary sign positions provides more specific, useful information than traditional concepts of dignity, detriment, exaltation and fall.

INTERPRETIVE RULES FOR PLANETS IN HOUSES

Rules for interpreting planetary house positions are discussed in Chapter Eight. This level of chart synthesis adds an additional layer of complexity to the chart narrative, for interpretations now need to incorporate the house in combination *with* the planetary sign position. Whereas planets in signs describe how a planet behaves and what it does; house positions show where the action occurs and what some of the outcomes might be.

Again, planets in houses can manifest in two general ways: as process and content. Process refers to how planets attempt to satisfy their motivating needs in the context of the house they tenant. Content is the outcome, which constitutes a blending of planet, sign, and house. In addition, planets in houses signify states that are situationally specific. For example, if an individual has a propensity for depression (a

Saturn state), then activation of this state is likely to be linked to circumstances associated with the house Saturn occupies. Saturn in the 7th may correspond to depression associated with failed partnerships or a general lack of intimacy.

Chapter Eight also discusses how house outcomes vary over time. Variations of outcome reflect the level of integration of factors that pertain to that house. A woman's Saturn in Scorpio in the 7th may initially manifest as a divorce caused by her partner's lack of fiscal responsibility; yet, by midlife she succeeds in utilizing her Saturnian proclivities to achieve mastery in Scorpionic matters pertaining to the 7th. A depressing divorce at age 29 may be succeeded at age 39 by an enduring and fulfilling relationship with a powerful man. Their relationship reflects a higher level meaning of Saturn in Scorpio in the 7th, e.g., they collaborate in a lucrative business that involves crisis management in the corporate world. Both outcomes equally reflect Saturn in Scorpio in the 7th, but at different levels of integration. As always, content mirrors process.

Just as the compatibility of planetary sign positions can be discerned by evaluating the zodiacal angle between ruled and occupied signs; so planetary house positions can be appraised in a similar manner. Moon in the 9th, for example, can be a problematic position due to the fact that Cancer, the sign the Moon rules, is quincunx Sagittarius, the sign associated with the 9th. Lunar actions are naturally inclined toward family, rootedness, and a sense of belonging; yet, if placed in the 9th, the Moon must fulfill these needs in a context that involves travel, foreign lands, and the pursuit of wisdom. A quincunxial dynamic connotes a problem that could be an enduring life challenge.

Aspects as Personal Myths

Planetary aspects are the focus of Chapter Nine. Up to this point, our literary metaphor has been limited to describing characters (planets), performing roles (signs) in specific settings (houses). Characters, however, have relationships with other characters, which are depicted by aspects. Just as signs and houses derive their meanings from the phases they signify within a 360 degree cycle, so also do aspects. Every aspect is a phase relationship within the synodic cycle of the two planets forming the aspect. A synodic cycle is the time it takes two planets to separate from the conjunction and eventually form another conjunction. This requires the faster moving planet to move ahead of the slower planet and make a series of twelve 30 degree angles—semi-sextile, sextile, square, trine, quincunx, opposition, quincunx, trine, square, sextile, and semi-sextile—before finally conjoining the slower planet again.

Each 30° phase relationship within the cycle constitutes an aspect that has a meaning analogos to the sign that represents that angle in the natural zodiac. In astrology, we are always dealing with iterations of the same twelve meanings. For example, when the faster of the planets moves 90° ahead of the slower planet, we call that an *opening square*. Since all aspects derive their meaning from the nature of the sign to which they correspond, this would be a Cancer angle. Cancer begins 90° from the vernal equinox (0° Aries); thus, it signifies the first (or opening) square of the zodiac. Accordingly, any actual opening square between two planets is essentially a Cancerian aspect.

An aspect symbolizes a type of dialogue between the participating planets that entails reciprocal influence. Each planet perceives and responds to the other in a manner that is consistent with the nature of the angle between them. Internally, these relationships are literally experienced as internal dialogues, or self-talk, which entail cognitive processes related to the individual's beliefs about fulfilling the needs of the respective planets. If Saturn is forming a closing square to Jupiter, for example, a person might harbor a belief that truth and justice can only be attained by hard work, perseverance and a willingness to endure periodic frustrations—perhaps a fitting aspect for a hardnosed lawyer.

Because planetary functions are motivated by specific needs, any relationship between two planets symbolizes a confluence or collision of motives. Either way, there is co-activation of the two planetary functions. If the planets form a soft angle (sextile or trine), then their motives and functions enhance one another. There is confluence; each function enriches the other's capacity to fulfill its motivating need. This, in turn, is reflected in positive cognitions pertaining to the respective needs and functions. However, if they form a hard angle (square, opposition, or quincunx), they are more likely to conflict; thus, there is a collision of needs. Each function tends to obstruct the other's capacity to achieve need fulfillment, which is experienced as grim cognitions pertaining to those functions.

Hard aspects generally manifest externally as a predicament or problem that requires effort to resolve. Things do not automatically go smoothly, as with the sextile and trine; rather, there is strife and struggle that may ultimately lead to significant achievement in matters pertaining to the respective planets. A Chinese proverb captures this succinctly: "The gem cannot be polished without friction, nor man perfected without trials." As with every story, conflict is essential to move the story forward. Without conflict, there is no story.

In myth and literature, a strong element of inner conflict is related to a corresponding outer conflict. Astrologically, external difficulties are symptomatic of internal conflicts that are struggling to resolve themselves. Hard aspects between planets not only symbolize a clash of motives; they symbolize cognitive structures (personal myths) made up of enduring ideas, beliefs, and expectancies by which an individual constructs a world and guides his behavior.

The word 'construct' warrants further comment. Current thinking in the cognitive sciences emphasizes participatory processes in knowing. People do not perceive reality passively or objectively, but actively through the conceptual filter of their personal theory of reality. In so doing, they co-construct the world since there is an interactive, interdependence between inner and outer conditions. Ideas fervently held not only shape one's perceptions, they operate like self-fulfilling prophecies—inducing other people to behave in conformity to one's preconceptions.

Personal myths are beliefs about one's capacity for meeting the needs of planets that comprise the aspect. These ideas originate in early, prototypical experiences, which are subsequently re-enacted in adulthood in an effort to complete unfinished business left over from childhood antecedents. Research in depth psychology has conclusively established that individuals are compelled at an unconscious level to repeat distressing childhood events in order to disconfirm the pathogenic beliefs that formed in their wake. In effect, old scenarios are re-enacted in hopes of creating new outcomes.

If this project is successful, it resolves old grievances, releases toxic residues, and liberates heretofore buried potentials. New skills and aptitudes emerge that constitute a higher level synthesis of the respective planetary functions, which are now utilized in the service of the angle that connects them. If Mars and Saturn form an opening (Cancer) square, for instance, the individual may express a capacity for controlled aggression as a martial arts master who trains woman in the art of self-defense. Mars and Saturn combine in a context that involves caring protection. There are many other potential outcomes, of course, but this serves to illustrate how two planets in aspect can combine to serve their connecting angle.

A dynamic approach to horoscope interpretation recognizes that individuals are always in process, which is to say they are, at least potentially, experiencing continuous growth and change. This is obvious from a purely developmental perspective in which all human beings undergo predictable, generic changes as part of the aging process. Beyond this, however, people are stimulated to grow in unique ways that are reflected by the dynamics of their birthchart and timed by transits and progressions to natal planets. All of this underscores that it is impossible to know exactly how a natal aspect is functioning until one has sufficient background information on the person, either gained through research or interview. An aspect cannot be interpreted in a one-size-fits-all way, for how it manifests is contingent upon its level of integration.

DISPOSITORS AND SIGNIFICATORS

Finally, Chapter Ten completes our narrative analysis by discussing the meaning of significators and dispositors. Planetary configurations are analogous to scenes in a movie. The planet is the actor performing a role (sign) in a situation (house) and in relationship to other characters whose needs have to be accommodated (aspects). If every planet were analyzed in just this way, we would have ten scenes running in parallel but not actually leading anywhere. This would be like watching a movie with multiple frames on the screen, each depicting a different actor in a particular situation but the scenes themselves would not be intelligibly related to form a coherent story.

In a real story, all the elements are functionally related so that there is a discernible structure to the action. *Plot structure* is the reoccurring sequence of events that give a story unity. Each character's action is in some way related to the action of every other character, such that all have a part to play in the sequence of action as a whole. Plot is not merely a repetition of similar incidents, but a progressive unfolding that gradually modifies awareness and leads toward resolution of the core conflict, both within and without.

An astrological chart can be read in a similar way. Planets are motivated to fulfill the need of the sign(s) they rule; yet, in a real chart, any sign can be on the cusp (beginning) of any house, which means the need of that sign is associated with the circumstances of that house. This adds an additional layer of complexity to signs as motivators of planetary action, for now we see that a sign is not merely a motive in itself, but a motive that is linked to particular circumstances. It is precisely this combination of need and circumstance that establishes the true motivation for a planet. Regardless of the house the planet occupies, it 'signifies' the house that begins with the sign it rules. If Aries is on the cusp of the 4th house, then Mars is the significator of the 4th irrespective of where it may be in the chart. Like a foreign ambassador whose primary loyalties are to his homeland, so a significator must perform its actions in the service of the house it signifies.

One can immediately see how the concept of signification begins to tie the chart together as a unified whole. This becomes even more apparent with planetary dispositors. Again, to use a narrative metaphor, every character has what is called a *back story*—a specific set of facts and factors that are chronologically earlier than the narrative of primary interest. Knowing the background of characters deepens our understanding of what motivates them to do what they do. Actions, in other words, can more fully be understood in the context of the actor's history.

Just so, every planet in the birthchart has a back-story that is related to the house it signifies and the planets that occupy the sign it rules. The planetary ruler is said to *dispose* those planets; i.e., a dispositor is a planet that rules the sign that another planet is *in*. All behaviors and experiences related to the disposed planet—as symbolized by its sign, house, and aspects—constitute the *reason for* the action of its dispositor. While a dispositor's actions will invariably be described by *its* sign, house, and aspects, the motivation for those actions refers back to the disposed planet. The behavior of the disposed planet activates its dispositor like a relay race in which one runner hands the baton to the next. In effect, the disposed planet is the back story that both motivates and helps to explain the dispositor's behavior in its current locale.

Dispositors not only indicate how one psychological tendency leads to another, thus symbolizing associative chains in feeling and thinking, they also indicate chains of events that seemingly occur *to* the person. If, for example, a man has Uranus in Virgo in the 7th house with Mercury in Scorpio in the 9th the problems he experiences with fidelity in traditional marriage may motivate him to investigate the sexual ethics of other cultures that give less priority to fidelity.

By itself, Mercury in Scorpio in the 9th might not be inclined to investigate that particular topic (there many other pursuits that would fit the configuration equally well). Let us imagine, however, that his marriage broke up because his wife was unwilling to tolerate his extramarital affairs—a common theme of Uranus in the 7th. Wishing to alleviate his guilt, he is driven to learn (Mercury) how European cultures (9th) are more forgiving of men that have mistresses (Scorpio). One can readily see how experiences symbolized by Uranus in Virgo in the 7th provide the motivational impetus for the subsequent behavior of Mercury in Scorpio in the 9th.

Unless a planet is in its own sign (the sign it rules), then it will have a dispositor, too. Planetary activation continues unfolding in domino-like fashion until it either comes to a planet in its own sign (final dispositor) or arcs back to a planet earlier in the chain, thus setting up a feedback loop. The seemingly infinite ways that planets can form chains of dispositors is testament to the uniqueness of every birthchart and the story it tells. Like the reoccurring sequence of events in *Groundhog Day*, each repetition brings with it a potential for new learning, elevation of awareness, and resolution of the core conflict.

SUMMARY

AstroPsychology is a transpersonal, growth oriented model that meets all the requirements of a modern personality theory. Utilizing a narrative metaphor, it conceptualizes the birthchart as an unfolding story in which fate both reflects and provides the necessary stimulus for the development of character. Each chapter addresses a stratum in the making of this story. Signs as motives, planets as functions, and houses as settings are the foundational principles; yet, all can be combined in ways that give a unique texture to the individual soul.

Astrological meaning is a multilayered phenomenon. At the root of the psyche are basic needs that motivate their planetary rulers to perform actions in the pursuit of need-fulfillment. When planets occupy signs, they express themselves in a manner that is consistent with the traits and values of those signs, while simultaneously activating their dispositors in a never ending sequence that makes up the plot of the life story. These dynamic processes play out their roles within specific settings (houses) and in relation to other planets (aspects) that have their own styles, agenda, and contexts for expression. Taken as a whole, the birthchart represents an evolutionary pattern, a fate that is fixed in its general parameters but flexible in its responsiveness to learning.

All this takes place inside a living, intentional cosmos that is immanent within every cell of nature's being. If planets are the visible representatives of archetypal fields that permeate Nature, then we are in them as much as they are in us. Astrological archetypes are the thought forms of *Anima Mundi*, the world soul, in the pattern of which every living thing is made. They inform our deepest feelings, thoughts, and yearnings—the interior of our souls—yet are evident as well in the fragrant breeze of a spring morning, the curve of our spine, birdsong and a neighbor's message, children's laughter, the Super bowl, an uncompleted task, and the joys and despairs of intimate relationship. Astrology reminds us that Psyche is *everywhere*.

Chapter Two

The Zodiac and the Psyche

THE MACROCOSM AND THE MICROCOSM

The zodiac is the foundation of the astrological language. Strictly speaking, it has no material existence in itself, but rather is a division of the Earth's orbit about the Sun into twelve equal sectors of thirty degrees each. Each sector forms one sign of the tropical zodiac. Because all the planets orbit the Sun on the same plane, and because the planets remain within eight degrees above or below this plane, the plane of the zodiac is actually a sixteen-degree band circling the Sun.

The tropical zodiac differs from the sidereal zodiac in that it is not based on the constellations; rather it is a time-space continuum formed of a succession of angles based on the ever-changing relationship of Earth and Sun. The mechanics of this relationship are somewhat complicated. The Earth's orbit about the Sun, called the *ecliptic,* is not in the same plane as the Earth's equator. This is because the Earth's axis tilts at an angle of twenty-three degrees away from its orbital plane (the ecliptic). If we consider the ecliptic the Sun's equator extended indefinitely out into space, and the *celestial equator* as the Earth's equator similarly extended, it is the interaction of these two planes that comprises the substance of the tropical zodiac (see Figure 1, next page).

There are four critical points of relationship between these two planes. These are the four angles, or cardinal points of the tropical zodiac. Corresponding to the seasons, these four points divide the year

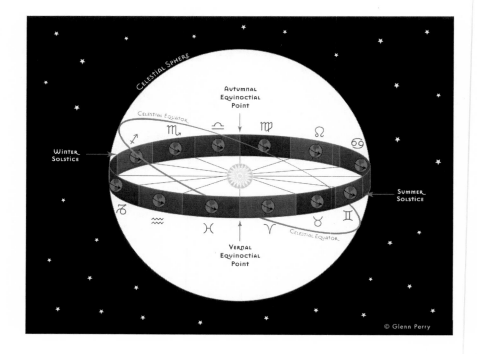

Figure 1: The Tropical Zodiac

Note when the earth is in Libra, the Sun is in Aries. Likewise with every other sign: it is the earth's position in the opposite sign that places the Sun in its proper seasonal sign, e.g., when earth enters Capricorn, it is actually the summer solstice, since the Sun will be entering Cancer. This entire process is self-contained with no reference to stars beyond our own Sun.

into quarters: At the vernal equinox—where the plane of the Earth's equator intersects the plane of the ecliptic—we have the first day of spring, or the beginning of the zodiac at zero degrees Aries. Next, we have the summer solstice—that point where the northern hemisphere is tilted at its maximum angle toward the Sun (the two planes being furthest apart)—thus marking the beginning of summer, or zero degrees Cancer. The situation repeats itself at the autumnal equinox with the planes again converging at zero degrees Libra, and then separating over the next three months to their maximum distance at the winter solstice, which marks the shortest day of the year at zero degrees Capricorn.

Technically speaking, the zodiac is a twelve fold division of the space-time continuum formed by the succession of angles between the celestial equator (Earth) and the ecliptic. More realistically, it is a symbolization of the year as expressed in seasonal phenomena. Considering each sign as one phase of this space-time continuum, the parallel between signs and seasons is exact: every sign is a metaphor of the process occurring in nature at the time to which it corresponds. Spring, for example, represents a phase of the year when heat is on the increase, motion accelerates, vegetation blooms, and new life pushes upwards in a struggle to be born. It is a time chiefly marked by beginnings. Similarly, Aries, the sign corresponding to the vernal equinox, represents the principle of birth, new beginnings, survival and action. We see this in classical Aries behavior, which is marked by the need to be first, to initiate, to pioneer new projects and assert oneself in a manner that demands unrestricted freedom *to be*.

Another good example of the qualitative similarity between signs and seasons is Capricorn. Marking the beginning of winter and therefore, theoretically, the coldest day of the year, Capricorn represents the principle of contraction. Days are shortest and heat is at a minimum. Here, dormant nature gives us the meaning of conservation and control. Capricorn represents the crystallization of forms, unlike Cancer (summer solstice), its polar opposite, where everything is fluid and soft. We speak of harsh, severe winters where everything is frozen and rigid. Nature is her most cruel and unsympathetic; life slows down; there is a sense of delay and limitation. From a psychological perspective, we might say that nature produces behavior consistent with herself, for Capricorn is described as cold, disciplined, austere, patient, frugal and thorough, to use just a few examples. Also, there is often a heaviness in Capricorn behavior that manifests as a serious and conservative approach to life; here, we find an instinctive appreciation for form, structure and organization. We could even describe Capricorn behavior as "winter-like," for all the words that apply to winter apply equally well to Capricorn.

This situation repeats itself for every sign of the zodiac. Signs are symbols of life processes reflected in nature. Each one represents a specific phase of the year as evidenced in seasonal phenomena. Inasmuch as human beings are a part and product of nature, they are a manifestation of these energies. For every phase of the year, there is a sign, and for every sign, a specific human drive. These drives are evidenced in certain types of behavior and events that reflect the underlying need, or instinct, of the sign.

Reduced to their essence, signs may best be described as abstract principles inherent in nature. Just as water vapor exists in an invisible state before it condenses into cloud, falls to Earth as rain and further cooled turns to ice, so the energy of a sign exists independent of its phenomena. It may manifest in humans as need, become known through behavior and culminate in event; yet, in principle, it precedes all these things. It is as if each sign were an invisible pattern of energy to which the shape and behavior of matter visibly conforms.

Signs may be likened to what Plato described as *Forms* or *Ideas* that exist as pre-patterned impulses in the mind of The Good—the ultimate state of reality. These Forms were thought to be alive and purposeful, yet, like gods, existed in realms too subtle to be detected by the senses. Since they could only be known through their effects, the various qualities of the phenomenal world were thought to be derived from these Forms. Beauty, for instance, could never be encountered in itself, but only as a property of some concrete thing that is beautiful. Where objects were ephemeral, qualities endured; the qualities evident in tangible objects being but fragile attenuations of the more intense and stable condition these forms enjoyed on their own plane.

Similar to Plato's Forms, Carl Jung's concept of archetypes also applies to zodiacal signs. According to Jung, an archetype is a universal thought form that manifests in primordial images and themes. While an archetype clothes itself in imagery that is familiar to the time and place in which it occurs, its meaning is the same across cultures. And although archetypes are structural elements of consciousness, they are not limited to human consciousness. An archetype can just as easily appear in the environment as an event or situation.

In the final analysis, an archetype is undefinable. It is a kind of formative field that is not limited to any particular shape or locale. Just so, astrological signs are more than the phenomena they body forth. These are but symbols of the deeper underlying principles contained within. Libra, for instance, is the sign connected with balance, symmetry, proportion, rhythm, grace—in short, that aggregate of qualities which makes for beauty. We may admire an exquisite painting or feel our spirit lifted by a song or ballet; yet, it is the quality of Libra within these experiences, and within ourselves, which makes us respond in kind and say "that's beautiful."

Just so, each sign radiates its own particular quality. While the emanations of a sign can vary a great deal in outer manifestation, in principle the sign remains the same; the quality endures. Human beings, animated by these principles, evidence their presence individually through dreams, behavior and events, as well as collectively through the great mythological, religious, and artistic outpourings of history.

THE STRUCTURE OF THE ZODIAC

As Jung liked to point out, at root our consciousness is collective; at our deepest strata we are all composed of the same fundamental energies. Similarly, in astrology, what we are studying in the zodiac is essentially the collective structure of the human psyche. This structure is a composite framework of twelve interdependent and interrelated drives, a complex web of energies called signs.

Technically, we can picture the zodiac as a circle divided like the slices of a pie into twelve equal segments. These segments, in turn, organize themselves into five distinct categories: (1) individual and collective; (2) the elements; (3) the modalities; (4) the polarities; and (5) perspective. **Individual** and **collective** signs show how the psyche is organized into six needs that emphasize differentiation from the whole, and six polar opposite needs that emphasize integration with the whole. The **elements** symbolize four distinct psychological functions, and the **modalities** symbolize three modes of action. Sign **polarities** signify a balance between expressive (yang) and suppressive (yin) tendencies in the psyche, whereas the category of **perspective** divides the psyche into three general groupings that symbolize the evolution of consciousness from more narrow, personal concerns to broader, more transpersonal ones. We will now consider each of these categories in turn (See Figure 2, p. 30).

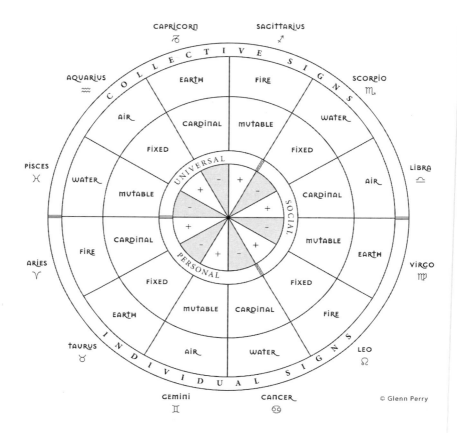

Figure 2: Zodiac Structure

Note that the inner circle depicts how signs alternate in polarity between yang (+) and yin (-). The next section shows how the first four signs are personal, the second four interpersonal (social), and the last four transpersonal (universal). The next division illustrates how the modalities of cardinal, fixed, and mutable proceed in sequence around the zodiac, beginning with cardinal, Aries. The next section depicts the sequence of the four elements. Finally, the outermost ring shows the six Individual and six Collective signs.

INDIVIDUAL AND COLLECTIVE

These two groupings of six signs comprise the broadest division of the zodiac. The first six signs, moving counterclockwise from the left side of the circle, take us from Aries through Virgo, or roughly March 22 to September 24. This six-month division between the two equinoxes marks out specifically that period of the year when days are longer than nights. Conversely, the second six signs, Libra through Pisces, or roughly September 25 through March 21, marks that half of the year when nights are longer than days. This, we find, has a curious significance.

Consider the phenomena of light and darkness: light illuminates differences. It highlights distinctions and emphasizes the boundaries that separate one thing from another. As darkness approaches, however, boundaries dissolve and distinctions blur. Finally, a uniform blackness prevails. Where once there were things, separate and distinct, now there is nothing, i.e., no things, or unity. Perhaps for this reason, light has traditionally symbolized the positive, conscious, yang, or individualizing factor of the universe; while, conversely, darkness represents the negative, unconscious, yin, or unifying factor.

These two groups of signs, individual and collective, are distinguished technically by the relative strength of lightness in the one and darkness in the other. Qualitatively, they are distinguished for similar reasons. The first six, Aries through Virgo, are the way of differentiation, or emphasis on the immediate rather than the long-range, on the parts rather than the whole. This group is about movement away from the collective and toward the individual; priorities center about the emergence of self from the whole, and on the establishment of separateness and uniqueness. From a developmental perspective, these signs signify the period from birth through young adulthood.

The second six, Libra through Pisces, evidence a distinct unifying trend. These signs are oriented toward social and universal concerns as the individual increasingly feels himself to be part of a larger world whose needs may supersede his own. Here, relatedness with others is the important thing. Rather than seeking immediate gratification for personal needs, the individual is drawn toward participation within a larger network of community interests. Vision broadens as priorities shift from short-range to long-range goals that benefit society as a whole. Developmentally, these second six signs mark the transition from the new adult status of Libra (marriage being one hallmark of adulthood), to the final complete absorption into personal anonymity with Pisces. This last sign signifies retirement and death of old age.

These two groups, sign to sign, are related through the interplay of complementary opposites; for every action of an individual sign, there is a corresponding antipodal collective sign that symbolizes a complementary yet opposite reaction. The two groups, we might say, compensate each other, each sign-pair being, as it were, two halves of the same issue. This becomes obvious when we consider them in mutual relationship.

1. Aries is my desires and needs (assertiveness); Libra is your desires and needs (cooperation).

2. Taurus is personal possessions and sensual gratification; Scorpio is shared wealth and erotic merger (social and sexual integration).

3. Gemini separates knowledge into concrete facts (empirical science); Sagittarius synthesizes facts into meaning, a statement of faith or belief (philosophy, law, religion).

4. Cancer is personal emotional needs (the urge to nurture and be nurtured); Capricorn is the world's needs, the urge to organize and manage the needs of the whole (the executive or administrator).

5. Leo is narcissism and recognition of the self as a separate being; Aquarius is altruism and recognition of the self as part of a larger whole (humanitarianism).

6. Virgo discriminates the parts from the whole, analysis; Pisces unifies or dissolves the parts into an undifferentiated whole (unification or dissolution).

Here, we see how each group of six signs corresponds to a pattern. The first six emphasize consciousness of self and differentiation from the whole; the second six stress consciousness of others and relatedness to the whole. Six individual and six collective, personality and commonality, self and others—human experience is forever the interplay of these two factors. The tensions that result lay the groundwork for evolution, for it is through the gradual and inevitable integration of opposites in the psyche that the individual is propelled in the direction of psychic wholeness, a process Jung termed *individuation*.

ELEMENTS

There are four elements in the zodiac—fire, earth, air and water. Each group is composed of three signs each: fire—Aries, Leo, Sagittarius; earth—Taurus, Virgo, Capricorn; air—Gemini, Libra, Aquarius; and water—Cancer, Scorpio, Pisces. In essence, the four elements depict the four functions of the psyche. A function is a primary way of experiencing the world: (1) we can experience the world actively by expressing ourselves (fire); (2) we can experience the world physically through the senses (earth); (3) we can experience the world mentally through our thoughts and perceptions (air); and (4) we can experience the world emotionally through feelings (water).

The four elements roughly parallel what Jung described in his psychology as the four functions, or types: intuition, sensation, thinking and feeling. The elements also correspond roughly to the four known states of matter—solid (earth), liquid (water), gaseous (air), and plasma (fire). As without, so within; the isomorphism of psyche and cosmos is handily depicted by the function the four elements play in the human psyche. Metaphorically, they are the psychological equivalents to the four states of matter, thus representing our link to the phenomenal world.

The sequence in which the four elements occur has a significance that goes beyond their meanings individually. The process—fire, earth, air and water—symbolizes a complete cycle of experience. If any of these functions are weak or missing (and the horoscope will show how), then the individual's capacity for fully experiencing his world will show a corresponding lack; it would be as if a link in the chain of experience were missing. Psychologically, this can have a crippling effect. Consider each of the elements in turn.

With fire, will is born. There is a fresh, naive innocence and desire to affect the world. Fire initiates action; it is creative energy rushing out to meet the world of form. Confident, exuberant, joyous, dynamic— fire has no sense of boundaries or restraint; anything and everything is possible. Fire gives faith in oneself, in others, and in the Universe.

With Earth, however, comes the first experience of limitation. Donning the garment of material existence, spirit becomes entrapped in matter: desire is born, the senses take command. Resources are not limitless, and there is the need to satisfy the demands of the physical body. With these demands comes the impulse to manipulate matter to personal advantage, to produce something in tangible form. Thus, Earth represents our capacity to be practical, realistic, and productive.

Having become absorbed in material existence, there is the need to pull back from the experience and conceptualize it. What is the nature of this world to which we have become attached? What is it, specifically, we have done? Air is the communicative, rational, cognitive function; it allows us to detach from matter and gain perspective. Air is the ability to learn and communicate. It is the spectator, the witness, the mediator. Without air we would not have sufficient objectivity to make distinctions, separate ourselves from our experience, and make the compromises necessary to live harmoniously with others.

Water follows air as memory follows experience. The lessons of air recede into the unconscious and become part of our storehouse of automatisms from the past, thus freeing us to learn new things. Water is intuition, automatic pilot, habit patterns built into our functioning. It also represents the psychic, feeling level inasmuch as it is receptive to the unknown realms that exist beyond the physical senses and discursive intellect. Similarly, no memory is without its attendant feeling; feelings are born out of the memory of prior experience. Attuned to the inner worlds of emotion and sentiment, empathy and compassion, its natural psychic openness makes it the most sensitive and vulnerable of the elements; in fact, it *is* sensitivity and vulnerability. In its most fundamental sense, water is the unifying element that binds us all together on a "gut" level. It is the urge to love and the need to be loved.

MODALITIES

Just as matter occurs in several forms, so energy has its characteristic actions or motions. These are called *modalities*, and are three in number: cardinal, fixed and mutable. Each category is composed of four signs each. The cardinal signs—Aries, Libra, Cancer and Capricorn—have an energy that might best be described as *centrifugal*, proceeding outward from the center. These signs pursue their needs by seeking something outside of themselves; there is a reaching, striving, goal-oriented quality.

The opposite is true for the fixed signs—Taurus, Leo, Scorpio and Aquarius. This group is characterized by *centripetal* energy—force drawing inwards towards the center. Magnetic is a good word to describe this quality; it invites you in rather than moving out from itself. One feels attracted to it, drawn into its center. Fixed signs have a tendency to be enduring, sustaining, constant, and even stubborn. There is a dogged determination about this group, where once committed to a definite course of action, it will persist unvaryingly until the final goal is consolidated.

The final modality—mutable—is a natural consequence of the first two. Its energy is *fluctuating*, dispersing outward in several directions at once. This is paralleled in the laws of physics: When an irresistible force (cardinal) meets an immovable object (fixed), energy is released (mutable). The signs that compose this group—Gemini, Virgo, Sagittarius and Pisces—are characterized by their flexibility and adaptability. Mutables are thus scattered, versatile, and changeable. Their capacity to adjust to the exigencies of a situation is rivaled only by their tendency to be inconstant.

THE POLARITIES

The polarities constitute a crucial division of the zodiac as they represent the separation between conscious and unconscious portions of the psyche. By polarities, we refer to those dichotomous energies variously referred to as yang, masculine, positive, light or Apollonian, and those referred to as yin, feminine, negative, dark or Dionysian. In the zodiacal model, the yang or positive signs represent the conscious portions of the psyche, while the yin or negative signs represent the unconscious. Just as days alternate with nights throughout the year, so signs of positive polarity alternate with those of negative throughout the zodiac. This can be illustrated by the first four signs: fire sign Aries (yang) precedes Earth sign Taurus (yin), which, in turn, is followed by air sign Gemini (yang), and then water sign Cancer (yin). Of the four elements, fire and air are yang, and Earth and water are yin. This same sequence of alternating yang-yin energies repeats itself throughout the remaining signs of the zodiac.

According to Jung, it is the constant interplay and tension between opposite poles of conscious and unconscious that makes for the integration of the psyche, a process he termed *individuation*. This was mentioned earlier in the section on Individual and Collective signs. We saw how these two groups were complementary opposites, and their relationship compensatory. With yang and yin polarities, we are again talking about opposites in the psyche that bear a compensatory relationship to one another; yet, the process is slightly different.

Signs opposite one another (Individual and Collective) represent a completion, while signs adjacent to one another represent a departure, a beginning or movement from one phase into the next. Each sign represents the next step in the process of conscious-unconscious unfoldment. As Jung described it, for every conscious attitude (yang) there is a counterpart unconscious (yin) attitude to compensate and balance it. Growth occurs through the dynamic exchange of energies within the psyche; conscious assimilates part of the unconscious, thus establishing a new balance or equilibrium between the two.

This principle, which is central to Jung's psychology, is beautifully illustrated in zodiacal symbolism. Each sign bears a compensatory relationship not only to the sign opposite it, but also to the sign that precedes it. Consider Libra and Scorpio. Libra, being an air sign, represents the yang or conscious part of the psyche, while Scorpio as a water sign is yin or unconscious. The essence of Libra is cooperation. As an air sign, it opts for separation and space between; differences are politely acknowledged and compromises affected to insure peaceful and harmonious relations. Libra, above all wants things to be *nice*. Scorpio, however, is not interested in things being nice, and thus compensates the light, charming banter of Libra with an intense, brooding quality. Scorpio's intention is to penetrate and expose the superficiality of Libra by creating a crisis that obliterates the differences that separate. It may do this in a devious, subversive manner, or by blatantly provoking a fight. The point, however, is that Scorpio wants union: not two partners, but one flesh. Death and regeneration is the issue here, not peace and harmony.

Scorpio, in turn, is followed by the fire sign Sagittarius that compensates the dark, daemonic qualities of Scorpio by emphasizing justice, ethics, truth and morality. This interplay between Yin and Yang signs repeats itself around the zodiac, constituting, as it were, the manner in which consciousness evolves or "folds out" of itself.

Behaviorally, there are some important differences between yang and yin signs. In general, we observe that yang signs are extroverted, oriented towards the outer world of objective events, people, and things. The emphasis is on the *active* expression of self. Yang signs tend to be open, direct, independent, and life-affirming. They represent the broadcasting system of the psyche, having to do with messages conveyed on either an action (fire) or intellectual (air) level. Yang is the mechanism that allows us to affect our universe, to cause things to happen "out there." In contrast, yin signs are introverted. The orientation is toward the inner world of subjectively perceived responses to environment. Hence, yin signs tend to be reflective, indirect, passive and doubting. They represent the feedback system of the psyche, having to do with messages received on either a sensory (Earth) or emotional (water) level.

Yin allows us to monitor the effects of experience. Thus, where yang signs are self-expressive, yin is more concerned with self-preservation. Similarly, where yang is spontaneous and assertive, yin is cautious and inhibited. Perhaps the key difference between the two polarities lies in their relationship to nature as a whole. Yang signs act on and interpret nature; yin signs submit to and unite with nature. In one, the approach is active/independent; in the other, receptive/dependent.

PERSPECTIVE

Perspective is an orientation in time and space. As each sign corresponds to a specific time-space phase of the yearly cycle, so each sign has its own unique time-space orientation, or "developmental perspective." By this, we mean that time and space are experienced differently for each sign of the zodiac, and this qualitative difference in perception is intricately tied to that sign's psychology or "point of view." Proceeding from Aries through Pisces, these different perspectives are divisible into three distinct groups: personal, social and universal. Each group is composed of four signs, or one sign each of the four elements. The first four signs are personal—Aries, Taurus, Gemini and Cancer; the second four are social—Leo, Virgo, Libra and Scorpio; and the last four are universal—Sagittarius, Capricorn, Aquarius and Pisces.

The personal signs—Aries through Cancer—are characterized by their egocentricity. These signs are relatively primitive with very little concern or awareness of other people. The focus is on the immediate gratification of instinctual needs; behavior is simple, childlike, oriented toward survival in the here and now. Their vision tends to be narrow and restricted, and time, if it exists at all, is experienced as passing very slowly. A year to the child of four seems an eternity. Developmentally, this group relates to the period from birth through puberty.

The social signs—Leo through Scorpio—are oriented primarily toward having relationships with specific others, whether this be peers, co-workers, spouse, or, to some extent, society at large. A key word here is *reciprocity*. The needs represented by these signs cannot be satisfied unless the individual takes into consideration the needs of others outside of himself. The need for validation, companionship, productivity, and power, all imply a need for meaningful involvement with other people. At this stage, vision has expanded to include the world of others. The individual experiences himself as part of a complex web of social relationships. Social signs are more sensitive to the reactions of others. Fads, customs, mores and taboos of society assume major importance. At this stage, life is experienced more as a coherent whole. One has a definite past and a more or less specific future. Concomitantly, one's experience of time has speeded up; years zip by relatively quickly in comparison to childhood. Developmentally, these signs encompass the period from adolescence (Leo) through the "mid-life crisis" of the early forties (Scorpio) when the individual experiences more fully his own mortality.

The universal signs—Sagittarius through Pisces—have a much more expanded perception of time and space than the first two. This group is concerned with ultimates—ultimate truth, ultimate order, ultimate love and compassion. Vision has expanded to the collective and transpersonal level. Whole epochs and nations are taken in at a glance. Humanity is viewed as an evolving whole, and the individual, in comparison, seems relatively insignificant. One's awareness of time has gone beyond the one-life stage; after-death states are now postulated, as well as a concern for the future of humanity as a race. With the signs Aquarius and Pisces comes a consideration of the infinite and the eternal—the transcendence of the spatio/temporal realm completely. In these later stages, time flashes by at a rate totally disproportional to earlier periods. Life, it seems, lasts "but the wink of an eye."

Fundamentally, these signs relate to the period from mid-life to old age.

Taking in the zodiac as a whole, we find that each sign corresponds to a developmental stage of life, these stages constituting a twelve-fold process that can be further organized into three distinct groupings: personal, social and universal. This idea parallels the principle of psychological epigenisis as formulated by Erik Erikson in his book *Youth, Identity, and Crisis.*[3]

According to this principle, all that grows has a ground plan, and from out of this ground plan the parts arise, each part having its time of special ascendancy until all parts have arisen to form a functional whole. Originally applied to biology in relation to phases of embryological development, Erikson's principle postulates that psychological growth proceeds in a similar manner.

Preliminary research suggests that while this may be true, the zodiac may be a superior system for differentiating and qualifying these various stages. Just as embryological development progresses from the simple cellular state to the complexity of the organism as a whole, so each sign increases in complexity (by incorporating the qualities of all signs that proceed it) as we move around the zodiacal circle. Similar to Eriksonian formulae, each sign-stage represents a specific task, the completion of which paves the way for the next sign.

We also find that within this process of personality unfoldment, each sign experiences time and space differently. At earlier stages of development, our vision is relatively narrow and time moves slowly. At later stages, time seems to have accelerated, and, concomitantly, vision has tremendously broadened. The implications of this phenomenon are rather interesting, yet deserve more space than we can afford at present.

Two things, however, are worth repeating: (1) as consciousness expands with age, our subjective perception of time and space changes with it: we see more in a shorter space of time—or, put simply, vision broadens as time accelerates; and (2) signs appear to be time-space phases that symbolize the steps of the evolutionary process. The year, upon which the zodiac is based, may actually be a microcosm of a larger cycle that encompasses the whole life.

The zodiac, in fact, may be the archetypal cycle for cycles in general. For instance, not only does the year serve as a microcosm of the

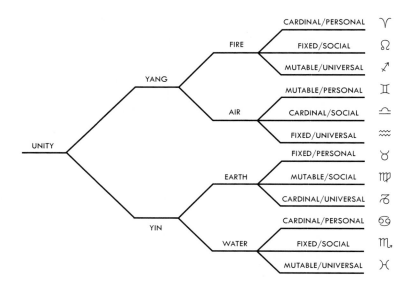

Figure 3: From Unity to Articulation of Parts

In Figure 3, "unity" stands for the transcendent whole, the macrocosm, out of which the parts of the zodiac emerge. These parts (archetypes) are like transcendent ideas in the mind of God, the expression of which culminates in the essential structures of consciousness as symbolized by the signs. The first division constitutes the differentiation of unity into the polar opposites, yin and yang, or the masculine and feminine principles of the Universe. From this fundamental polarity is differentiated the four elements, fire & air (masculine) and earth & water (feminine). These, in turn, further differentiate into the three modalities, cardinal, fixed, and mutable. There is also a threefold division of the elements into personal, social, and universal perspectives. The signs that result from the differentiation of unity into parts constitute the building blocks of consciousness. In various combinations, these building blocks make up the psyche that is cosmos, the microcosm that reflects the macrocosm. Every individual is a replica in miniature of the entire Universe. The task of evolution is to integrate the parts into a balanced and functional whole, and in so doing become one *with* the whole.

life cycle, but the life cycle seems to recapitulate the overall process of evolution, which, theoretically, occurs throughout many lifetimes. It even appears that the zodiac may symbolize the phases involved in the evolution of the race as a whole. This idea becomes clearer when we consider that Aries, for instance, is the mentality not only of the new-born infant but also of primitive man, while Pisces symbolizes the consciousness not only of the very old but of the saint or mystic as well.

ANGULAR RELATIONS

To complete our outline of the structure of the zodiac, there is one more idea that needs to be covered: that of aspects. Aspects relate to the quality of relationship between signs. We are still talking here about the collective psyche, however, and not the individual psyche. In order for relationships between signs to have personal significance, they would have to be triggered by planets occupying the signs involved. Mars in the sign Gemini, for instance, may be in aspect to Saturn in Leo, the planets serving as catalysts to the forces in question. We will consider the personal significance of aspects in later chapters. For now, we will simply examine the archetypal relationships between the various signs of the zodiac as they apply to all of us. The structure of the zodiac, in other words, can be regarded as a generic model of consciousness. Angles between signs show how the various parts of the human psyche are related to one another.

Since the circle is divided into 360 degrees, and each sign constitutes one-twelfth of the circle, relationships between signs are determined by multiples of 30 degrees. Major aspects are 0, 60, 90, 120, 150 and 180 degrees. These are called the conjunction, sextile, square, trine, quincunx and opposition respectfully. Consistent with our image of the zodiac as constituting the structure of the human psyche with individual signs as basic psychological drives, we find that the angular relationships between signs depict the various ways these drives interact—whether stimulating, constricting, harmonious, conflictual, or complementing.

The nature of these relationships is intricately tied to the polarity, element, modality and perspective of the signs involved. Even more to the point, an aspect derives its meaning from the nature of the sign to which it corresponds. In other words, it is the signs that form the first (or *opening*) and the last (or *closing*) aspects in relation to Aries that give us the meaning of the aspect. Gemini, for example, is the sign that forms the first sixty degree angle from Aries, or what we call an opening sextile. The nature of Gemini, therefore, corresponds to the meaning of an opening sextile. Likewise, Aquarius forms the last sixty degree angle in relation to Aries, and thus constitutes the meaning of the closing sextile. Just so, each sign represents a 30 degree phase in the overall 360 degree cycle of the zodiac, and this phase signifies an angle or *aspect*. Taking each aspect in turn, we find the following.

The **conjunction** (0 degrees) is not really an angle in that it signifies the relationship between planets that occupy close to the same degree of the same sign. Generally speaking, this angle has an Aries quality— egocentric, subjective, and spontaneous. Planets that are conjunct one another tend to operate as if they were joined at the hip. Because they don't see each other, they are like two instruments in a band that, while different, are playing the same notes of the same song. In other words, the planets are fused together and thus have a more aggressive, decisive quality. It is like two horses with blinders that are hitched to the same carriage; they are harnessed for the same purpose, are galloping in the same direction, and are moving *fast*. Thus the conjunction has a strong, uninhibited, vitalizing quality.

The **semisextile** (30 degrees) is considered to be a minor aspect; yet it is important in that it signifies the first 30 degree division from Aries. The semisextile represents the relationship between signs adjacent to one another. Being of different element, modality and polarity, these signs have little in common. Adjacent signs have a compensatory relationship; each sign evolves or "folds out" of the one that comes before. Because one is yang and the other yin, one sign is the unconscious of the other. The effect of this aspect is quite subtle and not readily apparent in either behavior or overt events.

Beginning with Aries, the first semisextile is with Taurus. Thus the nature of Taurus gives us a flavor of what the semisextile signifies. Taurus acts like a brake on Aries; it inhibits further action and takes stock of the current reality. Its nature is consolidating, slowing, and securing. What is the nature of the ground that has been conquered? What is of value here? If Taurus is compensatory to Aries, Aries is compensatory to Pisces, which constitutes the other sign that signifies the meaning of the semisextile. Pisces symbolizes the collective unconscious out of which the impulse to life emerges. Its nature is dissolving, flowing, and allowing things to be what they are. Like Taurus, it is the antithesis of action, which of course is the essence of Aries. In effect, Taurus restrains action by requiring a sustained, grounded focus on what *is*. Pisces restrains action by countering the impulse *to be and to go* with the impulse *to let go and let God*. Both Taurus and Pisces are counterbalancing, control processes that constitute a restraining influence upon the illusion of omnipotence that characterizes Aries.

The *sextile* relationship occurs between signs sixty degrees apart with one sign in between. Although of different element and modality, these signs are of the same polarity. They have enough in common to get along, while differing enough to be mutually stimulating. Generally speaking, the sextile relationship is observed to be energizing. The signs involved tend to combine and collaborate in a harmonious and fortuitous manner. As mentioned, the two signs that form a sextile to Aries are Gemini and Aquarius respectively. As air signs, they represent processes that enable the individual to understand and communicate about the nature of the planets that constitute the aspect. Sextiles, therefore, tend to present opportunities for learning and gaining perspective.

Signs 90 degrees apart are said to be in *square*. This aspect can only occur between signs of the same modality, yet opposite in element and polarity. While this aspect is certainly a stimulating and dynamic one, it also entails a struggle between conscious and unconscious. Consequently, it is one of the most difficult of all aspects to integrate. Squares tend to produce conflicts of an obvious and overt nature. The relationship is one of stress, tension, and struggle. Like chronic wounds, squares demand sustained attention. The dilemma of the square may become an issue that occupies the whole life. At the same time, the square aspect can be one of "divine tension," for it stimulates the signs involved to their utmost potential, thus often producing growth from the ability to contain and control the impulses involved.

As the sign that constitutes the opening square, Cancer gives us an understanding of the aspect, for Cancer exemplifies the inhibited, suppressed quality of the square. The fear that Cancer symbolizes is the fear of not belonging, of not being loved and accepted unconditionally.

Accordingly, the underlying tension that occurs between planets forming an opening square is rooted in the fear that expression of the planets involved could result in rejection. Capricorn is the sign that constitutes the closing square. The fear that Capricorn exemplifies is the fear of failure, of inadequacy, of not achieving anything of significance. It is precisely this fear that drives Capricorn to overfunction and overachieve. Likewise, the closing square can signify a fear that the signified planetary functions will operate in a dysfunctional manner and cause each other to fail to meet their respective needs. Again, this fear of failure produces the tremendous drive and ambition that characterizes the closing square.

The *trine* (120 degrees) occurs between signs of the same element and polarity, yet different modality. Trines connote relationships that are smooth, flowing and harmonious. One might consider the trine a kind of Zen aspect, for it seems to produce an easy, natural success that is obtained through the "effortless effort" which is the hallmark of Zen: "Sitting quietly, doing nothing, spring comes, and the grass grows by itself." Similarly, with the trine, things go well not because there is any struggle or effort involved, but simply because they have always gone well and will continue to do so. This expectation is implicit within the trine. Such confidence and faith is exemplified in the two fire signs that signify the opening and closing trines, Leo and Sagittarius. Leo mirrors the creativity and self-expression that characterizes the opening angle and Sagittarius corresponds to the buoyant optimism of the closing.

Perhaps the most paradoxical and incompatible of all relationships in the psyche, the *quincunx* (150 degrees) occurs between signs of different element, modality, polarity and perspective. Because they have literally nothing in common, there is often a sense of contradiction and absurdity between these signs that makes them extremely difficult to integrate. They usually relate to problems or covert conflicts that are (1) repressed yet periodically surface into problem/crisis situations; and (2) can only be resolved through a skillful blending of contrary circumstances. As the problem solver of the zodiac, Virgo perfectly correlates to the meaning of the opening quincunx. For it is the nature of Virgo to notice problems and work toward their solution. As the sign that signifies the closing quincunx, Scorpio is associated with crisis situations. Scorpio symbolizes a darkness and woundedness within the psyche that requires healing. Again, the closing quincunx perfectly correlates to this state of affairs, for the planets involved tend to produce a crisis in the areas of life they represent.

As mentioned earlier in the section on Individual and Collective signs, the *opposition* (180 degrees) signifies a relationship of complementary opposites. These signs are of the same polarity and modality but differ in element. The relationship is essentially one of completion, each sign being the "flip side" of the other; what one is missing, the other one has. On a personal level, this is often experienced as a "see saw" effect; the individual feels himself pulled in two directions at once. If the opposition is a particularly intense one, it presents an appearance of mutually exclusive needs (or situations) vying for dominance. Unlike the quincunx, however, the opposition presents a comparatively clear cut struggle; circumstances evolving out of this aspect result in obvious "either/or" type situations, the solution to which can only be achieved by doing "both."

Libra is the sign that correlates to the opposition, its essence being one of compromise, cooperation, and collaboration in establishing a sustainable relationship between two entities. In effect, the opposition is an aspect that requires harmonizing opposing planetary functions into a working partnership, which is precisely the need that Libra represents.

INTEGRATION OF THE WHOLE

Like the circuitry of an electronic computer, aspects tie the zodiac together into a functional whole; in effect, they denote the ways of the psyche, for they represent dialogues between the different needs and drives that make up the whole of the human being. These dialogues, and the circumstances which derive from them, manifest in a variety of ways. Just as signs represent archetypal needs and characters, so aspects portray archetypal relations between needs and the characters that embody them. The events we experience are thus an expression of psychic images and themes common to all humans, evidence of which can be found not only in everyday life, but also in myths, legends and fairy tales throughout history. Such archetypal stories are but personifications and dramatizations of the various needs and drives that comprise the human psyche. This is why astrology has always been intricately tied to mythology.

Ultimately, if we are to fully appreciate astrology from a process perspective, we must learn to see the zodiac as a dynamic whole. This means that no sign can be considered separate from any other, but only in relation to the part it plays in the unfoldment of a constantly expanding and integrating consciousness. We can, for instance, synthesize the components of yin polarity, cardinal modality, earth element and universal perspective and come up with the archetype known as Capricorn. But this is not enough; for part of what Capricorn *is*, is determined by what it is not. As Richard Idemon put it:

> It (Capricorn) cannot be properly understood without relation to its place in the entire schema, the process of twelve. For unless we understand where it is coming from (the qualities/signs that have proceeded it) and where it is going to (qualities and signs following) and what it is completed through (quality/sign opposite it) and so on, we have simply a static description that leads us down the well-worn path once more toward stereotype.[4]

We have seen how the zodiac can be organized into various categories—individual and collective signs, elements, modalities, polarities, perspective, and aspects. In an actual horoscope, these various components will all be present to greater or lesser degrees, depending upon the arrangement of planets. Planets are the distributors of zodiacal energies. An individual, for instance, may have six planets in fire signs, one in earth, three in air, and none in water. Similarly, this same individual may have the majority of his planets in collective signs, mutable modality, yang polarity and universal perspective. The relative distribution of planets in these categories would tell us a great deal about how this person orients himself to the world, as well as the strengths and weaknesses that invariably result from his particular constitution.

Further insight could be gained by looking at aspects. A cursory glance at the chart might reveal a preponderance of squares and oppositions, indicating a relatively challenging and driven life, or, perhaps, a plenitude of trines and sextiles, suggesting a relatively smooth flowing, stress-free life. In actuality, every individual will have his own unique blending of all the factors mentioned above.

The advantage of looking at personality in this manner is that the individual is not labeled in a linear way, e.g., as an introvert as opposed to an extrovert, but rather is seen in terms of the relative strength of one energy over another. We are not, therefore, a "this" as opposed to a "that," but both at once. We may have sixty percent of our planets in yang (extrovert) signs, and forty percent in yin (introvert) signs, but this makes us neither extrovert nor introvert; it simply shows where the personality falls along the continuum of extroversion-introversion. The same is true for the categories of elements, modalities and perspective; personality is not a matter of "either/ or," but "more and less." Astrology shows that the complexity of personality cannot be reduced to the static, linear notions of most psychological models. That is to say, we cannot be *typed*, for though we are all composed of the same fundamental energies, we are all unique. This uniqueness is reflected in our particular blending of zodiacal factors, and the degree to which we have integrated them.

The final point I wish to emphasize in this chapter is that the zodiac symbolizes a dynamic process intricately tied to the growth and evolution of the individual. No one sign is more important than any other; all contribute their energy to the compound we call the psyche, or soul. The individual, experiencing the results of these energies emanating out of consciousness and forming the events of his material existence, uses them as pivotal points to facilitate his own growth. The goal of the psyche, as symbolized by the zodiac, is the ever more effective and balanced integration of these energies into a dynamic and unified whole.

Chapter Three

Understanding The Legend

POLARITIES, ELEMENTS, QUALITIES, PERSPECTIVE

A s we saw in the last Chapter, there are several fundamental divisions in the zodiac that reflect the way the psyche is organized as a whole. These divisions include individual and collective signs, perspective, polarity, elements, and modality. In this chapter, we will take another look at these basic dimensions and begin to ascribe a deeper meaning to them. But first, let's take a look at what we call *the legend* in the birth chart. The legend is a way of measuring the relative strength or weakness of the chart's various dimensions for a specific individual. In so doing, a considerable amount of information can be gained at a glance. Just as an illustration often has a title or brief description below it (called the legend) that captures the overriding theme of the picture, so the legend enumerated beneath the horoscope summarizes the essence of the person it represents.

By assigning a numerical value of "one" to each planet in each of the five general categories, we can begin to quantify the relative strength or weakness of these various dimensions. For purposes of convenience, I include the Sun and Moon as "planets" when referring to the heavenly bodies that constitute our solar system, even though they are not really planets. However, because the Sun and the Moon tend to be experienced more strongly than the actual planets in the chart, a numerical value of "two" is assigned to each of them. A value of "one" is also assigned to the Ascendant and Midheaven (the meanings of which will be covered in Chapter Five), for they make an important contribution to overall personality dynamics as well.

Individual/Collective	Perspective	Polarity	Elements	Modality
Individual = 8	Personal = 6	Yang = 8	Fire = 5	Cardinal = 3
Collective = 6	Social = 4	Yin = 6	Earth =4	Fixed = 9
	Universal = 4		Air = 3	Mutable = 2
			Water = 2	

Figure 4: The Legend

Suffice to say that the strength of any dimension is reflected in the number of points that dimension receives. For example, if someone had his Sun, Mercury, and Ascendant in earth signs, then earth would receive a total of four points. Applying this rule to all the categories, we have a way of quantifying the relative strength of each of the five dimensions. The legend (Figure 4) depicts a chart with eight points in individual signs, six in personal, eight points in yang, five points in fire, and three in cardinal. Note that each category totals 14 points.

As you can see, the legend is a kind of snapshot of the chart with all its essential features laid bare. It becomes easy to see how subcategories like "personal signs" and "the element of fire" garner the most number of points in their category. As such, they constitute a "dominant" function or path of least resistance—something that feels natural and relatively automatic for the person.

Conversely, subcategories with few or no points depict functions that are potential shadows, complexes, or challenges in the life. These "inferior" functions tend initially to be undeveloped. They may be denigrated by the person or projected onto others where they are either scorned or admired. At some point, however, an inferior function might erupt chthonically from the underworld of the psyche and throw the person into crisis. Very often it becomes an area where the person *over-functions* and eventually gains a sense of mastery in the area that the inferior function symbolizes; i.e., it is precisely where the individual is most challenged that s/he is forced to develop.

INDIVIDUAL AND COLLECTIVE SIGNS

The most fundamental division of the zodiac is between the first six signs and the second six signs. The first half of the zodiac is concerned with the differentiation of self *from* the collective, whereas the second half is concerned with the integration of self *with* the collective. Aries through Virgo is an individualizing process with emphasis upon the parts rather than the whole. The focus is more short term than long term. Developmentally, the first six signs signify the growth of the self from infancy to adulthood, ending with the apprenticeship stage of Virgo where the individual develops a skill that allows for emergence into full adult status as a member of the community.

The second half of the zodiac is primarily concerned with the needs of the community and ultimately with all of life. As such, these signs are broader in their perspective, seeing how the parts must ultimately be joined together to form an integrated whole. The emphasis is more long term than short term. Personal gratifications can be delayed out of consideration for what is necessary and correct for the system of which one is a part. Relationship, sharing, ethics, duty, altruism, sacrifice—these are the main focus. Developmentally, the second half of the zodiac signifies the period from approximately 27 years through old age and death.

Each individual sign is polarized to a collective sign that is its complementary opposite. The goal of the psyche is to integrate self with others, individual with collective, in order to achieve psychic balance and wholeness.

INDIVIDUAL	COLLECTIVE
Individualizing, differentiating	Integrating, collaborating
Focus on parts, separating	Focus on whole, joining
Short term interests	Long term interests
Personal interests, self-focus	Community interests

PERSPECTIVE

The zodiac can be further divided into three perspectives or orientations in time and space—personal, social, and universal. Sometimes these divisions are referred to as personal, interpersonal, and transpersonal. The first four signs are personal, the second four social, and the last four are universal. Each group constitutes a distinct era in the individual's development from birth to death. As such, each era evidences a different set of concerns, values, and needs.

PERSONAL

Personal signs correlate to the period from birth through puberty, or from 0 to approximately 12 years of age. These signs—Aries, Taurus, Gemini, Cancer—are relatively selfish, childlike, and primitive in their outlook. They signify needs that can only be satisfied if the individual is focused on him or herself, i.e., needs for survival, food, clothing, language acquisition, and protection. Such needs are foundational, or basic, and must be met before the individual is ready to move out into the larger world.

During this period of time there is relatively little awareness of other people or their concerns. A child experiences itself more or less as the center of the Universe. The focus is on short term gratifications in the here and now. Personal signs are characterized by a relative lack of discrimination or differentiation; freedom, pleasure, knowledge, and belonging are pursued as ends in themselves, independent of the particular experience that provides for them.

Aries represents the freedom to act in the immediate moment (*my* impulses, *my* desires). Taurus signifies undifferentiated sensual gratification in the here and now (*my* pleasure, *my* security, *my* possessions). Gemini symbolizes the quest for undifferentiated information (*my* interests, *my* thoughts, *my* knowledge). And Cancer stands for undifferentiated love (*my* feelings, *my* mother, home, family).

Selfish, childlike, primitive	Basic, foundational, early
Simple, uncomplicated	Present focused, narrow vision
Egocentric, personal	Here and now consciousness

SOCIAL

By the time a child reaches adolescence, s/he has discovered the importance of social relationships and the legitimacy of other people's needs in addition to his/her own. The essence of social signs—Leo, Virgo, Libra, Scorpio—is the need for involvement with other people. Social signs embody the principals of mutuality, interdependence, and reciprocity. There is the awareness that one person cannot be satisfied without the other also being satisfied. Hence, to a certain extent, social signs are other-directed; they look for shared pleasures and mutual satisfaction.

Because social signs need validation from other people, they are prone to partisan values and "party politics." Political acts and principals may be dominated by a need for acceptance and validation from the group to which they belong rather than by an unbiased concern for the universal good of humankind as a whole.

With each social sign we move deeper and deeper into meaningful involvement with other people, until finally consummation is reached in Scorpio—complete fusion—followed by rebirth onto the universal level with Sagittarius. Each social sign needs people in a different way. Leo needs them for the attention they provide and for satisfaction of self-esteem needs—the need for recognition, approval, and validation. Leo symbolizes the need to feel special and important *relative to others*. Leo roles are the performer, the hero, the creative artist, and the boss (in the sense of someone whose will prevails). Leo also represents the need to appreciate others, to admire them, and to make them feel special, too. This "mutual admiration society" constitutes the relationship between lover/beloved, performer/audience, best friends, and playmates. Leo asks, "What can I do to attract attention and feel special? How can I make you feel important, special, and enjoyed, too?"

Virgo needs other people in order to feel useful and competent. Virgo asks, "What can I do for you? How can I be of help?" Roles here are the problem solver, the troubleshooter, the maintenance man, and the renovator. Relationships revolve around themes of servant/master, apprentice/master, worker/co-worker, and merchant/customer. "I am at your service," says Virgo.

Libra needs other people to maintain balance and relatedness. The essence of Libra is complementation, the need for partnership and for sharing with equal others. Roles are the diplomat, the business partner, the spouse, the public relations person, the arbitrator/mediator, and the charming host. Libra asks, "What can I do to bring about a state of harmony and beauty?"

Scorpio needs others for feelings of unity and integration. There is a need to fuse separate elements into an integrated whole, to reconcile division, and to bring about transformation through merger. Roles and relationships are the crisis intervener, risk taker (fireman, medic, emergency unit), power broker (boss, tyrant, dictator), healer (doctor, priest, shaman), involvement with corporate structures and shared financial relationships, erotic relationships, and all relationships with shadow figures such as criminals or underworld figures. Scorpio asks, "What can I do to feel deep, integrated and powerful?"

Other directed	Mutual, reciprocal
Interpersonal, giving	Interdependent
Sharing, participatory	Social, relational, cooperative
Partisan, factional	Community centered, provincial

Universal

By the time we move through the mid-life crisis of our early forties we have hopefully reached a point where we can begin to see the world and our place in it from a more detached perspective. The essence of universal signs—Sagittarius, Capricorn, Aquarius, Pisces—is concern for humanity as a whole. These signs see the big picture, how all the parts fit together into a whole that transcends individuals, communities, cultures, or any one group. Personal and social concerns are recognized as limited perspectives. Personal signs say, "Me, here, now." Social signs say, "Me and you together until death do us part." Universal signs say, "Everyone, everywhere, forever." In this respect, universal signs are humanitarian, idealistic, and visionary. They are concerned with human rights and what is needed for world justice, world order, world equality, and world peace.

Ultimate goals and values are the province of the universal signs. However, if an individual becomes too identified or attached to an ideal, there is the danger of extremism—the dictator (Capricorn), the demagogue (Sagittarius), the revolutionary (Aquarius), or the martyr (Pisces). Of course, these roles can be necessary during extreme times. Generally, however, if we have integrated these parts of our nature then we are content to make our own small contribution to an ongoing process infinite in time and scope. We don't have to accomplish the ideal on our own or in our own lifetime.

Universals care very much about things on a collective level, i.e., for the *principal* of a thing, but comparatively little on a personal or social level. Thus one's personal safety or finances, or one's marriage and children, can be sacrificed for the sake of a higher goal. With a heavy emphasis on universal signs there can be a kind of impersonal cruelty, someone who is relatively insensitive to individuals and loved ones because the transcendent ideal supersedes personal and interpersonal concerns. The individual is so obsessed with the vision of how things should be or could be that the personal, human part of things is lost. This is the type of person who will blow up a federal building in Oklahoma for a political ideal, or leave his wife in the middle of her pregnancy in order to do missionary work in Africa.

Sagittarius wants to educate and inspire humanity to higher standards of morality, justice, and wisdom. Hence Sagittarius is the sage, the teacher, preacher, demagogue, moralist, propagandist, or theorist.

Capricorn wants to make real the Sagittarian ideals of universal truth and justice. Thus Capricorn creates the necessary structures to implement and administrate the laws and codes that Sagittarius envisioned. This is bringing the ideal down to reality by organizing the physical world in such a way that it serves the greatest number of people possible. Capricorn's utilitarian perspective is exemplified in the figure of the administrator, the director, the president, executive, or bureaucrat.

Aquarius wants to throw out the old order of Capricorn and bring in a new order founded upon democratic principles of freedom, equality, and universal brotherhood. Aquarius is more *laissez faire*, hands off, and radical in its approach to order. The libertarian, the iconoclast, the revolutionary, the anarchist, and the utopian visionary are typical roles.

Pisces wants to be absorbed in the whole, to give up ego strivings and radiate selfless love to those who are suffering, lost, poor, or homeless. Here we have universal compassion and indiscriminate love producing the saint, the savior, the martyr, or the mystic. However, if a person is too strongly identified with this principal to the exclusion of being able to act in her own self-interest, we may have the tragic victim, the psychotic, or the addict who strives to become one with an idealized (but destructive) object—food, alcohol, drugs, or addictions to people and processes.

Ultimate values and ideals	Collective concerns
Visionary, utopian	Nonpartisan, humanitarian
Allocentric, altruistic	Philanthropic, selfless
Wholistic, transpersonal	Charitable, munificent
Impersonal, idealistic	Cannot see the trees for the forest

POLARITY

Polarity is a quality inherent in the zodiac. Every sign exhibits opposite, or contrasted, properties from the sign it succeeds. The two polarities are yin (receptive, feminine, negative) and yang (active, masculine, positive). All earth and water signs are yin while all fire and air signs are yang.

YANG SIGNS

Yang signs are oriented more toward self-expression and the outer world of objective events. Their gifts are sociability, expressiveness, creativity, and communication. They emphasize activity and thinking and are not sufficiently reflective to feel guilt. They are more likely to feel confidence and control over the situation, capable of meeting life's challenges directly.

Aries is the gift of courage and strength.

Gemini is the gift of gab.

Leo is the gift of pride, honor, and creativity.

Libra is the gift of grace and sociability.

Sagittarius is the gift of faith and righteousness.

Aquarius is the gift of perspective, of seeing whole.

There is a tendency to equate extroversion with health and introversion with illness. Thus fire/air gives the impression of being happier and healthier than earth/water. Too much yang, however, and the individual may become arrogant, insensitive, over-confident, scattered, and foolish. Fire/air has no understanding of the subtler realms of feeling and tends to lack patience, tact, empathy, and a capacity for self-reflection. Neither are they oriented toward personal growth, productivity, or self-improvement. The attitude is more complacent and self-satisfied.

YIN SIGNS

Yin signs constitute a controlling, restraining, consolidating energy and serve as a counterforce to yang energies. They keep the psyche from flying apart and overextending into the external world. Like psychic glue that keeps us from exploding or disintegrating, yin signs "ground" the psyche in the body and the emotions. Striving towards ideals of material security/perfection (earth signs), or emotional security/union (water signs), are characteristic of the negative signs. Earth-water gives us our capacity for sensitivity, inwardness, self-improvement, and productivity. Attached to the material and emotional realms, yin signs are work and conscience related. They express qualities of restraint and containment because they are oriented towards the demands and requirements of the environment. Just as yang signs constitute innate psychological gifts, so yin signs provide their own gifts.

Taurus is the gift of sensuality.

Cancer is the gift of sensitivity.

Virgo is the gift of competence.

Scorpio is the gift of healing and power.

Capricorn is the gift of responsibility.

Pisces is the gift of dreams.

Associated with suffering and thus fear, yin signs are cautious, deliberate and oriented towards self-preservation. These signs are doubting and inhibited because they feel more "attached" and thus more vulnerable to loss. The repressive, apprehensive nature of the yin signs causes them to be associated with psychological problems. They are more likely to be involved with feelings of depression, guilt, insecurity, anxiety, and inferiority. There is greater difficulty with trust and affirmation. In effect, they are "negative," which does not mean "bad," it simply means that yin is associated with caution, fear, and concern for one's wellbeing. Without such concerns, there would be little incentive for growth or self-improvement.

Taurus is the fear of not being secure or safe.

Cancer is the fear of rejection or abandonment.

Virgo is the fear of wrongness or making a mistake.

Scorpio is the fear of death and of violation.

Capricorn is the fear of imperfection and failure.

Pisces is the fear of disintegration and chaos.

Yang and yin alternate throughout the zodiac. Each sign is a compensatory response to the sign that comes before it. For example, each yin sign is the tension-maintaining, counter-balancing control mechanism of the sign that precedes it. This interrelationship reflects the innate psychic tendency toward balance or equilibrium between conscious and unconscious. Clearly, the optimal goal is a relative balance between yin and yang. Conscious and unconscious must be integrated for optimal functioning. With integration, there is a focused, directed spontaneity and a capacity for disciplined thinking and creativity.

YANG	YIN
Positive	Negative
Masculine	Feminine
Light	Dark
Conscious	Unconscious
Freedom oriented	Union oriented
Extroverted	Introverted
Active	Passive
Separating	Joining
Differentiating	Integrative
Initiating	Responsive
Spontaneous	Inhibited
Direct	Indirect
Open	Concealing
Confident	Doubting
Impulsive	Restrained

THE ELEMENTS

Elements constitute a four-fold grouping of motivational factors. Fire is motivated by the need for pure expression or action. Earth is motivated by a need to produce something in tangible form. Air is motivated by the need for social and intellectual exchange, while water signs are motivated by a need for emotional connection. The elements can also be thought of as the four major *functions* of the psyche. Fire is the function of action, earth of sensation, air of thinking, and water of feeling.

FIRE

Fire is the energy of spirit. It is *prana,* life-force, pure energy. Fire is the will to action. It gives one the courage to be, to express, and to expand. Fire animates and energizes. With fire strong in the chart, there is a sense that anything and everything is possible. There is zest and *joi de vivre.* Fire is life- and self-affirming. Aries affirms itself. "I am right. What I want is right." Leo affirms the other. "You are wonderful and I am wonderful and we are wonderful together." Sagittarius affirms the Universe. "This is the best of all possible worlds; God is just and life is good."

Fire signs are impatient with negativity. They are inherently opposed to it. Fire says, "I know what I want and I have the power to get it, so why don't you?" This is especially true for Aries and Leo, whereas Sagittarius will escape to a theoretical level and argue that whatever is happening is logical and meaningful and that one just has to think properly and everything will be all right.

Where fire is lacking there is often a lack of confidence and courage for self-expression. The zest, humor, and joy of life are diminished. With too much fire, however, there can be a self-absorbed, restless, impatient attitude toward life characterized by a relative insensitivity to other people's thoughts and feelings. The person may also overextend him/herself due to an overconfident, foolhardy disposition. Fire signs exhibit a certain naiveté, especially to limitation and suffering.

POSITIVE EXPRESSION	NEGATIVE EXPRESSION
Creative, expressive	Willful, domineering, arrogant
Confident, proud, vital	Egocentric, insensitive
Exuberant, enthusiastic	Overzealous, manic, fanatical
Dramatic, demonstrative	Showy, overwhelming
Joyful, happy, optimistic	Pollyanna, unrealistic, foolish
Assertive, bold, irrepressible	Aggressive, rash, impulsive
Energetic, bubbly, lively	Obnoxious, pushy, excitable
Dynamic, spirited, feisty	Impatient, contentious, selfish

EARTH

Earth represents the crystallization of spirit into matter. Thus earth signifies our capacity to handle the material world. All earth signs have the urge to produce something in tangible form. Earth signs are oriented toward what is basic, fundamental, and practical. Thus earth is not speculative, emotional, or visionary. It is solely concerned with what can be accomplished and used in a practical way. Accordingly, earth is primarily concerned with the effective utilization of resources and the enhancement of productivity. Earth asks, "Is it practical, will it work, can I feel it, see it, use it?"

Earth represents our attachment to the physical or desire world. It is our need for permanence and stability, and thus also our resistance to change. Earth has very little objectivity as a result of its attachments. It is inclined toward possessiveness and rigidity. This quality, in turn, can result in pain whenever things change, as they inevitably do. To the extent that we are attached to the material world, to the way things *are*, there can be suffering when things vary from their prescribed or predictable order. To earth, change is equated with loss of control and predictability.

Virgo and Capricorn are the "systems signs," as they are always look-ing for a better way to organize and get things done. Capricorn wants perfection now, and is the ultimate planner, whereas Virgo is content to find a flaw and fix it. Virgo is oriented toward fixing, improving, correcting. Taurus is not nearly so ambitious as Virgo and Capricorn. Its perspective is limited to what can be enjoyed *now* rather than later. Accordingly, Taurus is oriented toward appreciating whatever com-forts are available in the moment.

Taurus represents the urge to enjoy and possess the physical world, hence sensual and physical gratification. Virgo represents the urge to analyze and improve the physical world, hence the urge to efficient functioning and productive service to others. Capricorn represents the urge to control and perfect the physical world, thus the need to build a perfect structure and system. Capricorn's goal is to attain expert status and to fulfill one's public responsibilities.

POSITIVE EXPRESSION	NEGATIVE EXPRESSION
Practical, realistic	Unimaginative, conservative
Thorough, productive	Obsessive-compulsive
Reliable, conscientious	Perfectionistic, anxious
Methodical, systematic	Formal, plodding, slow

Materialistic, ambitious	Greedy, possessive
Enduring, persevering, patient	Rigid, unyielding, stubborn
Reserved, steady, grounded	Dull, phlegmatic, sluggish

AIR

Air symbolizes the conscious, reasoning mind, the power to learn and communicate. Air is the witness, the spectator, the transcendent function that serves as an objective mediator between the ego and the unconscious, or the self and environment. It is that part that can step above the immediate situation and view conflicts and process from a detached perspective. This provides the individual with a logical, rational faculty that promotes cooperation, compromise and harmonious social relations. The element air is an adjusting, adapting element that provides the necessary detachment and objectivity to function in social relationships.

Fire is compatible with air because it gives air the freedom, confidence and energy to act. Fire energizes the intellect into action. Earth and water inhibit the cool, abstract, theoretical nature of air by requiring physical practicality and emotional depth. By itself air often lacks deep emotion, tending toward superficiality, as well as having little conception of' the needs and limitations of the physical body.

Too much air inclines one toward excessive intellectualizing. So much time is spent observing life that a person strong in air may simply live in his head and never get anything done. Ideas are pursued for the sheer love of thinking and may become ends in themselves. The mind can be over-active, supercharged, leading to a world of vivid imagination and conceptual brilliance, yet at other times to a sense of reality totally out of touch with what is practical or possible. The nervous system is highly activated and extremely sensitive to the extent that the person may exhaust his/her nervous energy very rapidly.

Too little air can hinder the capacity to detach oneself from situations and be truly objective, resulting in learning difficulties as well as problems with communication and socializing. People with a lack of air rarely consider it to be a problem, however, because the mind does not know what it does not know.

POSITIVE EXPRESSION	NEGATIVE EXPRESSION
Intellectual, mental, rational	Overly intellectual, "heady"
Objective, impartial, detached	Cut off from feelings, schizoid
Abstract, theoretical, logical	Spacey, ungrounded
Cool, reasonable	Aloof, distant, insensitive
Communicative, engaging	Gossiping, verbose
Clever, witty, versatile	Flighty, superficial, inconstant
Conceptual, knowledgeable	Unrealistic, impractical

WATER

Water signs have to do with loving and the need to be loved, as expressed through the absorbing, blending, unifying nature of water. There is a general sense of needing to feel *connected*. Cancer's most basic need is to love in a personal, protective, nurturing context. Scorpio's urge is to penetrate, blend, and share on an equal level with peers. Pisces transcends personal and social/erotic love in a selfless, universal compassion that knows no limits or bounds.

Water signs are very sensitive, which means they are extremely responsive to stimuli. Feelings are tender, raw, easily hurt. Having no solidity or shape of its own, water is the part of us that may have difficulty differentiating between self and other. For this reason water is most compatible with earth, which gives it form and purpose. Earth-water blends are very nurturing.

Water signs are reflective and concerned with the past. This element signifies the assimilation of experience on an emotional level. Functioning becomes automatic and habitual. Having gone through the experience, water provides us with the capacity to feel sympathy, empathy, and compassion for the experience of others. We remember what it was like when we had a similar experience. Thus water is our *reflective* and *joining* capacity.

Water also represents the unconscious with its store of memories from the past, automatic response patterns and habits that have developed from repeated experience. The capacity to reflect and remember gives us the ability to process experience, keeping what is of value and letting go of the rest. Like a cow chewing on its cud, water brings back the past and works it over, seeking to assimilate what has been learned so that it is no longer necessary to spend conscious effort on the action. The experience can be relegated to the unconscious so that the individual can ready him or herself for a new beginning with fire, which inevitably follows water in an endless cycle.

Cancer is the *personal unconscious*. Here we are concerned with our own needs for nurturing, warmth, closeness, and love. With Cancer, we may be somewhat personally insecure, the major fear being loss of love or a sense of belonging. Cancer is the need for connection with a personal past, to a mother and a family that loves the individual unconditionally. Cancer requires the satisfaction of being connected on a personal, individual level. These are "family ties" or "the ties that bind."

Scorpio is the *social unconscious*. Here we are concerned with society's needs for an integrated and cohesive social order. To keep things integrated means eliminating that which is unintegrateable. This gives rise to that which is forbidden as expressed in societies' unwritten laws and taboos. Scorpio signifies social insecurities and fears, such as the fear of being shunned, ostracized, or "eliminated" (killed, fired, destroyed) if we violate social taboos or for some reason cannot be integrated into an existing system. Scorpio is also the principle that connects us to our ancestral past. We are born into and inherit the traditions and beliefs of a clan, tribe, or community. To the degree that the individual integrates him or herself with the community, s/he attains social power. One of the ways we experience this integration is through shared financial relationships, or "financial ties," such as investments, taxes, insurance, and inheritance.

Pisces is the *collective unconscious*. Here we are concerned with the collective needs of humankind and a need to feel oneness with the Universe at the deepest level of our being. Pisces is a nondiscriminatory, self-sacrificing love, compassion, and forgiveness. The most spiritual of all signs, and the most intuitive, Pisces can also be associated with a vague sense of anxiety that things may unravel, disintegrate, and collapse into the chaos from which we all have come. To the degree that we lack faith in some sort of unifying "higher power," there will be a vague, haunting fear of a return to chaos. Pisces is the principal that unites us with our primordial past, that past which we share simply because we are human. This is the deepest level of the psyche wherein we are connected to all life and feel bound to care for all life.

Water is the most vulnerable of the elements. It is due to our need to feel loved and connected that we are susceptible to emotional pain. Because water is associated with unconscious, habitual response patterns based on past experience, it is the part of the psyche that has most to do with unconscious motivation, i.e., behavior that is influenced by factors outside of awareness—irrationality, unconscious compulsions, repressed memories, and the like. Water has the most difficulty trusting and affirming life. Again, it is the relative absence of our connections with others that produces emotional pain. Suffering is basically a water phenomenon.

Cancer is associated with fear of rejection and not belonging to a family. Scorpio is associated with fear of abuse, violation, and betrayal of trust on a social level. There is also a fear of being ostracized or "eliminated" by one's community because of a subjectively perceived "badness." Whatever one is ashamed of constitutes the Scorpio component of consciousness. Pisces may suffer from an inability to affirm the Universe. There can be a sense of tragedy and/or victimization. Comparing the present imperfect reality against the ideal of infinite love and beauty, Pisces may seek to escape from reality. The fear is that the vision is unrealizable and that separation from the Universe/God is unbridgeable.

Too little water indicates a person who may be out of touch with feelings, or who may get off on the feelings of others—vicarious feeling relationships. Such people may appear cold, uncaring, aloof, or insensitive in some way. Emotional rapport escapes them, and they can be cut off from others on an emotional level without realizing it. Or they may have a distrust of intuitive knowledge. Feelings still occur on an unconscious level and influence behavior regardless of whether or not the person is aware of it. Such people may be unusually fearful of pain, the logic being, "If I can't feel, I can't suffer." When pain is finally encountered, it can overwhelm the person because he or she has not developed a capacity to contain and tolerate it.

Water is the cleansing, healing, purging energy, and lack of it may indicate a build-up of toxicity in the emotional body, which may eventually show up as sickness on a physical level. If experience is not assimilated at an emotional level, and psychological waste is not eliminated through a sharing of feelings, it may lead to a state of auto-toxicity and resultant sickness. Too much water can indicate excessive sensitivity, dependency, and insecurity. Because an extreme need to connect may cause a blurring of boundaries, water is susceptible to confusion of personal identity.

POSITIVE EXPRESSION	NEGATIVE EXPRESSION
Sensitive, vulnerable, open	Oversensitive, easily hurt
Emotional, deep feelings	Overemotional, maudlin, tragic
Intuitive, psychic	Confused, illogical, irrational
Sympathetic, empathic	Merging, rescuing, no boundary
Unifying, absorbing	Amorphous, unclear
Indirect, aware of subtleties	Manipulative, deceptive, covert
Flowing, receptive, yielding	Undefined, chaotic, helpless
Caring, compassionate	Needy, smothering, clinging
Healing, containing	Suffering, martyr syndrome

MODALITY

Each element expresses itself in three different ways—as cardinal, fixed, or mutable. These modes constitute different styles or types of expression of the basic elements/functions.

CARDINAL

Cardinal signs are Aries, Libra, Cancer, and Capricorn. Cardinality is a style of expression that involves centrifugal movement out from a center towards a goal state. Satisfaction of the need is gratified by reaching out to something, starting things, getting things moving. Yang cardinal signs (Aries and Libra) move directly out from their own space to get what they want. Introverted or yin cardinal signs (Cancer and Capricorn) manifest indirectly, yet tenaciously. The needs of all cardinal signs necessitate taking some form of action for their satisfaction. Aries is pure cardinality, a direct, unrestrained out-rushing force. As cardinal water, Cancer cautiously reaches out to make an emotional connection. Cancer typifies "passive action" to elicit a caring response. As cardinal air, Libra listens aggressively, seeks social contact, and draws people out in order to establish and maintain a relationship. As cardinal earth, Capricorn may be somewhat reserved, yet is relentless in its striving for success, status and distinction.

POSITIVE EXPRESSION	NEGATIVE EXPRESSION
Generating, initiating	Too many irons in the fire
Striving, reaching, pursuing	Overactive, overcommitted
Goal driven, outreaching	Uncentered, dissatisfied

FIXED

The fixed signs—Taurus, Leo, Scorpio, and Aquarius—are magnetic rather than outreaching. This is centripetal force, energy drawn inwards to a center. Accordingly, fixed signs manifest by attracting and controlling. They stabilize, concentrate, and preserve what was started in the cardinal phase. With a magnetic tendency, centripetal signs are the binders of the zodiac. The energy that was flung out and made available in the cardinal phase is now accessed, bound, and utilized in the fixed. The more emphasis on fixity in the chart, the more the person will endure a situation no matter how difficult or frustrating. There is great staying power.

Getting stuck in some sort of impasse or power struggle also typifies someone with too much fixity. For example, we might say "he's in a fix," meaning a situation from which he can't readily extricate himself. The problem is a lack of adaptability and flexibility, as in "something has to give." With Taurus Rising, Saturn in Taurus, and four planets in Leo including the Sun and Moon, the Yugoslavian dictator Slobodan Milosevic is a good example of someone with too much fixity.

Each fixed sign is resistive in some way. Taurus resists change in general, i.e., anything that threatens its security. Leo resists any affront to its ego, thus exhibiting "stubborn pride." Scorpio resists any attempt at control or violation and thus exemplifies the indomitable "diehard." And Aquarius resists the status quo, thus embodying the obstinate rebel who opposes tradition and authority on principal. If fixity is lacking in the chart, the individual may lack concentration, stamina, or perseverance.

POSITIVE EXPRESSION	NEGATIVE EXPRESSION
Concentrating, consolidating	Freezing, getting stuck
Conserving, sustaining	Hide-bound, rigid, unyielding
Steadfast, focused, enduring	Stubborn, retentive, inflexible
Tenacious, persistent	Obstinate, closed-minded

MUTABLE

Gemini, Virgo, Sagittarius, and Pisces are mutable signs. The energy is spiralic or distributing outwards in multiple directions. As such, mutability is dispersing and flexible in its mode of expression. These signs are characterized by their adaptability more than anything else. A heavy mutable emphasis may indicate someone with a multiplicity of interests who is pulled in several different directions. There can be a tendency toward inconstancy, change, restlessness, and scatteredness. This may result in the jack-of-all-trades or the dilettante who lacks the persistence to really accomplish much.

If there is too much mutability, the person may have difficulty sustaining a clear focus on what he or she really wants out of life, i.e., what his or her primary values, goals, and interests are. Finding a direction and moving towards a precise goal is problematic. He or she may feel lost or confused or ambivalent when it comes to pursuing an objective. Or s/he may be frantically over-extended, or lack a sense of what is realistically possible. If s/he is deficient in fixed signs and thus does not have a strong center, there can be much worrying and fretting with a tendency toward nervous exhaustion.

POSITIVE EXPRESSION	NEGATIVE EXPRESSION
Adaptable, adjustable, flexible	Inconstant, changeable, erratic
Mental, communicative	Nervous, distracted, restless
Versatile, variable, multiple	Diffused, overextended
Dispersive, distributing	Scattered, depleted, confused

SUMMARY

Like the elements, polarities, and perspective, the modalities form a functional unity. Each form of energy necessarily implies and balances the other two. An apt metaphor is the phases of an internal combustion engine. Cardinal signs signify the initial spark or outward explosion that gets things moving. This outward explosion encounters fixed boundaries that compress the energy back inwards—the fixed signs—which, in turn, causes a dispersion of energy directed toward multiple ends—turning the crankshaft, recharging the battery, and the myriad tasks that are required to propel the system forward. This last phase would be mutable. Thus we see how each mode of energy requires the other two.

Chapter Four

Signs as Astrological Archetypes

MOTIVATIONS, CHARACTERS, STAGES, TRAITS & THEMES

I n the previous chapter, we explored the meaning of the zodiac and
compared signs to universal principles inherent in nature (archetypes). These principles have their expression in human behavior.
The zodiac, therefore, is the foundation of the astrological language,
forming as it were the letters of our alphabet. This language is essentially divided into four parts: signs, planets, houses, and aspects. Each
of these parts is a different expression of the same universal principle,
or archetype. For every sign, there is a planet, house, and aspect that
correspond to that sign. Planets are "rulers" of signs and houses because
the planet is the dynamic, active version of that archetype.

As the prime movers of the psyche, planets represent psychological processes, or functions, geared toward the satisfaction of the sign
(need) they rule. They are the verbs of the astrological language. Their
expression is relatively active, although they can manifest as states,
attitudes, and events, too. Houses represent specific areas of life experience. They are the concrete externalization via events of the planets/
signs to which they correspond. Houses, therefore, are circumstantial,
situational and contextual. Signs, themselves, serve two functions.
First, a sign symbolizes a need that underlies and motivates its ruling
planet. In this regard, the sign functions as a noun, e.g., the need for
autonomy. Second, a sign functions as an adverb descriptive of how a
planetary process operates when a planet is *in* a sign.

A simple example should make this clear. As a motive, Aries symbolizes the need for autonomy. Whenever this need is activated, it motivates its ruling planet, Mars, to act in the service of this need. Mars represents the verb to assert; yet, Mars may be in any of twelve signs. If it is in Pisces, it may assert weakly; if in Capricorn it could assert systematically; if in Leo it will assert dramatically, and so on. Here we see how the sign functions as an adverb that modifies the natural function of the planet that is in that sign.

In their various combinations, signs, planets and houses provide the basis for a complete astrological sentence. For the time being, however, we are going to focus exclusively on signs. Once the essential principles of signs are understood, everything else in astrology will make more sense.

There are three distinct ways of looking at signs: (1) as process, (2) as behavior, and (3) as content. **Process** has to do with the underlying needs and drives which the signs represent. **Behavior** is the traits and attributes that characterize the sign. **Content** refers to the external events that derive from and reflect the nature of the sign. In terms of a psychological language, signs as process perform a noun function, e.g., Leo is the *need* for validation, approval, and self-esteem. When signs are referred to in their behavioral function, i.e., as modifiers of planets, they take on the role of adverbs. For instance, if the planet Mercury were in the sign Libra, Libra would color the expression of Mercury; Mercury would express itself in a Libran manner. As an event, this relationship may manifest in some concrete experience such as writing a dance routine, or being asked to design the cover of a book. We will explore more fully this distinction between process, behavior, and content in subsequent chapters.

SUN SIGNS

Before we go on, it is necessary to underline a point made earlier in this book. The human psyche, or personality, is a composite structure made up of all twelve signs. The peculiarities of temperament and disposition have more to do with the manner in which these signs are arranged and activated within the psyche (by planets) than with any one sign in particular. Confusion results from the tendency to classify individuals according to Sun sign alone.

The function the Sun plays in the solar system—that of being its inner core, its hub, the massive central organ which provides life, light and energy to the whole—is analogous to the function the Sun plays in the psychology of the individual. In astrology, the Sun represents the will or ego; that part of us which consciously chooses one thing over another. Of all planets, it is perhaps the most crucial in terms of identity formation. The sign in which it is placed has much to do with self-concept and personality expression. The individual will tend to identify himself, i.e., his character or temperament, with the principle of his Sun sign. Moreover, the nature of the sign the Sun tenants will be directly affected by solar qualities of expressiveness and creativity.

Yet, a person is much more than Sun sign alone, for this is but one part of his total nature, which is comprised of all twelve signs to varying degrees of emphasis. To fully appreciate the significance of signs as motivators of personality, it is necessary to reduce them to their essences; that is, to the instinctual needs they represent. This is impossible if we personify them, e.g., "she's a Leo," which suggests that one sign forms the whole of the human personality.

Sign	Descriptive Terms
Aries	Assertively, directly, boldly
Taurus	Stable, calm, sensuous, steady
Gemini	Curious, intellectually, chatty
Cancer	Softly, tenderly, caring, protective
Leo	Dramatic, creatively, playful
Virgo	Efficiently, competently, helpful
Libra	Intimate, kindly, aesthetic
Scorpio	Powerfully, passionately, erotically
Sagittarius	Bluntly, optimistic, truthfully
Capricorn	Seriously, organized, disciplined
Aquarius	Insightful, detached, abrupt, cool
Pisces	Imaginative, selflessly, empathic

Figure 5: Signs as Behavioral Traits

SIGNS AS DESCRIPTIVE OF BEHAVIOR

The most obvious characteristic of signs is their descriptive function, and this is what is emphasized in most astrology books. As mentioned in the preceding paragraph, signs have been more or less personified in popular astrology. The result of this distortion is that we do not describe Leo behavior, we describe Leo individuals, e.g., "He [Leo] is a show-off and likes to be the center of attention; he is quite extroverted." It is misleading to depict signs in this manner. By equating signs with people, facets of the psyche are blown up into whole persons and the metaphorical meaning of the sign is lost. This is evidenced in the prevailing tendency to ask individuals, "what sign are you?" And the individual might respond, "I'm a Leo," which simply means that the Sun is posited in Leo and that the outward manifestation of personality has taken on the flavor of this sign.

As the central organ of identity, the Sun's expression is conditioned by the sign in which it is placed. Yet, we are talking about two different things: planet and sign. No matter what the planet, its manner of expression is going to be affected by the sign it is in; thus, we could have Mars in Leo, Venus in Leo, or Mercury in Leo. Whatever the planet, however, its intrinsic manner of expression is going to be modified by the Leonian tendency toward warmth, extroversion, flamboyance and the like. So with Mars, we could say, "I assert myself dramatically;" with Mercury, "I communicate in a flamboyant style;" and with Venus, "I seek companionship in an outgoing, extroverted manner."

Like a membrane through which the energy of a planet flows, a sign modulates a planet's natural frequency. Since any planet can be in any sign, combinations are legion; the interaction of sign and planet producing behavior particular to that interaction. In this context, the sign becomes an adverb modifying the expression of the verb, the planet. With Jupiter in Virgo, for example, we could say that the person's approach to religion (Jupiter) is critical, thoughtful, and skeptical (Virgo).

For any given sign, it is possible to list dozens of terms descriptive of that sign's manner of expression. The sign Gemini, for example, has to do with thinking and discourse. Behavior typical of this sign would focus on the adroit and skillful use of language as a means of labeling, classifying, and communicating responses to environmental stimuli.

Sign	Motivational Need
Aries	Survival, being, autonomy
Taurus	Stability, security, pleasure
Gemini	Learning, communication
Cancer	Nurturance, caring, belonging
Leo	Validation, approval, self-esteem
Virgo	Efficiency, competence, service
Libra	Intimacy, relatedness, beauty
Scorpio	Transformation, sexuality, power
Sagittarius	Meaning, truth, expansion
Capricorn	Structure, perfection, order
Aquarius	Perspective, insight, change
Pisces	Transcendence, unity, bliss

Figure 6: Signs as Basic Needs

Hence, Gemini is a metaphorical construct for the words "chatty," "curious," "rational," and "empirical," to name just a few. If we took the planet Mars, which stands for the verb to assert, and put it in Gemini, we would have a person who is intellectually assertive, or who asserts through words, facts, and knowledge. Figure 5 on page 71 lists some of the key descriptive terms relating to the twelve signs.

SIGNS AS MOTIVATIONAL DRIVES

In their noun (process) form, signs are best described as motivational drives, or needs. They represent the underlying energy behind the expression of personality. All behavior, therefore, must be understood in the context of the need that behavior serves. Accordingly, the need of a given sign is inferred from behavior that is characteristic of that sign. While this behavior might be expressed in a variety of ways, or not expressed at all (depending on other factors in the chart), the underlying need would remain the same. Consider the person with Sun in Taurus. Typically, he would express himself (Sun) in a slow, deliberate manner (Taurus). We may notice a calm, steady exterior. He is practical, earthy, sensual and perhaps somewhat stubborn. This is not a person, we notice, who takes well to sudden change. Inertia characterizes his every move. From these and other characteristics, it is not difficult to identify the basic need beneath Taurean behavior—the need for safety, security, and sensual gratification.

Since the Sun is the dominant symbol of personality expression, the need of Taurus would be very evident in the personality, being right on the surface, as it were. The individual might even appear as a veritable embodiment of the need Taurus represents, this fact being reflected in behavior, voice tone, body posture, and life style. Yet, even if there were no planets in Taurus, the need for safety and security would be there. It might not be so obvious in the personality, but it would still be influencing behavior. The strength or weakness of a given sign is determined by (1) how many planets are in that sign—the more planets the stronger the urge; and (2) the relative position of the "ruling planet" of that sign. We will consider the importance of ruling planets in later chapters. At this point, I wish only to emphasize that signs are motivational drives that underlie the functioning of specific psychological functions as symbolized by the planets. The basic motivational needs that the signs symbolize are listed in Figure 6 on the previous page.

SIGNS AS EVENTS

Events (content) emanating from a given sign have to do with the external manifestation of that sign's energy, i.e., the actual concrete experiences through which the need of a sign seeks satisfaction. A case in point would be Sagittarius. Reduced to its essence, Sagittarius represents the quest for meaning, purpose and significance. It is the need to believe in something greater than oneself, and, further, the need to express and promulgate these beliefs. From this need come concepts of right and wrong beliefs, and, thus, ethics, morality, and law. The search for the "truest truth" soon leads us into the area of values and quality; something is either more true or less true than something else; things are better or worse, right or wrong.

Because the need for meaning and values is a fundamental urge of humankind, whole institutions spring up in response to it: churches and temples provide a place to honor and worship gods—the religious embodiments of truth; philosophies provide elaborate theories on the nature of Man and the Universe; metaphysical systems purport to reveal the underlying causes and purposes of existence; and universities grant access to the accumulated knowledge and traditions of learning

Sign	Event Manifestation (Primary Themes)
Aries	Adventures, new projects, competitions, fights, hard labor
Taurus	Money & goods, possessions, sensual pleasures, relaxing
Gemini	Books, learning, information, communications, writing
Cancer	Home, family, mothering, caretaking, feeding, nourishing
Leo	Play, games, entertainment, creativity, parties, romance
Virgo	Work, services, crafts, utilities, diet & health, tasks, chores
Libra	Marriage, social relations, contracts, art, aesthetics
Scorpio	Sex, death, taxes, corruption, pain, healing, financial ties
Sagittarius	Religion, philosophy, higher education, ethics, law, travel
Capricorn	Career, ambition, authority, status, duties, obstacles, limits
Aquarius	Groups, causes, humanitarianism, technology, reform
Pisces	Spirituality, sickness, loss, idealism, escape, drugs, charity

Figure 7: Signs as Events

that have been bequeathed throughout the ages. The eternal quest for meaning, indeed, takes many forms.

On a more mundane level, yet still in service to the same need, there are the legislative and judicial bodies of government that regulate the behavior of the citizenry according to whatever is considered to be right, true and morally proper at the time. Truth cannot always be delivered from the pulpit, however, or justice from a judge's bench, but must be written as well. This gives rise to the distinctly Sagittarian profession of publishing. The dissemination of truth also finds its way into the business world as promotion and advertising. Here again, the concern is with values and qualities, e.g., "this product is better/worse than this product."

The search for and expansion of knowledge is accomplished not only through the written and spoken word, but through travel as well. Seeing how other cultures conduct their affairs is an age old method for broadening our understanding of the world. Wanderlust is thus another characteristic expression of Sagittarian energy.

These categories of experience—religion, philosophy, scholarship, law, publishing, advertising, promotion, and travel—serve to illustrate the many forms a single archetype can take, yet still remain true to itself. People engaged in the aforementioned activities are all expressing, in one form or another, the same fundamental principle. These activities provide a vehicle for the Sagittarian quest for meaning and values. Thus, Sagittarius is said to "rule" these aspects of life. Their manifestations are mundane derivatives—hence, symbols of Sagittarian energy.

Each sign, similarly, rules over its own area of experience. Rulerships are actually based on a kind of factor analysis. A factor is a condition or circumstance cooperating with other conditions or circumstances in bringing about a specific result. In effect, the result is a product of factors that have a high degree of correlation. Travel, philosophy and religion, for instance, are factors that correlate to the search for truth and wisdom, which ideally *results* from these activities. Promotion, advertising and law are factors that correlate to values; law and religion correlate to ethics. Sagittarius is simply a metaphor which brings all of these factors together under one heading. Sagittarian activities and conditions (factors) cooperate to bring about truth, wisdom, values, and ethics. These results constitute the primary "theme" of the sign. To the degree that a given sign is strong in the chart, its theme will be more or less evident in the person's life.

Taken as a whole, the zodiac provides the ultimate taxonomy, for there is literally nothing that cannot be classified under the auspices of one or another of the signs. By organizing phenomena according to their qualities, astrology becomes a representational system of life itself. In Figure 7 on page 75, a brief listing is provided of the more common manifestations, or themes, of the archetypes we call signs.

ZODIACAL SIGNS AS SUBPERSONALITIES

There are additional ways to think about signs. In the next section, I provide an outline summarizing how each sign constitutes a psychological need, a primary archetype, a developmental stage, and a behavioral pattern. Perhaps most importantly, however, an astrological sign (and the planet that rules it) can be described as a subpersonality that resides within the psychic compound Jung called the *Self*—the totality of the psyche. Accordingly, whenever I utilize a pronoun such as *it*, *he*, or *she* when referring to a sign, this caveat should be kept in mind. The being I am referring to is not a human being, but an archetypal one.

Note also when reading the following sections how the need of a sign, its corresponding archetype, developmental phase, and behavioral pattern are all self-consistent. For example, the behavioral tendencies of a sign are geared toward a specific goal or target state as signified by the need of the sign. Leonian behavior, for example, is perfectly suited to attain self-esteem. Likewise, the archetype of a sign presents various images or characters that symbolize the core needs of the sign. And a sign's developmental stage shows how the behavior and need of a sign can be understood in the context of that sign's orientation in time and space.

ARIES

Planetary Ruler:	Mars
Corollary House:	First
Corollary Aspect:	Conjunction
Polarity:	Yang
Element:	Fire
Modality:	Cardinal
Perspective:	Personal

Psychological Need

Survival	Autonomy	Immediate Gratification
Life/Existence	Independence	Action/Doing, Novelty
Being	Freedom	Activity/Movement

Archetypal Characters

Warrior, Fighter	Pioneer or Beginner	Noble Savage
Impetuous Child	Infant or Young Man	Adventurer
Competitor	Opponent	Explorer

Developmental Phase

Birth to 18 months. Sensori-motor stage in Piaget scheme. Primary narcissism. Process of separation/individuation up to rapprochement. Sense of omnipotence. Need for basic trust (Erikson). Undifferentiated self. No separation between self and objects. Pure impulse. "I am the world. Me, here, now."

Behavioral Traits and Themes

Innocence: Like a newborn child, Aries behavior seems to be naturally innocent and unsophisticated. Everything is seen and experienced through fresh eyes. For this reason, Aries is the archetype of the "noble savage."

ingenuous	naïve	primitive
natural	uncivilized	innocent
simple/childlike	fresh	unpretentious

The will to be: Aries signifies the birth of self as a separate being. Although there is no sense yet of being a separate self or of having a clearly defined identity distinct from others, there is a strong impulse to survive as an autonomous entity. This principle is, of necessity, directly opposed to cooperation (Libra) and in conflict with externally opposed authority (Capricorn). Everything having to do with "doing it alone" is Aries.

autonomous	invincible	willful
independent	indomitable	self-sufficient
self-reliant	self-directive	self-governing

Perpetual motion: Aries behavior seems to be characterized by enormous reserves of physical energy. One has the image of wild horses galloping across a field, or rams squaring off for a joust. Aries is similar to what Freud described as the *id* or *libido* (psychic energy), which seeks immediate satisfaction of sexual and aggressive impulses. Aries is characterized by a relatively raw, unrestrained, primitive energy, from which it derives its strength.

energetic	hot-blooded	strong
enthusiastic	vital	ardent
fiery	vigorous	spirited

Births and beginnings: As the first sign of the zodiac, and corresponding to the first day of Spring, Aries represents the principle of birth, or beginnings. Perhaps for this reason, it is a marked characteristic of this sign to start more than can be finished. Seeing the world with fresh eyes awash with wonder at every new observation of human capacity, Aries is filled with a sense of "I can do that!" Fundamentally a sign of action, Aries seems to be primarily oriented to starts and diametrically opposed to completions (Libra).

initiating	active	eager
pioneering	decisive	quick
enterprising	action-oriented	impulsive

Undifferentiated self: Because Aries experiences time and space in a manner similar to the newborn infant, there is little differentiation between self and environment. Accordingly, the capacity to wait, to plan ahead, to endure frustration, or to patiently persevere, is relatively absent. This makes sense when one considers that for Aries nothing exists except the immediate present. There is no memory of a past, and no conception of a future. Consequently, Aries demands immediate gratification because only the *now* exists.

impulsive	instinctual	non-reflective
spontaneous	straight & direct	unquestioning
impetuous	abrupt	unrestrained

Knows no fear: Since there is nothing perceived as separate from Aries, and therefore nothing opposed, Aries has no conception of fear or limitation. Everything and anything is possible. The Nike ad line *"Just do it!"* is a perfect expression of Aries. This point of view exemplifies the superman mentality—a kind of omnipotent over-optimism. Typically, Aries will attempt more than can be accomplished, start more than can be finished, promise more than can be delivered, and will seldom look before leaping. More than any other sign, however, at the end of the life Aries can say "no regrets." For whatever else happens, it will not be for lack of trying. A particularly apt word for Aries is *courage*.

fierce, fearless	bold, forthright	brash, reckless
courageous	audacious	brave
daring, defiant	dauntless	intrepid

Aries, god of war: In the home of a friend of mine is a poster showing a newly-hatched baby chick struggling to emerge from its shell. Beneath the image are inscribed the words, "Arise, go forth, and conquer." Not surprisingly, my friend is a Sun sign Aries. The sign is naturally warlike precisely because the impulse to war is linked to the impulse to survive. And Aries quite simply is the impulse for life, for survival, and for doing whatever is necessary to assure it. If frustrated or thwarted, Aries is notoriously quick to anger (no frustration tolerance), which makes sense when one considers that Aries experiences frustration as *a threat to survival*. Yet, there is no vindictiveness or carrying a grudge. Aries fury is quickly spent and quickly forgotten. If Aries could speak, it might say "I want what I want and I want it right now!" Perhaps the best word to describe this quality is *fierce*.

aggressive	fierce, fearless	contentious
assertive	belligerent	angry
adamant, resolute	combative, feisty	offensive
demanding	desiring	impatient
volatile, warlike	quick-tempered	pugnacious

Egocentric: The term *egocentric* can be defined as "self-centered; interested primarily in oneself and one's own concerns and indifferent to the concerns of others." Recall that the infant does not differentiate itself from the outside world and thus has little awareness of the effects its actions have on other people. Likewise, Aries has little awareness of other people. Being a self-starter and sure of its own direction, Aries is sometimes equated with "leadership," but Aries leads only in the sense of being the first to be going somewhere. If others follow, that is of little interest to Aries. There is only one thing of real interest to Aries, and that is *itself* and the freedom to act on whatever impulse is occurring in the present moment. Needless to say, this unbridled instinct for self-gratification can be offensive to people. Accordingly, Aries has a reputation for being somewhat brutish, insensitive, and out for himself. A classic example in film is Marlon Brando (Sun Aries) as Stanley Kowalski in *Streetcar Named Desire*.

abrasive	rough	insensitive
crude	intrusive	brutal
pushy	narrow	discourteous
outspoken	arrogant	blunt
brazen	rude	antisocial

TAURUS

Planetary Ruler:	Venus
Corollary House:	Second
Corollary Aspect:	Opening Semisextile
Polarity:	Yin
Element:	Earth
Modality:	Fixed
Perspective:	Personal

Psychological Need

Safety & Security	Self & Object Constancy
Predictability	Stability (Homeostasis)
Pleasure	Sameness & Familiarity
Comfort	Sensual Gratification

Archetypal Characters

Earth mother	Settler, Squatter	Couch Potato
Fertility Goddess	Homesteader	Glutton
Demeter, Ceres	Sensualist, Hedonist	Epicurean
Young Woman	Voluptuary	Satyr

Developmental Phase

Eighteen months to approximately four years. Anal stage in Freudian model. Late sensori-motor and early preoperational learning in Piaget scheme. Rigidity of thought. Centration or "frozen thought." Rapprochement. "Paradise lost" and resultant concern with security and attachments. Attainment of object permanence along with self and object constancy.

Behavioral Traits and Themes

Voluptuous manner and sensual focus: No sign is more deserving of the epithet "earthy" than Taurus. With Jupiter in Taurus on the Ascendant, Mae West said it best when she purred, "Too much of a good thing can be wonderful." There is something innately attractive and beautiful about Taurus. One feels drawn to it in a gentle way. It is not necessarily a glamorous beauty, but it is a natural one, like a French milk maid or a rugged outdoorsman—perhaps the Marlboro man (minus his cigarettes). In more extreme cases, it can be downright lustful, even lascivious. In certain of his movies, Jack Nicholson embodies this dimension of the sign.

natural beauty	sensuous	earthy
attractive	voluptuous	inviting
touchable, huggable	luscious	physical

Focus on pleasure, security, and sensual gratification: Taurus is not only attractive, but *attracting*. The well-known Taurus attribute of materialism and possessiveness is indicative of the need for physical security. The accumulation of goods, and strong attachments to things and people, illustrate the dominant Taurean concern for safety. One of the sign's chief attributes is its ability to acquire, save, and conserve money and possessions. Pleasure and contentment are equated with "having objects," especially people to whom the individual is attached (thus Taurean possessiveness). In fact, Taurus represents attachment behavior and its developmental corollary: self- and object constancy.

acquisitive	pleasure-oriented	materialistic
accumulative	comfort-seeking	attaching
hoarding	indulgent	possessive

Taking things at face value: Piaget characterized preoperational thought as "frozen." He noted that children between two and five have a tendency to "centrate," i.e., focus on one salient feature of an object or event and ignore other features. The rigidity of thought that typifies this period makes it difficult for children to "put two and two together." They focus instead on immediately observable states of matter with little or no understanding of how things *change* from one state to another (lack of reversibility). There is still a considerable amount of egocentricity at this stage, which reflects the child's inability to deal with several aspects of a situation at the same time. The fact that toddlers cannot readily understand how things change is reflected in their obsessional concern with physical security and stability, a preoccupation which makes understanding any kind of change difficult. All of this is typical of Taurus' perceptual sensibilities as well.

concrete	basic	simple
unimaginative	physical	uncomplicated
dense	tangible	slow

Calming presence: Because Taurus has to do with the need for stability and security, it is characterized by a natural calmness. In fact, one of the most salient features of the sign is its mellow, laid back quality. Gary Cooper is a good example; or recall (if you can) the soothing voice of the singer, Perry Como. Taurus is both comfortable and comforting. No sign is less likely to get ruffled or agitated.

calm, content	sober, reserved	soothing
mellow, serene	solid, stable	gentle, docile
sedate, unruffled	secure, settled	tranquil, placid
comforting	pleasant	safe, innocent

Familiarity breeds comfort: Taurus' love of comfort makes it naturally resistant to change, for change is equated with loss of predictability and certainty. Taurus is like the homeostatic mechanism of the psyche that guards the system against losing its sense of equilibrium. It assures that the familiar, steady ground of the known will continue to provide its comforts and securities. No sign is more steadfast and tenacious than Taurus. "Slow and steady as she goes," is a Taurean platitude. The Taurus part of us wants to gain immunity from any unforeseen circumstance or potential danger that may arise. Accordingly, the sign is quite content to allow things to remain as they are, no matter how unsatisfying they may actually be. When psychoanalysis was all the rage in Europe during the middle of the century, the German poet Rilke was asked if he had considered it. "I am afraid," he said, "that if my demons leave me, my angels will take flight as well." Just so, Taurus will tenaciously cling to the known in an effort to avoid losing whatever good might potentially be lost in the process of change.

steadfast	predictable	familiar
methodical	patient, enduring	slow & steady
consistent, plodding	tenacious	dependable
persistent	persevering	reliable

Playing it safe: All behaviors that are geared toward physical safety and security are Taurean. No sign is more "stick in the mud" or unadventurous than Taurus (recall that the adventurer is an Aries archetype, which Taurus compensates). Comfort is of much greater interest, and is more highly valued, than anything else. Accordingly, Taurus has a reputation for being a bit of a couch potato, i.e., sluggish and comparatively dull. This can be maddening if the situation calls for moving forward. Yet, if "holding down the fort" is the goal, stock it with a bunch of Taureans and it will be impregnable.

conservative	reactionary	reticent
conventional	regressive	hesitant
restrained	suspicious of change	lethargic, lazy
cautious	deliberate	dull, sluggish

Extremely resistant to change: Carried to an extreme, Taurus can be almost pathological in its fear of change. Loss of security and attachment is its worst nightmare. It is interesting to note that with Borderline Personality Disorder it is precisely the failure to attain self and object constancy that produces the clinging, insecure behavior that typifies the disorder. Likewise, if our Taurean sensibilities are not well integrated, there can be extremes of jealousy, possessiveness, and obstinacy. Such extremes appear to compensate for an inner lack of security.

retentive	stubborn, obstinate	inert, reluctant
clinging	intractable	fixed, stiff, rigid
bull-headed	immovable, resistant	unwilling

GEMINI

Planetary Ruler:	Mercury
Corollary House:	Third
Corollary Aspect:	Opening Sextile
Polarity:	Yang
Element:	Air
Modality:	Mutable
Perspective:	Personal

Psychological Need

Information	Rote Learning
Knowledge (Facts)	Mental Stimulation
Data, Input	Language & Communication

Archetypal Characters

Messenger (Hermes)	Student, Pupil	Dilettante
Herald, Reporter	Observer	Amateur
Puer Aeternus	Scientist	Peter Pan

Developmental Phase

Four to seven years. Kindergarten through 2nd grade. Piaget's late preoperational and early concrete operations period. Detaching from senses and forming mental representations of concrete world. Learning to read and write. Language development. Questions, questions. Explosion of learning and talking/reporting about what is known (messenger).

Behavioral Traits and Themes

Learning machines, walking database: One of the most salient qualities of the Gemini personality style is its bright eyed, bushy tailed, ever alert, constantly inquiring mind. Gemini is like "Johnny Five," the delightful living robot in the movie *Closed Circuit* who craved more and more "input." A virtual learning machine, Gemini can pick up information and repeat it back again with a skill that can be astounding. Yet, this openness and eagerness to acquire more and more information gives Gemini a nervous, restless quality, like a bird that jerks its head from side to side, exquisitely sensitive to incoming stimuli.

nervous, restless	hyperactive, busy	bright, learned
mercurial, quick	effervescent, eager	keen, alert

Need for undifferentiated learning: I once had a Gemini client come in for an astrology consultation. When asked if there was anything specific that she wanted me to focus on, she replied, "No. Just teach me. I want to learn!" In other words, she did not want to learn about anything in particular, she just wanted to learn in general. She was not even that concerned about whether she learned about herself, for learning about astrology was equally stimulating. Needless to say, it was an easy and enjoyable time for both of us. The point is that Gemini represents the need for undifferentiated information. Accordingly, it is the most curious, most observant sign in the zodiac.

curious, inquisitive	exploratory	mental
observant, aware	investigative	cerebral
classifying, labeling	experimental	knowledgeable

Joe Friday, "Just the facts, ma'am": Because Gemini signifies a relatively early stage in cognitive development, the ability for abstract thought is negligible. Although a voracious learner, Gemini is less interested in opinion than in concrete facts and empirical data. As a personal sign, it is still egocentric and has difficulty seeing other perspectives. Accordingly, Gemini has little capacity for abstracting meaning or judging value, which is Sagittarius' province. Like other personal signs, Gemini is relatively amoral, or premoral would be more accurate.

factual	simple, concrete	amoral (premoral)
parroting	empirical	nonjudgmental
literal, rote	imitative	superficial
indiscriminate	linear thinking	shallow

Precocious—quick to learn a variety of new things: Something that immediately stands out is Gemini's dexterity in both thought and action. Not surprisingly it is between the ages of four and seven— the Gemini stage—that children develop the hand-eye coordination that enables them to play sports. Prior to this age, coordination is simply not adequate. On a mental level, Gemini displays the same quickness in coordinating words and concepts. Language and communication are comparatively easy. The ability to quickly grasp the essence of something enables Gemini to readily adapt to changing circumstances (unlike Taurus, which has great difficulty adapting to new conditions). Accordingly, the sign gives the impression of knowing a little bit about a great many things, while not knowing very much about any one thing. Depth, in other words, is sacrificed for breadth of learning.

adaptive, flexible	skillful, agile	dexterous, dual
adroit, versatile	coordinated	quick learner

Reporting—the messenger of the zodiac: C-3P0, the eloquent ambulatory computer of *Star Wars* fame, is another good example of the Gemini archetype. Knowledgeable about different cultures, planets, languages, customs, and spacecraft, C-3PO was the perfect messenger and translator. As a protocol droid, he was particularly gifted in languages, being conversant in several million of them. Yet, one of his more annoying qualities was that he did not know when to stop talking, the result of which was that more than once he had to be "shut down" so that Luke and Han could focus on the task at hand. C-3PO also provided a certain amount of comic relief, fretting and chatting away like an overgrown mechanical child. This is typical of Gemini, which is notorious for its flippant attitude, clever wit and light banter, as well as for not knowing when to shut-up!

communicative	verbal, chatty	light, humorous
conversant	garrulous	clever, witty
loquacious	glib, facile	pun-loving

Little depth or constancy of attention: Like any other sign, Gemini's problems result from its strengths being over-expressed. When Gemini overfunctions it tends to become scattered and ungrounded, as if the person cannot keep up with his or her own mind. The most extreme example of this is children diagnosed with Attention-Deficit Hyperactive Disorder (ADHD), a condition that is fairly common among children in the Gemini stage. The syndrome is characterized by a short attention span, distractibility, and inability to complete tasks. All of these traits are typically Geminian. Significantly, ADHD is referred to as a "learning disorder." The mind is so overactive that it cannot effectively assimilate information.

Another variation on this theme is the archetype known as *Puer Aeternus,* which appropriately means "eternal youth." Like an overfunctioning Gemini, Puers are characterized by their silliness, lack of commitment, inconstancy, flightiness (often having flying fantasies, like Peter Pan), irresponsibility, lack of discipline, superficiality, hyperactivity, and inability to judge right from wrong.

changeable	scattered, flighty	dilettantish
fickle, inconstant	undisciplined	ungrounded
unreliable	light, trivial	frivolous

CANCER

Planetary Ruler: Moon
Corollary House: Fourth
Corollary Aspect: Opening Square
Polarity: Yin
Element: Water
Modality: Cardinal
Perspective: Personal

Psychological Need

Nurturing, Mothering	Emotional Security
Belonging & Tenderness	Caring & Protection
Sympathetic Understanding	Warmth & Closeness
Unconditional Love	Acceptance & Support

Archetypal Characters

Mothers, Nannies	Dependent Child	Wombs, Nests
Caretakers, Cooks	Chameleon	Containers
Nurturing Figure	Homemaker	Protectors

Developmental Phase

Eight to twelve years. This is the latency phase of childhood, "the quiet interlude." The birth of the emotional self occurs during this period; there is now the capacity to "contain" rather than "act out" feelings, along with greater internal locus of control. Children become more introverted, quiet, calm, pliable, receptive, and reflective. Able to introspect and evaluate feelings, there is increased empathy for others. Memory awakens and the cognitive capacity for "reversibility" becomes possible. For the first time children are able to understand the concept of transition. There is also consolidation of the super-ego (self-inhibition). This is primarily a period of building a foundation for self-expression.

Behavioral Traits and Themes

Maternal instinct: Cancer symbolizes the love that a mother has for her child. It is devoted, unconditional, and protective. As a personal sign, the love is very personal; the basis of the mother's love for her child is the fact that it is *her* child. There is an emotional bonding and identification between mother and child such that the child will eventually internalize and transform the maternal relationship into a capacity for self-care. No sign is more tender, caring and loving than Cancer.

nurturing	motherly, maternal	tender, soft
loving	affectionate	kind, gentle
loyal, devoted	doting, giving	warm, caring
protective	smothering	containing

Sensitive to feelings: Cancer is the ability to connect with others emotionally, to be sensitively attuned to feelings, whether one's own or the feelings of another. This sensitivity allows for affective attunement, sympathetic understanding, and emotional connection. Cancer, therefore, is like a great receptor that absorbs information on an emotional level.

sensitive	receptive	accepting, open
feeling oriented	intuitive	absorbing
emotionally responsive	perceptive	impressionable

The Chameleon or magic mirror: Because there is such a strong need to establish and maintain emotional contact with others, Cancer has a tendency to take on the color of its environment. It is extremely sensitive and responsive to stimuli on an emotional level, and tends to absorb the emotional tone or mood of its surroundings. This can make it difficult for Cancer to differentiate its own feelings from those of others. Thus Cancer is often described as moody and changeable in its emotional states.

reactive, responsive	Chameleon-like	adapting
adjusting, absorbent	inconstant	moody
mirroring	reflecting	changeable

Soft and fluid: Like water, Cancer tends to conform to the shape of its container. In fact, it is still only when it is being contained, thus water flows downward until it reaches a container—a pond, a lake, or an ocean. The profound sensitivity of Cancer combined with its need to be loved and "held," makes it extremely susceptible to the influence of others. Note that this trait is diametrically opposed to Capricorn rigidity.

impressionable	pliable, moldable	compliant, malleable
irresolute, inconstant	easily influenced	vacillating

Moving like a crab—taking the circuitous route: Although Cancer is a cardinal sign, its watery nature makes it very indirect in its manner. Since Cancer is loath to approach someone directly, it creates a situation where the other must react. Ideally, the response that Cancer evokes will enable it to feel accepted and gain what it wants. Imagine a shy boy circling the girl of his interest without ever approaching her directly, eventually she sees him, there is a sidelong glance as the boy smiles bashfully and looks away, the sequence repeats itself, and eventually there is sustained contact. The nonverbal message is essentially, "can I get close to you?" This style or strategy can be employed in any number of situations.

indirect, circuitous	manipulative, shy	lurking, sidelong
concealing, suppressed	roundabout, allusive	devious, covert

Socially inept, shy, withdrawn: Cancer's extreme susceptibility to rejection makes it difficult to relate to others on a social level. It is much more comfortable relating one to one, or being in a situation where it can express caring concern. Lightness, frivolity, and play are not its strong suit. Cancer is the classic introvert, tuned into the inner world of feelings, fantasy, and imagination. The emotional pulse-taker, Cancer's chief concern is "how am I feeling now?"

timid, insular	passive, inhibited	quiet, reflective
sensitive, docile	introverted, shy	self-protective

Living in the past—remembering one's roots: Cancer represents memory. In one sense, it symbolizes the need to have a past to remember. Accordingly, Cancer is associated with all things pertaining to origins, foundations, and roots, for these represent a source of emotional security, provide a sense of belonging, and evoke memories of love, acceptance, and protection. Attachment to the past often takes the form of collecting and holding on to things that symbolize the "good times," e.g., mementos, souvenirs, keepsakes, relics, tokens, and the like. These are usually stored in an old shoe box or chest along with family pictures and baby toys. Cancer tends to romanticize the past. It is also inclined to demonstrate great loyalty to that which it regards as home or homeland.

sentimental, maudlin	clannish, close knit ties
patriotic, loyal	romanticizing the past
preserving, clinging to past	traditional, historic

Dependent behavior: As the need for unconditional love, Cancer symbolizes dependency needs. Although the word "dependent" has all kinds of pejorative connotations, the fact remains that people need to depend upon one another for love and support. There is a healthy expression of dependency needs. Yet, because this very basic and fundamental need is so often frustrated, deficiencies occur that may result in the need being over-expressed or too intensely felt. Thus Cancer is extremely vulnerable to rejection. This quality is often represented by the archetypal "southern belle" who is apt to faint whenever overwhelmed by feeling.

dependent	delicate, easily hurt	vulnerable, fragile
clinging	weak, insecure	possessive

LEO

Planetary Ruler:	Sun
Corollary House:	Fifth
Corollary Aspect:	Opening Trine
Polarity:	Yang
Element:	Fire
Modality:	Fixed
Perspective:	Social

Psychological Need

Validation of identity	Approval	Play & Creativity
Self-esteem	Attention	Self-expression
Positive self-image	Admiration	Enjoyment

Archetypal Characters

Hero, Heroine	Performer	Egoist, Peacock
Star, Starlet	Creative Artist	Party Animal
King or Queen	Romantic Beloved	Playmate

Developmental Phase

Twelve to eighteen years. Adolescence. Identity crisis. Need for consolidation and validation of identity. Need to differentiate from the family matrix and consequent rebellion against parental authority. Insistence upon choosing own values, beliefs, and customs. Experimentation with various roles and identities. Attraction to heroes and role models. Formal operations, capacity for abstract thought. Deepening of self and other awareness. Peer relations assume major importance; the need for self-esteem is paramount. Socializing, partying, and courtship behavior. Obsessive concern with appearance, image, and popularity. Self-consciousness and egocentricity. Need to be an individual yet accepted by peers. Urgent need for attention and validation.

Behavioral Traits and Themes

The Peacock: There is an innate sense of self-importance in Leo, almost a peacock quality. Behavior is characterized by an unquestioning confidence and self-assurance. One has the impression of royalty or star-quality. This is often compensatory, however, for a fear of being merely ordinary.

proud, confident	admirable	dignified, stately
regal, noble	praiseworthy	snobbish, snooty
commendable	superior	pretentious

Intensely social: With Leo, the quality of self-love is awakened, as well as interpersonal love. Accordingly, Leo is enormously effective at giving others a sense of being liked, appreciated, and enjoyed. As with the Sun, there is a feeling of being bathed in radiant warmth whenever Leo focuses its attention on you. I've had Leo friends who actually broke out into applause whenever they approved of something I did, which was often—not because I was particularly deserving, but because it was their nature. As a fixed sign, Leo wins you over by attracting. And what is so attractive about Leo is the sheer power of its joy, positivism, and good will. Leo is truly *le joi de vivre.* The "Good Time Charlie," no sign is more likable than Leo.

amiable, likable	warm, sunny, radiant	vital, dynamic
affable, jovial	gregarious, joyful	happy, fun
magnetic	attractive, captivating	vivacious

Need for validation: The saying, "everyone loves a lover" is applicable to Leo. Recall that Leo signifies the need to feel important, special, and unique. When this need is projected onto others, Leo treats them accordingly. Again, there is the ability to get others to like themselves. Leo behavior, therefore, is unconsciously intended to win people over; it is, in effect, "winning behavior." This type of behavior is best exemplified in courtship and romance wherein the goal is to get the beloved to associate his or her good feelings with being in the company of the suitor.

romantic, courtly	chivalrous, gracious
generous, affectionate	gallant, magnanimous
stroking, flattering	appreciative, laudatory

Mirror, mirror on the wall, who's the fairest of them all: Behind the need for validation is that which needs validating—identity. The Leo part of us requires the reassurance of acceptance as proof of the validity of our created self-image. At this level, we know ourselves only through the responses of others. As the poet Robert Burns put it, "we see ourselves as others see us." The danger with Leo is that other people can be reduced to members of an audience. Regardless of the motivation, however, no sign is more adept at gaining attention and winning approval. There is natural flash and showmanship.

creative, expressive	demonstrative, outgoing
confident, optimistic	dramatic, flamboyant
extroverted, flashy	self-assured, positive

Born to rule: The desire for the limelight and the presumption of importance often result in Leo gravitating toward positions of authority. Also, since Leo represents the motive force behind volition, or will, there is a natural "willfulness" to this sign. Making decisions comes naturally. What may also come naturally is making decisions for others, i.e., telling them what to do. Thus Leo has a reputation for being a bit bossy at times. The French emperor, Napoleon, whose name has become almost synonymous with tyrant, is perhaps the best historical example of this tendency.

authoritative	overbearing, bossy	imperious
commanding	domineering, lordly	paternalistic
forceful	directive	tyrannical

Desire to impress: When the need for validation is carried to extremes it can result in an over concern with appearances. Leo tends to be somewhat preoccupied with externals, i.e., with popularity, impressions, image, and the like. Thus it loves to put on a good show and impress others with its style if not its substance.

conceited, vain, smug	extravagant, ostentatious
grandiose, inflated	showy, lavish
affected, phony	bombastic, boastful

Good time Charlie: A major driving force in Leonine psychology is the quest for the good time. We could call it the mundane version of the hero's quest, for its goal is plain: *to simply enjoy being oneself*. And if Leo can get you to enjoy yourself in the bargain, all the better. The pursuit of happiness and the avoidance of sadness constitute its main activities. This is reflected in the Leo association with play, sports, games, parties, romance—those activities normally associated with fun and happiness (a good card game is Leo's version of heaven). It also shows up in Leo's well known aversion to hard work and discipline. Striving for advancement and improvement would imply that Leo is not OK just the way it is.

playful, merry	lazy, slovenly	averse to work
pleasure-seeking	indolent, inert	party animal

Psychological blind spot—susceptibility to flattery: Leo can be a notoriously poor judge of character for a number of reasons: (1) their need to be liked predisposes them to see the best in others: and (2) they are susceptible to flattery for the same reason. Both of these tendencies make Leo easy prey to hucksters, sycophants, fawners, deceivers, and others who prey upon its weakness to flattery. In short, Leo tends to be relatively blind to the faults and failings of other people.

uncritical, short-sighted	easily duped, too trusting
indiscriminate, naïve	unquestioning of others
too accepting	susceptible to flattery

The Divinity Complex: Ego needs for approval and validation can be so strong that admitting fallibility is quite difficult for Leo. It is extremely rare for this part of our nature to admit wrongdoing, retract an opinion, back down from an argument, or apologize for making a mistake. Leo takes itself very seriously and becomes demoralized by criticism or humiliation. This sign of stubborn (fixed) pride is prone to such ego defense mechanisms as denial, rationalization, projection, and repression. Also, Leo is likely to exercise a double standard, or what we might call "the divine right of kings," i.e., giving oneself absolute clemency in wrongdoing yet being absolutely unforgiving to enemies.

narcissistic, egocentric	presumptuous
justifying, rationalizing	defensive, pig-headed
contemptuous if criticized	obstinate, prideful
unforgiving to enemies	self-aggrandizing
headstrong, willful	arrogant, dismissive

VIRGO

Planetary Ruler:	Mercury
Corollary House:	Sixth
Corollary Aspect:	Opening Quincunx
Polarity:	Yin
Element:	Earth
Modality:	Mutable
Perspective:	Social

Psychological Need

Efficient functioning	Service, Usefulness
Competence, Proficiency	Improvement
Discrimination	Betterment, Correction
Health & Fitness	Problem Solving, Utility

Archetypal Characters

Efficiency Expert   Spinster, School Marm
Trouble Shooter   Doubting Thomas
Fix-It Man/Woman   Faultfinder
Craftsman   Analyst, Critic
Apprentice, Novice   Worry Wart

Developmental Phase

Nineteen to twenty six. The novice stage of adulthood. Apprenticeship. Developing a skill, trade, or craft. Joining the work force. Being of service to the community. This is a comparatively modest, humble time of life.

Behavioral Traits and Themes

The Good Worker: Virgo represents the need to be useful, thus there is a distinctly pragmatic orientation with this sign. As both a social and an earth sign, the emphasis is on being of service to others. Favorite Virgo expressions are, "What can I do for you? How can I be of help?" Virgo is associated with the exchange and distribution of goods and services.

efficient, competent   pragmatic, practical
responsible, diligent   industrious, skillful
utilitarian, helpful, useful conscientious, reliable

Systems mentality: The urge to efficient functioning makes Virgo particularly interested in finding better ways of accomplishing tasks. Usually this involves dividing the job up into steps, ordering the proper sequence, and undertaking each step one by one. The assembly line method of industrial production is a good example. Virgo's perspective is that anything worth doing is worth doing better. And if it can be done better, Virgo will find a way to do it. Virgonian overfunctioning is exemplified in obsessive-compulsive disorder.

systematic, methodical   painstaking, calculating
technical, exacting   orderly, routine
perfectionistic, thorough   economical, thrifty

Inferiority Complex: If Leo is the sign of the superiority complex, Virgo compensates by feeling inferior. If Leo appreciates, Virgo depreciates. Because the nature of the sign is focused on "wrongness," there is a natural humbling effect when attention is turned upon the self. Virgo's intent is to notice and correct mistakes in order that improvement can be brought about. Applied to the self, this can be expressed in a tendency toward self-criticism or self-deprecation. Like most yin signs, Virgo is not particularly comfortable in social situations. The prissy, love-starved telephone operator "Ernestine," the character invented by Lily Tomlin (who is a Sun sign Virgo) is a classic Virgo archetype.

humble, modest	aloof, uptight
prim & proper	self-critical, self-conscious
socially uncomfortable	prissy, restrained
shy, reserved, inhibited	unassuming, unpretentious

Doubting Thomas: There is a careful, "look before you leap" quality to Virgo. It tends to hang back, examine things closely, question assumptions, and hold judgment in reserve. Being an earth sign, it is reluctant to accept things on faith alone. There is a "show me" quality to Virgo; it demands proof and tangible evidence. It ponders, mulls, and cogitates. Being square Sagittarius and opposed Pisces, there is no sign with a greater tendency toward agnosticism than Virgo.

skeptical, doubting	cautious, careful, hesitant
irreligious, disbelieving	questioning, scrupulous
mundane, secular	agnostic, empirical

Can't see the forest for the trees: With Virgo, discrimination is awakened. The parts take precedence over the whole. Whereas Gemini is content to know *what* something is, Virgo wants to know how it works, what it is used for, how it is made, and how it can be used to make things better. As an earth sign, yet ruled by Mercury, Virgo probes below the surface in order to differentiate the parts from the whole—like taking apart a radio to see how it works. This perspective might be called reductionist or atomistic. Certainly it is *analytical*. It is the details that matter to Virgo. This narrowing of vision often manifests physically in the eyes literally being close together, with a vertical furrowed line between the brows as if one were peering into a microscope at a nasty virus—the skeptical, examining look. Charlie Sheen is a good example. The expression is one of being *troubled*.

analytical, probing	discriminating
scrutinizing, examining	differentiating
detail conscious	separates and compares
reductionist	narrow vision

Problem-solving mechanism: The purpose behind all of Virgo's probing and examining is efficiency. Once it is determined how something works, Virgo tries to figure out how it can be improved. Virgo is really the imperfectionist. It does not want things to be perfect; it wants to discover mistakes so it can make things better. "What's the problem here?" is a Virgo phrase. Intrinsic to the sign is the need to search out and uncover the flaws in things and people so that, once found, they can be corrected. Virgo is the repair and maintenance system of the psyche.

critical, fault-finding	complaining, nagging
picky, finicky	worrisome, irritable
strict, carping	fixing, adjusting
correcting, improving	dissatisfied, discontented
intolerant of error	rennovative, repair-minded

Health and fitness experts: Virgo's urge to efficient functioning makes it naturally interested in how the body works. Accordingly, Virgo is inclined to study things like anatomy, body chemistry, and physiology. A chief preoccupation with Virgo is diet, which shows up as an interest in vitamins, health supplements, vegetarianism, and the like. Virgo occupations include the dietitian or nutritional consultant. Health and fitness, preventive medicine, and concern with personal hygiene are classic Virgo interests.

fastidious, neatnik	sanitary, hygienic
clean & orderly	meticulous
health & diet conscious	hypochondriachal

LIBRA

Planetary Ruler:	Venus
Corollary House:	Seventh
Corollary Aspect:	Opposition
Polarity:	Yang
Element:	Air
Modality:	Cardinal
Perspective:	Social

Psychological Need

Harmony	Intimacy	Fairness
Beauty	Partnership	Peace
Balance	Social Relatedness	Equality

Archetypal Characters

Venus/Aphrodite	Peacemaker	Social Butterfly
Love Goddess	Diplomat	Charming Host
Beloved	Mediator	Artist

Developmental Phase

Twenty-six to thirty-five. Emergence into full adult status as a "social equal." Interest in marriage and partnership starts during this phase. Establishment of linkages with the community through networking and public relations. One's work identity is more established. Parties are not the raucous "beer bash" of adolescence, but more the "cocktail" variety for intermingling in "polite society." Increased ethical sense.

Behavioral Traits and Themes

Social relatedness: Libra is the first of the collective signs and is therefore a sign of social awareness. The primary need is for relatedness; thus, Libra behavior is geared toward establishing congenial ties with others. In the *I Ching* it is written, "Affection, as the essential principle of relatedness, is of the greatest importance in all relationships in the world." One of Libra's principal talents is drawing people out and engaging them in conversation. Johnny Carson, perhaps the greatest of all talk show hosts, is a Sun sign Libra. Whereas Leo is concerned with being "interesting," Libra is concerned with being "interested" *in the other*. The primary attributes of Libra have to do with attracting people and putting them at ease.

engaging, interested	ingratiating, sociable
inviting, enticing	affectionate, kind
attractive, agreeable	cheerful, amiable
friendly, nice	charming, pleasant

Miss Manners: Libra is concerned with the rules of conduct. Every culture has its customs, mores, and conventions that constitute the "social contract" for that culture. Cultural expectations assure that conduct among members of society conforms to what is generally agreed to be in good taste and considerate of others. The Libran impulse acts as a sort of social lubricant, smoothing over differences and mediating conflicts. One of Libra's primary assets is awareness of rules of etiquette, manners, and politeness. Such refinements of character make for the smooth and harmonious functioning of a culture.

polite, gracious, refined	etiquette-conscious
tactful, diplomatic	well-mannered, courteous
cultured, cultivated	smooth, artful

The urge to beauty: Libra is deeply appreciative of the beautiful in art or nature. This aesthetic refinement allows for an instinctive appreciation of balance, harmony, symmetry, rhythm, proportion—in short, that aggregate of qualities that makes for beauty and which pleasurably exalts the mind. Unlike Taurus, which is connected to the senses, the beauty of Libra is of a more abstract (air) nature. Music, dance, and painting fit here. This quality of Libra manifests behaviorally as grace of movement and beauty of expression.

appreciative of beauty	artistic, aesthetic
lovely, exquisite	beautiful and beautifying
graceful, elegant, serene	appealing, tranquil

The Scales of Justice: With Libra, the principle of fairness is awakened. Whereas Aries is a sign of action, Libra is the sign of cooperation—acting together in partnership. Libra is painfully aware that there are always "two sides to every story." As a social-air sign, Libra is concerned with mental exchange. There is an innate interest in what makes other people unique, or *different*. Thus opposing points of view hold a fascination for Libra. As a developmental stage, Libra represents the ascendancy of our capacity for objective awareness. The sign symbolizes the capacity for socialized speech wherein communication is adapted to the level and interests of the other. An instinctive diplomat, there is a natural capacity for compromise, fairness, and accommodation with Libra.

fair, just, ethical	thoughtful, accommodating
detached, objective	considerate, cooperative
balanced, impartial	mediating, arbitrating

Sickeningly Sweet: Because Libra focuses primarily on other people, with the intention of granting equal rights and opportunity, there can be an intellectual detachment that makes this sign difficult to pin down. Libra evidences a cool indifference to self; the view is impartial and unbiased. Yet, if the ability to see both sides is carried to an extreme, Libra can become equivocating, wishy-washy, and indecisive. Too much compliancy in the personality invites others to become overly aggressive in an attempt to balance the interactional system. Libra's "peace at any price" philosophy actually backfires by evoking selfish, abusive behavior in the other. For this reason, an overfunctioning Libra is the astrological equivalent of Dependent Personality Disorder.

placating, appeasing	superficial, shallow
equivocating, hesitant	conciliatory, compromising
indecisive, wishy-washy	noncommittal, irresolute
acquiescent, compliant	two-faced, fence-sitter
evasive of contention	peace at any price

SCORPIO

Planetary Ruler:	Pluto
Corollary House:	Eighth
Corollary Aspect:	Closing Quincunx
Polarity:	Yin
Element:	Water
Modality:	Fixed
Perspective:	Social

Psychological Need

Transformation, Healing	Integrity, Coherence
Death & Regeneration	Power, Potency
Sex (Penetration & Merger)	Elimination, Catharsis
Assimilation, Integration	Purification, Cleansing

Archetypal Characters

The Wounded Healer	Shadow Figures, Stranger
Shaman, Witchdoctor	Monsters, Evil
Sorcerer, Wizard, Witch	Daemonic, Demons
Psychotherapist	Underworld Figures
Financial Wizards	Dictators, Terrorists
Secret Agent, Spy	Femme Fatale
Detective, Investigator	Criminals, Villains
Black Widow, Prostitute	Paranoid, Fear Monger

Developmental Phase

Thirty-six to forty-five. Mid-life crisis. Dark decade of the soul. Facing one's mortality and "seeing the dark at the end of the tunnel." Possible death of parents. Sense of time running out, facing one's unlived self, one's shadow, one's compromised integrity. Disintegrating the self (death and rebirth process) and subsequent self-renewal. Giving up stereotypical role identity and becoming more authentic. Deepening, healing, and owning one's power.

Behavioral Traits and Themes

Eroticism: There is something innately erotic and sexual about Scorpio behavior. It is a non-verbal, intensely penetrating quality that exerts a powerful hypnotic attraction. As a fixed sign, there is a magnetic energy; as a water sign, it is silent and deep. Scorpio *is* erotic love.

erotic, sexual	hypnotic, magnetic
alluring, provocative	intriguing, mysterious
penetrating, exciting	fatally fascinating

Fear of being overpowered and controlled: Scorpio penetrates, but is itself impenetrable. No sign is more guarded, suspicious, and distrustful. There seems to be a fear of being subjected to some external control or some infringement upon one's will. This fear produces a mobilization of defense and vigilance against the perceived threat of danger. Scorpio knows instinctively that secrecy is the basis of power and that silence serves power best.

guarded, suspicious	paranoid, vigilant
secretive, distrustful	withholding, impenetrable
icy, cold, silent	brooding, grave

Internal police state: Scorpio tends to exhibit a rigid, controlled behavior that has much in common with repression. The person appears to be in an internal state of siege, as if some objectionable inner impulse is going to burst through the defenses and take over the self. Thus there is a tight, intense, compacted quality to the personality. Self-control and mastery of forbidden impulses—murderous rage, suicidal feelings, illicit sexual desires, destructive or criminal impulses—is at the core of Scorpio. Though these feelings need to be acknowledged and integrated, they cannot be acted out without endangering oneself or others.

controlled, contained	deep, dark, prohibited
repressive, conflicted	intense, seething, pent up
concentrated, compacted	taboo, forbidden

The urge to merge: Scorpio represents the sex drive, pure and simple. There is a yearning for deep, intimate contact with another person or entity. This requires a willingness to lose control and give oneself over to the desire for union. The sexual drive can be sublimated into any number of outlets, e.g., religious conversion, financial and political power, or even criminal pursuits. Any activity that involves a passionate and intense desire to have union with something outside the self—with money, with territory, with a company, with the enemy, or with one's own forbidden desires, is Scorpionic. In effect, Scorpio is the urge to be transformed through union with all that is feared and resisted.

sexual, passionate, intense	consuming desires
devouring, engulfing	desirous, yearning
covetous, rapacious	compulsive, overwhelming

The territorial imperative: The sexual energy of Scorpio has to do with the tension of reconciling opposites into a new unity. Scorpio, in effect, is the integrative mechanism of the soul. It represents the principle of longing for union with the unknown. If one is unwilling to be transformed in the process, however, and thus unwilling to be penetrated and changed by integrating what lies outside the boundaries of the self, then an alternative measure is to seek power *over* the feared thing—whether this is a person, a company, or a territory. When Scorpio is operating in an unintegrated way, it strives to control that which it perceives as a threat to the current regime. In so doing, a counterfeit integrity is achieved, the price of which is potential revolt by the controlled object.

powerful, controlling	coercive, influential
intimidating, forceful	domineering, compelling
autocratic, dictatorial	despotic, tyrannical rule

The death instinct: Freud wrote about the death instinct (*thanatos*), by which he meant any impulse aimed at destruction of the self and primarily appearing as a *repetition compulsion*, i.e., a compulsion to act out an earlier painful traumatic experience. In other words, thanatos referred to self-destructive behavior. However, what I mean by "death instinct" is the impulse to integrate whatever one fears, whatever has power *over* one, and in so doing *die and be reborn* into a new identity.

The pull toward integrating the shadow is the erotic energy that Scorpio symbolizes. The part of us that resists this process is generally the conscious part of the personality, e.g., the ego, which then necessitates that Scorpio operate subversively. Scorpio undermines, subverts, and corrupts precisely because it is antagonistic to whatever is holding it down; therefore, it attacks the autonomy of the ego in what appears to be an act of self-destruction. Unless one is willing to embrace the dark, the uneasy division between self and shadow cannot be resolved.

When the internal fear is projected and substituted for an external threat, we have the well-known defensive behavior of the paranoid. Scorpio's more benign forms are embodied in professional risk takers who embody the impulse to flirt with and even conquer death. At its darkest level, Scorpio manifests as the true denizen of the underworld—the sexual pervert, the prostitute, the criminal, the insurrectionist, terrorist, saboteur—in short, all that society regards as destructive and evil.

sabotaging, undermining	subversive, corrupting
dangerous, destructive	hostile, morbid, corrupt
perverse, deviant, criminal	evil, antagonistic

Tactical Maneuvers: Because Scorpio is associated with things hidden, forbidden, or taboo, it does not operate openly for fear of reprisal. Scorpio's *modus operandi* is akin to tactical maneuvers. While it can be calculating and intentional, it is almost never direct or spontaneous. Strategic, as in acts of war, is more the Scorpio style. Also, because it is innately attuned to whatever may be dark and hidden in the system within which it is embedded, Scorpio is acutely aware that to reveal or disclose the secret could be dangerous.

covert, sly, underhanded	power-gaming, tactical
devious, crooked, crafty	strategic, plotting, scheming
manipulative, cunning	sleazy, insidious
discreet, hidden	sneaky, furtive, conspiring

Murderous Rage: Fear that a traumatic experience could be potentially overwhelming and destructive to the self may lead to repression of the trauma along with its associated affects, images, and meaning. For example, the experience of having been violently abused becomes something one is *afraid* to remember precisely because it is linked to a number of negative ideas, e.g., "one is bad and deserved what happened," "people are evil and not to be trusted," or "life is hell and not worth living." These ideas, in turn, are associated with frightening affects such as shame, pain, fear, rage, and revenge. Such affects are repressed not only because they are frightening, but because they cause behavior that is destructive to oneself and others. Repression, therefore, results in a state of internal tension.

In projection, this internal tension is transformed into tension vis-à-vis the external world, into biased anticipation of the external world, and finally into conviction about the external world. This may ultimately explode into the cold rage and homicidal impulses that we witness when otherwise good people become possessed by their own fears and hostilities and violently act them out toward innocent people. The movie *Falling Down* with Michael Douglas is a good example.

violent, explosive	homicidal, murderous
volcanic, incendiary	irrational, unwarranted
extreme, over-the-top	vengeful, vindictive

Evil and the daimonic: Scorpio symbolizes the wound in the psyche and thus is associated with fear, pain, and shame. This may simply be a minor injury that results from a hurtful remark or minor affront to one's pride. Or it can be a more serious wound as when someone has been abused or betrayed. Scorpio's style in expressing pain is rarely straightforward. Unlike Aries who responds directly and immediately, Scorpio will hold back and wait for a strategic opportunity. When the response does come, it is likely to be unexpected and cutting. Scorpio naturally tunes in to where the other person is most vulnerable. Sarcasm, ridicule, derision, jibes, barbs, caustic comments, pot shots, and underhanded remarks are preferred forms of Scorpio hostility. If the original injury is sufficiently serious, Scorpio can be cruel and vindictive. This needs to be understood, however, in the context of the wound that underlies the behavior. Scorpionic hostility is actually an attempt to rid oneself of pain and shame by evoking in the other what is subjectively felt within. It is a projection of "badness" outward into the other person.

If one externalizes Scorpio, then there is invariably the perception of evil in the outside world. This is actually a distortion of the impulse for transformation. Instead of embracing one's pain and seeking to heal it, the source of the pain is externalized and then subjugated. In other words, an external threat is substituted for an internal fear, and an external solution is sought over an internal one. If an individual is sufficiently convinced that the *other* guy is evil, he might rationalize that "the end justifies the means" and that he must "fight fire with fire." So Scorpio gets in the first blow in an act that appears to be completely unprovoked. Remember Jim Jones and the People's Temple in Guyana. Stories of people becoming the very thing they fear is one of the most popular themes in film and literature. This suggests that fear of evil is at the root of evil.

evil, wicked, demonic	sarcastic, cutting, venomous
diabolical, devilish	hurtful, spiteful, hateful
vindictive, vengeful	threatening, scary, malevolent
cruel, terrible, ruthless	caustic, trenchant

The detective, secret agent, therapist, investigator: Anyone engaged in the process of ferreting out secret information is expressing the Scorpio drive. Scorpio represents the need to penetrate the sham and the pretense, expose the truth, get at the heart of the matter, and reveal the underlying reality. The ultimate object of Scorpio's perception is what we commonly call "the clue." This suspicious, probing style reflects Scorpio's tendency to perceive danger, whether real or imagined.

piercing, probing, searching	intuitive, perceptive
exposing, revealing	suspicious, biased
scrutinizing, examining	uncovering, disclosing
blunt, confrontational	sharp, penetrating
accusing, ferreting out	cynical, wary

Agents of transformation: In its most positive sense, Scorpio is the great integrator, the divine alchemist who restores unity to the soul. This regenerative influence is personified by members of the helping professions who engage people in a process of healing. Doctors and therapists of all persuasions are Scorpio exemplars. The wounded healer is perhaps the most pure expression of the Scorpio archetype. The transformative process, or healing cycle, involves three stages—penetration, assimilation, and elimination, the result of which is integrity, renewal, and empowerment. Individuals are not the only entities that Scorpio heals. The same process can occur collectively, politically, financially, or in numerous other ways. Any system, in effect, can be reformed, cleansed, or healed.

healing, regenerative	reforming, cleansing
transformative	assimilating, integrating
purifying, unifying	eliminating, empowering

SAGITTARIUS

Planetary Ruler:	Jupiter
Corollary House:	Ninth
Corollary Aspect:	Closing Trine
Polarity:	Yang
Element:	Fire
Modality:	Mutable
Perspective:	Universal

Psychological Need

Truth	Hope	Justice
Meaning, Significance	Wisdom	Expansion
Morality, Ethics, Virtue	Purpose	Travel

Archetypal Characters

Teacher, Professor	Zeus, Jupiter
Preacher, Minister, Priest	Demagogue, Politician
Theorist, Prophet, Futurist	Moralist, Lawmaker
Traveler, Explorer	Pollyanna Optimist
Wiseman, Guru	Missionary, Propagandist
Promoter, Advocate	Super salesman

Developmental Phase

Forty-five to fifty-six years. Age of increasing influence and wisdom, especially over the young. Average age of people in upper echelons of business and politics is 54. Time for teaching, advising, guiding, and seeing true—the "consultant." Gail Sheehy calls it "the age of insightfulness and philosophic concern." Deeper understanding and improved judgment constitutes the "wisdom of age." Arrival at true "integrity," i.e., approval of oneself ethically and morally, independent of other's standards (Erikson and Kohlberg). Desire for truth and justice is paramount. Also, time of personal expansion, maximum income, kids out of the house, and freedom to travel. Increase in general contentment and positive attitude toward spouse and children, "feeling that life is good." Age of becoming a grandparent.

Behavioral Traits and Themes

Enthusiasm—to be filled with God: Jovial Sagittarius is perhaps the most enthusiastic sign of the zodiac. The word "enthusiasm" comes from the Greek and means "to be filled with God." The roots are *en* "in," and *theos* "god." The keynote here is faith. Sagittarius symbolizes faith in life, faith in God, and faith in the Universe. The underlying conviction is that we live in an ordered and intelligent cosmos presided over by a just and beneficent higher power. Everything is meaningful and "just" as it should be; we have only to discern the obvious for life to be wonderful. If such optimism is carried too far, however, we can have the pollyanna type who naively expects everything to turn out right despite all evidence to the contrary. Voltaire's irrepressible Professor Pangloss in his satire *Candide* exemplifies this trait.

jovial, cheerful	humorous, gregarious
life-affirming, positive	exuberant, enthusiastic
hopeful, optimistic	buoyant, irrepressible
trusting, full of faith	fervent, ardent
zealous, spirited	naïve, pollyanna

The teacher-theorist: Sagittarius signifies abstract thinking, which should be distinguished from concrete thinking (Gemini). The natural polarity between fact and theory is represented in the Gemini-Sagittarius opposition. Morality is a direct consequence of our ability to think on a long-range, abstract level and to include others in the equation, not just ourselves. The far-sightedness of Sagittarius gives it the ability to discern consequences for the future of humanity. By understanding the consequences of actions taken in the present, we are able to formulate laws, principles, moral codes, and ethical standards.

As a mutable sign, Sagittarius symbolizes that *truth is a relative, changing thing*. What is true is contingent upon the facts (Gemini) of the situation and the context within which they are viewed. Sagittarius *expands* the frontiers of knowledge by synthesizing pieces of information in such a way that it constitutes an advance in the sum total of existing knowledge. The capacity to abstract principles or laws from facts represents "the higher mind" of Sagittarius. Meaning is not self-evident, but is a construction that emerges from a synthesis of facts.

The analysis of cause-effect relations is also distinctly Sagittarian. Such analysis gives rise to hypotheses, theories, and ultimately laws, for it enables the thinker to predict outcomes. This capacity to *see* the future, to prophesize or predict on the basis of existing conditions, to deduce outcomes from probable causes, is a Sagittarian activity. Advisors and consultants are Sagittarian, as are philosophers and moralists. In fact, predicting outcomes from causes is the basis of religion and morality, for wisdom and morality are born out of an understanding of time. The fundamental Sagittarian question is, "if I do this now, what will happen later? Will the consequences for myself and others be bad (painful) or good (pleasurable)?"

philosophical, religious	deductive, hypothetical
high minded, intellectual	theoretical, abstract
speculative, presumptuous	future-oriented
insightful, logical	reasonable, wise
interpretive, inferential	farsighted, prophetic

The Great Debater: There is a definite "know it all" quality about Sagittarius that operates independent of the relative worth of its opinions. Sagittarius is infused with such a quality of "knowingness" that the individual feels compelled to share what he knows even if there is little evidence to support his claims. While such knowledge may merely be ill-founded opinion, having an opinion is an end in itself for Sagittarius. Even if the beliefs of Sagittarius are unsupported by evidence, there is still a certain joy in formulating a theory. Ideally, one's beliefs should be open to change based on the introduction of new facts. Again, Sagittarius is a mutable sign. Difficulties occur when beliefs become rigid, dogmatic, and incapable of adjusting to new information. As Manly Hall put it, "what is generally called knowledge is merely an opinion, on a level of illusion." The expression, "he's full of hot air" was undoubtedly made in reference to Sagittarius. Foghorn Leghorn, the Disney cartoon character, is a Sagittarian caricature who embodies this quality.

bombastic, pompous	truthful, honest, frank
argumentative, dogmatic	windy, preachy, tactless
rhetorical, eloquent	inflated, opinionated
straightforward	disarmingly direct

Righteous and high-minded: Sagittarius represents our need for an ethical belief system. What is truly ethical, however, must go beyond what is merely good for the individual or community. Ethics must be applicable to all of humankind. "The greatest good for the greatest number" is a Sagittarian sentiment. Whereas social signs are concerned with conforming to the agreed upon standards of the culture, i.e., "cultural relativism," universal signs are concerned with principles and laws that transcend one's social milieu and group loyalties.

Sagittarius is judgmental in the sense that it is concerned with linear notions such as good/bad, right/wrong, and true/false. As a fire sign and a universal sign, Sagittarius is not particularly sensitive to feelings (quincunx Cancer). There is such a powerful commitment to virtue and truth that other considerations recede into the background. Justice is blind, as they say, and logic can be very cold. Yet, the innate enthusiasm and righteousness of the sign will often persuade others to "do the right thing."

ethical, moralistic, just	intolerant, unsympathetic
righteous, virtuous	lecturing, proselytizing
uplifting, persuasive	judgmental, principled
propagandizing, brainwash	inspirational, oracular

The intrepid traveler of the globe and of the mind: Rather than being limited to the concrete or the actual, Sagittarius is concerned with *the possible*. It is always asking and wondering what might be true, what might be possible to achieve. This hopeful, exploratory quality drives the individual to seek broader horizons and greener pastures. Sagittarius symbolizes our need to expand beyond our present limits, not only intellectually but physically as well. Sagittarius is symbolized by the archer who points his arrow toward the heavens. The inspired idealism of the sign thrusts us ever forward and upward toward a higher state.

expansive, adventurous	travel-loving, restless
idealistic, inspired	excited, on-the-move
roving, exploratory	farsighted, moving on

The Good Samaritan: All fire signs have a positive attitude. As a universal sign, Sagittarian love extends outwards to all of humanity. Thus Sagittarius is philanthropic, which literally means "lover of humankind." The innate faith and optimism of the sign causes it to see the best in people, whom are regarded as generally good. This is compensatory to the previous sign, Scorpio, which suspects the worst in people. Notorious for its do-gooding, Sagittarius is motivated to support activities that it believes to be in the public interest. In addition to its religious and philosophic predilections, Sagittarius is naturally political.

generous	philanthropic	beneficent
benevolent	good, wonderful	charitable
civic-minded	public-spirited	open-handed

Biting off more than you can chew: Driven by a need for constant expansion, Sagittarius' main problem is *over*expansion. This can take a variety of forms. Optimism carried to an extreme becomes merely foolishness. If enthusiasm turns to exaggeration, one becomes unreliable. Overconfidence can result in grandiose schemes and reckless extravagance. And the desire to expand one's horizon's may, if undisciplined, lead to wanderlust. Or the individual may merely live in his head and become an ivory tower scholar out of touch with the real world.

Often Sagittarius has difficulty putting into practice what comes out of its mouth so effortlessly. Hypocrisy is just a misstep away from idealism. Yet, exaggeration combined with blind optimism can be enormously persuasive. People are eager to believe someone who believes in themselves. Problems occur when Sagittarius cannot deliver on what has been promised. The Sagittarian tendency to overextend and promise more than can be delivered leads many unsuspecting souls to ruin, e.g., get-rich-quick schemes and fraudulent land deals are typical. Legal difficulties result when victims seek to recoup their losses.

This overreaching, grandiose quality typifies what psychologists call manic disorder. The disorder is characterized by an elevated mood, delusions of grandeur, pressure of speech, flight of ideas, distractibility, and excessive involvement in pleasurable activities which have a high potential for negative consequences, e.g., going on a shopping spree.

extravagant, profligate
unreliable, inconsistent
foolish, irresponsible
thriftless, indulgent
grandiose, manic

excessive, philandering
wasteful, improvident
undisciplined, scattered
hypocritical, unrealistic
overextended, spread out

CAPRICORN

Planetary Ruler: Saturn
Corollary House: Tenth
Corollary Aspect: Closing Square
Polarity: Yin
Element: Earth
Modality: Cardinal
Perspective: Universal

Psychological Need

perfection, excellence	success, accomplishment
structure, limits, form	order, organization
control, authority	responsibility
prestige, status	mastery, achievement

Archetypal Characters

Father (figure)	Authority Figure
Wise Old Man, Senex	Establishment
Administrator, Executive	Control Freak
Governor, Bureaucrat	Scrooge, Miser

Developmental Phase

Fifty six to sixty eight. Period of highest career achievement. Becoming supreme authority. The zenith of one's life (climacterium). Sense of having built something of lasting value and of having made an impact on future generations. Also, acceptance of limitations of life; one can go no further. Antithesis of success is despair (Erikson). May experience profound regret for what one has done or not done with one's life. The final reckoning. If despair, can lead to depression (involutional melancholia) characteristic of the age. Suicide rate rises dramatically during this phase of life. Also, hypochondriachal concerns may dominate. One must beware of pessimism/negativity.

Behavioral Traits and Themes

Serious and Somber Mood: Because Capricorn is concerned with perfection, the most salient feature of the personality is gravity. Capricorn takes itself very seriously. As a yin sign, it is rather inhibited and reserved. As an earth sign it is heavy and formal. And as a universal sign, there is the weight of the world upon its shoulders.

controlled, cold, stoic	distinguished, mature
serious, grave, somber	dry, dull, dour, ascetic
austere, tight, mechanical	formal, heavy, taciturn
inhibited, reserved	undemonstrative

Climb the highest mountain: One of the symbols of Capricorn is the mountain goat, and for good reason. No sign is more adept at climbing to high places than Capricorn. The sign symbolizes the drive for distinction, status, and perfection. There is a never ending struggle to get to the top and thereby gain *control*. Capricorn is the gourmet of the zodiac; nothing but the best will suffice. Consequently, Capricorn exerts a continuous pressure on the psyche to do more, achieve more, become more—*to be the best*. We might call it "the urge to prevail." As a language tense, Capricorn is "future perfect."

ambitious, driven	hardworking, dedicated
deliberate, relentless	status-conscious
patient, enduring	concentrated, focused
climbing upwards	persistent, persevering
dogged, determined	aspiring, industrious

The drive for excellence: As mentioned, Capricorn is the gourmet of the zodiac. Because it is concerned with quality, Capricorn disdains the common and the average. Perfection is the goal. Yet, because perfection is an unattainable absolute, people in the grip of Capricorn often feel inadequate, even inferior. The standard is so high that it is difficult if not impossible to attain; yet, the standards are unrelenting and compel the individual to persevere.

A subjective sense of being "behind in the race" can make Capricorn an exceedingly anxious sign. Spontaneity and playfulness are sacrificed in the insatiable pursuit of success. Capricorn can hold others to the same strict standards that it holds for itself. Accordingly, the sign has a reputation for being critical and demanding. The "taskmaster" is a Capricorn archetype.

perfectionistic, exacting	demanding, harsh, severe
authoritarian, stern, strict	obsessive-compulsive
admonishing, pressuring	anxious, fastidious
technical, critical	ruthless, intolerant

Systems Oriented: Capricorn has an innate talent for understanding the principle of order. Time and space are structured in a way that allow for maximum efficiency. Usually, this structure will involve some sort of hierarchy, with Capricorn at the top (naturally). There is a talent for organization, time management, and administration. Capricorn instinctively knows that anything that needs to be accomplished can be reduced to a system with tasks laid out in a particular sequence. Schedules and deadlines make sense to Capricorn. Likewise, the idea of finding a method, technique, or formula for accomplishing a goal has intuitive appeal. There is a natural understanding of the necessity for rules, regulations, and limits. As a universal sign, Capricorn's perspective tends to be long-range. "Good planning" is the keynote here; long-range goals are Capricorn's *forte*.

orderly, administrative	systematic, structured
shrewd, planful	efficient, methodical
economical, organized	thorough, painstaking

The Disciplined Achiever: No sign is more geared for success than Capricorn. Its *modus operandi* is perfectly suited to achieve the goal, whatever the goal may be. In a very real sense, Capricorn behavior defines what it means to be an achiever. In fact, without some of the qualities mentioned below—discipline, responsibility, determination—it would be difficult to achieve success in any field.

disciplined, reliable	productive, stable
conscientious, dedicated	responsible, dutiful
determined, resolute	dependable, diligent
solid, grounded, steady	realistic, practical

Perseveration: Once committed to a course of action, it is difficult for Capricorn to change strategies or shift focus. In fact, new information may be regarded as potentially distracting. There is a tendency, in other words, to stick with what works even when it is not working well. Rather than considering new possibilities, methods, or alternatives, Capricorn simply tries harder. If carried to an extreme, perseverance becomes perseveration—the inability to shift focus. Like an aircraft carrier whose momentum and massive weight make it difficult to slow down and change direction, there can be a loss of volitional control and impaired ability to choose.

conservative	traditional	orthodox
rigid, inflexible	conventional	cautious, careful
intractable	immovable	persevering

Principle of contraction: Capricorn is painfully aware of the discrepancy between its present state and the goal of perfection for which it strives. This can be experienced as a chronic sense of deprivation or lack. Inherently pessimistic, Capricorn fears things will get worse before they get better. Symbolizing the principle of contraction, the sign evidences an inordinate miserliness when it comes to managing finances. The tightwad of the zodiac, Capricorn has a reputation for being cheap, greedy, and selfish. The character that best correlates to this dimension of the archetype was personified by Ebenezer Scrooge in Charles Dickens' *A Christmas Story*.

prudent, thrifty, frugal	materialistic, avaricious
stingy, cheap, miserly	greedy, selfish, tight
economizing, moderate	pessimistic, negative

Living Machines: When out of balance with its opposite sign, Cancer, Capricorn behavior looks suspiciously like obsessive-compulsive personality disorder (second only to Virgo in this regard). So intent is the need to be perfect that the individual may try to live according to a fixed system of rules and formulae. Resembling "living machines," their choices are motivated not by personal preferences or whims subjectively felt, but by technical indicators external to themselves.

A painting, for instance, is bought not because of the sense of beauty and aesthetic pleasure it inspires, but because the artist is famous, the critic's review impressive, or the price tag high. For Capricorn, subjective feelings are less trustworthy than objective indicators of quality. Cancerian hunches, feelings, impressions, and intuitions are regarded not as valuable sources of information but as nuisances that are potentially distracting. Cut off from its "insides," Capricorn can lead a haunted, doubting existence plagued with loss of conviction. Not only does the sign find it difficult to trust or understand its own feelings, it can be equally insensitive to the feelings of others.

callous, hardened, rigid	worrying (is it the best?)
cold, indifferent, unaffected	doubting (is it right?)
unsympathetic, merciless	skeptical, questioning
mechanical, programmed	insensitive, thick-skinned

Tendency toward depression: If out of touch with feelings and thus cut off from emotional contact with others, Capricorn can lead a lonely, deprived existence. A life consecrated to externals—success, status, achievement—does not necessarily lead to love and happiness, a lesson that may be difficult for Capricorn to learn. Capricorn's greatest problem is a tendency to overcompensate for its perceived deficiencies by struggling to distinguish itself as superior. Yet, if the individual sacrifices human contact and caring to external goals and achievements, this can only reinforce the loneliness that motivated the ambition in the first place. The expression, "it's lonely at the top," may strike a resonant chord to a hyper-Capricorn type who eventually discovers that the price of success is loss of love and family (Cancer). This, of course, was the lesson that Ebenezer Scrooge learned.

It is precisely Capricorn's perfectionism and pursuit of excellence that makes it vulnerable to depression. Plagued with a haunting sense of inferiority for which it overcompensates by striving for status and success, Capricorn needs external confirmation to ward off feelings of failure. If sufficient success is not attained, Capricorn cannot overcome its inherent sense of "not being good enough," and plunges into guilt and despair.

brooding, lonely	melancholy, sad
socially awkward	depressed, gloomy
taciturn, reticent	uptight, withholding

AQUARIUS

Planetary Ruler:	Uranus
Corollary House:	Eleventh
Corollary Aspect:	Closing Sextile
Polarity:	Yang
Element:	Air
Modality:	Fixed
Perspective:	Universal

Psychological Need

awakening, revelation	perspective (wholistic)
enlightenment	overview (panoramic)

liberation, emancipation   objective outlook
change, progress   breakthrough, reform

Archetypal Characters

Trickster, Jokester   Prometheus, Reformer
Court Jester, Wise Fool   Rebel, Revolutionary
Free Spirit, Nonconformist   Radical, Iconoclast
Objective Witness   Outraged Idealist
Utopian Visionary   Mad Scientist/Genius
Eccentric Oddball   Innovator, Inventor

Developmental Phase

Sixty eight to eighty. Retirement age, time to withdraw and sum up one's life. Seeing one's life as a whole; gaining broad perspective on things. Detachment from symbols (jobs, roles, positions) that previously defined identity. Radical objectivity. Eccentricity of old age. Outspokenness. Detachment from ego identity and thus lack of concern for what other's think. Seeing oneself as part of vast unfolding of human history, past and future. Freedom and independence to do anything. May be new openness to experiment. Spouse may die. Crazy Grandpa or Grandma. Withdrawal, detachment, and isolation may result from loss of identity, friends, or spouse. Can be overcome by too many changes.

Behavioral Traits and Themes

The Eternal Watcher: We might call Aquarius the eternal watcher, or simply the witness. Like a broad-angle lens, Aquarius allows us to step above the situation and view conflicts and process from a detached perspective. There is the capacity for ultimate objectivity with Aquarius because there is little attachment to the outcome of what one sees. Consequently, there is the rare ability for "seeing true." Friendly, though in an impersonal way, Aquarius has an unconditional acceptance of all that is human.

Unlike Leo, Aquarius is not susceptible to flattery. Nor is it concerned with making people feel important or special. Aquarius sees past the ego's defenses and into the inner core of the person. Sometimes there is a subtle sadness in this view, as if Aquarius can see something in you that you are not yet ready or capable of seeing yourself. It is this same broadness of view and tolerance for the weaknesses, foibles, and failings of humankind that gives Aquarius its wacky, whimsical sense of humor. No sign is more apt to poke fun at the pretensions of the ego. This, in fact, is the basis for the Aquarian archetype of the trickster.

cool, detached, cut off	dispassionate, impartial
objective, impersonal	distant, aloof, remote
observant, watching	unbiased, unprejudiced
has world sadness	whimsical, wacky

Agape, Brotherly and Sisterly Love: As a universal sign, Aquarius represents the principle of brotherly and sisterly love, or what the Greeks called *agape*. This is the love that one individual feels for another simply because the other is human. Platonic love is another term for it, by which Plato meant a higher form of love that ascends from passion for an individual to contemplation of the ideal. Unlike romantic love (Leo) or erotic love (Scorpio), Platonic love is free from sexual desire and does not need to be reciprocated. This kind of love transcends distinctions such as nationality, race, or creed by recognizing the common core within all people that binds humanity together as a whole. Aquarius does not judge, "like me good, not like me, bad," as Leo does. Rather Aquarius perceives and, indeed, expects every individual to be totally unique. Differences are automatically acknowledged and accepted. Instead of getting caught in the trap of conformity to a social or cultural standard, Aquarius transcends differences that artificially separate one group from another by identifying with the essence of humanity itself. The Aquarian perspective, therefore, allows the individual the freedom to acknowledge his or her capacity to exhibit *any* behavior. Like the poet Terrance, Aquarius can say "nothing that is human is foreign to me."

accepting, broad-minded	friendly, collegial
open-minded, tolerant	egalitarian, not snobbish
non-judgmental, liberal	impersonal (love)

Divergent vs. convergent thinking: Divergent vs. convergent thinking pertains to the discovery that certain individuals who are unusually creative—divergent thinkers—are able to entertain a wide range of possible answers to a question precisely because they do not worry about their success or failure or how others might regard them. Similarly with Aquarius, there is a tremendous capacity for original thinking because this part of the psyche is not concerned with validation or approval (Leo) and therefore is radically open to another level of mind. Aquarius is known for its uniqueness of perspective, originality, and eccentricity. At this level there is no concern for whether one measures up to externally imposed conditions of acceptance. Thus the individual is *free* to be anyone or anything; behavior does not need to be consistent and identity is not limited to a particular style or outlook.

The Aquarian need for progress and **change** often manifests as erratic behavior, such that Aquarius sometimes seems strange and unpredictable. As the embodiment of the trickster archetype, Aquarius delights in mocking the pretensions of the ego—whether one's own or others'. This is not surprising, considering that Aquarius is opposed Leo, the sign of the ego. From an egoic perspective, Aquarian behavior can be shocking and upsetting. The singer, Eartha Kitt (Sun Aquarius), was socially ostracized for ten years after telling President Lyndon Johnson and his wife in no uncertain terms what she thought about the Vietnam war. Her outburst during a White House dinner party was so shocking it made headlines throughout the country. Another pure expression of the archetype was the character of "Maude" in the 1972 cult film *Harold and Maude*.

The enlightened view that Aquarius represents may cause the individual to feel cut off and separate from the rest of the world. This seems to be one of the liabilities of the sign, for those who march to the beat of a different drummer march alone. Their very "seeing" sets them apart from those who do not see. It is not unusual for people to feel threatened by Aquarian behavior, for the very nature of the sign is to provoke or shock people into changing.

atypical, different	controversial, bizarre
eccentric, unusual	resilient, free, flexible
original, novel, fresh	nonconformist, separate
unconventional, unique	idiosyncratic, peculiar

The mad scientist: Aquarius is the need for breakthrough into a new and better world. Like the titan Prometheus, Aquarius is driven by a divine discontent and wants to steal fire from the gods, i.e., liberate humanity from ignorance and awaken it to a more enlightened state. Accordingly, Aquarius is forever promoting the new, the untried, and the untested. Their forward thinking tendency, talent for discovery, and continuous impatience with traditional methods and procedures, causes Aquarius to be naturally drawn to new advances in technology. Computers and modern science are Aquarian playgrounds. The ability to see novel possibilities and generate new ideas gives Aquarius a certain brilliance in comparison to more ordinary minds. The sign represents our capacity for wholistic thinking, i.e., to instantly see how all the parts of a system make up the whole. This synthesizing, wholistic perspective is related to radical insight, the "ah ha" experience that shocks the mind and advances knowledge into new and often unexpected directions.

experimental, inventive	innovative, ingenious
futuristic, cutting edge	progressive, avant garde
forward thinking	original, advancing

Utopian visionary: Having moved beyond the illusion of separateness and, therefore, the need to prove oneself important and distinct from others, Aquarius is concerned with the ideals and aspirations that characterize humanity as a whole. Aquarius is not content to accept things as they are, but wants to explore what is ultimately possible for humankind. It is the untapped potential of the human spirit, or "the further reaches of human nature" as Abraham Maslow put it, that engages Aquarius' interest.

This idealistic striving for a better world in which all people recognize one another as brothers and sisters is evident in the Aquarian proclivity for humanitarian and altruistic acts. It is vitally important to Aquarius that human rights not be violated due to the petty squabbles, provincial thinking, and unreasonable fears that keep humanity divided against itself. The Aquarian ideal of a self-governing, democratic world order naturally gravitates the sign toward involvement in movements and reforms wherein like-minded individuals are bound together for a common cause.

humanitarian, humanistic	allocentric, unselfish
democratic, altruistic	idealistic, visionary
universal, utopian	group oriented

The Outraged Idealist: Aquarius is the need to break free from external controls, limits and authority. With everything accepted and integrated as part of oneself, and therefore nothing to be defended against, Aquarius is infused with an intrinsic morality and an abiding faith in its fellow humans. Aquarius symbolizes our capacity for enlightenment, and enlightenment can be defined as "absence of darkness." The dark side has been relinquished from the terrors of self-made fears and the self has been liberated to reunite with that One in which we all "move and have our being."

Understood in this context, it is easy to appreciate Aquarius' hostility toward authority and control. Unlike Aries, whose freedom-impulse is connected to its concern for survival, Aquarian freedom derives from a need for liberation from oppressive structures. The utopian vision of Aquarius sees all humans as brothers and sisters whom, if left alone, will naturally do what is right. External control is therefore unnecessary. Living for the whole in cooperative harmony is the Aquarian ideal, and the strongly Aquarian personality will embody and act out this ideal at every opportunity.

Since to be controlled by the arbitrary standards of a regulatory body conflicts with this ideal, Aquarius rebels against authority. The very existence of a regulatory agency contradicts the Aquarian world view—that every individual is intrinsically good and will naturally do what is necessary for the good of the whole. It is the apparent distrust that those in authority feel toward their fellow humans that necessitates laws and controls and therefore militates against the Aquarian ideal of universal freedom.

It is not just rebelliousness, therefore, that marks the Aquarian drive, but rebelliousness oriented toward freedom and independence from externally imposed authority. Where Capricorn is "you should obey," Aquarius says, "We are all free to disobey." Of course, there can be no genuine freedom without responsibility, which is why Capricorn precedes Aquarius in the zodiac. The concept of responsibility is presupposed in Aquarius.

rebellious, radical	anti-authoritarian
iconoclastic, anarchic	revolutionary
discontent with status-quo	nihilistic, disruptive
anti-establishment	dissenting, agitating
insurgent, resistive	social activist

The Open Vessel: The symbol of Aquarius is the image of a man bent down on one knee balancing an upturned urn upon his shoulder. The vessel, it should be noted, is open at both ends. The image signifies our human capacity for serving as a container and channel for universal consciousness, which flows downward from heaven to earth. As always with astrological symbolism, the metaphor is apt. For Aquarius does indeed seem to serve as a vehicle for the expression of universal mind.

Unlike the other two air signs, Gemini and Libra, the perspective of Aquarius has shifted to an entirely abstract realm, a dimension of mind observing mind; idea interacts with idea in computer-like fashion until a critical mass is reached and the intellect makes a quantum leap to another level of understanding entirely. Seeing how the whole is a synthesis of many parts, Aquarius appreciates the necessity of all things in the broad process of evolution. This kind of wholistic thinking is in many respects beyond morality. One might call it *transmoral,* for morality is built into the sign yet transcended at the same time.

Dane Rudhyar once wrote that "total understanding can only come out of total acceptance." Consider the trial of OJ Simpson in 1994-95. From a Sagittarian perspective, the important thing was whether Simpson was guilty or innocent. Many who thought Simpson was guilty were morally outraged over his acquittal. Yet, Aquarius would view the same outcome from an entirely different perspective. Taking a more long range view, Aquarius recognizes that the Simpson trial constitutes a phenomenon that transcended the issue of murder and the guilt or innocence of Simpson as an individual. The trial was about *more* than murder, says Aquarius, it was about disconnect that exists between blacks and whites within the larger culture. This, in effect, was the larger issue of which the Simpson trial was merely a subset.

Aquarius might reason that if the outcome of the Simpson trial *shocked and awakened* the white community to a new awareness of the plight and sentiments of blacks in America, then perhaps more good will have been accomplished by Simpson's acquittal than his conviction. For had Simpson been found guilty, the white community would not be surprised and would not think too deeply about the race issue. It was precisely Simpson's acquittal that sparked ongoing discussion and debate about the different cultural experiences of whites and blacks in America. Why was it that 88% of blacks thought Simpson to be innocent, while 64% of whites thought him guilty? The media merely played up the conflict and even suggested that the Simpson trial *set back* race relations, but Aquarius would argue that a system *must step back to leap*, that evolution is always preceded by regression. Thus whatever anger and conflict the trial sparked was a necessary antecedent to the new awareness that will eventually result.

Whereas murder would be rightfully condemned in Sagittarius, Aquarius would examine the phenomena dispassionately and seek to gain an understanding of the behavior by viewing it in a broader light. What was the relationship between the victim and the perpetrator? What were the earlier and deeper factors within the life of the murderer that culminated in such a violent act? What meaning does the event have for victims of violent crimes? From an Aquarian perspective, there is no tragedy or right and wrong. Thinking has become circular rather than linear; no one is blamed or judged. The mind is thus freed to consider aspects of the phenomena that it otherwise could not see.

This kind of thinking can have a quality of brilliance. Having gone beyond an egocentric and moral perspective, Aquarius is our link to Universal Mind. Ego has surrendered itself to the whole and thus the individual becomes an open receptacle for the influx and outpouring of universal energies. It is not the individual who acts but the whole which acts through him. Aquarius is beyond choice. Personality has become a vehicle for the irruption of divine wisdom. What is expressed, therefore, may have a quality of revelation to it. It reveals, shocks, startles, awakens, and illumines. Aquarius can be the "wise fool," for it tends to blurt out the truth regardless of how upsetting it may be to others.

enlightening, illuminating   startling, controversial
ingenious, brilliant   shocking, disturbing

stimulating, shattering
revealing, awakening
abstract, electric
outspoken, tactless

synthesizing, super logical
irritating, upsetting
sudden, spontaneous
comprehensive

The Absent Minded Professor: The Aquarian drive for freedom and change combined with its disdain for limits and structure does not bode well for organizational planning. Again, the concept of structure is built into Aquarius. Being but a hollow vessel for the outpouring of universal wisdom, Aquarius disdains planning things in advance or adhering to a schedule. Too confining! Aquarius might argue, "in the long run, what does it matter?" Wedded to the infinite, its head in the clouds, Aquarius will quietly mail its lunch, put its keys in the icebox, and run off to the latest space exhibit at the local planetarium in the midst of dinner. It is a quality that seems oblivious to any need for order or stability. Since the Universe is running the whole show anyway, and doing quite well at that, why should Aquarius worry? Why do anything at all? Accordingly, the sign has a reputation for producing loners, oddballs, and eccentrics.

Unlike Leo or Capricorn, Aquarius feels very little need to achieve a position of importance in the world or to produce anything in tangible form. Relatively indifferent to praise or criticism, Aquarius is characterized by a marked lack of personal ambition. If carried to an extreme, this can result in a condition known as schizoid personality disorder. The essential feature of this disorder is a pervasive pattern of indifference to social relationships and a restricted range of emotional experience and expression. People with this disorder often appear cold and aloof. They seem vague about their goals, indecisive in their actions, and impaired in their ability to develop an occupation. On the other hand, they may, in some instances, be capable of high occupational achievement in situations that enable them to perform under conditions of social isolation.

abrupt, disconnected
disorganized, jumbled
absent-minded, erratic
schizoid, isolated

unpredictable, brusque
unstable, scattered
undependable, inconstant
indifferent, loner mentality

PISCES

Planetary Ruler: Neptune
Corollary House: Twelfth
Corollary Aspect: Closing Semi-Sextile
Polarity: Yin
Element: Water
Modality: Mutable
Perspective: Universal

Psychological Need

transcendence (of duality)
unitive consciousness
sacrifice, surrender
holiness, sanctity

infinite love & beauty
atonement & forgiveness
oneness with life/nature
bliss, rapture

Archetypal Characters

Savior, Messiah
Mystic, Holy Person
Poet, Dreamer, Artist
Flake, Dingbat, Imbecile
Medium, Psychic
Alcoholic, Drug Addict

Martyr, Scapegoat, Saint
Victim, Dupe, Casualty
Sick, Weak, Helpless Type
Fraud, Deceiver, Cheat
Rescuer, Codependent
Psychotic, Schizophrenic

Developmental Phase

Eighty to the end of life. Maximum expansion of time and space, or collapse of boundaries separating time and space. "Not me, not here, not now." Lives in imagination, "dream time." Possible confusion or disorientation. Passivity, senility, may drift into unconscious. Loosening of memories and associations. Time of loss and suffering. Grief as people die all around. End of life. Possible isolation (retreat) or institutionalization. Decay and deterioration of body. Sickness and incapacitation. Possible increased spirituality as individual prepares for death and reunion with source.

Behavioral Traits and Themes

The Space Case: The most striking characteristic of Pisces is its passivity. There seems to be a distinct absence of zest, vigor, or vitality.

Perhaps this is a consequence of the Piscean need for letting go to the collective unconscious. There is a sense that all is as it should be and that one has only to flow with the real—the ultimate reality. Pisces symbolizes our capacity to be empty, selfless, and one with God. It is the antithesis of action or effort.

quiet, shy, retiring	otherworldly, ethereal
passive-submissive	vapid, vacuous
transparent, floating	soft, fluid, liquid
dreamy, spacey	flat, spiritless, insipid
fragile, delicate	weak, lifeless, vacant

Flowing with the real: "Let it be," "go with the flow," "let go and let God." Such expressions reflect the Piscean impulse for surrender in selfless love to the Universe. Pisces signifies flow states, desirelessness, and effortless effort. As a universal water sign, it seeks to become one with the whole. This is not a personal love, but a love that is all encompassing and indiscriminate. Nothing and no one can be excluded for it is the nature of Piscean love to be all-inclusive. With acceptance of everything and identification with nothing, desires cease. For when all that exists is perceived as part of oneself, what is there left to be desired? One already *is* everything. Such an undifferentiated oneness with the whole creates a sense of unitive consciousness. Unlike Virgo, which wants to dissect reality and compare the present imperfect reality against the ideal, Pisces *is* the ideal already realized.

allowing, accepting	desireless, effortless
compassionate, forgiving	yielding, flowing
surrendering, opening	indiscriminately loving
empathic, sensitive	all inclusive love

Rescue Tendencies: Because Pisces represents an all-inclusive, indiscriminate love and compassion, it is very sensitive to all that is tragic in the world. To the extent that we are, as Jesus stated, "our brother's helper," we share in the collective guilt of humankind that results from neglect of the poor, the disabled, the aged, the homeless, and the sick. It is the nature of Pisces to identify with the victims of society and strive to help those who seem incapable of helping themselves, whether they are actually incapable or not. And that's the problem. This selfless, loving quality of Pisces often leads individuals to involve themselves on a personal level with people who are simply self-destructive. When this occurs, Pisces often ends being victimized by the victim. The self-help movement in psychology has labeled such behavior "co-dependency," meaning the helper actually reinforces the dependency of the supposed sick one. In actuality, there is identification on an unconscious level between the helper and the helpless. This may stem from unconscious guilt on the part of the Piscean person who feels personally responsible for the suffering of the victim.

rescuing, saving	bleeding heart
co-dependent	redemptive love
weepy, tragic	unconscious guilt

Everything is nothing: When boundaries dissolve and distinctions cease to have meaning, a state of uncertainty prevails. Recall how Gemini and Virgo are dualistic in that they want to distinguish one thing from another. The duality of subject and object, or self and other, is the fundamental division upon which self-awareness depends. Conversely, Pisces is our impulse to transcend duality. The attainment of unitive awareness means that phenomena are no longer perceived as separate and distinct, for all has been subsumed by a larger reality. Such a perception is difficult to convey with words since words by their very nature are separative and distinguishing. Accordingly, Piscean communication relies upon *images* to convey meaning. Symbol and metaphor is the language of Pisces, especially as these are contained in allegories, fairy tales, dreams, legends, myths, and stories. Images, of course, are inherently ambiguous for their meaning is dependent upon the context—the whole—in which they occur. Anything that is intangible, ineffable, murky, or amorphous is Piscean.

symbolic, metaphorical	vague, obscure, unclear
formless, shapeless	imaginal, figurative
cloudy, foggy, hazy	global, diffusive, circular
archetypal, mythical	intangible, ineffable
incoherent, ambiguous	allegorical, apocryphal
amorphous, indistinct	nebulous, fuzzy, murky

The Mystic-Psychotic continuum: In Buddhism, consciousness is tentatively described as the relation between subject and object, or self and not-self. The two terms are relative, one implying the other; that is, subject cannot exist without object, and *vice versa*. The ego, or *satva* in Buddhist terminology, exists only because it accepts this polarity. Egoic consciousness naturally divides reality into opposites— self and not-self, good and evil, hope and fear, life and death. These pairs of opposites are mutually dependent, for one cannot cease without destroying the other. Buddhism holds that liberation from duality is contingent upon the ability to recognize that such opposites are ultimately a trick of the mind, a self-created illusion (*maya*), the reconciliation of which allows for unitive consciousness and liberation. By neutralizing opposites through awareness, the illusion of duality is extinguished and the individual attains *nirvana*.

While all of this is classically Piscean, it helps us to understand what happens when such a state occurs prematurely, i.e., before the individual has developed a strong and stable identity. In order to give up the self, the self has to be fully mature and differentiated. This is one of those lovely little paradoxes that typify Pisces. Self-awareness is contingent upon recognition of duality. To have a separate identity the boundaries that separate self from other must be relatively clear and distinct. If these boundaries have not been sufficiently developed, then the self remains undifferentiated and submerged in the unconscious. This can lead to a profound sense of disorientation, loss of reality, and identity-confusion. In its most extreme form, this correlates to psychosis wherein the individual cannot distinguish what is inside from what is outside. Voices, hallucinations, visions, and delusions entail the projection of one's internal state onto the environment. Subjective and objective reality becomes merged and life becomes a waking nightmare. In short, Pisces is the state both of the mystic and of the psychotic, depending upon the level of self-realization. Most of us exist somewhere on a continuum between the two.

bewildered, befuddled	diffusive, disoriented
mixed up, helpless	confusing, chaotic
puzzling, distorted	crazy, psychotic, insane

Escapist Tendencies: Piscean behavior is characterized by a certain vacillation, or ambivalence. Having no point of view of one's own, and therefore the capacity to see all points of view simultaneously, there is a sense of being lost in a sea of possibilities. Again, there is no point of reference from which to choose. To decide one thing is to negate its opposite, which Pisces cannot do. This is the meaning of the Piscean symbol of two fishes bound together yet swimming in opposite directions. For Pisces, all points of view are equally valid. This dilemma is captured by the Sufi story of Nasruddin.

> Nasruddin was listening to a court case in his capacity as judge. After the plaintiff concluded his arguments, Nasruddin said, "yes, I do believe you are right." However, when the defendant finished his logical and eloquent speech, Nasruddin exclaimed, "yes, I do believe you are right!" And when his bailiff burst out, "you can't agree one man is right and also agree with the opposite opinion," Nasruddin replied, "yes, I do believe you are right."

Since Pisces affirms everything, there is little capacity to choose one thing over another. In fact, there is little desire to do anything at all. No sign is more passive, submissive, and indecisive than Pisces. Unable to take a clear stand and thus compelled to acquiesce, Pisces is easily influenced by wills that are stronger. A common Piscean figure is the weak minded dolt who does the bidding of some powerful Plutonic figure.

Pisces tends to be malleable, ambivalent, and indecisive. Having a distinctly other-worldly character, it has little incentive for dealing with the mundane realities of this world. Whereas its opposite sign, Virgo, is busily engaged in solving problems and maximizing efficiency, Pisces regards such pursuits as intolerable drudgery. It is the ideal of infinite love and beauty that beckons to Pisces. There are a variety of avenues for pursuing this ideal—meditation, prayer, retreats, communing with nature, or escaping into the world of the imagination through Piscean arts like music, dance, poetry, or film. And if reality intrudes too aggressively on one's dreams, there is always drugs and alcohol to numb the senses and weave a protective cocoon about one's private world.

indolent, procrastinating
ambivalent, vacillating
irresponsible, escapist
weak-willed, feeble

indecisive, malleable
absent-minded, spacey
impressionable, naive
self-abnegating

Alice In Wonderland Mentality: The yearning for an ideal, magical reality is so strong in Pisces that it can be difficult for the sign to acknowledge the more unpleasant realities of concrete existence. The material world of facts and events, such as a painful loss or failure, may be suspended or distorted to conform to wishful thinking; thus, the so-called "real world" may seem decidedly unreal, whereas the realm of dreams and fantasies is experienced as more real. A salient characteristic of the sign, therefore, is its capacity to distort or deny reality.

If confronted directly as to the facts of the situation, Pisces may resort to deception, deceit, or obfuscation in order to protect the fantasy. In short, whatever does not conform to the ideal may be distorted or ignored, and this Pisces can do without conscious intent. The elusive, slippery quality of the sign is a natural consequence of its association with the unconscious and the imagination.

elusive, evasive
illusionary, fanciful
deceitful, deceptive

camouflaged, hidden
slick, slippery
tricky, false, beguiling

Paradoxical Thinking: The essence of Pisces is the need to transcend duality and reconcile division into a common unity. As the story of Nasruddin illustrates, this can be confusing. The western mind has been trained in Aristotelian logic which declares that a thing cannot be what it is and what it is not at the same time. "A" is not "non-A". This is Virgo reasoning, or analysis, which can only perceive in distinctions and contradictions. It does not perceive the whole. But eastern philosophy teaches that the whole is actually an interplay of opposites such that nothing exists without its opposite also existing; the two are related and inseparable. Paradoxical logic, therefore, holds that "A" and "not-A" do not exclude each other but are, in fact, two faces of the same reality.

With Pisces there is an experience of consciousness at a level above cognition. The seeker and the thing sought for gradually converge, mingle, and become identical. Whereas Sagittarius can form concepts about ultimate reality and formulate laws as to how to live in harmony with it, Pisces seeks a direct experience of God. As a water sign, Pisces strives for an internal, emotional participation in absolute reality rather than an outer description of it. There is the realization that ultimate reality cannot be captured in words, for it is ineffable and incommunicable. As the Tao says, "it is neither this nor that." Or, as Meister Eckhart proclaimed, "God is the negation of negations...a circle whose center is everywhere and whose boundaries are nowhere." The word "mystic" derives from the Greek root *mu*, meaning silent or mute—*muo*, meaning literally "I shut my mouth." All of this is described by Pisces which, as the last sign of the zodiac, embodies a silent and unfathomable mystery.

ineffable, mystical,	contradictory, illogical
unfathomable, abstruse	incommunicable
enigmatic, paradoxical	irrational, mysterious
esoteric, cryptic, arcane	concealed, unknowable

Depth Creativity: The creative inspiration that flows from Pisces is of a different sort than Leo or Libra, both of which are creative in their own way. Leo rules the performing arts, while Libra gives expression to all forms of beauty. But Piscean creativity has a quality of the transcendent and sublime. It is especially wedded to the image, which wells up from the unconscious like a dream. Painting, photography, and film are particularly Piscean. Music, too, as well as dance, can give expression to the Piscean impulse to lose oneself in the creative act. Poetry paints pictures with words, music translates feeling into sound, and dance allows sound to flow into movement. Myths, parables, allegories, and fables are also appropriate vehicles for the release of Piscean creativity.

symbolic, metaphorical	sublime, elevated, lyrical
artistic, creative, musical	imaginative, poetic, idyllic

Completion—the final attainment: As the last sign of the zodiac, Pisces represents completion or return to the source from which all life flows. The circle closes upon itself. In Hindu philosophy, this is referred to as *mahamudra*, the grand orgasm with the Universe. Buddhists call it *nirvana*, the absolute and final extinction of individuality without loss of consciousness. And in Christian theology, the image of heaven captures the essence of the quest. With Pisces one yearns to be a servant of the whole, a divine channel, a vehicle for expression of the numinous. Out of this surrender to the divine there is the experience of bliss, ecstasy, and transcendence of all pain and limitation. While few of us are able to attain such a lofty state, it is well enough to understand that some hint of this yearning will always be evident in Piscean behavior.

On a more mundane level, Pisces symbolizes our quest for the ideal, which initially occurs on the level of imagination. The fantasy, or dream, of consummate love, power, beauty, courage, knowledge, or skill is inspired by the Piscean dimension of consciousness. Accordingly, this sign is associated with all things elegant, refined, and archetypal.

ideal, absolute, ultimate	refined, elegant, exquisite
blissful, ecstatic	holy, mystical, spiritual
unitary, joyous	inspiring, transcendent
saintly, messianic	radiant, luminous, blessed

I have stated that although Pisces is inspired by faith in a transcendent ideal, it is also prone to deception, weakness, vacillation, and denial of reality. It is important to understand the relationship between these traits and to appreciate why they are self-consistent with the nature of the sign. Because Pisces symbolizes our desire for a transcendent ideal, i.e., for infinite love and beauty, it is reluctant to recognize anything that deviates from this ideal. Denial of reality operates as a defense against the pain of loss of oneness—oneness with life, with the Universe, and with God.

Because this ideal necessarily emerges from the imagination (the collective unconscious), there is a natural tendency toward fantasy with this sign. So if reality deviates too markedly from the ideal, it is easy to substitute fantasy for reality—hence, the tendency toward deception. Deception involves a substitution of a preferred reality for an actual reality. And because the sign strives to reconcile duality into a unified whole, it has difficulty making decisions, which necessarily cause separation *from* the whole, i.e., the preferred state of oneness—hence the tendency toward vacillation. Pisces is a weak sign in the sense that it signifies our capacity for surrender, letting go, and trusting in a higher power to work through us. This makes the sign easily influenced by stronger wills that frequently are not divine in their intentions. Thus Pisces is often the dupe or victim.

If Pisces is operating in a relatively integrated way, there is bliss, inspiration, and idealism, but also a plaintive longing for reunion with the divine. This acute and painful awareness of separation from a higher and better place necessarily gives Pisces a somewhat resigned, mournful quality. From a Pisces perspective, anything that deviates from the ideal borders on tragedy. Thus, much of the time Pisces suffers from its awareness of the inherent, inescapable tragedy of human imperfection.

SUMMING UP

There are essentially five ways that signs have been described In this chapter. First and foremost, each sign can be described as a set of psychological needs with several members, e.g., Aries symbolizes needs for survival, autonomy, and action. As a basic drive/motive, a sign performs a noun function in an astrological sentence.

Secondly, signs can be understood as constituting a set of archetypal characters that embody the underlying need(s) of the sign. Libra, for instance, symbolizes the love goddess, peacemaker, and artist, for these roles personify Libran needs for relatedness, harmony, and beauty. A sign's function as an archetypal character should not be underestimated, for we are inhabited by these archetypal entities, each of which embodies a full range of needs, feelings, desires, characteristics, and talents.

Additionally, each sign-entity—god or goddess if you will—enjoys a certain degree of autonomy within the psyche, and thus we ignore their voices at our own peril. For if their respective functions are not honored, they will most surely manifest externally in a form that breeds problems and suffering. Conversely, as their gifts are integrated and actualized, the roles they assume on internal and external levels will evolve accordingly, e.g., Leo may change from egoist to hero, Scorpio from criminal to healer, and Sagittarius from windbag to wise man.

A third aspect of signs is that they represent developmental stages. This is an important, little understood feature of signs that conveys a great deal of meaning. For these inner gods have personalities that correspond to distinct ages in the human life cycle. Signs that are strongly emphasized in an astrological chart will incline the individual to see the world in a manner that corresponds to that age-period. People who are strongly Piscean, for instance, often have an affinity for geriatrics and may behave like old people before their time!

The dominant traits and concerns of signs are age appropriate for the developmental stage corresponding to that sign. Infants (Aries) are necessarily selfish, egocentric, and concerned about survival. Toddlers (Taurus) are preoccupied with attachment needs and are easily forgiven for wanting things to stay the same. Seven year olds (Gemini) are naturally fickle, shallow, and frivolous. Latency age children (Cancer) turn inwards and become more vulnerable to rejection. Adolescents (Leo) are unavoidably narcissistic, willful, and defensive. Novice adults (Virgo) worry about job skills and employability. Marriage and partnership are dominant concerns of thirty-year olds (Libra), while mid-life adults (Scorpio) obsess about death and power. Afterwards, they become increasingly interested in justice and moral imperatives (Sagittarius). Sixty year olds (Capricorn) are expected to be conservative, traditional, and to uphold the status quo. The 70's (Aquarius) mark a period of radical change as individuals detach from old identifications. And dementia/senility is a common hallmark of attaining age 80 and beyond (Pisces).

A fourth dimension of signs is their function as behavioral descriptors. The fundamental action of a planet will invariably be modified by the traits and characteristics of the sign it occupies. In this regard, the planet functions as a verb—a form of action—that is qualified by the sign, which functions as an adverb. If the Moon is in Sagittarius, I can justly say "I respond intellectually," the lunar verb being *respond* and the Sagittarian adverb being *intellectually.*

Finally, the fifth dimension of signs is that they represent content, i.e., specific themes, lessons, or concerns that tend to manifest in external events. Whereas process is the underlying drive and behavior of the sign, content is the concrete circumstances, institutions, things, and events that reflect the meaning of the sign. These outward manifestations provide the vehicle through which the need of the sign seeks satisfaction. An adventure, for example, provides a vehicle for Aries to experience freedom and novelty. Money provides Taurus a means for obtaining security. Gemini satisfies its need for learning by attending classes, while Cancer feels nurtured when enjoying a fine meal at a favorite restaurant.

In the following Chapter, we will explore how planets are the active agents of basic needs and how they symbolize specific psychological functions.

Chapter Five

Planets as Archetypal Processes

ACTIVE AGENTS OF BASIC NEEDS

In this chapter, we are going to examine how planets are the active agents of sign-needs and how they symbolize specific psychological functions. Generally speaking, we can divide the language of astrology into two areas: process and content. Process constitutes the psychodynamics of the birthchart and has to do with the underlying motives, conflicts, beliefs, goals, and choices that characterize a person's inner life. Because process can be defined as a series of operations conducive toward a goal, it is dynamic; it is the active movement of consciousness as it progresses from motive to action. Content, on the other hand, is the *outcome* of psychological functioning. It shows up in a person's lived experience—relations with other people, things, and events. Whereas process *is* psychological functioning, content is the consequence of psychological functioning, an epiphenomenal by-product of psychic life.

Process has four *inner* dimensions: motive, function, emotion, and target state. Content has four *outer* dimensions: person, place, thing, or event. Behavior is the ninth dimension and has qualities of both process and content, for behavior is the connecting link between inner and outer experience. Any behavior, by definition, involves some sort of interaction with an outside environment. Since the same astrological variable can symbolize any of nine dimensions, a key idea is that content mirrors process; intrapsychic dynamics are reflected in the nature and quality of one's outer experiences. Jung's theory of synchronicity

137

is central to astrology because it provides an explanatory mechanism for how inner and outer experiences are related. Synchronicity, in turn, rests on Jung's concept of the archetype, which he described as having *psychoid* properties, i.e., an archetype can manifest simultaneously as both an intrapsychic factor and an environmental condition.

Because archetypes can manifest in diverse ways across the entire spectrum of human experience—from inner motivation to outer event—they are protean entities that serve as unifying psychological principles. In this chapter, an astrological theory is presented that outlines the key dimensions of planetary archetypes. First, we will look at planets as archetypal processes and explore why a single planet is capable of depicting several different parts of psychic structure, e.g., motive, function, and emotion. Next, we will look at how different facets of outer experience—content—are symbolized by the same planetary archetypes. Finally, each individual planet will be explicated in terms of the nine dimensions of the relevant archetype.

PROCESS

THE ARCHETYPAL ORIGINS OF MOTIVATION

Any adequate theory of personality must of necessity explain human motivation. Theories of motivation strive to account for the springs of human action, cataloging the intrapsychic forces that impel mental and bodily activity. A motive can be defined as an impulse, desire, or drive that incites a person to action. Deriving from the Latin *movere,* meaning "to move," motives move people; they account for the "why" of behavior, i.e., its underlying impellants.

This is especially important for astrology, as our model has frequently been accused of being deterministic due to the belief that astrologers attribute causality to external forces such as stars and planets. However, if one accepts the premise that the underlying impellants of behavior are universal archetypal principles, as reflected in planets and embodied in human beings, then astrology may be one of the few nondeterministic systems in the field of psychology today. One thing is certain: if astrology is to be given serious consideration as a viable personality theory, it must provide a credible account of human motivation.

Recall that Jung considered the archetype to be the deepest, most primitive element of the psyche. Likewise, the founder of humanistic psychology, Abraham Maslow, alleged that basic instinctual needs such as survival, safety, belonging, and self-esteem are the motive springs of human consciousness. In our astrological model, however, these terms are more or less equivalent. To paraphrase Jung, the archetype is the self-portrait of the need, i.e., it is an image, or symbol, of a human motive. While Jung never organized his system of archetypes into a precise model of clearly defined motivational correlates, it was clear that he regarded archetypes as motivating dynamisms. These transindividual entities were thought to be attributes of a Universal Psyche *and* the human psyche. Each archetype is an autonomous, dynamic nucleus of concentrated psychic energy—a god within—that is inherently intelligent and intentional. Archetypes, in effect, are the innate ideas of both psyche and cosmos; human beings are populated by Platonic *Forms* that shape our thoughts, feelings, and perceptions.

What we are proposing here is that zodiacal signs and their respective ruling planets constitute a twelve-drive model that connects human motivation to core archetypal processes that are immanent at every level of Nature. Every psychological need is an extension of a basic organizing principle in the Universe. As a symbol of a universal principle, an archetype cannot be precisely defined or reduced to a single image, for there can be more than one image for any motive just as there can be more than one word for a need.

As a symbol of transformation, for example, a Scorpio archetype might manifest as a shaman (one who transforms), a villain (that which needs to be transformed), or a monster (representing fear of transformation). Likewise, as a symbol of the need for change and liberation, Aquarian characters include tricksters, rebels, mad scientists, and eccentric oddballs. Obviously, we do not run into all of these archetypal characters in real life; monsters, thankfully, are confined to the landscapes of our dreams. The point is that every archetypal manifestation is a metaphor for a motive, and often depicts the degree to which that motive is integrated within the psyche. If the Scorpio archetype is dishonored within, so that the individual suffers an excessive fear of transformation, then that archetype is likely to manifest outwardly in behavior or events that take a monstrous form—spousal abuse, sexual molestation, being the perpetrator or victim of a crime, and other unpleasant manifestations that characterize an unintegrated Scorpio-Pluto.

Signs as Motivational Needs

In Chapter Three, the signs of the zodiac were described as psychological needs and archetypal principles. It bears repeating that the need of a sign can be inferred from behavior that is characteristic of that sign. By observing various behavioral traits of a sign, and applying inductive reasoning, one can discern where the behavior is leading *to*, i.e., the goal of the behavior, which is always satisfaction of some specific need. Consider, for example, the traits of Aries: assertive, direct, fearless, impatient, independent, combative, and so on. There is a logical consistency to these traits that suggests Aries behavior is oriented in a particular direction—toward *freedom of being*. We can conclude, therefore, that Aries symbolizes the need for freedom, autonomy, or simply survival. Ultimately, there is nothing Arian that cannot be understood in the context of this need. Likewise, if we consider the traits of Libra—engaging, charming, nice, cooperative, considerate, and fair—we can reasonably assert that Libra represents the need for *relationship*. Again, there is nothing Libran that cannot be understood in the context of this need.

Of course, there are additional words that capture different nuances of a sign-need. Like an archetype, a sign's motive cannot be reduced to any singular word; rather, it is more a category of need. The underlying need of each sign is like a diamond with different facets, each facet requiring a different word that is self-consistent with every other word describing the need of that sign. Capricorn, for instance, can be described as the need for perfection, order, structure, control, authority, and success—all of which have obvious correlations. Taken together, we can more easily grasp the drive that Capricorn symbolizes.

To summarize, a complete analysis of the zodiac suggests that there are twelve fundamental, innate, inborn needs that correlate to the signs. These signs obey a precise, developmental sequence such that earlier sign needs take precedence over later ones. Aries, for example, represents the need for survival, Taurus for safety, Gemini for learning, Cancer for belonging, Leo for self-esteem, and so forth. Each of these needs correlates to a developmental epoch, within which the need of that sign is in its ascendancy; i.e., it is the primary developmental thrust of the period. Accordingly, astrology presents a hierarchically organized, twelve-stage, twelve-drive model of motivation. At the heart of the theory is the assertion that people act in the service of their needs.

PLANETS, FACULTIES & FUNCTIONS

Strictly speaking, planets do not actually symbolize motives; rather, they symbolize psychological functions that are oriented toward satisfying the needs of the signs they rule. Signs are motives; planets are their active agents. A planet (including the Sun and Moon) symbolizes a psychological faculty, which can be defined as an inherent power or ability to perform a function. A function is the normal, proper, or characteristic *action* of any thing, human or otherwise. Planetary faculties perform functions—asserting, attracting, thinking, listening, creating, serving, engaging, and so forth. Planets, therefore, are functions that involve certain *actions*, and these actions are motivated by needs. This implies that motivation and function are as inseparable as a rocket and its fuel tank.

Each sign-planet pairing can be regarded as a motivational system. When we talk about the body, we refer to specific systems: the cardiovascular system, the gastrointestinal system, and the endocrine system. Likewise, there are psychological systems as well. Aries-Mars rules the competitive/assertion system, Taurus-Venus the security/stability system, and Capricorn-Saturn the control/mastery system. A sign-planet is a "motivational system" because it entails an interaction between two components of the psyche—sign and planet. As needs, signs motivate their ruling planets to perform specific functions, and these functions involve appropriate *actions* that serve the underlying motive.

A planet's functions can be inferred from actions that characterize its nature. Again, we can infer functions via inductive reasoning. By observing characteristic actions of a planet, one can discern where the actions are leading to, i.e., the purpose of the behavior. An action is any behavior that is goal-directed, or is done for a reason. Some actions are readily observable, whereas others are more psychological in nature. For example, if a normal and proper Neptunian action is *to empathize*, then one of Neptune's functions is the capacity for empathy. Note that a planetary function is the nominalization of the verb-form of that planet. One simply turns the verb/action of the planet into a noun—to empathize (verb/action) converts to empathy (noun/function). Another characteristic Neptunian action is *to transcend;* thus, the corollary Neptunian function is *transcendence.*

Recall that functions are always in the service of needs. Again, every sign is "ruled" by a certain planet. This simply means that for every need represented by a sign, there is a planet (function) devoted to the fulfillment of that need. Planets, then, are psychological processes geared toward satisfaction of specific needs. Signs and planets form verb-noun pairs, as it were, the planet being the active agent (verb) of the sign (noun) over which it "rules."

Saturn, for instance, is the planet that rules Capricorn. The noun form of Capricorn might best be described as the drive for perfection in material form—or, put more simply, the need for order, structure and control. Saturn, as the verb form and active agent of Capricorn, would fulfill its need by ordering, structuring, and controlling within the behavioral environment. Since Saturn signifies the verbs to order, to structure, and to control, it follows that Saturnian functions are *order*, *structure*, and *control*. Again, planets symbolize particular categories of activity, which are oriented toward the fulfillment of motivating drives. Each planet is a distinct type of actor, who acts in accordance with a set of motivating values. Saturn, for example, symbolizes activities that are related to goal achievement, ambition, and seeking status, which are *its* motivating values.

The point here is that needs symbolized by signs provide the motivation that trigger the functions represented by planets. How and whether that planetary function satisfies its need is indicated by a host of additional factors including the planet's sign and house position and its aspects to other planets. The degree to which a planet can satisfy its sign-need is a measure of that planet's functionality (or dysfunctionality). This is a topic that will be explained more fully in subsequent chapters.

PLANETARY EMOTION & TARGET STATES

At the heart of the proposed theory is the simple assertion: *needs motivate.* Once a felt need begins to dominate awareness, that person is motivated to engage in behaviors that satisfy the need. A theory of motivation, therefore, must deal with human feelings and emotions, as feelings/emotions are inseparable from the motivational process. People act out of anger, fear, love, excitement, pride, shame, aesthetic pleasure, and so on. Emotions are "archetypal voices" of sign-planet motivational systems and function as barometers of need satisfaction.

If planets could talk, each would have a characteristic imperative; each would have has its own distinct internal voice.

Aries-Mars: "Just do it! Go for it! It's your *right*. Nothing can stop you now!"

Taurus-Venus: "Settle down. If it feels good, enjoy it. Pleasure yourself. Mellow out."

Gemini-Mercury: "That's interesting; define and classify it. Put on your thinking cap."

Cancer-Moon: "Listen, turn inward; what are you feeling now?"

Leo-Sun: "Let it shine, baby. Express yourself. Let's have some fun!"

Virgo-Mercury: "Be careful, there's a problem here. Figure it out."

Libra-Venus: "Turn on the charm and *engage*. Consider, compromise, cooperate."

Scorpio-Pluto: "Face your fear and take it to the limit; do or die. Get down and dirty."

Sagittarius-Jupiter: "Just do the right thing. It's all good. Keep the faith, baby!"

Capricorn-Saturn: "Bear down and focus. Concentrate. Control yourself."

Aquarius-Uranus: "Expect the unexpected. Stay open and detached."

Pisces-Neptune: "Let go and let God. Surrender. Trust the Universe."

The above examples illustrate how we experience the planets as a form of self-talk. These are our inner voices, the archetypal imperatives that tell us what to do through specific emotional signals that are converted into symbolic language. For example, we might feel angry (Mars) and then say to ourselves, "I've got to stand up for myself; he can't do that to me!" If we feel attracted (Venus), we might think:

"Be nice; let them know you are interested." Each planetary state has its own agenda and behavioral imperative. One can also experience conflicting emotions and voices as evidenced by hard aspects between planets, a subject we will take up in later chapters.

In systems theory, the relationship of emotion to motivation would be described in terms of calibration and target states. Every individual has a range of permissible feeling for a given motivational system, e.g., for Capricorn-Saturn, we tolerate a certain amount of failure or lack of success, beyond which we are motivated to achieve. The term for this fixed range is the *calibration,* or "setting" of the motivational system, like a setting on a thermostat. Just as a thermostat automatically responds to temperature changes and activates switches controlling heating mechanisms, so human beings automatically respond to changes in affective states and respond by activating corrective behaviors.

With the Capricorn-Saturn system, if a person feels he is falling too far behind in his goals, he will tend to try harder; if he feels he is way ahead of schedule, he may, for the moment, relax and focus on some other need until he again feels an urgency to achieve. Each sign-planet in astrology has a desired state, e.g., Capricorn-Saturn would be a state of order, control, success, and so forth. Note that a target state constitutes fulfillment of the governing need for that sign-planet system.

The degree of realization of the preferred state is continually monitored by a reference signal—an affect—which specifies the amount of deviance from the "target state." When a disturbance arises in the environment that has a destabilizing effect on the desired state, this effect is registered as a varying reference signal. The degree of variance from the target state represents a measure of *error;* the indication of error is then used to trigger a behavior that opposes the error. Thus, changes in action (output) are opposed to the effects of disturbance (input) in exact measure as to the degree of error from the target state.

To put this in astrological terms, imagine an individual with a strong Capricorn-Saturn component to his personality, the target state of which is a feeling of success and superior status. Of late, however, he has been under functioning on the job. Eventually his boss tells him that he is being demoted due to inferior performance. This is the *disturbance;* his affective response includes feelings of anxiety, guilt, and failure. As a reference signal, these affects vary markedly from the target state of success. To the extent that he feels unsuccessful, he is likely to compensate by working harder, staying focused, putting in extra time, and so on. His improved performance is calculated to counteract the feelings of guilt and failure that have been evoked by his demotion. His goal is to re-establish a feeling of success.

A primary goal of any system—human or otherwise—is to restore balance (homeostasis) by counteracting disturbance and re-attaining its target states. An emotional variable that has slipped out of its prescribed bounds is the system's equivalent of motivation in the sense that it leads the individual to search for a means to bring it back into line. In Chapter Six, we will look more closely at the affective (emotional) range of each sign-planet system. The point here is that an organism does not simply respond to an environmental stimulus in a direct, linear fashion; rather it controls its responses by virtue of intrinsic reference signals—*emotions*.

The relative strength of a motive can be inferred from how a planet is constellated in the chart as a whole, i.e., its sign and house position and the aspects it forms to other planets. Although these topics will be covered more thoroughly in later chapters, a brief comment may apply here. If a planet receives many aspects and/or is in its own sign or house, then the affects related to that planet will be strongly experienced and will constitute a dominant motive. One cannot tell merely by looking at the chart whether the planetary function is well integrated, only that it will be a dominant affect. Such a planet may symbolize a chronic "mood," for a mood is a relatively stable pattern of feeling—a kind of global affective response pattern that is more diffuse and enduring than an affect. It may not be a response to a specific event, but rather expresses itself in certain qualities of feeling that saturate a person's every perception, thought, and behavior.

For example, if the planet is Jupiter, the person may be perpetually optimistic; if Saturn, the native could be chronically gloomy, if Mars, continuously angry, and so on. These affects would repeatedly activate the corresponding planetary function to engage in some behavior that attempts to satisfy the need which the emotion conveys. Such a pattern of behavior would constitute a dominant trait.

People become aware of basic needs through the processing of information from the environment and from their own physiology. They experience these needs as emotional states that motivate them to act in state-specified ways, i.e., to choose behavioral goals that will result in the desired state of need satisfaction. They tend to persist until the goals are achieved and the needs are satisfied. If their behavioral strategies prove effective, then goal attainment will result in need satisfaction and termination of the behavioral sequence. Otherwise, individuals are compelled to reevaluate their strategy and decide on a new goal or a new approach.

Astrologically, this process can be understood by relating sign-planet motivational systems to specific affects that are experienced on a range of intensity. Each sign-planet system has a target state, or preferred feeling, that is experienced as a varying reference signal. Deviation from the target state evokes a disturbing affect, which, in turn, stimulates a corrective planetary action that is calculated to achieve the desired feeling. Planets, therefore, symbolize flowing goal-oriented movements that constitute a series of operations conducing toward an end. Such processes involve continuous change until the goal state is reached.

SUMMARY

Current theories of personality postulate that human beings are intrinsically motivated to satisfy a variety of innate, psychological needs. It was speculated that these needs have their origin in archetypes, which constitute universal ordering principles immanent at every level of Nature. As primordial images, archetypes are metaphors of human motives. Because archetypes can manifest through internal and external events at the same time (synchronicity), environmental conditions motivate people from without just as needs motivate from within. Synchronistic events are purposeful in the sense that they stimulate the growth of consciousness by confronting the individual with the consequences of his or her own behavior.

The zodiac not only symbolizes the structure and dynamics of the psyche, it also represents the innate drive toward wholeness. As an integrated totality, the zodiac depicts a hierarchically organized, twelve-stage, twelve-drive model of motivation. Each sign constitutes a basic psychological need.

CONTENT

Many people today still consider astrology's primary value to be its capacity to forecast events. Predictive, event-oriented astrology has a long and respected tradition, its major branches being **horary,** which answers specific questions, **electional,** which "elects" favorable times to begin an enterprise, and **mundane,** which studies the relation of planetary cycles to political and cultural trends. Event-oriented astrology works precisely because planetary archetypes have a tendency to manifest not only through human behavior but also through the events humans experience. From a psychological perspective, however, the *meaning* of an event is considered more important than ability to predict the event itself. The psychological astrologer is interested in (1) how events reflect the psyche of the experiencer; and (2) what the event's purpose might be in the larger framework of personal growth and evolution.

There are four ways an archetype can manifest externally—as a person, place, thing, or event. An event can be defined as a *segment of time* in which something occurs of a particular quality; i.e., an event is a significant occurrence, happening, or outcome. Actually, the term "event" constitutes a higher order class of which "people, places, and things" are members, for the people we meet, the places we go, and the things we acquire are events in themselves.

Events are referred to as *content* because they constitute the prime subject matter of life. Content is contained in awareness, as when we focus our attention on a spouse (person), live in an ashram (place), worry about our bank account (thing), or go on a vacation (event). Clearly, these four dimensions tend to overlap and represent somewhat artificial distinctions. A woman can pay attention to her husband while vacationing at an Ashram in India and worry about her bank account all at the same time. For our purposes, however, it is useful to distinguish people, places, things, and events as different dimensions of our lived experience.

Content is always in some way a product of a planetary action. We may fight someone (Mars), attract goods (Venus), investigate a topic (Mercury), protect our children (Moon), or go to a university (Jupiter). Sometimes events appear to happen *to* us, as if we bear no responsibility for their occurrence. A woman is raped, a man's car is stolen, or a natural disaster destroys the family home. From an astrological point of view, however, such events cannot be mere random occurrences. A core principle in astrology is that consciousness generates conditions consistent with itself. We must remember, however, that individual consciousness is always embedded within a larger consciousness—the objective psyche—which may have purposes that supersede the intentions of its individual members. Since we are indissolubly part of this larger consciousness, our every thought, decision, and action has consequences that reverberate throughout the whole and eventually come back to us in the form of an event. Painful events may not simply be retribution for past sins, but opportunities for strengthening under-functioning parts of the psyche.

Sometimes it is necessary to take a long range view when attempting to understand the significance of an event. While many of the events we experience appear quite different, every life has a pattern that originates in childhood. Early experience leaves a powerful imprint and becomes a kind of template for later experience. This is due, in part, to the ideas that developed in response to these early events. Once established, core beliefs function like self-fulfilling prophecies, generating conditions that have the same or similar quality as the ones that occurred in childhood. Cognitive patterns that developed during one's formative years continue to influence decisions and behavior right into adulthood. Ultimately, these internal patterns form the pattern of our everyday life; they construct the very fabric of our existence, showing up in our jobs, our relationships, and our finances. Everything of significance bears their mark. Pattern is the endlessly repeating story of our lives.

When interpreting an astrological chart, therefore, it behooves the astrologer to pay close attention to the nature and quality of a person's lived experience. For each and every event can be seen as a metaphor for some intrapsychic factor that may be operating outside of awareness. The outer world is psyche turned inside out. Events are derivatives of consciousness; content mirrors process; fate is soul spread out in time. In the remainder of this section, we will explore how archetypes can be discerned behind the persons, places, things, and events that characterize an individual's everyday life.

ARCHETYPAL CHARACTERS

An archetype can manifest externally as a character in three different ways—as a personality type (e.g., narcissist, obsessive), a role (e.g., mother, sibling, employee), or an occupation (e.g., accountant, professor). While all persons that we meet embody one or another archetype, there is no single way that an archetype manifests. Rather, there is a plethora of ways that are modified by that planet's sign, house, and aspects, as well as by the degree to which that archetype is integrated within the individual. Every planet in astrology symbolizes both an inner and outer character, and the nature of the inner character is reflected in the outer one.

Inner characters make their presence known through the moods, attitudes, internal dialogues, postures, and impulses that characterize different psychological states. As such, these inner characters constitute identities, or sub-personalities. Externally, these same archetypal figures make their presence known through the personalities, roles, and occupations of the people we attract. These individuals, too, will be characterized by moods, attitudes, and behaviors that reflect *their* psychological states. What is so odd about astrology is that a planetary configuration describes the nature of the outer character just as accurately as it describes some facet of one's own personality. See Figure 8 for a list of archetypal characters associated with each sign-planet system.

Consider, for example, the archetype of Mars. We are possessed by this identity whenever we feel aggressive. "I can do it; nothing can stop me now," is the voice of Mars. There is an impulse to fight, to be free, to assert one's *right to be.* Externally, Mars will show up in a form that reflects the way it is constellated within the individual. The external Mars person will behave in a way that either parallels or compensates the way Mars is expressed by the native. If the native is uncomfortable with his warrior identity and is afraid to *be* it (overmodulated Mars), then the warrior archetype may manifest externally in a compensatory way; someone will act aggressively, or selfishly, or brutally toward the person. Or, the native may be plagued with someone who similarly lacks the capacity to assert.

Conversely, if Mars is undermodulated and the native has poor control over his warrior spirit, then Mars may show up in a compensatory way where people assert in an underhanded, passive, or covert manner toward the individual. Equally likely when Mars is undermodulated is that other people will act in a similarly primitive, impulsive, or thoughtless way. Hostilities are out in the open and there are continual fights and competitions until the native learns to better integrate his warrior spirit.

Characters symbolized by planets will be particularly busy in the houses these planets tenant. If Mars is in the 6th house, then co-workers are apt to embody Mars. However, if Mars is in the 8th house, one's partners may embody Martian traits in the bedroom or in the way joint finances are handled. Wherever Mars resides, circumstances arise that provoke the native to anger or assertion and thereby give him ample opportunity to integrate Mars to a higher degree. Again, depending upon how Mars is integrated and constellated overall, i.e., its sign, house, and aspects, the degree of difficulty will vary accordingly. As a general rule, however, Mars characters will behave in a manner that either reflects or compensates the way Mars is expressed by that individual.

Mars' roles are fairly straightforward. Anyone who competes against the person, challenging her to fight, encouraging her to assert, violating her rights, or in some way threatening her survival, is embodying a Mars function. Mars can be a competitor, an adversary, a rival, an opponent, or a fellow combatant. The warrior archetype can also show up as a survivalist, a daredevil, militant, adventurer, or explorer. The more Mars constitutes a dominant trait in the people one attracts, the more it is likely to be a strong component of the native's personality as well—or *needs to be*. If the native struggles over the way other people express their need for independence, freedom, or survival (doing it to excess or not enough), then this indicates the native is having *internal* problems with Mars as well, expressing it either too little or too much. Life will always provide circumstances that stimulate the person to develop skills in precisely those areas that present problems.

Although we have been focusing on Mars here, the same principle applies to the other planets as well. Each planet symbolizes a separate identity in the sense that when we are *in* that archetype we experience the whole chart through its eyes. If circumstances evoke Venus such that Venus momentarily takes over and possesses the person, e.g., he feels affectionate, attracted, and loving toward someone, then the Venus-identified person will experience the rest of his chart as if he *were* Venus. If Venus is opposing Saturn, he will begin to anticipate that his love will not be reciprocated; if Venus squares Mars, he will worry that his beloved is too selfish. In other words, the planets to which Venus forms hard aspects will show up externally in a form that frustrate or inhibit what Venus wants.

While aspects will be covered more thoroughly in subsequent chapters, the point here is that not only does each planet constitute a separate identity, it also symbolizes specific other persons with whom we interact. One can interpret a planet either way—as the self, or as a significant other person who embodies that function. In both instances, the planet will manifest in a manner that is consistent with its placement in the chart.

To return to the above example, if natal Venus is opposed Saturn, the Venus-possessed person is apt to perceive others as withholding or rejecting (in other words, as too Saturnian). Note, however, that this outcome occurs only when the person is predominantly identified with her Venus. If she identifies with her Saturn function, then the opposite may occur: she perceives potential lovers as too Venusian – needy, compliant, wishy-washy, saccharine, and so on. Whichever side of the polarity the native assumes, the lover may assume the opposite such that the behavior of both participants is equally consistent with the meaning of the aspect.

Likewise, if the Venus-possessed person has Venus square Mars, then his love interest will behave as if he *she* had Venus square Mars, too, but she will tend to embody the Mars side, which the Venus-identified man has for the moment projected, e.g., she may be abrasive, demanding, or feel restricted by his desire for intimacy. Of course, the argument could be made that the individual who actually has the aspect is behaving in a way that evokes exactly that behavior in the other which is expected. Aspects signify beliefs, and beliefs operate like self-fulfilling prophecies. From a synchronistic perspective, however, at least part of the reason for the experience is that the native has unwittingly sent out a casting call and advertised for someone who fits his script. The Universe is only too happy to oblige.

Sign-Planet	Archetypal Characters
Aries-Mars	Warrior, competitor, rival, young man, adventurer, pioneer, noble savage, sociopath
Taurus-Venus	Hedonist, settler, earth mother, voluptuary, builder, young maiden, money maker
Gemini-Mercury	Messenger, herald, reporter, student, amateur, dilettante, librarian, sibling, neighbor, punster
Cancer-Moon	Mother, women, dependents, caretaker, cook, protector, historian, Realtor, patriot, the public
Leo-Sun	Hero, father, men, performer, star, playmate, buddy, romantic interest, audience, narcissist
Virgo-Mercury	Efficiency expert, fix-it man, trouble shooter, doubting Thomas, novice, analyst, critic
Libra-Venus	Beloved, partner, spouse, diplomat, arbiter, artist, host, social butterfly, beautician, ally
Scorpio-Pluto	Healer, shaman, criminal, tyrant, stranger, financier, evil person, sex object, prostitute
Sagittarius-Jupiter	Teacher, guru, prophet, traveler, demagogue, moralist, optimist, promoter, sales person
Capricorn-Saturn	Authority figure, father, executive, manager, superior, expert, professional, taskmaster
Aquarius-Uranus	Witness, trickster, rebel, radical, humanitarian, inventor, eccentric, free spirit, liberator
Pisces-Neptune	Savior, victim, martyr, alcoholic, addict, mystic, fraud, poet, dreamer, psychic, wimp

Figure 8: Archetypal Characters

Knowing which part of a person's chart someone else is playing has two diagnostic advantages. First, one can infer the *purpose* of that person in the life of the native. If the external character embodies a predominantly Saturn function, e.g., as an authority figure, then there may be challenges and opportunities for developing the Saturn function within the native. Second, the precise nature of one's experience with the external character provides *feedback* that reflects the state of integration of the corresponding psychological function, while at the same time stimulating it to further growth.

A common example would be the role of a parent in a child's life. It appears that part of the child's fate is to complete unfinished business from the parent's life that is reflected in either the Moon (mother), or Sun (father). It never ceases to amaze me how the placement of the Moon not only describes the native's history with the maternal figure, it also describes the history of the maternal figure herself. How the mother was affected by experiences prior to the birth of her child seems to get passed on to the child as a kind of psychic inheritance. The child's experience with the mother is internalized and then worked with continuously over the course of the lifetime. If the mother was depressed, the child inherits the depressive tendency and must heal within herself what remained unresolved in the mother.

The same could be said of the Sun and the child's experience of the father. The position of the Sun in the chart suggests a theme in the life of the father that may constitute "unfinished business." Like two runners in a relay race, the father hands the baton to his son/daughter whose fate then becomes to run his/her leg of the race—i.e., to advance the cause and, hopefully, to achieve in his/her own life whatever the father left unfinished in his own. The key to the specifics of the challenge is revealed by the sign, house, and aspects of the Sun. The child must literally "out do" the father by actualizing his/her *solar* potential to a higher degree; he or she must attain a higher level of creativity, self-esteem, confidence, and capacity to love with a full and open heart. The situation may repeat itself when that child becomes a parent, such that each subsequent generation must carry forward the evolutionary trajectory of the family line.

ARCHETYPAL PLACES

A place is an *area of space* of a particular quality set aside for a purpose. Each planet fulfills a purpose in that it expresses an action that is designed to satisfy a motive and attain a goal. However, purposes require places in which the appropriate actions can occur. For example, Mercury symbolizes a process of learning, which often requires a school—a place of learning; the Sun signifies the creative impulse, which might require a theater or studio; Uranus signifies a group of like-minded people bound together for a common cause, hence a convention center or meeting hall would be a fitting place.

The upshot is that not only do planetary archetypes symbolize characters that perform actions; they also represent the places in which

Sign-Planet	Purpose	Place
Aries-Mars	Assertion, survival	Stadium, arsenal, battlefield, desert, boxing ring, race track, front line
Taurus-Venus	Security, comfort	Bank, park preserve, farm, storage facility, massage center, garden
Gemini-Mercury	Learning, reporting	School, library, book store, newsroom, station, road, passageway
Cancer-Moon	Belonging, nurturing	Residence, restaurant, hotel, shelter, reservoir, reservation, river
Leo-Sun	Creativity, play	Theater, playground, place of fun or entertainment, sports arena
Virgo-Mercury	Service, health, work	Workplace, office, garage, employment agency, health clinic, lab
Libra-Venus	Partnership, beauty	Bridal suite, art gallery, ballroom, beauty salon, arbitration office
Scorpio-Pluto	Healing, regeneration	Abyss, cave, brothel, morgue, bathroom, sewer, operating room
Sagittarius-Jupiter	Expansion, justice	University, church, courthouse, embassy, airport, foreign land
Capricorn-Saturn	Success, structure	High office, office building, mountain, skyscraper, top of anything
Aquarius-Uranus	Change, awakening	Conference room, fraternity house, convention hall, internet
Pisces-Neptune	Unity, endings	Places of confinement, rest home, retreat, bar, asylum, sanctuary

Figure 9: Archetypal Places

these actions occur. Linking places to planets is a simple matter of observation and deductive reasoning.

If we know that Neptune symbolizes the transcendent function, then we can deduce that Neptune rules places that support transcendent activities, e.g., rescue missions, retreats, convents, meditation centers, and the like. Next, we can test our hypothesis by observing whether, in fact, Neptune manifests as these kinds of places wherever it is constellated in the chart. Of course, there can be more than one place befitting a planetary archetype. In each instance, however, the place is appropriate for one or more of the activities that typify that archetype. Since Neptune is also associated with escapism, victims, the aged, and people who must be secluded, Neptune rules hospitals, bars, crack houses, rest homes, prisons, mental institutions, and other places where people go to escape, get high, recover, rehabilitate, fall apart, or end their lives. While a planet may not literally manifest as an actual place, its location in the chart can color a house environment so that it feels "as if" the place was there, e.g., Neptune in the 4th can make one's home feel like a retreat; with Mars in the 7th one's marriage may seem like a boxing ring; and with Pluto in the 10th one's career may appear to take place "underground."

Figure 9 (page 154) presents a brief listing of some purposes and places associated with each planet. While the list is by no means exhaustive, it illustrates how the purpose of a planet finds expression in various locales. The value of knowing a location's corresponding planet brings us back, once again, to Jung's notion of synchronicity. If a woman is working in a hospital as a nurse, then both her occupation and her working environment correspond to Neptune. Since her life experience appears to highlight this planet, we are cued to check the status of Neptune in her chart, i.e., its sign, house, and aspects. Clara Barton, who gained the title of "Angel of the Battlefield" for her work as a nurse during the American Civil War (she later founded and then served as president of the American Red Cross for 22 years), has Sun conjunct Neptune in Capricorn in her 10th house.*

If a client reports that she is feeling drained and exploited at her job in the hospital, we can translate her report into a psychological language of process. What are the beliefs, attitudes, and behaviors that create her experience with the hospital? For these, too, will be indicated by Neptune's placement. If we note, for example, that Neptune squares Mars in her chart, we can hypothesize that her capacity to say "No" and act in her own self-interest (Mars) is in conflict with her capacity for compassion and selfless service (Neptune). Accordingly, she may not have proper boundaries when it comes to caring for others and is therefore vulnerable to exploitation. In fact, this is a very common situation in the field of nursing.

---

* Sun conjunct Neptune indicates that she identified (Sun) with the victimized (Neptune) and sought to rescue them by being stoic, disciplined, and responsible (Capricorn). Its placement in the 10th house suggests that she would become renowned for this type of selfless service.

Again, in subsequent chapters we will explore more fully how to interpret planetary configurations like the above. The point here is that whatever place corresponds to a planet, the native's experience within that locale can be traced directly back to the corresponding psychological function. The astrologer thereby has a ready means for discerning the attitudinal and behavioral antecedents that generate the outer condition.

ARCHETYPAL THINGS

Planetary principles tend to crystallize into various things, with each planet representing a class of things. While a thing can be an abstract behavioral quality, like belligerence, for our purposes things can be defined as **inanimate** objects, like a wallet, or **animate** objects like a pet. Those things that a planet "rules" must necessarily be consistent in their function and quality with the psychological principal of the corresponding archetype. For the warrior archetype, a Mars thing would be a weapon. For the archetype of beauty, a Venus object would be jewelry. A book would be a clear manifestation of Mercury, whereas for Jupiter it could be a religious relic. The pride and strength of a lion is a good symbol for the Sun, whereas the lethal sting of the Scorpion is apt metaphor for Pluto.*

Again, a planet correlates to a class of things, all members of which symbolize that planetary quality. Saturn, for example, constitutes a class of objects that includes bones, barriers, blockades, corporations, clocks, buildings, handcuffs, measuring devices, bricks, scaffolds, and frames. Note how all these things evidence the Saturn principle of structure, time, and control.

Things that make up real-life events can be interpreted in the same manner as objects in dreams. If one dreams of driving a car downhill and suddenly finding that the brakes are out, an interpretation would be that the dreamer is feeling out-of-control in his real-life actions; that "things are moving too fast." The same event could conceivably have the same meaning in one's waking existence. A car is a means of *moving forward,* and thus has a Mars connotation. Breaks, on the other

---

* Certain animals, of course, have long been associated with specific signs-planets, for their traits and aptitudes symbolize abstract, psychological qualities.

Sign-Planet	Planetary Things
Aries-Mars	Weapon, missile, ammunition, tool, face, head, iron, scissors, sharp objects, adrenals
Taurus-Venus	Couch, possession, sweets, mortar, object of art, savings, ornaments, cow, sculpture
Gemini-Mercury	Book, newspaper, arms, mail, phone, printer, cabs, dictionary, nerves, radio, language
Cancer-Moon	Souvenir, memento, biography, breasts, fluids, silver, womb, container, boat, pot, food
Leo-Sun	Scepter, award, medal, prize, trophy, gift, gold, heart, games, toys, game ball, lion, peacock
Virgo-Mercury	Pets, vacuum, toothbrush, calculator, microscope, vitamins, utensil, device, intestines
Libra-Venus	Scales, object of art, contract, treaty, beautiful things, embroidery, valentine, kidney
Scorpio-Pluto	Wound, bomb, corpse, bodily waste, genitals, rectum, reptiles, toilet, debt, a will, finances
Sagittarius-Jupiter	Bible, advertisement, a law, passport, code of ethics, diploma, religious icon, liver
Capricorn-Saturn	Bones, barrier, corporation, clock, building, handcuffs, ruler, scaffold, frame, gavel
Aquarius-Uranus	Airplane, computer, technology, an invention, antennae, satellite, group/ club, modem
Pisces-Neptune	Alcohol, drugs, fish, gas, oil, fog, photography, mask, parasite, decay, garbage, feet

Figure 10: Archetypal Things

hand, serve a Saturn function; they retard, inhibit, and slow things down for purposes of control. If a person has a Mars square Saturn aspect, then the failure of his breaks has an obvious correlation to the aspect and may hint, synchronistically, at a needed change in attitude. Perhaps he should better regulate his actions, be more patient, and not push so hard to accomplish goals—all challenges of Mars square Saturn.

Things, in effect, are symbols of archetypal principles. One must always distinguish an archetype from the things that symbolize it. The image of a Greek god, for instance, is itself a thing that stands for the archetype behind it; i.e., the image is not the archetype but an expression *of* the archetype. Likewise, when an expensive car is referred to as a "status symbol," we are saying that the car stands for abstract qualities such as wealth, excellence, superiority, and high achievement. Knowing the astrological meanings that "things" have helps us to think symbolically and to appreciate the deeper, synchronistic import of everyday events. Figure 10 (page 157) lists several objects that serve as symbols, or metaphors, for the psychological qualities associated with each sign-planet.

PLANETS AS EVENTS

As stated earlier, an event can be defined as a segment of time in which something occurs of a particular quality. An event is a significant occurrence, happening, or outcome. A core principle of astrology is that character produces events consistent with itself. This is supported by Jung's concept of synchronicity, which implies that any idea held long enough will attract whatever conditions it needs for its expression.

For example, the physical manifestation of Saturnian energy often comes as obstacles, hindrances, limitations, delays, burdens and a chronic sense of lack. At least some of these events may be a direct consequence of an internal attitude of fear, i.e., dread of failure, which is produced by a belief that one is not adequate to the task. The individual, anticipating things will go wrong, tends to experience the very thing he expects—failure and deprivation. The quality of the event thus becomes a symbol of the attitude from whence it derives its form and energy. This is the key to understanding how astrology works.

Sign-Planet	Planetary Events
Aries-Mars	Beginnings, adventure, competitions, violations, fights, battles, accidents, injuries, fire
Taurus-Venus	Accumulation of goods & money, experiences that provide pleasure, security & comfort
Gemini-Mercury	Learning experiences, communications, short journeys, relations with siblings/neighbors
Cancer-Moon	Experiences with mother/women, being nurtured (fed, loved), acceptance or rejections
Leo-Sun	Experiences with father/men, fun & games, parties, recreation, romance & courtship
Virgo-Mercury	Work related events, relations with co-workers, health concerns, problems to be solved
Libra-Venus	Social events, attractions, relations with partners, contracts & lawsuits, art & leisure
Scorpio-Pluto	Crises, shadow encounters, evil, wounding, death, power struggles, healing, reform
Sagittarius-Jupiter	Good luck, teacher & grandparent relations, travels, conferences, religious events
Capricorn-Saturn	Relations with authority, obstacles, delays, stress/pressure, career successes & failures
Aquarius-Uranus	Shocking events, sudden change, revelations, group relations, revolutions, causes
Pisces-Neptune	Charity, being victimized, spiritual pursuits, fraud, losses, retreat, dreams, psi events

Figure 11: Planetary Events

To be even more specific in regard to chart content, we have to consider the sign that a planet occupies. This would provide an important clue to the manner in which both the attitude and the event manifest. Saturn in Pisces might express a sense of inadequacy with regard to conditions of suffering. Anyone who is sick, disabled, addicted, mentally ill, victimized, or in need of charity may constitute a source of anxiety. The person may grow up wanting to rescue someone who is ill, but feel inadequate. A tragic condition may exist that requires selfless, compassionate service; yet, the child is overwhelmed by the enormity of the task.

Eventually s/he may overcompensate and become an authority on Piscean matters. Perhaps s/he becomes a head nurse in a hospital that cares for individuals with bone (Saturn) Cancer (Pisces). Or s/he could master a spiritual discipline like meditation, or an artistic discipline like singing – "s/he had perfect pitch." There are countless ways a given combination of planet and sign can manifest. Although it is impossible to know exactly what will happen, whatever does will fit the range of possibilities. There will be numerous circumstances that flow from the combination, and while these circumstances may be different in detail, they are of the same or similar quality.

While planets correlate to general types of events, real events are invariably hybrid creatures that partake of more than one archetype. To fully appreciate the significance of an event, one must see it as the summary product of complex interlocking factors as reflected in planetary sign positions, house positions, and aspects.

Figure 11 lists some typical events that correlate to each planet. Again, however, the reader should keep in mind that events are never the product of any one archetype; rather, an event emerges out of the interaction of several archetypes. Each planet adds its own unique quality, yet is but a contributing factor in a collaborative process. Archetypes are the strands of meaning out of which the fabric of our lives are woven. Each planetary archetype interweaves with other archetypes until something unique is created—*a life*.

To use another metaphor, events are like still images in a film; they are frames of meaning that are created out of the interactions of various characters. Each archetype is a character that has a potential for certain kinds of action. When these internal characters come together, their various potentialities combine to create an event that reflects the interaction. Yet, the event itself is but a frame in a larger, ongoing story that constitutes a whole life. Like still images of a film, each event has its own integrity and quality but is merely a portion of an unfolding narrative that emerges at a higher level of organization. In Chapter Nine on dispositors, we will examine how this higher level reflects both character and narrative (plot) structure.

Summing Up Content

Content has been defined as the outcome of psychological functioning. As such, it occurs in four dimensions—person, place, thing, or event. Although content is a derivative of planetary action, it is not always clear how a native's lived experience results from her psychic structure. One hypothesis is that the chart symbolizes the child's *prototypical* experiences of early childhood. Core beliefs that result from childhood operate like self-fulfilling prophecies, creating events that recapitulate childhood prototypes. These patterns tend to repeat until the person is able to learn from self-created experience and shift his beliefs in the direction of greater health and wholeness.

A planet can manifest as a character in three ways—personality type, role, or occupation. While inner characters constitute sub-personalities, or part-selves, outer characters appear in guises that reflect the native's relative integration of the corresponding archetype. Struggles with outer characters provide the impetus for strengthening that archetypal dimension of the psyche.

Planetary archetypes are also associated with specific places. A person's primary areas of life experience suggest the planets that correlate to those places constitute key psychological processes. Places provide appropriate contexts for the expression of planetary actions. Additionally, the quality of a person's experience within a place correlates directly to the attitudes and beliefs symbolized by the corresponding archetype. The diagnostic implications of such correlations are far reaching, as the astrologer merely needs to listen to the client's story to infer the underlying intrapsychic factors that support it.

Inanimate and animate objects are yet another category of experience that corresponds to planets. Each planet "rules" a class of things, all members of which have analogous properties. Because things symbolize archetypal processes, they have meanings similar to dream objects. Like pieces of a puzzle, they fit together to create emergent meanings that reflect how reality is being constructed; i.e., the nature of the things one attracts reflect certain core ideas around which experience is internally organized. This complex tissue of beliefs makes up the structure of the native's personal narrative.

Because this structure crystallizes into objects that intrude upon awareness, things make conscious one's internal story. If someone experiences a chronic lack of money, for example, this may reflect an internal belief in *scarcity*—commonly called "poverty consciousness." This belief would show up in his chart as a particular configuration that would cue the astrologer to the existence of a possible negative pattern. By inviting the client to explore the nature and origins of his beliefs about money, the astrologer may assist the client in developing a new story that allows for greater prosperity.

Events constitute the final category of experience ruled by planets. An event was defined as a segment of time in which something occurs of a particular quality. Again, the quality of the event reflects the nature of the archetypal processes that generate it. Events are never the product of one archetype, but are hybrid creatures that emerge from the interweaving of several archetypes. Additionally, events constitute a higher order class of which characters, places, and things are members.

Planetary archetypes function as unifying psychological principles. Not only do they manifest as external characters, places, things, and events, they also represent psychological needs, faculties, emotions, states, and behavioral acts. When one considers the almost infinite number of ways that archetypes can combine to produce the vicissitudes of inner and outer experience, one can appreciate astrology's power as a psychological language. As a model of the psyche, astrology unequivocally demonstrates the primacy of consciousness. The external world is effect, not cause; events are symptoms of, not reasons for, who we are.

PLANETARY DIMENSIONS

In the following section, I outline the various dimensions of each planet. First, I cite the psychological need that is the underlying motivation of the planet. Secondly, I describe the planet as a psychological process, or verb. Thirdly, I note the psychological faculty the planet symbolizes. And lastly, I list some of the psychological states and external outcomes that correlate to the planet.

The Sun ☉

Active agent of the Leo need for

Validation of Identity	Positive self-image
Self-esteem	Approval, Admiration
Creative self-expression	Enjoyment, Recreation

Sun as process represents the verbs

To create, to express	to entertain, to perform
To intend, to decide	to choose, will, identify
To defend (self-esteem	to rationalize (behavior)
To court approval	to approve (of someone)
To romance, to impress	to validate (someone)

As psychological faculty or capacity

Self-expression, Creativity	Identity, Self-concept
Volition, Will, Intention	Ego, self

As psychological state or event

The target state of the Sun is pride and confidence. What it seeks to avoid is shame or humiliation of any kind. The Sun needs to be noticed, thus it tends to engage in activities and behaviors that draw attention to itself, which is perfectly healthy and natural. To enjoy oneself is to express oneself, and this is what the Sun seeks—self-expression, creativity, play, and performance. The Sun's position in the chart shows where and how the individual seeks an audience to validate his or her identity. Solar activities correlate to romance and courtship, play, fun and games, sports—in short, any activity that involves self-performance. Again, the sign and house position of the Sun indicate how and where we enjoy ourselves and how/where we seek to impress others.

If the Sun is well integrated, it tends to produce positive states—joy, pride, confidence, and affability. However, if is not well integrated, the individual may overcompensate and display arrogance, grandiosity, egotism, vanity, and self-inflation. These are examples of undermodulated solar states. Overmodulated solar states include low self-esteem, deflation, reticence, uncertainty, and lack of self-confidence.

The Moon ☽

Active agent of the Cancer need for

Nurturing, Mothering
Belonging, Acceptance
Sympathetic Understanding
Warmth & Closeness

Emotional Security
Tenderness
Unconditional Love
Caring & Protection

Moon As process represents the verbs

to nurture and protect
to care for, sympathize
to love unconditionally
to feel, to contain

to listen (to feelings)
to react habitually
to understand, to resonate
to remember, to react

As psychological faculty or capacity

Receptive Function
Listening Response
Memory

Nurturing Faculty
Emotional Conditioning
Personal Unconscious

AS PSYCHOLOGICAL STATE OR EVENT

The goal state of the Moon is a sense of belonging and closeness. What it tries to avoid is rejection. Accordingly, the Moon's placement indicates how and where the individual seeks to experience loving feelings—both toward and from others. Related themes include nurturance and dependency issues, experiences involving need for understanding and support, themes of vulnerability, sensitivity, and tenderness, and where there may be emotional conditioning from the past. Other issues include self-protectiveness, domestic issues, and experiences involving mother/woman in the native's life. Activities may involve some sort of caretaking, nurturing and protecting, providing a safe haven for others, feeding, housing, and the like.

If the Moon is well integrated, the individual will find it easy to express tenderness, listen sympathetically, and talk about feelings. Conversely, undermodulated lunar states includes excessive emotionality and dependence upon others, oversensitivity, and clinging neediness. If the Moon is overmodulated, the person is likely to be uncomfortable with feelings and unable to express tender caring. At the root of this condition is an inordinate fear of rejection.

Mercury ☿

As a planet, Mercury is the ruler of two signs, Gemini and Virgo respectively. Accordingly, Mercury strives to meet the needs of both signs.

Active agent of the Gemini need for

Information, News	Learning, Education
Mental Stimulation	Communication
Knowledge (facts & data)	Language

Active agent of the Virgo need for

Efficient functioning	Competence
Proficiency Service,	Usefulness
Problem solving	Improvement
Discrimination	Health & fitness

Mercury represents the Gemini verbs

to learn, to study	to notice, to observe
to label, to classify	to question, to inquire
to inform, to recount	to communicate, to report

Mercury represents the Virgo verbs

to analyze, to examine	to scrutinize, to dissect
to reduce (to parts)	to serve, to improve
to correct, to fix	to renovate, to maintain
to criticize, to find fault	to systematize

As psychological faculty or capacity

Cognition, Reason	Speech, Communication
Thinking, Rationality	Intellect, Mind

As psychological state or event

When serving the **Gemini** need, Mercury's target state is one of curiosity and interest. What it seeks to avoid is boredom or disinterest. This can manifest as an insatiable desire to learn. Verbosity results from an equally strong need to report what one has learned. If the need for learning is overdone, there can be restlessness and a tendency toward scatteredness. Mercury's physical manifestations include taking

classes, learning about new things, and becoming somewhat of a dilettante if the learning capacity overfunctions—i.e., a jack-of-all-trades
and master of none. Other typical manifestations include involvement
in communications media, writing, reporting, journalism, classifica-
tion of knowledge, filing information, and the like.

When serving the **Virgo** need, Mercury's target state is a sense of
being useful and productive. Related states include efficiency at work-
related tasks, competence in getting the job done, skillfulness in
completing tasks, and general overall helpfulness. If the person tries
too hard to be helpful, then criticality and fault-finding may result,
especially if there is something or someone that needs fixing. Physical
manifestations include any kind of work or service, fixing things that
break down, correcting mistakes, being a trouble shooter or efficiency
expert, work in crafts, trades, merchandising, and especially the health
field—e.g., diet and nutrition.

Venus ♀

Like Mercury, Venus is also the ruler of two signs, Taurus and Libra.

Active agent of the Taurus need for

Safety, Security
Self & Object Constancy
Sensual Gratification
Sameness, Predictability
Stability, Homeostasis
Pleasure & Comfort

Active agent of the Libra need for

Harmony, Beauty, Balance
Social Relatedness
Intimacy, Companionship
Fairness, Equality

Venus represents the Taurus verbs

To attract, to acquire
To have, to possess
To soothe, to comfort
to secure, to conserve
to procure, to obtain
to pleasure, to gratify

Venus represents the Libra verbs

To beautify, to harmonize
To cooperate, to consider
to balance, complement
to relate, to engage

To mediate, to arbitrate   to attract, to join with
To negotiate, compromise   to socialize, to partner

As a psychological faculty or capacity

Self & Object Constancy   Aesthetic Function ("taste")
Internal Security   Artistic Sense
Psychological Stability   Social Ability
Self-Soothing   Capacity for Intimacy

As psychological state or event

In serving the **Taurus** need, the target state of Venus would be equanimity, which is related to safety, comfort, and pleasure. The states it tries to avoid are pain, insecurity and instability. Related to this basic goal state are experiences involving the accumulation of goods and money that provide for security, serenity, and sensual gratification, e.g., the person obtains the means for purchasing a fishing boat which provides endless hours of pleasure. If Venus is overdone, however, there are a number of states and behavior that can result—grasping, possessive behavior, self-indulgence, laziness, lethargy, sloth, gluttony, and greed.

In serving the **Libran** need, Venus' target state is intimacy and cooperation. The individual seeks experiences that involve collaboration. Having to do things alone is avoided, i.e., lack of engagement with others. As one of my Libran clients put it, "I don't mind being independent; I just don't want to have to do it alone."

Desired states would include feelings of affection, love affairs, partnerships of all sorts, a sense of grace and charm, diplomatic relations, social connections, networking and the like. In addition, Venus also signifies the aesthetic ideal. Thus states of harmony, beauty, and artistic appreciation would also be sought. If carried too far, Venus can produce superficiality, shallowness, equivocation, and over dependency upon others for feelings of love and connection. If underfunctioning, it correlates to experiences of open conflict, disagreements, disputes, or even lawsuits.

Mars ♂

As active agent of the Aries need for

Survival, life, being	Autonomy, Independence
Freedom, liberty	Immediate Gratification
Action/Doing	Activity/Movement

Mars as process represents the verbs

to act, to do	to assert, to affirm
to begin, to venture	to initiate, to pioneer
to activate, to vitalize	to fight, to battle
to dare, to endeavor	to inflame, to excite

As a psychological faculty or capacity

Assertion	Competitive Instinct
Survival Instinct	Drive, Initiative
Aggression, Id	Libido Instinct

As a psychological state or event

The goal state of Mars is pure aliveness, the joy of being alive. What it seeks to avoid is deadness, which generally means any threat to its survival. For example, Mars would experience lack of freedom or lack of movement as a life threatening condition. Above all else Mars needs to *keep moving*, especially toward what it wants.

The impulse to attain the immediate, short term goal—the reward—trumps all other considerations. Accordingly, Mars is notorious for its lack of restraint, absence of social skills, and general insensitivity to other life forms. Corollary states are vitality, decisiveness, impetuousness, impulsiveness, omnipotence (no sense of limits), recklessness, anger, frustration (if thwarted), and aggression.

Physical manifestations of Mars energy include new enterprises or projects, adventures, accidents, fights, violence, quarrels, headaches, high blood pressure, mechanical ability, engineering skills, and work with tools or cutting instruments. Any "do-it-yourself" type work that involves hard, physical labor is Martian.

Jupiter ♃

Active agent of the Sagittarius need for

Truth, Wisdom	Purpose
Meaning, Significance	Virtue, Morality, Ethics
Justice, Right	Expansion, Travel
Hope, faith, trust	Belief in a higher power

Jupiter as a process represents the verbs

To theorize, to hypothesize	to speculate, to interpret
To conclude, to generalize	to infer, to deduce
To abstract, to believe	to teach, proclaim
To proselytize, preach	to advertise, sell, promote
To moralize, judge, debate	to affirm as right or true
To predict, to prophesy	to counsel, to advise
To trust, hope, have faith	to expand, travel, broaden
To overextend, exaggerate	to overestimate, to overdo

As a psychological faculty or capacity

Higher mind	Deductive Reason
Moral Judgment	Conscience, Virtue
Capacity for Hope	Capacity for Faith

As a psychological state or event

The target state of Jupiter is one of hope, faith, and enthusiasm. It is an expansive feeling that flows from an abiding trust in the intelligence of the Universe. The antithetical state is one of doubt, loss of faith, or cynicism. When Jupiter is functioning properly, there are a number of experiences that result—good luck, good fortune, and a sense of abundance.

Jupiter is our "fairy godmother complex." It indicates our capacity for hope and whether we expect things to go well. This may manifest in states of optimism and acts of generosity, philanthropy, and good will. Jupiter also correlates to experiences of foresight, long-range views, and wisdom. It is naturally philosophical, ethical, and moral in its outlook. It rules consulting or advisory positions.

If Jupiter is overfunctioning, a number of states and problems may result, such as dogmatism, self-righteousness, presumptuousness, and a tendency toward being overly judgmental. There may be missionary zeal and a desire to convert others to one's opinions. Too much faith can result in grandiosity, a manic fervor, acts of extravagance and overindulgence, improvidence, gambling, and general foolishness. The individual may have great expectations that are not grounded in reality. This may cause him to overextend, exaggerate his position on important matters, expect too much from others, promise too much to others, and generally become a victim of his own blind optimism.

Saturn ♄

Active agent of the Capricorn need for

Perfection, Excellence	Success, Accomplishment
Prestige, Status	Structure, Limits, Form
Order, Organization	Control, Authority

Saturn as a process represents the verbs

to achieve, to produce	to succeed (accomplish)
to persevere, to persist	to execute (the plan)
to consummate, to fulfill	to structure, to order
to organize, to discipline	to manage, to govern
to plan, to systematize	to control, to maintain
to perfect, to master	to crystallize, to mature
to obsess, to concentrate	to focus, to deepen
to conserve (tradition)	to economize, be prudent

Saturn as a complex represents the verbs

to fear (failure/inadequacy)	to obstruct, to retard
to suppress, to inhibit	to slow, to delay, to block
to restrict, to constrict	to contract, to tighten up
to crave (due to deficiency)	to overcompensate
to try too hard, to obsess	to overfunction, to overdo

As a psychological faculty or capacity

Ambition, Authority	Self-discipline
Self-control	Duty & Responsibility
Respect for rules & limits	Productivity

As a psychological state or event

The target state of Saturn is a sense of mission accomplished, of a job well done, of *success*. Related to this target state is the need to feel organized and "together" in the process of pursuing the goal of success. The sense of being "on top of things" is a Saturn target state, and alludes to the Saturnian quest for being on top, i.e., the boss, authority, or president.

What Saturn fears most is failure. In fact, the accomplishment of success is to some extent a natural compensation for the fear of failure. All of Saturn's more positive states—ambition, patience, discipline, determination, perseverance, expertise, status, and ultimate honors and distinction—can be regarded as compensatory for an inner fear of failure, inferiority, inadequacy, or deprivation. Saturn, therefore, is associated with responsibilities, serious business, duties and obligations, and a felt pressure to succeed. Saturn may also be experienced as a state of craving or anxious longing in that area of the life where the planet is most active.

If Saturn is overfunctioning, then the native may fall prey to unrelenting standards that drive the person to try too hard. This may result in workaholism or an inability to enjoy the fruits of one's labor. If the natural and healthy anxiety that accompanies Saturn is suppressed, however, the individual may procrastinate and avoid responsibility. Or he may simply give up, allowing negativity and pessimism to control behavior. An internal state of fear can correlate to certain outer conditions such as experiences of limitation, delay, deficiency, obstacles, blocks, and restrictions. If the individual perceives these conditions as unalterable and interminable, then the more extreme negative states of Saturn will be felt—utter failure, personal defectiveness, depression, loneliness, isolation, gloom, guilt, melancholy, despair, and sadness.

Uranus ♅

Active agent of the Aquarius need for

awakening, revelation
perspective (wholistic)
objective outlook
change, progress, reform

enlightenment, illumination
overview (panoramic)
altruism, humanitarianism
liberation, breakthrough

Uranus as process represents the verbs

to awaken, to enlighten
to liberate, to emancipate
to objectify, to release
to progress, to advance

to reveal, to illumine
to free from outmoded ways
to change, to reform
to innovate, to invent

Uranus as complex represents the verbs

to shock, to shatter
to rebel, to agitate
to perturb, to destabilize
to separate, to distance

to startle, to jolt, shake up
to disrupt, to upset
to rupture attachments
to break up, to break away

As a psychological faculty or capacity

Observing Ego
Wholistic Thinking
Radical Insight, Change

Universal Mind
Objective Witness
Altruism, Humanitarianism

As a psychological state or event

Uranus' goal state is one of universal love, or what the Greeks called *agape*. It is a state that is attained when the perspective that gives rise to it is realized. Such a perspective is one of radical insight or self-realization, a super objective awareness that sees in a flash of illumination how all things work together for good.

Having realized this, Uranus wants to share the news by engaging in acts that awaken others. Humanitarianism, altruism, and movements that reveal the interconnectedness of all things are favorite Uranian pastimes. Recognition that the whole always takes precedence over the part is typically Uranian. Likewise, there is an abiding concern for the future welfare of collective humanity.

Uranus tends to bring about breakthrough, revolution, revelation, or discovery, one way or the other. It is associated with states of sudden change, disruption, the unexpected, and destabilization, all of which may cause shock and upset. It is also associated with eccentricity, the bizarre, abnormality, and controversy. Broadcasting, radio, television, computers, electronics, advanced technology, and science in general are ruled by Uranus.

The planet stimulates positive reforms via some original contribution or invention that advances the system in a new direction. The system that advances may be anything—a marriage, a business, a field of study, an art, a culture, a political system, or an institution. If carried to an extreme, Uranus can produce a divine discontent that may manifest in iconoclasm, anarchy, rebellion, revolt, dissension, or nihilism.

Neptune Ψ

Active Agent of the Pisces need for

Transcendence of Duality	Unitive Consciousness
Oneness with Life/God	Infinite Love & Beauty
Holiness, Bliss, Rapture	Atonement & Forgiveness
Charity, Altruism	Surrender, Non-attachment

Neptune as process represents the verbs

to transcend, to merge	to flow, to melt, to yield
to surrender, to sacrifice	to let go and let God
to abdicate, to renunciate	to empathize, to forgive
to accept and allow	to love impersonally
to love selflessly	to martyr oneself for others
to rescue victims	to imagine, to envision
to dream, inspire	to envision, to fantasize
to elevate, to heighten	to intuit or channel (psi)
to glamorize, idealize	to enchant, beguile

Neptune as complex represents the verbs

to escape, to space out	to go unconscious, deny
to be helpless, to collapse	to dissolve into chaos
to vacillate, procrastinate	to submit, to defer to others

to abdicate responsibility	to self-destruct, to sabotage
to confuse, to mystify	to bewilder, to befuddle
to delude, to deceive	to camouflage, to disguise
to disappear, to retreat	to distort, to elude, to hide

As a psychological faculty or capacity

Transcendent Faculty	Collective Unconscious
Imagination & Fantasy	Empathy & Forgiveness
Intuition, Psi Ability	Dreams, Idealism

As a psychological state or event

The target state of Neptune is a blissful, transcendent awareness of the unity of life. While such a state is difficult to attain (let alone maintain), we can see traces of it in most Neptunian pursuits. On the positive side, spiritual aspirations in general are Neptunian so long as the goal is participation in ultimate reality rather than merely intellectualizing about it. Meditation, yoga, retreats, and prayer are the usual forms. Anytime a person is moved to feel empathy, compassion, or forgiveness for another, he or she is experiencing Neptune.

Psychic experiences such as telepathy, precognition, or clairvoyance are other forms the planet takes. If a person feels inspired by transcendent feelings of oneness with the divine, or has a vision of infinite love and beauty, they are experiencing the higher side of Neptune. Kind heartedness and a legitimate wish to relieve suffering are other healthy expressions, as is a willingness to surrender in faith to that which is beyond personal control. The latter gives rise to experiences of flow, plasticity (adaptability), and 'effortless effort' in the pursuit of objectives.

A less pleasant but perhaps more common experience of Neptune is victim/savior states, both sides of which are Neptunian. While there are many genuine victims that are deserving of help, e.g., survivors of airplane crashes, people with life threatening illness, or children who are victims of sexual abuse, many others are "apparent" victims who are simply self-destructive, usually due to unconscious guilt that may show up as drug or alcohol addiction. Typically one person—the rescuer/martyr/savior—tries to help the apparent victim. Whenever the rescuer assumes responsibility for the victim's life, especially if the victim is capable of helping themselves, then the rescuer is acting out a Neptunian impulse. Often this is motivated by the rescuer's denial of his own psychological problems, which are then projected into a suitable carrier—the apparent victim. Oneness is achieved by the victim having deferred responsibility to the savior, who remains unconscious to his own motivations and underlying psychological problems. Whereas the victim acts out the Neptunian impulse by an act of self-destruction, the savior acts out the Neptunian impulse by the act of saving. Individuality on both sides is sacrificed in the enmeshed state that results.

We might say that the victim *de-selfs,* i.e., goes unconscious, and thus avoids having to make the difficult choices and decisions that being an individual requires. By denying reality, by escaping or avoiding responsibility, by vacillating and procrastinating, or by assuming a state of relative passivity and helplessness, the individual surrenders his life not to God, but to fate. And fate usually shows up in the form of a person who preys upon the victim's weakness by deceiving, exploiting, sabotaging, betraying, or abandoning the victim. A second wave of fate then appears in the form of a social worker or a homeless shelter or simply a caring person—anyone who is willing to extend a helping hand. A particularly virulent form of victim/savior states occurs in the dance of the dependent/co-dependent who remain fused together in not so blissful oneness until one of them decides to stop the game. Failure to achieve this may result in 'compassion fatigue' (burnout) for the savior, death for the victim.

Subjective states involving confusion or delusion are also Neptunian. Confusion is often in the service of denial, and operates as a defense. For various reasons, the person is unconsciously seeking to avoid a disturbing truth. When states of confusion occur on a more or less regular basis they are indicative of individuals who have not been able to develop a strong, differentiated self. Neptune, however, can be experienced by anyone who has been a victim of subterfuge, deceit, deception, treachery, or fraud. Such experiences may simply be in the service of deepening the victim's capacity for empathy and understanding of suffering—or, perhaps they are a spur to greater discrimination.

While most people have been disillusioned at one time or another, the stronger forms of Neptunian pathology occur in those unfortunate souls who live in a more or less constant state of delusion, such as schizophrenics. Common experiences of loss, tragedy, grief, and sickness are other passages into Neptune. Note that it is usually when people are in a state of suffering or grief that they are most likely to express their spiritual longings through prayer or meditation.

Neptune can also be experienced through imagistic art forms such as painting, photography, or film. Poetry, music and dance are yet other forms the muse may take, especially when these forms give expression to a transcendent ideal.

Pluto ♇

Active agent of the Scorpio need for

Transformation, Healing
Catharsis, Release
Purification, Cleansing
Integrity (Integration)

Death and Regeneration
Purging, Elimination
Power, Potency
Sex, Merger, Fusion

Pluto as a process represents the verbs

to empower, impassion
to deepen, intensify
to penetrate, merge, fuse
to integrate, to assimilate
to regenerate, renew
to heal, to purify
to restore, to reform
to metamorphose, mutate
to cathart, release

to compel, possess
to eroticize, arouse
to probe, to pierce
to incorporate, metabolize
to transform, convert
to purge, to cleanse
to transmute, to remake
to eliminate (toxins)
to expel, to exterminate

Pluto as complex represents the verbs

to fear, to dread
to repress, to ward off
to project as evil/bad
to scheme, to plot
to force, oppress, terrorize
to corrupt, pervert, darken
to entice, seduce, tempt
to destroy, to revolt

to distrust, to suspect
to repudiate, to disown
to control, to manipulate
to intimidate, to coerce
to scare, frighten, alarm
to degrade, to demean
to subvert, to undermine
to annihilate, to kill

As a psychological faculty or capacity

Power, Potency   Sexuality, Eros
Integrity (Integration)   Healing Ability

As a psychological state or event

The target state of Pluto is one of power or wholeness, though it is a different kind of wholeness from that which Uranus or Neptune seeks. Pluto wants to feel whole *inside* rather than with the whole of humanity or nature. This internal wholeness is what we might call integrity—a state of concentrated force within the psyche that results from the psyche being integrated. To the extent this occurs, there *is* a deep, penetrating quality to the individual's connections with others, marked by a relative absence of fear.

Integrity occurs when there are no wounds too painful to heal, no repressed memories too frightening to recall, no traumas stuffed away in a state of suspended animation in some dark corner of the mind. If such divisions do exist, Pluto rules the processes of transformation and healing that result—these include the peak experience, catharsis, purging, and cleansing. Pluto also correlates to all the requisite fear and suffering that such painful experiences entail. For Pluto is both death and rebirth.

Again, Pluto is not particularly interested in attaining transcendent states of oneness with all life; however, it does want to feel united with its immediate environment. This is because one's local surroundings are the repository of projections, and it is precisely what one projects, i.e., one's shadow, that creates an uneasy division between self and other. Thus Pluto is associated with power struggles and control issues, for it is the shadow contents of consciousness—one's unhealed wounds—that usually come back to haunt us in the form of a relationship predicament.

If the individual is unwilling to suffer or to change through an encounter with the shadow, then Pluto may manifest in attempts to control or even destroy what has now become the enemy. The less virulent forms of such control are coercion and intimidation, such as extortion, blackmail, kidnapping, and mob rule. The more extreme forms degenerate into paranoia, violence and destruction. Rape, murder, terrorism, and tyranny are all Plutonic.

To the extent that the shadow is projected, one suffers fear and disempowerment. If the individual over identifies with the Pluto component of consciousness to the exclusion of other parts of the psyche, he or she will become possessed by the shadow and metamorphose into that which is feared; the good Dr. Jekyll becomes the bad Mr. Hyde. It is the individual's attempt to resolve his fear that actually causes him to fall into his shadow, for one can see in the phenomenon a belated attempt at integration. Shadow states usually involve some kind of criminal or evil act, underworld association, compulsion, perversion, or subversion.

Anyone who is engaged with the shadow or underworld elements of society is performing a Pluto function. This includes people working in the healing professions—doctors, therapists, social workers—as well as people who descend into the underworld to confront the shadow directly. Examples include police, detectives, FBI agents, CIA operatives, vigilantes, spies, infiltrators, undercover agents, informers, investigators, and all others involved with fighting evil.

Other manifestations of Pluto involve sexuality, erotic encounters, and feelings of passionate intensity. Passion seems to be what humans feel when they are about to be transformed by an experience with the unknown. It is perhaps for this reason that sexual arousal and anxiety are both characterized by the same physiological responses; i.e., we are aroused by what we fear because of a need to integrate it. "Do or die" extremism is also Plutonic, as occurs when individuals are willing to die for their convictions.

Chapter Six

Houses as Psychological Environments

ESTABLISHING THE SETTING OF THE STORY

J ust as signs correspond to a twelve-fold division of the earth's orbit about the Sun, so houses derive from a twelve-fold division of the earth's rotation on its axis. Accordingly, the structure of astrological houses parallels the organization of the zodiac. Each house represents a two-hour phase of the twenty-four hour daily cycle. The Rising sign, or Ascendant, marks the time when the Sun rises in the east to start the day, or approximately 6:00 a.m. Each house, in turn, unfolds at two-hour intervals. Proceeding clockwise and following the apparent path of the Sun, the cusp of the 12th house would start two hours after sunrise or approximately 8:00 a.m., four hours after sunrise would start the 11th house, six hours (12:00 noon) the cusp of the 10th, and so on.

Eventually, as one rounds the circle, there is a return to the cusp of the 1st house. Planets and signs can fall in any of the twelve sectors, depending upon one's time of birth.

PSYCHOLOGICAL STRUCTURE OF THE HOUSES

In the same way that houses parallel the structure of the zodiac on a physical level, so they also parallel the zodiac on a psychological level. The first house corresponds to the first sign of the zodiac, the second house to the second sign of the zodiac, the third to the third sign, and so on throughout the twelve signs. The psychological meanings of the houses parallel in physical circumstances the more abstract meanings of the signs to which they correspond. Houses, in short, represent departments of life experience. They are the mundane derivatives of sign principles, i.e., the situational, experiential, or earthly manifestation of that archetype. As such, a house provides a context for the actions of planets.

A planet in a house is like an actor upon a stage. The psychological function of that planet—the role it plays in the life drama—is most noticeably expressed within the circumstances of the house it tenants. The Sun, for example, will perform the role of "hero" or "ego" within the context of the house it occupies.

Each house corresponds to a specific sign, planet, polarity, element, modality, and perspective. The first house corresponds to the sign Aries, the planet Mars, yang polarity, fire element, and personal perspective. Regarding modalities, the parallel terms for houses are **angular**, **succedent**, and **cadent**, which mean more or less the same thing as cardinal, fixed, and mutable. For example, angular houses correspond to activities that involve moving out toward a goal, i.e., asserting (1st), grounding (4th), engaging (7th), and achieving (10th). Succedent houses are concerned with concentrating and focusing the activities that were initiated in the angular houses. Their function is to preserve (2nd), consolidate (5th), transform (8th), and collectivize (11th). And like mutable signs, cadent houses classify (3rd), adjust (6th), disseminate (9th), and dissolve (12th) processes and constructs that were solidified in the succedent houses.

The meaning of the circumstances and activities that belong to a particular house are closely associated with the sign and planet that corresponds to that house. Consider the 5th house, which corresponds to the fifth sign, Leo. In its noun form, Leo represents the need for validation and approval. The 5th house simply represents those specific types of experiences through which this need is most easily and readily satisfied. 5th house experiences are all of a similar type or quality—courtship and romance, all forms of creativity and self-expression, theater, play (parties, hobbies, fun and games, sports), children, gambling and speculation. All of these activities satisfy the basic Leo need for validation and approval.

Romance, for instance, is an experience wherein we feel special, flattered and admired. Through creativity we are essentially producing replicas of ourselves; the creative work becomes a kind of metaphor through which identity is released. The praise that hopefully follows serves as culminating fulfillment of the act. Similarly, in theater the actor uses the role as a vehicle through which he expresses himself and (ideally) wins the respect and applause of the audience. Play is much the same, its purpose being to serve as medium for self-expression. If we win the game (sports event, contest), then our objective is again fulfilled.

Children, in a Leo/5th house sense, are seen as extensions of parental egos; they are our "creations" and thus our representatives. Naturally, parents want to be proud of their children. Gambling and speculation provide the final arena through which Leo seeks satisfaction. When we gamble, we are going for the payoff. Whether this be money, a date with the girl of our dreams, the applause of an admiring audience, or the successful sale of a personal work of art, the payoff is essentially the same—the feeling that we are "OK," even wonderful, that the world loves us and appreciates us just as we are.

SCENES AND SETTINGS OF THE LIFE STORY

From a narrative perspective, a house is similar to what is commonly referred to as the setting in a play or story. A setting is the location in time and space of the physical background of the action. The actors in our life drama, of course, are the planets. A planet's character is revealed through its potential for certain kinds of action, both good and bad. Because planets have relationships with one another (aspects), just like characters in a drama, houses constitute the stages upon which these characters play out their roles.

The proper function of a setting is to help motivate action. The same is true in astrology. For example, if we place Venus in "the underworld" (8th house) and surround her with all sorts of dangerous and evil 8th house figures (rapists, criminals, gangsters), the native may be motivated to reform her environment in order to keep from being destroyed by it. Perhaps she falls in love with a criminal and must regenerate within herself, and within her partner, a capacity for love. In this manner, a setting is central to the meaning of the story.

Each house has a certain atmosphere, which is a loose metaphor for the total feel or mood of a setting. A house, in effect, symbolizes an environment replete with characters, props, mood, and events. The 10th house, for example, presents us with authority figures, limits and rules, a serious mood, and events that center about the pursuit of long term, career goals. The 1st house, on the other hand, is inhabited by fellow combatants in the fight for survival; it is more akin to a battlefield or field of adventure in which our will to survive is tested. First house activities orient around a theme of personal freedom—can we act decisively in our own self-interest; can we boldly assert our rights? Of course, in an actual birthchart, there are twelve possible settings within which the action of the life can unfold. Each house represents a department of experience and forms a context for the expression of the planets that reside in that house.

A planet in a house symbolizes a character in an environment, thus a "scene" in the overall story. Because houses provide their own characters, a planet in a house helps to define the nature of the characters that normally reside there. The planet, in effect, becomes superimposed over the usual characters of that house.

Earlier I gave the example of Venus in the 8th. Because the 8th house is an area of wounding, the usual figures we meet there are often in pain. These include people in crisis, "dark" characters, criminals, underworld figures, prostitutes, and others who in one form or another are mired in shame. Venus, on the other hand, symbolizes a person to whom we are attracted—a potential lover and partner. But if we associate such a person with those who are wounded and in pain, what does this imply about our Venus object? If someone has Venus in the 8th, she may attract partners who are damaged in their capacity to love, and will thus experience the usual outcomes that result from this condition—partners who avoid vulnerability due to a fear of intimacy, or who betray, abuse, and violate her trust. Yet, Venus in the 8th also symbolizes *her* capacity to trust and love. Any planet that tenants the 8th house must be healed. Eighth house planets, therefore, are wounded healers, at least potentially. Accordingly, whomever she attracts will provide her with opportunities for regenerating her (and their) Venus function.

Another example is Mars in the 10th. Here the "boss" (10th house figure) is likely to be perceived as bold, pioneering, egocentric, perhaps a bit reckless and headstrong, impatient with rules, and so on—all characteristics of Mars. Mars in the 10th also indicates how the native will approach authority figures and generally behave toward people in positions of leadership. Again, the same description applies—bold, aggressive, reckless, headstrong, impatient with rules, and so on.

To some extent, a planet in a house is going to change or influence what is happening in that house. Planets both define and alter their house environments. Normally the mood of the 10th is serious, conservative, and formal; yet, by placing Mars in the 10th the mood is considerably altered. Now one's career becomes a launching pad for a new enterprise, an exciting place where profession becomes an adventure. Having a career may feel like waging a war—opponents must be vanquished; one's courage and mettle is put to the test. Rather than working respectfully within the limits, old ways are challenged and new practices are aggressively advanced. The native approaches goals like a warrior who has to defeat any and all rivals; thus, Mars in the 10th suggests a competitive, spirited approach to goals.

Yet, because Mars is notoriously impulsive, one's career may be marked by an endless series of new beginnings. While good at initiating projects, the native may lack sufficient follow through to build a solid, enduring foundation for long term success. In other words, the 10th house requires discipline and perseverance, and these are precisely the qualities that Mars lacks. A possible solution would be for the person to choose a career that capitalizes on Mars' strengths, e.g., a career that requires courage and daring, a bold, enterprising spirit— and that provides ample opportunity for adventure!

When interpreting a planet in a house, try to imagine how each "planetary character" might behave in the house/setting it occupies. The more planets in a house, the more that setting will be a central backdrop in the unfoldment of the life drama. If there is a preponderance of planets in a few houses, it is the natural circumstances and activities of those houses that are going to be central to the life story. For example, many planets in the 8th indicate someone who is preoccupied with wounding-healing, crisis, death-rebirth, sexuality, investments, fear and pain, and/or the underworld.

Here is a brief listing of the houses and the particular activities to which they correspond.

First House (Ascendant)

Planetary Ruler: Mars
Corollary Sign: Aries
Polarity: Yang
Element: Fire
Modality: Cardinal (Angular)
Perspective: Personal

The 1st house represents the *beginning* of life and thus the surface or outer edge of personality. It shows how we initiate activity and assert ourselves in the world. Like the spark of life, it is unthinking, unplanned *action*, our initial impulse, our first step forward. Like the sign Aries, it is so unconscious and instinctual that the individual may not be fully aware of this aspect of the personality.

The 1st house has a special significance in that its cusp shows the sign that was rising on the eastern horizon at the moment of birth; thus, it is called the 'Rising Sign', or 'Ascendant'. This sign is strongly associated with how the person asserts in the world, and denotes a general theme that is indissolubly linked to destiny and will remain one of the central defining features of their existence.

Signs and planets in the 1st also describe how others see us, especially their first impression. Because the 1st house correlates to physical appearance, it is like "the wrapping on the package," our advertising, body language, or the clothes we wear—that which both ornaments and protects the interior self. It can also be described as one's persona or mask and is associated with the face and head.

Because Mars is the natural ruler of the 1st house, it is an area of life fundamentally concerned with survival. Planets in the 1st (as well as the Rising sign) suggest what the individual needs and does in order to survive as a separate entity. These signs and planets may function more or less independently; e.g., Moon in the 1st suggests the individual must nurture himself rather than depend on others. This is what the person tends to do alone. Likewise, planets in the 1st may indicate those activities that involve periodic new beginnings, e.g., Venus in the 1st symbolizes someone who initiates new relationships quite easily, but may find it difficult to sustain them over the long term.

Individuals with many planets in the 1st house tend to place a high priority on adventure, competition, freedom, and independence. However, like the Fool in the Tarot deck, 1st house planets tend to operate instinctively and recklessly. If the behavioral style of a 1st house planet is *too* successful, the individual may get stuck in his mask and remain relatively unconscious of deeper dimensions of his real self. An extremely successful mask may give one a sense of omnipotence, just like in the movie *The Mask.* If there are many 1st house planets, there can be a recurrent theme of initiating new projects and getting off to a fresh start. As a developmental stage, it correlates to birth and the first 18 months of life.

Second House

Planetary Ruler: Venus
Corollary Sign: Taurus
Polarity: Yin
Element: Earth
Modality: Fixed (Succedent)
Perspective: Personal

This department of life describes attitudes toward physical resources, money, and possessions. It shows how we go about meeting needs for security and attachment. Signs and planets in the 2nd symbolize one's earning and spending habits. The concept of "ownership" is key, for the 2nd house describes whatever one has accumulated, acquired, stored, or saved. With Mars in the 2nd, the native may be impulsive in spending money and thus have difficulty saving. With Saturn there, just the opposite may be true: the native is naturally conservative, even stingy in how s/he manages resources.

Planets in this house symbolize one's perceptions of the physical world and all that it has to offer—from wealth to poverty. Do we trust that the world will meet our physical needs? Is it a safe place? Can we get what we need to feel secure? Expectations can range from "poverty consciousness" to "prosperity consciousness." Factors in the 2nd show how we go about meeting security needs and also that which gives us security, e.g., Jupiter in the 2nd may associate security with having advanced academic degrees or membership in a church.

With Venus as the natural ruler of the 2nd, this house is also associated with the need for pleasure and sensual gratification. One's attitude toward the body and its desires for touching and physical contact are described by the 2nd. Likewise, one's attitudes toward the earth—ecological concerns, agriculture, the environment, deforestation, and other matters affecting the earth are associated with this house.

If a person has many planets here, he or she could be inordinately concerned with safety, security, stability, money, possessions, and physical pleasure.

The 2nd correlates to the "toddler" stage of life, from eighteen months to approximately four years. Planets here can suggest issues associated with the development of self and object constancy.

Third House

Planetary Ruler: Mercury
Corollary Sign: Gemini
Polarity: Yang
Element: Air
Modality: Mutable (Cadent)
Perspective: Personal

The 3rd house is our communications department. It has to do with activities that involve the assimilation and transmission of information. The 3rd house describes our attitudes toward anyone in the immediate environment with whom we can communicate. It also describes the nature of these people. Traditionally, this meant schoolmates, siblings, and cousins in childhood and neighbors in adulthood. However, with modern technologies of communication—radio, television, telephone, faxes, email, and the internet—this can literally mean anyone on the planet who is a source or recipient of information.

The primary focus in this area is on *learning*. This includes reading, studying, and acquiring data in general. The 3rd house describes our experience of primary education, from kindergarten through high school, as well as the quality of day to day thinking. Rote learning, journal keeping, and all types of messages received and sent correlate to the 3rd house.

Individuals with a loaded 3rd house place a heavy emphasis upon communication. They want to stay "informed" and will seek experiences that are mentally stimulating. Also, they may identify with the role of messenger and seek positions in society as journalists, reporters, or some other occupation that involves the transmission of data. As a developmental stage, the 3rd house describes the period from approximately four to seven years.

Fourth House

Planetary Ruler: Moon
Corollary Sign: Cancer
Polarity: Yin
Element: Water
Modality: Cardinal (Angular)
Perspective: Personal

The 4th house essentially describes the home environment, both past and present. Planets and signs in the 4th symbolize our approach to nurturance, care, and protection. The 4th house provides clues as to the nature of one's family of origin. To what extent did the individual experience a sense of belonging? Of being understood, supported, and loved? How did the individual respond to his or her family? The 4th house describes attitudes and beliefs about family ties and support.

As the Moon rules this house, it may symbolize an aspect of the individual's experience with the mother or nurturing figure. In a more general sense, it provides clues about the individual's heritage and family lineage, one's *roots*. Circumstances and conditions that pertain to private life are central to the 4th house. It is where we seek the "refueling" and emotional support that equips us to go back out into the world. It is our "home base."

A strong 4th house suggests someone to whom home, family, foundations, and a sense of belonging are of primary importance. The individual may identify with being a caretaker in some sense, e.g., restaurant work or homecare. On a mundane level, it correlates to the homeland (patriotism), land in general, property, and real estate. It describes the nature of our experiences during the period from seven to twelve years old.

Fifth House

Planetary Ruler:	Sun
Corollary Sign:	Leo
Polarity:	Yang
Element:	Fire
Modality:	Fixed (Succedent)
Perspective:	Social

The 5th house is our personal playground, our own theater of creative self-expression. It is here that we seek playmates to engage in activities of mutual performance. It describes our attitudes toward fun, parties, recreation, entertainment, games, hobbies, romance, creativity, and play in general. This is the area of life wherein we seek validation and approval for who we are, i.e., our ego identity.

In the 5th house, the goal is to enjoy oneself as well as others. It is where we strive to have a "good time" with friends and peers. The 5th house suggests "what we bring to the party." Factors in the 5th may describe our projections onto an imaginary audience. Will people like us? Will they approve of who we are and what we express? It especially describes our assumptions about courtship and what we expect to happen.

Concerns about winning and losing are central to the 5th. Will we win our beloved's heart or will our heart be broken? Likewise, sports belong to the 5th house, for they are a form of play in which we seek to win and prove our worth. Gambling and speculation are yet other "games" that pertain to the 5th. In gambling we hope to win and demonstrate favored status. The bearing and creation of children is a 5th house activity, too, for one's children can be a source of pride or shame. Individuals with a strong 5th house will display a greater than average interest in the above activities.

As a developmental stage, the 5th house pertains to adolescence, the period from twelve to eighteen years old. This is the time when people are most intensely engaged in those activities that properly belong to the 5th house—parties with peers, "best" friends, romance and courtship, sports and recreation, and creative self-expression.

Sixth House

Planetary Ruler:	Mercury
Corollary Sign:	Virgo
Polarity:	Yin
Element:	Earth
Modality:	Mutable (Cadent)
Perspective:	Social

The 6th house describes the work environment. It symbolizes that department of life wherein the individual has a job to do. This job ranges from mundane, day to day tasks such as brushing one's teeth and washing the dishes to regular responsibilities at work. Whether one is self-employed, an employee, or an employer, factors in the sixth symbolize our attitudes toward work. It suggests both the kind of work we are inclined to do and the probable outcomes of our efforts. In short, one's employment history is described by the 6th. The goal is to function in an efficient and competent manner and provide a service to the community. Factors in the 6th house describe the gifts we bring and the challenges we face in our efforts to be useful and helpful to others. This house also symbolizes our experience with employees and co-workers. Are they competent, efficient, reliable? And how do they regard our efforts?

One's approach to problem solving in general is described by the 6th. We might call it the house of *self-improvement*. For it is here that we must conduct a thorough analysis of the situation (or ourselves), make the necessary adjustments and modifications to assure efficiency, and correct whatever mistakes impair optimal performance. Signs and planets in the 6th suggest the way we approach problems and also the problems that must be solved. Mars in the 6th suggests an energetic, independent approach to problem solving. Yet, the problem to be solved may be Mars itself, e.g., a reckless, impulsive, impatient style that impedes efficiency and good planning.

The 6th house is the repair and maintenance department of the psyche. It not only symbolizes our daily work environment, it also correlates to our daily health and what we do to maintain it. Diet, nutrition, exercise, personal hygiene, and preventative medicine are related to the 6th. Other concerns of the 6th have to do with pets,

which in a sense are in our employ. A strong 6th house suggests someone who is very work-oriented and concerned with being helpful to
others. As a developmental stage it correlates to the apprenticeship
phase of life, or 18 to 26 years old when we enter the work environment and begin to develop specific job skills.

Seventh House

Planetary Ruler: Venus
Corollary Sign: Libra
Polarity: Yang
Element: Air
Modality: Cardinal (Angular)
Perspective: Social

Intimate relationships constitute the main theme of the 7th house. It
is here that we meet our partner, whether business or marital. One's
approach to partnership and companionship is suggested by factors
in the 7th house. With Venus as the archetypal ruler of the 7th, the
key requirement is love, compromise, and cooperation. For unless
the individual is willing to accept differences and collaborate toward
mutually satisfying outcomes, the partner is likely to turn into the
open enemy—which is an alternative meaning of the 7th. The 7th
house describes potential difficulties and conflicts that could impede
intimacy and, worse, result in litigation and prosecution.

Contracts, agreements, and potential lawsuits all belong to the 7th
house. Not only does this house describe our basic attitude toward relationship; it also describes the nature of the partner that we are likely to
attract. Factors in the 7th house constitute aspects of the psyche that
tend to be projected and objectified in the person of the partner. These
factors may be either a source of attraction or of animosity. Frequently
they are both. The partner, in other words, embodies that part of the
psyche that we need to love and accept in order to establish balance
within ourselves. To the degree that we are able to do this, relationships are enhanced.

On a more general level, the 7th house describes our social relations
or "public relations." Networking, socializing, and conformity to the
customs and mores of our culture are reflected by the 7th house. Other

activities that take place within this house are mediation, diplomacy, arbitration, and negotiation. A final meaning is any involvement with activities that pertain to beauty and art. A loaded 7th house suggests an emphasis upon aesthetics, partnership and social relations. Developmentally, the 7th house corresponds to the period from 26 to 35 years of age.

Eighth House

Planetary Ruler:	Pluto
Corollary Sign:	Scorpio
Polarity:	Yin
Element:	Water
Modality:	Fixed (Succedent)
Perspective:	Social

The 8th house is our personal underworld, the house of transformation. Its contents have to do with sex, death, and power, all of which are related. Experiences of deep merger and joining require individuals to die to their separate selves and be reborn into a more complex, integrated state. This kind of transformation, whether it is psychological, sexual, or financial, can lead to renewal and empowerment.

Traditionally, the 8th house indicates the "results of partnership," that is, the consequences of merging one's life with another—sexually, emotionally, and financially. The signs and planets that tenant this house will reflect the person's attitude and approach to such matters. If there are fears and difficulties, then these will be reflected in the nature of the 8th house planets and signs.

Psychological wounds that require healing are symbolized by the contents of the 8th. In effect, the planets that occupy the 8th constitute both the approach to transformation as well as that which needs to be transformed. These wounds may be embodied in the nature of the partner (projective identification), or reflected in the issues that come up between partners. Challenges may include psychological issues that impede trust and get projected onto the partner; e.g., the shadow may be embodied in some aspect of the partner's personality or behavior. Sexual conflicts and money issues are other 8th house themes.

8th house experiences are not limited to marital partnerships, but can extend into any relationship that involves deep emotional sharing, crisis intervention, healing, or financial ties. These include healing relationships of all types (doctors, therapists), crisis intervention (paramedics, fireman, police, detectives), involvement with death and danger (morticians, disease experts, scientists involved with atomic power), and financial connections (accountants, controllers, stockbrokers, tax attorneys, IRS agents). Taxes, wills, inheritances, investments, insurance, and debts are 8th house phenomena.

The individual's approach to things that are taboo, forbidden, or dangerous to express is also indicated by factors in the 8th. How do we deal with such painful and destructive emotions as jealousy, envy, hate, vindictiveness, rage, and greed? How do we deal with trauma and emotional injury? What is our degree of interest in such matters and what do we associate with them? Ideally, such feelings (and their associated beliefs) are acknowledged, contained, and eliminated over time. Again, factors in the 8th symbolize both our approach to forbidden feelings as well as that which is forbidden.

Planets and signs in the 8th house suggest whatever is dark and repressed within the individual. Since we need to move *through* these experiences, the 8th house indicates how we negotiate transitions. What is our attitude toward death and rebirth, transformation, and crises that may produce profound changes? And what is the nature of these crises? A strong interest in such matters may create interest in the occult, magic, uncovering nature's secrets, after-death experiences, scientific research into the nature of life and matter, psychic research, and other related phenomena.

To the extent that the native successfully negotiates the challenges of the 8th house, he/she becomes powerful in a constructive way. To the extent that the native attempts to avoid the vulnerability that accompanies this area of life, he/she is either disempowered or may overcompensate by seeking to obtain power *over* people and situations. This latter strategy generally results in what we call *evil*—crime, perversion, coercion, violence, and tyranny.

Developmentally, the 8th house corresponds to the mid-life crisis, which generally occurs somewhere between 35 to 45 years of age.

Ninth House

Planetary Ruler:	Jupiter
Corollary Sign:	Sagittarius
Polarity:	Yang
Element:	Fire
Modality:	Mutable (Cadent)
Perspective:	Universal

The ninth house is our department of philosophy, religion, and higher education. Experiences in this house help us to develop our fundamental beliefs about life. The ideal here is to develop a deep and abiding faith in the Universe. Such faith should infuse one with hope for the future—one's own and that of humankind—and a conviction that all experience serves a higher purpose. Our approach to matters of faith will be described by 9th house factors.

In a narrower sense, the 9th house involves our efforts to understand the nature of right and wrong. The ethical standards and moral values that regulate behavior are largely a consequence of experiences in this house. Accordingly, 9th house factors symbolize our approach to truth, meaning, and ultimate values. To what extent are such concerns relevant to our lives? How important is higher education and knowledge? If the individual attends college (or teachers therein), 9th house planets suggest one's approach to higher learning and even the nature of the studies undertaken. In other words, factors in the 9th indicate both our approach to truth and the nature of that truth itself, e.g., one's religious predilections, philosophical beliefs, ideology, moral doctrines, and perception of God.

Planets and signs in the 9th characterize the particular kinds of experiences we have with clergymen, philosophers, moralists, teachers, mentors, gurus, and legislators. Our attitude toward "the laws of the land" is reflected here as well, especially concerns about legality and justice.

The dissemination of knowledge is another 9th house activity. This includes teaching, preaching, publishing, promotion, and advertising. Anything that expands the mind is part of the 9th house. This includes whatever broadens the intellect and increases our understanding of life—travel to distant lands, interest in other cultures and people, or consciousness raising seminars and conferences. Being a consultant or advisor is a 9th house occupation, especially if the advice is about how one can best orient to the future. As a developmental stage, the 9th house describes the period from 45 to 56 years.

Tenth House (Midheaven)

Planetary Ruler: Saturn
Corollary Sign: Capricorn
Polarity: Yin
Element: Earth
Modality: Cardinal (Angular)
Perspective: Universal

The 10th house is the executive mansion. It describes our vocational potential, career goals, and the way we handle and express authority. The dominant goal in this area of life is *success* in one's chosen profession. This is where we strive to make an impact and leave behind something of value to succeeding generations. Our relative success or failure in this regard will determine our standing in the community, i.e., our reputation and public image. To the extent that one is successful, this house describes honors gained, recognition, status, achievements, and distinction.

The cusp of the 10th house is called the Midheaven, or *medium coeli* (M.C.). Like the Ascendant, the Midheaven has a special significance in that it reveals the sign that was culminating at the moment of birth. This sign will be strongly associated with how the person establishes that career for which he or she becomes publically known. The word 'career' in this context should not be taken too literally, for one can 'make a career' out of anything that entails an enduring goal toward which the native labors diligently. Such striving may or may not entail achievement in a public, conventional sense, e.g., with Pisces on the 10th the individual might strive to excel at voluntarism, content with an anonymous role in a charitable cause. This is not a traditional 'career' but it may constitute her highest achievement with or without public recognition.

In general, factors in the 10th characterize one's attitude and approach to career, however that might be defined. 10th house planets symbolize both the *way* we pursue our career and also, to a lesser extent, the *type* of career we pursue. It is through the attributes of the signs and planets that tenant this house that we hope to gain success and recognition. Again, not all long-term goals are associated with a career in a formal sense. Signs and planets linked to the 10th may simply symbolize what we seek to accomplish over the long term, and how we go about doing it.

Attitudes toward authority are a dominant concern of this house. The initial authority one encounters is generally the father; hence, the 10th house describes the individual's experience with the father with regard to his role as an authority, disciplinarian, and provider.* Later authority figures may be perceived in a manner that is patterned after this original model. If one has positive experiences and associations with the father, this may increase the likelihood of becoming a success and authority in one's own profession. In any event, the extent to which one becomes an authority and the way one handles authority is described by factors in the 10th house.

Developmentally, the 10th house describes the apex of one's career, or the period from 56 to 68. This is when the individual is most likely to distinguish him or herself for career achievements.

Eleventh House

Planetary Ruler: Uranus
Corollary Sign: Aquarius
Polarity: Yang
Element: Air
Modality: Fixed (Succedent)
Perspective: Universal

The 11th house is where we express our concern for humanity at large. Any interest, cause, or movement that transcends our individual lives and has significance for humanity as a whole is signified by the 11th house. *Fellowship* is a dominant theme here. Accordingly, this is where we get involved in clubs, associations, fraternities, lodges, leagues, and organizations that are dedicated to a *group* cause. Such values or

---

* A father has dual roles. As a solar figure, he is the child's playmate, first friend, and greatest fan. As a Saturnian figure, he is the rule maker, authority figure, and that person who embodies virtues necessary to be successful in the outer world.

ideologies may be religious, political, social, environmental, intellectual, or any other type. The important thing is that they involve a group of like-minded people bound together by a common interest.

Planets in the 11th describe the way we approach such concerns and the type of cause that compels our allegiance. The goal here is *to join with others* and support something that has significance beyond one's personal concerns.

The 11th house signifies matters that are at the cutting edge of change—visions for the future, altruistic acts, humanitarian objectives, technological innovations, radical politics, and revolutionary aims. Planets and signs here reflect how we approach change, and the content of that change. If Jupiter tenants this house, the revolutionary aim may involve religion, the legal justice system, or higher education. If Mars, it could be a martial arts movement or cause. The Moon or Saturn here might reflect a reactionary approach to change and a wish to return to a simpler, more traditional time.

Although the 11th house is often described as the house of "friends," the friends of the 11th are not friends of the heart or bosom buddies, which are to be found in the 5th house. Rather, they are colleagues and associates with whom we share certain values and aspirations for collective humanity. What these values are, and the way they are approached, is described by factors in the 11th house.

This house signifies the period from approximately 68 to 80 when individuals enter the retirement years and frequently become involved with groups of like-minded people, support causes, and promote projects that have collective value.

Twelfth House

Planetary Ruler: Neptune
Corollary Sign: Pisces
Polarity: Yin
Element: Water
Modality: Mutable (Cadent)
Perspective: Universal

The 12th house signifies the collective unconscious, which is both the source and end of individual existence. To experience this level of reality requires that one transcend any sense of separateness, individual identity, or personal self-interest and merge in sacrificial love with the whole of nature and the Universe. This house is associated, therefore, with all things mystical or spiritual—meditation, prayer, retreats, convents, monasteries, places of silence and solitude where people contemplate their relationship to God.

Because this house is associated with sacrifice and transcendence, planets in the 12th suggest both that which is sacrificed and that which serves as a vehicle for transcendence. In other words, not only is one's *approach* to spirituality indicated by 12th house factors, but also that which must be sacrificed *en route*. Mars in the 12th, for example, may associate a physical discipline like *Tai Chi* or fighting for a spiritual ideal as the path to God. This planet also indicates what needs to be sacrificed in the sense that one's capacity for self-assertion would be best utilized when fighting for the helpless, the victimized, or the underdog.

The 12th house signifies our participation in the whole of life; thus, it requires a kind of all-inclusive selfless love. This is where we care for those who are unable to care for themselves—the aged, the sick, the disabled, the mentally ill, the homeless, victims of crime, accident victims, abused children, stray animals—in short, anyone or anything that is helpless. Training the occupationally handicapped, providing services for the aged, caring for the disabled, working with addicts, doing charity work, hospital work, or any other service that involves caring for others less fortunate than the self, is a 12th house activity.

Locations for 12th house activities include rehabilitation centers, prisons, hospitals, convalescent homes, homeless shelters, group homes (residential treatment centers), hospice, and orphanages. Note that these are all places where people are contained because they cannot, for the moment at least, be productive members of society. Factors in the 12th house symbolize the way we go about doing such work and, to a certain extent, the nature of the work itself.

For example, Venus in the 12th may involve acts of loving kindness to those who feel unloved. I know a massage therapist with Venus in the 12th that gave massages to AIDS victims. She literally provided a loving touch. Again, planets in the 12th house need to be sacrificed on a personal level and utilized for the greater good of the whole. This does not mean that the individual cannot expect to have personal needs satisfied that are associated with that planet. The challenge is to utilize the planetary function for the greater good of the whole without necessarily denying one's own needs that the planet represents.

If a 12th house planet is not consecrated to a spiritual or humanistic ideal, then that planet may be "lost" to the individual, i.e., not available to consciousness. The person may deny or repress that function due to guilt, fear, or shame. This is related to the 12th house notion of secret enemies. Subjectively, signs and planets in the 12th may operate subversively or unconsciously and sabotage the individual's conscious intentions. They could constitute weaknesses, operate in a feeble, dysfunctional manner, or simply be missing in action. Saturn in the 12th, for example, could mean the individual is unable to pursue success without in some way sabotaging herself.

Objectively, these same planets could manifest in the personage of someone who deceives, abandons, or sabotages the individual. For example, Saturn may symbolize a dysfunctional, alcoholic father for whom the child unconsciously feels responsible. To be more happy and successful than the father may evoke unconscious guilt; thus the child sabotages himself out of identification with or loyalty to the paternal model. Any planet or sign in the 12th may be a source of self-undoing (self-sabotage) due to unconscious guilt bound up with that function or need. If sufficiently self-destructive, the individual may end up in a hospital, a prison, or some other 12th house institution of confinement. A classic 12th house act of self-undoing is drug or alcohol abuse.

Yet another way the process manifests is to try and recover the lost function by locating its dysfunctional expression in someone else— preferably a victim of some sort. Loss of boundaries and a tendency to become enmeshed with a victim is a common 12th house theme. Planets in the 12th may signify those people whom the individual feels compelled to save, rescue, or redeem because of an unconscious identification with the victim. Accordingly, victim-savior relationships, co-dependency, and compassion fatigue fall into this category. The individual can play out either role, being the savior on one occasion and the victim on another. Very often these roles become so interchangeable that it is difficult to distinguish between the two, e.g., the savior is betrayed by the victim and becomes a victim oneself.

Of course, if the planet becomes well integrated, then the native may rescue others by virtue of setting a good example. The native may be a charitable, truly spiritual individual who experiences compassion for all living things. Again, planets in the 12th must be utilized in a compassionate, relatively selfless manner without becoming self-sacrificial. For example, if the Moon is in the 12th, the person may care for the homeless or the aged but is not compelled to deny his or her own self-care out of irrational guilt.

Because the 12th house is associated with the deepest strata of the unconscious, it is also the house of dreams, imagination, and fantasy. Accordingly, another way that individuals can utilize 12th house energies is through some form of transcendent creativity. Poetry, music, dance, painting, photography, filmmaking, and storytelling—anything that involves image and symbol—are various ways that 12th house planets can be positively utilized. Again, the *approach* to this realm of imagination, as well as the particular *kind* of creative products that result, is symbolized by the nature of the planet. Working with the unconscious directly through dream analysis, hypnosis, intuition training, or research into psi phenomena is yet another way of expressing 12th house energies.

Developmentally, this house corresponds to the age 80 and beyond when we all become victims of old age, retire more-or-less completely from public life, suffer mental or physical decline, and are most likely to be institutionalized recipients of compassion.

Chapter Seven

Interpretive Rules for Planets in Signs

STYLES OF ACTION AND TYPES OF OUTCOME

I n this chapter, we are going to take a look at what I call astrological grammar. If the reader shudders at such a prospect, let me say
only that astrology is itself a language, albeit one that uses symbols
rather than letters. In translating these symbols into words, however,
an implicit grammar is revealed. While it may initially seem awkward
to think of astrology in this way, knowing a few simple rules will
increase one's ability to speak the language immeasurably. It will also
assure correctness of interpretations, deepen understanding, and keep
the practitioner from getting lost in the maze of information that the
chart reflects.

When I speak of *grammar*, I am referring to that branch of learning that investigates the formal features of a language and the rules
that govern its usage. *Syntax* has to do with construction of sentences,
and is the central concern of grammar. It consists of linguistic rules
for determining the proper arrangement of words. For example, in an
astrological sentence we have at least four parts: the native (subject),
the planet (verb), sign (adverb), and house (object). With Venus in
Cancer in the 6th house, I could say, "She relates sensitively at work."
She is the subject, *relates* is the Venus verb, *sensitively* is the Cancerian
adverb, and *work* is the 6th house object of the action. From this simple
statement, we can extrapolate a range of additional meanings, e.g.,
that she utilizes her social talents at work by being kind, caring, and
protective, making sure that policies are fair, that people get along,

and that the work environment reflects a pleasant, home-like atmosphere in which to conduct business.

While this interpretation is astrologically correct, the complexity of the sentence may be intimidating. Frankly, I would not want to break it down into grammatical parts! Yet, this more elaborate statement is merely an extension of the simpler, rule-bound sentence that preceded it: "She relates sensitively at work." This underscores my point that once the core idea of an astrological configuration is properly delineated, one can extend indefinitely its various entailments without sacrificing correctness of interpretation.

In deconstructing the language of astrology it becomes apparent that signs and planets are more Protean than Procrustean. In other words, they change form to interact with one another in myriad combinations and meanings. The syntax of astrology is such that signs and planets are polymorphous, capable of expressing the same idea in various ways, each expression having its own emphasis and tone. This changeability takes various shapes through what are called *parts of speech*. Every astrological term is inherently at least one part of speech and can often act the part of two or three parts of speech by its usage in different instances.

For example, Mars can be utilized as verb or a noun. Recall that a **verb** is any word that expresses an action, while a **noun** is the name of a subject of discourse, e.g., a person, place, thing, idea, or quality. If I say, "He asserts passively," then Mars is the verb, *assert*. However, by converting the verb into a noun that defines a psychological function (i.e., a thing), I can say, "For him, assertion is difficult." Now Mars becomes a noun, *assertion*, which I can describe in terms of its sign position. Signs can function as nouns too, e.g., Aries is the need for *freedom*. But signs can also function as **adverbs** that qualify verbs. Adverbs describe the quality of the action. If Mercury is in Aries, then Aries describes the quality of Mercury's action, e.g., "I communicate *directly*."

There are essentially five ways that a planet in a sign can be delineated. While the rest of this Chapter will detail these five ways, I will list them here to give the reader a quick glimpse of the terrain we are about to cover. Of the five ways, three describe the why and how of action (process) and two describe the empirical consequences of action (content).

COMBINING PLANETS AND SIGNS

1. Planets as Functions, Signs as Complements

A planet is an organ of consciousness, and as such symbolizes a class of related psychological functions. The sign position of the planet can serve as an adjective or noun that describes the way these functions operate.

2. Planets as Archetypal Characters, Signs as Adjectives

A planet is an autonomous, intentional psychic entity—an archetype—that represents a specific mode of being. The sign position of the planet qualifies the nature of this archetypal being.

3. Planets as Verbs, Signs as Adverbs and Adverbial Clauses

A planet describes a particular kind of action. The planetary sign position qualifies the nature of this action, i.e., it answers the questions "how," "why," and "in what manner."

4. Planets as States, Signs as Domains

A planet symbolizes a range of related states, which include specific moods, affects, and attitudes. The sign position of the planet signifies the domain, i.e., that specific field of human activity, within which the individual experiences these states.

5. Planets as Verbs, Signs as Complements

A planet signifies an action, whereas its sign position describes the object of this action, i.e., the sign carries out the intention of the verb and completes its meaning by answering the question "what?"

PLANETS AS NOUNS

In the above list, the first three ways that planets function in signs are **processes**. These constitute the whys and how's of behavior, and as such describe underlying psychodynamics. In the immediate sections to follow, we will explore how planetary processes operate as nouns that are modified by sign positions.

PLANETS AS PSYCHOLOGICAL FACULTIES

A planet's primary expression as a noun is the specific psychological faculty it represents. Recall from Chapter Four that a **faculty** is the inherent power or ability to perform a **function**. In this regard, planetary names, like Mars, Mercury, or Venus are analogous to the names we give our physical organs like kidney, liver, or heart. The liver, for example, is a faculty that has a number of related functions: generation of digestive enzymes, control of metabolism, immune system regulation, storage of glycogen, and production of antitoxic substances. Just so, a planet is a faculty that has various functions. A planet's functions can be determined by nominalizing any of its verb forms, i.e., converting a planetary process into a noun. If the Sun signifies the verb, "to express," then one of its functions would be "self-expression." Related functions include intentionality, creativity, and play. Lunar functions include listening, containing, and caring.

Although some attempt has been made to correlate planets to psychological faculties as they are described in various personality theories, it is my contention that no equivalent term exists in any of these theories that captures the full spectrum of functions that a given planet symbolizes. We could, for example, say that the Sun symbolizes the ego, or Mars the id, or Pluto the shadow, but each planet has additional properties that go beyond the delimited meanings these psychological terms convey, e.g., Mars is like the *id* in Freudian psychology, but also signifies our survival instinct, competitive drive, capacity for assertion and independence, and ability to initiate new projects—e.g., to found an organization, start a business, or embark on an adventure. As a faculty, Mars is more complex than what Freud meant by *id*.

Most terms that refer to psychological faculties have no clear astrological correlates. From an astrological perspective, constructs like intellect, ego, id, superego, shadow, complex, and mind refer to emergent properties that result from the combining of two or more planets. As such, they are hybrid entities, e.g., Freud's concept of the superego has attributes that partake of both Saturn and Jupiter. The ego has properties that blend the Sun, Mercury, and Mars (at least). The id has qualities that are similar to Mars and Pluto. Jung's concept of the shadow is similar to what we mean by Pluto and Saturn. Some terms, like "intellect," are so general they would seem to be diffused through the whole chart, e.g., all the air signs, along with Mercury, Jupiter, Sun, and Uranus represent different facets of what we mean by "intellect."

NOMINALIZING PLANETS: FACULTY TO FUNCTION

As stated, planets signify abilities, or capacities, to perform specific functions. A planetary faculty, therefore, is best described by listing its various functions. It bears repeating that a function is the normal, proper, or characteristic *action* of any thing. Again, the quickest way of determining a planet's functions is to take any verb form of the planet and convert it into a noun, e.g., if Mars is "to assert," then the function becomes "assertion". This is called *nominalizing* the verb/planet.

As an organ of consciousness, each planet is geared toward satisfaction of a specific psychological need. As such, planets signify processes that express themselves in particular types of action; i.e., a process is an action expressed for the sake of fulfilling a need. Saturn, for example, *controls* in order to meet the need for structure and order (Capricorn). To *control* is a verb. However, if we nominalize this verb, we come up with the function of "control." As a psychological function, the planet becomes a noun that answers two questions: (1) *what* is being done? and (2) *what* is doing the doing? In the case of Saturn, the answers are (1) *controlling,* and (2) the function of *control.* Additional Saturn functions would include achievement, organization, discipline, planning, mastery, conservation, structure, and order, all of which are nominalizations of Saturnian verbs.

If each planet signifies a psychological faculty, it is the function of that faculty to perform an action designed to bring about a result. As a psychological process, each planet signifies a class of verbs. Jupiter, for example, signifies the verbs *to judge, to theorize, to interpret,* and so on. In each instance, the verb can be nominalized—converted into a noun that signifies the psychological function. "To judge" becomes *judgment,* "to theorize" becomes *theory*, and "to interpret" becomes *interpretation*. We can then say, for example, that Jupiter signifies the functions of judgment, interpretation, and theorizing.

Sometimes it's possible to move to a yet higher level of abstraction and use a term that signifies the functions themselves. For example, if Jupiterian functions include moral judgment, interpretation, and hypothesis formation, we could simply call Jupiter the Higher Mind. Venus processes include beautifying and harmonizing; thus we could call Venus our Aesthetic Function. In general, however, the name must refer back to one or more functions—nouns—that characterize the planet. When identifying a planetary function, it is best to choose words that capture the most general features of the planet. For example, the most general functions of Neptune would probably be transcendence, imagination, empathy, and idealism. In Figure 12 below, I list one general process and function for each planet.

FACULTY	PROCESS	FUNCTION
Sun	To intend	Intentionality
Moon	To nurture	Nurturance
Mercury	To learn	Learning
Venus	To attract	Attraction
Mars	To assert	Assertion
Jupiter	To interpret	Interpretation
Saturn	To organize	Organization
Uranus	To awaken	Awakening
Neptune	To imagine	Imagination
Pluto	To transform	Transformation

Figure 12: Process and Function

PLANETS AS SUBJECTS, SIGNS AS SUBJECT COMPLEMENTS

Once a planetary function is identified, it then becomes possible to make statements about that function, e.g., how it operates and its capacity to meet the need it governs. For example, we can say something about the person's *capacity* for assertion, or learning, or nurturing. In other words, a planet's position in the horoscope—its sign, house, and aspects—provides information about its *degree of functionality*; i.e., its capacity for doing the job it is designed to do. Some sign positions, for example, are going to enhance the planet's functionality, while others will compromise it. Once the planet is nominalized—converted into a function—we can begin to assess its functionality by analyzing its sign position. Here are a few simple examples:

Mars in Aries:

My *instinct for survival* (♂) is strong (♈).

Venus in Capricorn:

When it comes to *marriage* (♀), I can be rather cold and calculating (♑).

Mercury in Pisces:

Cognition (☿) is a weak (♓) function in my chart.

In effect, the function becomes the **subject** of the sentence, and the sign position becomes the subject complement. A subject complement is a noun or adjective that renames or describes the subject. If we are talking about Saturn in Aries, we could make a statement about control as the subject, e.g., "Control is like wielding a weapon." For Mars in Taurus, we might say, "Aggression can be profitable." For Mercury in Capricorn, "Knowledge confers status." In each case, the subject is completed by a **noun** that describes the planetary function by comparing it to a thing or quality—*weapon, profitable, status*. Of course, when we are making statements about individuals, there is an implied "you" as the real subject. In describing Saturn, for example, we could say, "For you, control is like wielding a weapon." Any statement about a planet in a chart is implicitly a statement about the individual whose chart is being interpreted.

Again, when a planet's sign position is utilized as a subject complement it can be either a noun or an adjective. If the sign is converted into an **adjective**, it renames or describes the noun—the planetary function—by telling us *what kind* of function it is. Once a planet is nominalized, you merely need to ask the question "what kind?" and begin inserting adjectives that correlate to the meaning of that sign position. If we are talking about a *thinking* function (☿), an adjective should tell us what kind of thinking is occurring—e.g., *deep* (♏), *broad* (♒), *focused* (♑), *analytical* (♍), *creative* (♌), and so on. Similarly, if we convert the verb form of Saturn "to achieve" into the function of *achievement*, the sign position of Saturn should tell us what kind of achievement. Saturn in Gemini might be "His achievement was of an *intellectual* variety. In Aries, "He was known for his *pioneering* achievements in the field of physics." In Libra, "His *artistic* achievements were noteworthy," and so on.

When a sign functions as a **noun** that complements the subject, then it generally operates as an abstraction—i.e., a quality, attribute, mental state, emotion, or behavior that renames or describes the function. For example, if Saturn were in Scorpio, one could say: "Control is a necessary evil." Here the Scorpio word *evil* is a noun/quality that complements the Saturn function of *control*. With the Sun in Pisces, one could say: "Your identity seems diffuse and confused." Here, the Piscean nouns *diffuse* and *confused* complement the solar function of *identity*. Whether used as an adjective or a noun, a planet's sign position qualifies the *way* that function functions (or *dys*functions). Here are more examples.

Mars in Capricorn:

My *instinct for survival* (♂) is honed to perfection (♑). In the military, I always received low marks for *aggression* (♂) because I was too cautious (♑). (What kind of instinct for survival? The kind that is *honed to perfection*. What kind of aggression? the kind that is *cautious*).

Venus in Scorpio:

When it comes to *self-soothing* (♀), I cannot do it, as I get overwhelmed by anxiety (♏). I guess I have little *self or object constancy* (♀). (what kind of self-soothing? The kind one *cannot do*. What kind of self or object constancy? The kind that is *little*).

Mercury in Pisces:

Cognition (☿) is a weak function in my chart, as I become confused (♓) by all the possible meanings of a word. My *thinking* (☿) is a little fuzzy (♓) at times.

Venus in Gemini:

Socializing, for her, was *merely an opportunity to gossip*. (answers *what kind* of socializing?)

Jupiter in Aquarius:

His *morality* was of a *liberal* sort. (*liberal* qualifies the function/ noun *morality*, thus answering the question *what kind* of morality?)

Uranus in Sagittarius:

The *change* his generation sought to bring about was *religious;* they were a group of religious reformers. (*religious* qualifies the function *change,* which answers the question *what kind of change?*)

Jupiter in Virgo:

When it comes to exercising *judgment*, I can be quite *critical.* My *theory* is quite *complex* and *explicit*, capable of accounting for the minutest details. A good *interpretation* should be *precise, economical*, and *reductionistic*. (Note how the adjectives *complex, explicit, precise, economical,* and *reductionistic* modify the function-nouns *judgment, theory,* and *interpretation*).

Sun in Virgo:

My *creativity* is of a practical sort; I entertain my co-workers in order to relieve job related stress. (*practical sort* modifies *creativity*).

Moon in Gemini:

Listening does not come natural to me, for it so stimulates my mind that all I want to do is talk! (what kind of listening? the kind that *does not come easy* and that stimulates talk.)

Neptune in Scorpio:

My *imagination* is intense, full of paranoid fantasies. *Dreams* are occasions for acting out forbidden sexual scenarios. (what kind of imagination? what kind of dreams?).

ARCHETYPAL RELATIONSHIPS BETWEEN PLANETS AND SIGNS

When interpreting planetary sign positions, it is important to discern the archetypal relationship between the sign the planet occupies and the sign the planet naturally rules. For example, if Mars rules Aries, but is *in* Pisces, then the archetypal relationship is semi-sextile. For any planetary sign position, always ask *what might be the challenge or difficulty of that placement? Or, what might be the ease or advantage of that placement?*

Generally speaking, the quality of the planet-sign relationship is consistent with the meaning of the angle that naturally exists between the signs involved—semi-sextile, sextile, square, trine, quincunx, or opposition. For example, Mars in Sagittarius (natural trine relationship) has the advantage of asserting (Mars) in ways and for reasons that are moral (Sagittarius), but Mars in Capricorn (natural square relationship) faces the difficulty of striving for freedom (Aries) in ways that don't violate the rules and limits of the prevailing order. How can you be spontaneous *and* obedient at the same time? It's a contradiction, thus a conflict. For Mars in Capricorn, assertion is problematic because feisty Mars becomes a bit conservative, reticent, and inhibited. The Warrior is forced into an authority role. It is still a warrior, but it has to combine it with caution and long term planning. What would Hercules be like as a boss?*

Difficult placements involve planets that are in signs to which their ruled sign is naturally square or quincunx. This often involves a clash between yin and yang energies, so there is tension, stress, and inhibition. For example, if the Sun is in Taurus (square relationship), the Sun's expressiveness is restrained because Taurus is naturally inhibited and hesitant. If Saturn is in Libra (square relationship), Saturn has difficulty taking control because Libra is oriented toward fairness and equality. Jupiter in Cancer (quincunx) presents a problem in that Cancer is too subjective, emotional, and narrow in its focus to accommodate the expansive, theory-building, philosophical nature of Jupiter.

A moderate placement would be the opposition because while the principles of planet and sign are potentially conflictual, they are also complementary, e.g., Jupiter in Gemini can theorize about learning and language, explore a variety of different religious models, and expand its understanding of cognition itself. Planetary placements in signs to which they are naturally sextile or trine tend to work more easily, and there is a relative absence of stress and conflict in the way the planet expresses itself.

The archetypal relationship between the sign(s) a planet rules and the sign the planet occupies may give important early clues about key themes in the native's life. While I do not make value judgments as to whether a sign position is good or bad, this technique does clarify the

---

* This way of evaluating planets in signs often contradicts archaic concepts of exaltation, fall, and detriment. In traditional astrology, Mars is regarded as a malefic planet because of its aggressive, warlike nature. Because Mars' placement in Capricorn inhibits its natural spontaneity, this was considered 'good' and so Mars was thought to be exalted in Capricorn. But such logic only applies if one accepts the flawed premise that Mars is an 'evil' or 'malefic' planet.

ease or difficulty of functioning for that planet as well as the nature of the challenge or gifts that might apply.

This way of evaluating planetary sign positions is more efficacious than resorting to traditional judgments like exaltation, fall, or detriment. Any planet that is in a sign opposite to the one it rules is said to be in **detriment**, meaning that sign is allegedly detrimental to the planet's optimal functioning. Conversely, if the planet is in its **exaltation**, then it is in the sign from which it presumably gains maximum power, i.e., its functioning is optimized. However, if it's in the sign opposite its exaltation, then it is in its **fall**, which the ancients likened to a person in exile: the planet is weakened and distorted. Concepts like detriment, fall, and exaltation, however, are arbitrary value judgments that some individual or group of individuals once deemed valid. Just because a concept is old does not make it right. As the philosopher Manly Hall once said, "What we generally call knowledge is merely an opinion, on a level of illusion." That being said, I will venture an opinion here: medieval concepts like detriment, fall, and exaltation are anachronisms ill-suited for a psychological, growth oriented astrology. I don't even agree with most of their judgments.

To illustrate my argument, let us examine one planet in its alleged exaltation—Jupiter in Cancer. In a classic text from the 20th century that repeats the traditional dogma, Sakoian and Acker (1973) attest that Jupiter gains power in Cancer because it expands the nourishing, family oriented love that Cancer symbolizes. One could argue, however, that any sign could benefit from Jupiter's benevolence (in fact, one can put a positive spin on *any* planet-sign combination). Yet, the sign that Jupiter rules—Sagittarius—is actually quincunx Cancer in the natural zodiac. This suggests a dilemma for Jupiter in Cancer. Jupiter is expansive, Cancer is inhibited; Jupiter is philosophical, Cancer is emotional and provincial; Jupiter loves travel, Cancer wants to stay at home. In short, Jupiter in Cancer is problematic. Shy, introverted, provincial Cancer stifles the natural exuberance, expansiveness, and philosophical nature of Jupiter. This is equivalent to a politician having to make some tough, moral decisions about upcoming legislation that would benefit the larger community; yet, the proposed legislation might create an inconvenience for his own family—so he gets all emotional and argues shrilly against the bill. While this is a hypothetical example to be sure, it serves to illustrate the inherent dilemma of Jupiter in Cancer.

To assess the ease or difficulty of a planetary sign position, one has to do some creative thinking; that is, figure it out for oneself and then test one's formulation in the laboratory of personal experience. Observe individuals that have Jupiter in Cancer; note closely what happens when Jupiter is transiting this sign. It is too easy to merely fall back on archaic formulations and not question the actual merit of the opinion.

PLANETS AS ARCHETYPAL CHARACTERS, SIGNS AS ADJECTIVES

Another way planets perform a noun function is when they are presented as **archetypal characters**. Each planet is a meta-archetype symbolizing a class of archetypes. Pluto, for example, symbolizes the archetypes *shadow, monster, villain, stranger, witch, healer, tyrant, rapist, vampire, and devil,* all of which are related. The archetype, as Jung stated, is the self-portrait of the instinct; it is a metaphor designating a psychological function. That there can be more than one archetype for a given planet indicates that a faculty can manifest in a variety of different but related forms, depending upon its level of integration.

It is useful to think of planets as archetypal characters, for they do not merely signify psychological processes but also environmental events—people with whom we interact. Remember that every variable in astrology has both a subjective and objective dimension; it manifests within and without, and the "without" is always a metaphor for how that variable is operating internally. An unintegrated Pluto may initially take the form of a *criminal* with whom the native develops a relationship. As Pluto does its transformational work upon the psyche, however, it may later manifest as a *mysterious stranger* and ultimately as a *powerful healer*.

A planet's sign position qualifies the form that the archetype might take; in other words, it types the type. Pluto might be a healer, but what kind of healer? The sign functions as an adjective modifying a noun—the planetary archetype. Convert a planet into an archetype and then ask, "What kind?" Saturn—what kind of *wise old man?* Uranus—what kind of *revolutionary?* Jupiter—what kind of *teacher?*

Saturn in Aries:

As an *old man*, he was not only wise but *bold* as well. Ever the *fierce warrior*, he was an *authority figure* for the young soldiers. (*Bold* answers the question, what kind of wise old man? *Fierce warrior* answers what kind of authority figure?)

Uranus in Cancer:

This *revolutionary* was a reactionary, for he opposed change and sought to reinstate traditional family values that were a throwback to the 19th century. As a *utopian visionary* he awakened us to the plight of children in this country, advocating the need for collective care.

Jupiter in Leo:

She was a dramatic *teacher* who entertained while she educated. Marshall Applewhite was a charismatic *prophet* of false hope. Don King is a confident if not boastful *promoter*.

PLANETS AS VERBS

A **verb** is a type of action, and as such it carries the momentum in a sentence. Verbs assert, move, impel, and report on a condition or situation. They give sentences vitality. In astrology, planets are the true verbs of our language. While a sign can motivate and qualify the expression of planets, it can never *do* anything of itself. Planets, on the other hand, are always active even though they can be described as psychological functions, e.g., *assertion, thinking, or nurturance*. In effect, planets are *doings*; each planet does something different: Mars *asserts*, Venus *attracts*, Mercury *reports*, the Moon *nurtures*, the Sun *performs*, Jupiter *expands*, Saturn *controls*, Uranus *awakens*, Neptune *transcends*, and Pluto *transforms*.

As a verb, a planet can connote a physical or psychological form of action. A physical form of action denotes some kind of physical activity. Pluto, for example, might destroy a federal building in an act of terror. Jupiter might stand on a soap box and deliver a rousing speech. A psychological form of action, however, is more abstract, subjective, and internal. While less visible, it tends to precede physical forms of action. The Sun, for example, symbolizes the verb *to intend,* which underlies any actual choice an individual may be observed to make.

PLANET/SIGN	PSYCHOLOGICAL	PHYSICAL
Mars ♈	Vitalize	Fight
Venus ♉	Soothe	Caress
Mercury ♊	Think	Write
Moon ♋	Care	Feed
Sun ♌	Intend	Express
Mercury ♍	Analyze	Fix
Venus ♎	Consider	Compromise
Pluto ♏	Distrust	Murder
Jupiter ♐	Believe	Teach
Saturn ♑	Plan	Manage
Uranus ♒	Perceive	Protest
Neptune ♓	Empathize	Rescue

Figure 13: Inner and Outer Actions

Saturn is *to plan*, which necessarily precedes implementation of the plan. Some examples of physical and psychological verbs are listed in .

Keep in mind that a planet cannot be understood in terms of any one verb; rather, planets are meta-verbs signifying a whole class of actions that are in various ways related. Saturn, for example, signifies the verbs *produce, achieve, plan, execute, structure, order, control, perfect, conserve, suppress, delay, obstruct, restrict,* and *overcompensate.* One can readily see how each of these verbs is a variation on a theme. Depending upon a planet's sign, house, and aspects, one or another of its verbs may be more suitable to convey a meaning most pertinent to what is actually observed.

PLANETS AS VERBS, SIGNS AS NOUNS/NEEDS

It is important to recognize that a planetary verb conveys an intention. This intention is to satisfy the need that motivates its particular kind of action, e.g., Uranus *enlightens* in order to satisfy the Aquarian need for *awakening;* Jupiter *theorizes* in order to satisfy the Sagittarian need for *truth;* Mars *asserts* in order to satisfy the Aries need for *survival.* Because each planet is oriented toward satisfying the need of the sign it rules, it is motivated by that sign. In this regard, the sign that a

PLANET/SIGN	PSYCHOLOGICAL MOTIVE
Mars ♈	Survival, Being, Autonomy
Venus ♉	Stability, Security, Pleasure
Mercury ♊	Knowledge, communication
Moon ♋	Nurturance, caring, belonging
Sun ♌	Validation, approval, self-esteem
Mercury ♍	Efficiency, competence, service
Venus ♎	Intimacy, relatedness, beauty
Pluto ♏	Integration, transformation
Jupiter ♐	Meaning, truth, expansion
Saturn ♑	Structure, perfection, order
Uranus ♒	Perspective, insight, change
Neptune ♓	Transcendence, unity, bliss

Figure 14: Core Motivations

planet rules performs a noun function—it is a thing, a motive. Figure 14 lists some words that convey the core, underlying motivations of each planet:

Planets are not only motivated by psychological needs, but by goal states that constitute a subjective sense of need satisfaction. For example, Mars signifies a number of different actions, all of which lead to a state of aliveness—the target state of Mars. To the degree that a planet's target state is not attained, the individual will suffer the negative version of that state. For example, to the degree that one does not feel a joyful aliveness, one may feel dead, depleted, or discouraged, which are negative states of Mars. To the extent that one does not feel hopeful, one is apt to feel hopeless, which is the negative state of Jupiter. In Figure 15, I list words that correspond to positive and negative states for each planet.

By defining planets as actions that are motivated by basic needs and target states, we can construct simple astrological sentences. The form of the sentence is to state the underlying need, the action taken to satisfy the need, and the target state the action is designed to attain. While there is an obvious similarity between a need and a target state,

PLANET/SIGN	POSITIVE	NEGATIVE
Mars ♈	Aliveness	Deadness
Venus ♉	Safety	Insecurity
Mercury ♊	Knowledgeable	Ignorance
Moon ♋	Belonging	Rejection
Sun ♌	Pride	Shame
Mercury ♍	Useful	Incompetent
Venus ♎	Intimate	Disharmony
Pluto ♏	Powerful	Paranoid
Jupiter ♐	Hopeful	Hopeless
Saturn ♑	Successful	Failure
Uranus ♒	Altruistic	Indifferent
Neptune ♓	Inspired	Confused

Figure 15: States

and sometimes the same word applies to both, there is a subtle but important difference between the two. A motivating need is experienced as an impulse, a drive *to do* something that fulfills the need. A state is generally an affect that reflects the degree to which a need is fulfilled. For example, if one satisfies the Capricorn need for structure, one feels organized. However, if one does not fulfill this need, a sense of failure, despair, and stress may result. The negative state triggers the impulse to perform a corrective action so that the need can be fulfilled and the desired state attained. Here are a few examples that describe how a planet's motivational need, behavioral process, and target state are all related.

Sun:
To develop self-esteem, I *express* myself with the intention of winning approval and gaining pride.

Moon:
Because I want to belong, I *care* about others and try to be sensitive to their needs so that we can be close.

Mercury:
Stimulated by an insatiable curiosity, I *study* people with the intent of learning about the psyche.

Venus:

Since security is my primary goal, I *accumulate* as much as I can, and waste as little as possible, in order to feel safe.

Mars:

My goal is to survive, but I feel most alive when *fighting* for my rights.

Jupiter:

Because I cherish wisdom, I *teach* comparative religion. Believing in a benevolent higher power fills me with hope.

Saturn:

I am driven by a desire for perfection, so I *persevere* until I *achieve* my ultimate goal—*success.*

Uranus:

Motivated by a need for perspective, I *detach* from my egocentric views, see the folly of self-importance, and thus feel more altruistic and humane.

Neptune:

Inspired by a love of God and an image of transcendent wholeness, I *surrender* to His will in hopes of achieving eternal bliss.

Pluto:

Racked with pain and desperate for healing, I *coerced* the doctor to give me medicine. Soon I felt whole again.

PLANETS AS VERBS, SIGNS AS ADVERBS

We have seen how verbs are parts of speech that convey action. Adverbs, on the other hand, comprise a class of words that modify verbs. For example, the sentence "I run fast" is comprised of a verb, "run," and the adverb "fast." Note than an adverb answers the question, "how?" For example, *how do you run?* If we define a planet as a verb and a sign as an adverb, then the simplest form of a complete astrological sentence is a planetary action modified by its sign position. Remember, an adverb modifies—changes, enhances limits, inhibits, intensifies, or muffles—the expression of the verb.

Just so in astrology, a sign qualifies the expression of the planet that resides in that sign. The sign always answers the question: "*How* do you [verb]?" An analogous situation would be an actor playing a role. Imagine Clint Eastwood in a film. No matter what movie he is in, Clint Eastwood is always himself—yet, he could be a cowboy, a detective, or a soldier. Or consider the illustrious British actor, Anthony Hopkins. In *Remains of The Day,* he played a butler—a Virgo role. In *Nixon,* he played the former president—a Capricorn part. In *Silence of the Lambs,* he played a psychopathic psychiatrist (the irrepressible Hannibal Lecter), clearly a Scorpio role. So we have Anthony Hopkins in Virgo, Capricorn, or Scorpio. He is always Anthony Hopkins, but his behavior is altered by the nature of the role (sign) he is in. Likewise in astrology, a planet retains its character no matter what sign it is in; yet, the sign operates like a role that qualifies the planet's expression. Here are some examples of signs as adverbs.

Mars in Taurus:
I assert *steadfastly*, wearing down my opponent with sheer persistence.

Mars in Gemini:
I assert *intellectually*, wielding words like swords.

Mars in Cancer:
I assert *softly*, being careful not to offend.

Mars in Leo:
I assert *playfully*, winning others over with my charm.

Of course, for sentences to make sense, one must combine verbs and adverbs in ways that are intelligible. If Mars is in Pisces, there is no point in saying "I assert *imaginatively*" even though the words "assert" and "imaginatively" are correct for Mars and Pisces individually. When you put them together, however, they are merely confusing. What does it look like to assert imaginatively? Conversely, if one says "I assert passively," the speaker's intent is considerably less obscure. For "passive assertion" is a common phrase and still consistent with the meaning of Mars and Pisces. It is not difficult to envision someone who asserts in a vague, unclear, rather feeble manner.

One can also take a planetary verb and follow it with the adverb *by being,* which in turn is followed by one or more adverbs that correlate to the planet's sign. In this sense, the sign is an adverbial clause—a group or words—that modifies the planetary verb.

Mars in Virgo:
I assert by being *critical* and *analytical*, seeking the most efficient way of obtaining my objective. (*critical* and *analytical* are adverbs).

Mars in Sagittarius:
I assert by being *persuasive* and *life-affirming*, convincing others to do my bidding through the sheer force of my enthusiasm.

Venus in Cancer:
I negotiate by being *caring* and *concerned*, making sure both sides feel that their interests are protected.

PLANETS AS VERBS, SIGNS AS ADVERBIAL CLAUSES

Whereas a simple adverb is one word that describes a verb, an adverbial clause is a group of words that describes a verb. Signs function as adverbial clauses when more than one word—a clause—is utilized to qualify a planetary function. An adverbial clause can describe "how," "why," or "in what manner" a function is operating. With Mars in Taurus, it would be proper to say, "I assert myself by holding my ground," or "I assert myself in order that I can retain my property," or "I assert myself in a slow, deliberate manner." The first clause tells "how," the second explains "why," and the third describes "in what manner."

Sun in Capricorn:
He expressed himself *as if he were already president of the company.* [Describes how]

Mercury in Libra:
She speaks *in a cordial, refined way*, much like the British upper classes. [Describes way, or manner]

Moon in Pisces
She listens *out of compassion for their suffering.* [Describes why]

Jupiter in Aries:
He preached *because it allowed him to mask his anger with righteousness*. [Describes why]

Moon in Virgo

She nurtured her children *with a method that was precise, efficient, and cold,* as if she were raising little robots. [Describes method, or manner]

Mars in Pisces

He fought *in order to save the children,* even if it cost him his life. [Describes why]

CHART CONTENT

When we interpret planets in terms of motivations, functions, goals, and behavioral styles, we are talking about a dynamic *process* that relates to the intrapsychic world of the individual. This is astrology's subjective dimension, or *psychodynamics.* However, when we interpret planets in terms of events—results, outcomes—then we are talking about *content* that refers to the interpersonal world of the individual. This is astrology's objective dimension—empirically observable experience. Chart content manifests as environmental *events* that constitute the external manifestation of psychic energy. These are the actual concrete experiences through which the sign/need seeks satisfaction. Again, events include relations with people, places, and things. An event, however, is invariably linked to a psychological state that results from how the individual is organized internally. In Figure 16, I list different states that apply to each planet, as well as various events that might correspond to that state.

Note in Figure 16 that state and event are synchronous with one another; the individual feels the state when experiencing the matching event. This would be the equivalent of having a planet in its own sign, e.g. Sun in Leo. Try to imagine, however, a planet in a sign with which it naturally conflicts, such as Mars in Scorpio (a quincunxial relationship, since Aries is quincunx Scorpio). In this case, a person may feel excited and spontaneous in situations that require vigilance and circumspection. One would not want a surgeon, for example, becoming excited and spontaneous while performing an operation. This planetary sign position represents a challenge, for unless the natural exuberance of Mars is damped by Scorpio, the person is apt to feel and act in a manner inappropriate to the situation.

PLANET	STATE	EVENT
Sun	Pride	Performing in a contest
Moon	Belonging	Enjoying Christmas with one's family
Mercury	Curiosity	Listening to talk radio
Venus	Pleasure	Fine dining with one's beloved
Mars	Excitement	Cliff climbing and bungee jumping
Jupiter	Faith	Expanding one's business into new territory
Saturn	Doubt	Downsizing one's business
Uranus	Dissent	Engaging in social protest against war
Neptune	Grief	Discovering that one's mother has cancer
Pluto	Paranoia	Being stalked by a crazy former lover

Figure 16: States and Events

PLANETS AS STATES, SIGNS AS DOMAINS

Each planet can be associated with specific psychological states that form a continuum from positive to negative. When I refer to a state, or "state of mind," I am referring primarily to a mood or affect state, e.g., pessimism, optimism, anger, detachment, pleasure, joy, worry, and the like. States are closely linked to content because they are outcomes—manifestations—of intrapsychic processes; like events, they are more or less directly observable (unless an individual tries to hide what he is experiencing). A state of mind can manifest in a person's general attitude, voice tone, facial expression, as well as verbal and nonverbal communications. For example, when we refer to someone as being in a state of anger, we can visualize what this looks like—a hostile attitude, raised voice, fierce expression, accusatory tone, belligerent posture, and so on. Planetary states include:

Sun:
Pride (vs. shame), confidence (vs. self-doubt), playfulness, expressive, creative, arrogance, conceit, certainty (vs. uncertainty)

Moon:
Nurtured, close, connected, protective, belonging, tenderness, sympathy, dependency, rejected

Mercury (as ruler of Gemini):
Curiosity, interest, attentiveness, restlessness, nervousness, scatteredness, distraction.

Mercury (as ruler of Virgo):
Productive, useful, helpful, efficient, competent, critical, worried, troubled, negative, obsessive

Venus (as ruler of Taurus):
Safety, security, comfort, pleasure, indulgent, serenity, ease, laziness, stubborn, resistant

Venus (as ruler of Libra):
Kindly, cooperative, obliging, social, balanced, harmony, beautiful, attractive, serene, peaceful

Mars:
Joy, excitement, vitality, energy, omnipotence, impatience, irritability, anger, competitiveness, selfishness, aggression

Jupiter:
Hope, optimism, faith, enthusiasm, trust, great expectations, mania, righteous, virtuous, judgmental

Saturn:
Success, mission accomplished, patience, control, determined, pressured, driven, duty bound, obligated, stressed, inadequate, deficient, inferior, defective, pessimistic, gloom, despair

Uranus:
Altruistic love, sudden flash of insight, realization, perspective, detached overview, liberation, dissent, agitation, upset, startled, shock, unstable, schizoid detachment

Neptune:
Selfless love, unitive awareness, empathy, compassion for suffering, forgiveness, inspiration, irrational guilt, passivity, confusion, uncertainty, grief, victimization, helplessness, denial, delusion

Pluto:
Powerful, passionate, intense, centered, erotic, fearful, jealous, envious, paranoid, possessed, pain, shame, hostile, vengeful, destructive

A planet's psychological state tends to manifest in the domain of the sign it occupies. A domain is a sphere of activity, function, or concern. Another word is *field*, meaning an area of human activity and interest that functions as a background, e.g., the field of history (Cancer), aesthetics (Libra), or religion (Sagittarius). In this regard, a sign is a domain or field that signifies a specific area of human activity.

To determine how a planetary state might manifest in a specific zodiacal field, ask: how might this state be related to the affairs ruled by the sign the planet occupies? For example, if the Sun is in Virgo, and the Sun's target state is one of "pride," how might pride be related to Virgo? Perhaps the individual feels a sense of pride in a job well done? Mars in Libra might feel "angry and aggressive" in matters pertaining to fair play, the needs of others, contractual agreements, and equal rights. Jupiter in Cancer might feel "optimistic" that the larger system (God, the church, the legal system) will care for citizens, protect children, and preserve "family values." Saturn in Sagittarius might feel "pessimistic" about whether justice will be served. Each planet is going to achieve a "state of mind" within the domain of the sign it occupies.

Sun in Scorpio:
Charles Manson seemed *proud* of his ability to manipulate people to perform acts of murder.

Moon in Pisces:
Hillary Clinton feels *tender* toward the plight of families that are unable to provide health care for their children.

Mercury in Aries:
Adolph Hitler was *interested* in claims professing the supremacy of the Aryan race.

Venus in Capricorn:
Howard Stern has *affection* for guests on his radio talk show, for they are instrumental to his success.

Mars in Aquarius:
Lee Harvey Oswald was *angry* that his revolutionary communist agenda was being suppressed by the federal government.

Jupiter in Leo:

Having *faith* in the power of the pulpit to dramatize the plight of refugees in Bosnia, Pope John Paul is a champion of the oppressed.

Saturn in Gemini:

Determined to learn all that he could and convinced that knowledge was the key to success, Freud was conversant in eight languages.

Uranus in Cancer:

Oprah Winfrey was *shocked* to learn that the way beef is brought to market in this country constitutes a serious health hazard.

Neptune in Sagittarius:

During the 1970's when Neptune was in Sagittarius, people were *inspired* by the mystical religions of the east.

Pluto in Virgo:

The 60's was an era characterized by *crisis* in the workplace; discrimination and unfair labor practices created widespread *unrest* among minorities.

A planet may experience a variety of different yet related states within the same sign. For example, Jupiter states of hope, faith, enthusiasm, optimism, righteousness, and zealousness can all be experienced in relation to the sign of Libra, e.g., a person might *hope* that the incidence of divorce is reduced, have *faith* that God is fair, feel *enthusiasm* for art, express *optimism* that diplomacy is the key to world peace, become *righteous* when agreements are broken, and be possessed by *zealousness* when negotiating contracts.

Because a planet symbolizes an entire class of states that can attach themselves to any number of different outcomes, astrology has enormous flexibility as a language. This same flexibility, however, is also what makes it inherently ambiguous. In forming an interpretation of any planet-sign combination, keep in mind that the individual is likely to experience a wide range of possible meanings over the course of a lifetime. Nevertheless, this range of outcomes will display an intelligible pattern that is organized by the symbolism of the planet-sign blend. Martin Luther King, for example, had Saturn in Sagittarius. Note in the following description how many different states and outcomes flow from the Saturn-Sagittarius combination.

Martin Luther King was very *serious* about his religious and political studies. He was *determined* to master the great legal documents of American history—the Declaration of Independence, the Constitution, the Bill of Rights, and the Emancipation Proclamation. Perhaps this was due, in part, to his *doubt* that justice would prevail for blacks in the American system. He was *driven* to show that much of conventional morality and traditional law was oppressive to minorities. At times he was wracked with *despair* over the difficulty of achieving a truly moral outcome, and he was *pessimistic* that he would live to see the legal and political legislation that was necessary for the realization of racial equality. *Anxious* over his legal battles and feeling *inadequate* in his ability to convince fellow blacks to follow his moral imperative of peaceful resistance, he struggled against the *despair* that threatened to engulf his mission. Yet, at other times he was *patient* and willing to work hard for the *success* he craved—success on legal, moral, and religious grounds that would serve as a platform for the realization of a higher truth: that all men *are* created equal regardless of race, color, or creed.

PLANETS AS VERBS, SIGNS AS COMPLEMENTS

A planet's sign position not only tells us *how* the planet is doing its thing, it also tells us *what* the outcome might be. A sign, in other words, fulfills the part of speech known as the *complement*. A complement completes the meaning of the verb, carrying out its intention. Rather than being descriptive like adjectives and adverbs, complements answer the question *what?* The planet is a verb when it describes an action that the subject (the native) performs. The complement then functions as a direct object because it receives the action of the verb and answers the question "what?"

Mercury: I think.	I think *what?*
Mars: I assert.	I assert *what?*
Saturn: I achieve.	I achieve *what?*

A complement is a noun because nouns also answer the question "what?" You may recall from high school English that a noun is a word that names a person, place, thing, event, or abstraction. Abstractions include emotions, ideas, qualities, attributes, states of mind, functions, and other things you can grasp but can't quite put your finger on. Thus, a sign can function as a complement by symbolizing a person, place, thing, event, or abstraction.

> Mercury in Taurus: I study *millionaires* (person).
> Mars in Pisces: I fight in *bars* (place).
> Saturn in Virgo: I produce *vacuums* (thing).
> Venus in Scorpio: I arbitrate *crises* (event).
> Jupiter in Leo: I teach *self-esteem* (abstraction).

In order to speak the language of astrology fluently, it is necessary to memorize appropriate keywords. In the examples above, I used only one word to indicate the complement, but a fuller interpretation could utilize a variety of complements. For example, with Jupiter in Leo, I could say:

> He teaches acting to adolescents at the local theatre. In an effort
> to increase their confidence and self-esteem, he awards certificates
> of merit to all who complete the course.

In this example, Leonian complements are included in each category: person (adolescent), place (theatre), thing (certificate of merit), event (acting), and abstraction (self-esteem). Again, once the basic rule is understood, one can develop a theme to a fuller extent. In Figure 17, I list complements in all five categories for each sign.

In the previous section on states and domains, we explored how planets can manifest as psychological states—affects, attitudes and expectations—that are expressed within and toward circumstances ruled by the signs they occupy. In this section, we are exploring how a planet can manifest as empirical content, or "action outcomes," such as particular kinds of activities, interests, and concerns. Again, the particulars of this content will be colored by the sign the planet occupies. The sign, in other words, *complements* the verb (activity) that the planet symbolizes; i.e., it is the direct object of the verb.

When interpreting a planet in this way, think of the planet as a verb, and then ask *what* is that planet going to (verb)? For example, what is Venus going to beautify; what is the Sun going to create; what is the Moon going to nurture; what is Jupiter going to teach; what is Saturn going to perfect? If Mars fights, what does Mars fight/assert *for*? If Mars is in Capricorn, it might fight for authority; if in Aquarius it might fight for

Sign	Person	Place	Event	Thing	Abstraction
Aries	warrior	stadium	fight	weapon	anger
Taurus	farmer	storage bin	massage	wallet	comfort
Gemini	student	school	message	dictionary	curiosity
Cancer	caretaker	home	meal	souvenir	tenderness
Leo	playmate	party	play	game	happiness
Virgo	apprentice	workplace	problem	microscope	worry
Libra	partner	art exhibit	wedding	painting	fairness
Scorpio	healer	crisis unit	crisis	scalpel	power
Sagittarius	guru	university	lecture	pulpit	optimism
Capricorn	boss	mountain	promotion	girder	ambition
Aquarius	associate	meeting hall	rebellion	computer	revolution
Pisces	mystic	retreat	illness	drug	spirituality

Figure 17: Signs as Complements

a cause; if in Pisces, it might fight for the underdog. If Venus beautifies, what does Venus beautify, or attract? Venus in Cancer might beautify the home, or it might attract a sensitive mate. If Jupiter believes, what does Jupiter believe *in?* Jupiter in Taurus might believe in only that which is observable to the five senses; thus the person might embrace a philosophy of materialism. The person's highest good or ultimate value might be "proper utilization of the resources of the physical world." If Saturn organizes and perfects, what exactly might Saturn want to organize and perfect? Saturn in Virgo might want to organize and perfect a method or technique for achieving a particular goal. If it is in Aquarius, it might want to organize and perfect a humanitarian project of some sort.

As complements, signs function as nouns that signify people, places, things, events, or abstractions. In other words, a planet in a sign not only shows *how* the person is acting; it shows *what* the person is doing. A planet, of course, can also manifest as an objective condition or phenomenon, such as a parent, spouse, career, creative project, or the like. For example, Mars in Leo may symbolize a fellow competitor who competes in a noble manner—perhaps a good sport who fights for love and honor. Leo is the complement that describes Mars as a character in the native's life story.

In the following sentences, the reader is advised to consider how the

228 • INTRODUCTION TO ASTROPSYCHOLOGY

interpretation may be descriptive of both the native and the people with whom the native interacts. In other words, a planet may indicate not only what a person does, but what others are doing *with or to the person*. It may also symbolize how the native perceives his or her world, i.e., what does s/he project onto the world?

Mars in Taurus:

He *fights* to hold on to what he owns. (*to hold on* is *what* he fights for).

Mars in Leo:

She is *competing* for the lead in the school play. (*the lead* is *what* she is competing for).

Venus in Aries:

She *attracts* rough and ready types—soldiers, fighters, adventurers. (*rough and ready types* are *what* she attracts).

Mercury in Sagittarius:

He *talks* about theories, concepts, and ideas, though he is not always sure of his facts.

Sun in Libra:

Tatiana *identifies* with all that is beautiful, but especially the ballet.

Moon in Pisces:

Her mother *protected* stray animals, wayward children, the aged and infirm, and three alcoholic husbands.

Jupiter in Scorpio:

Dr. Kevorkian *moralizes* about the right to die. The infamous Nazi surgeon, Joseph Mengele, *taught* that pain was a necessary evil for the purification of the Aryan race.

Saturn in Aquarius:

Before Luke was born, his father *organized* the first rebel alliance.

Uranus in Leo:

It was Luke's generation, however, that successfully *rebelled* against the emperor.

Neptune in Libra:

Disney films often *idealize* marriage, giving the illusion that couples marry and live happily ever after.

Pluto in Virgo:

The Pluto in Virgo generation *purged* the food industry, giving us the natural foods alternative—fruits and vegetables uncontaminated by toxic pesticides.

A planet symbolizes a class of verbs that can attach themselves to any number of different complements. Again, this is what gives astrology its flexibility and ambiguity as a language. It bears repeating that when interpreting a planet-sign combination one must anticipate that it will manifest in a variety of ways over the course of a lifetime. Nevertheless, this range of variable outcomes will display an intelligible pattern that is consistent with the symbolism of the planet-sign mix. In the following example of Michel Gorbachev, who has his Moon in Leo, notice how different lunar verbs can be used with different Leo complements.

Michel Gorbachev, the great Russian leader, *listened* to many potentates who were inflated with their own self-importance. By *reflecting* a true understanding of their concerns, he was able to *sympathize* with their wounded egos and *contain* the rage that resulted from their narcissistic injury. Citizens felt that he truly *cared* about the self-esteem of all Russians. For example, he was able to *protect* many creative artists who were abandoned when the Communists fell from power. By appreciating everyone and rejecting no one, Gorbachev *nurtured* a national pride and self-respect that had been deflated by half a century of political neglect.

Do you see how the lunar verbs *listen, reflect, sympathize, contain, care, protect,* and *nurture* all have different complements; yet, the different outcomes reveal an intelligible pattern? In each instance, the complement reflects a Leonian theme—potentates inflated with self-importance, wounded egos, narcissistic injury, self-esteem, creative artists, national pride, and self-respect. I don't know Gorbachev personally, but I can speculate that the above is true merely by relating lunar processes to Leonine complements.

PUTTING IT ALL TOGETHER

In previous sections, I have deconstructed the language of astrology by relating signs and planets to *parts of speech*. We have seen how planets can function as nouns and verbs, and how signs can function as nouns, adverbs, adjectives, and complements. Ultimately, however, we will need to combine these linguistic parts into a flowing narrative. In the following interpretation of Mars in Aquarius, I weave together a narrative that contains the following linguistic parts.

1. Mars as a psychological function (noun) with Aquarius as a complement.
2. Mars as an archetypal character (noun) with Aquarius as an adjective.
3. Mars as a psychological process (verb) with Aries as need/ target state (noun).
4. Mars as a psychological process (verb) with Aquarius as an adverb.
5. Mars as a psychological process (verb) with Aquarius as an adverbial clause.
6. Mars as a psychological state (noun) with Aquarius as a domain.
7. Mars as a psychological process (verb) with Aquarius as an adverbial clause and a complement.

See if you can identify these seven linguistic devices in the narrative below:

> In your chart, Mars is in the sign of Aquarius. As a psychological function, Mars signifies aggression, or your survival instinct. With Mars in Aquarius, your aggression tends to be somewhat detached, cool, and oriented toward changing situations that have become too stagnant and predictable. Your instinct for survival is unusual in that you can objectively perceive a situation and know instinctively where it is headed.
>
> Your inner warrior can be whimsical and capricious in that you sometimes act in ways that shock people into new perspectives; no one knows what you are going to do next.

In order to survive as an independent entity, you fight to preserve your rights and enjoy the feeling of being alive. You assert unemotionally, however, detached and seemingly indifferent as to how things turn out; for you are intuitively aware that your actions have consequences and implications that go beyond you as an individual. Accordingly, you have a tendency to act in a progressive, humanitarian manner and may feel impatient with others who are too preoccupied with their own petty concerns to see the big picture.

An enlightened warrior, you fight to bring about changes in the community and have an ardent desire to awaken people to perspectives that preserve individual freedoms.

Here is an analysis of the seven linguistic features listed in the above narrative.

1. Mars as a psychological function (noun) with Aquarius as a complement.

As a psychological function, Mars signifies aggression, or your survival instinct. With Mars in Aquarius, your aggression tends to be somewhat detached, cool, and oriented toward changing situations that have become too stagnant and predictable. Your instinct for survival is unusual in that you can objectively perceive a situation and know instinctively where it is headed.

Mars is identified as a psychological function, *aggression* and *survival instinct* (nouns), which are qualified by the adjectives *detached, cool,* and *unusual.* As adjectives, these words answer the question, "what kind of aggression? what kind of survival instinct?" The phrase *and oriented toward changing situations that have become too stagnant and predictable* is an Aquarian complement of the verb *tends to be,* because it answers the question "tends to be *what?*" Likewise, the clause *you can objectively perceive a situation and know instinctively where it is headed* is an Aquarian complement of the verb *can* and further qualifies the Aquarian adjective *unusual.* The complement answers the question "can *what?*"

2. Mars as an archetypal character (noun) with Aquarius as an adjective.

> Your inner warrior can be quite whimsical and capricious in
> that you sometimes act in ways that shock people into new per-
> spectives; no one knows what you are going to do next.

As an archetypal character, Mars is referred to as an inner *warrior*, which
is qualified by the Aquarian adjectives *whimsical* and *capricious*. The
remainder of the sentence is comprised of two clauses: (1) *you sometimes act
in ways that shock people into new perspectives;* and (2) *no one knows what you
are going to do next.* Both of these clauses describe typical Aquarian behavior and thus act as modifiers of *warrior.* Thus the entire sentence answers
the question, "what kind of warrior?" In effect, this is an *Aquarian* type
of warrior that is whimsical, capricious, shocking, and unpredictable.

3. Mars as a psychological process (verb) with Aries as need/target state (noun).

> In order to survive as an independent entity, you fight to pre-
> serve your rights and enjoy the feeling of being alive.

The phrase *to survive as an independent entity* is the psychological need of
Aries. This need motivates Martian behavior, as described by the mars'
verb *fight*. The phrase *to preserve your rights and enjoy the feeling of being
alive* is the complement of *fight* while also describing the target state
of Aries/Mars.

4. Mars as a psychological process (verb) with Aquarius as an adverb and adverbial clause.

> You assert unemotionally, however, detached and seemingly
> indifferent as to how things turn out; for you are intuitively
> aware that your actions have consequences and implications
> that go beyond you as an individual.

As a psychological process, Mars signifies the verb *assert,* which is modified by the adverbs *unemotionally, detached,* and *indifferent.* The adverbial
clause, *for you are intuitively aware that your actions have consequences and
implications that go beyond you as an individual,* typifies Aquarian behavior and serves as a modifier of the verb *assert,* i.e., it explains why the
person asserts.

5. Mars as a psychological process (verb) with Aquarius as an adverbial clause.

> Accordingly, you have a tendency to act in a progressive, humanitarian manner and may feel impatient with others who are too preoccupied with their own petty concerns to see the big picture.

Have a tendency to act describes Mars as a psychological process, whereas the Aquarian adverbial clause *in a progressive, humanitarian manner* acts as an adverbial clause in describing the manner of the action.

6. Mars as a psychological state (noun) with Aquarius as a domain.

> …and may feel impatient with others who are too preoccupied with their own petty concerns to see the big picture.

Impatient is a Mars state of mind, whereas *too preoccupied with their own petty concerns to see the big picture* is an Aquarian domain, i.e., "the big picture" is an Aquarian perspective. Aquarius is concerned with awakening others to a broader perspective, but Mars gets *impatient* when this does not happen immediately.

7. Mars as a psychological process (verb) with Aquarius as an adverbial clause and a complement.

> An enlightened warrior, you fight to bring about changes in the community and have an ardent desire to awaken people to perspectives that preserve individual freedoms.

Mars is an archetypal character—*warrior*—modified by the Aquarian adjective *enlightened.* The mars verb *fight* is qualified by the Aquarian clause *to bring about changes in the community and have an ardent desire to awaken people to perspectives that preserve individual freedoms.* As an adverbial clause, it explains "why" the person fights; as a subject complement, it answers the question, "fights for *what?" Criterion*

FIVE CRITERIA FOR PLANETS IN SIGNS

By deconstructing meaning statements in the above manner, we can develop a systematic understanding of astrological grammar. Not only does this enable us to understand the rules of astro-syntax, it also establishes criteria for what constitutes a good interpretation. There are at least five criterion that need to be met when interpreting planets in signs: (1) the psychological function of the planet needs to be clarified;

(2) the motivation behind the behavior should be explicit; (3) the behavior itself should be described in clear, unambiguous terms; (4) a planetary affect state should be related to the domain of its sign position; and (5) the empirical consequences of a planet's actions should be related to a theme of its sign position.

1. *The psychological function of the planet needs to be clarified.* Too many interpretations make the mistake of attributing qualities to the person without clarifying that the statement relates to a specific *part* of the person. When interpreting Moon in Gemini, for example, it is neither useful nor accurate to state, "you are witty, talkative, and curious about people," for such a description fails to account for the psychological function involved, i.e., *to listen, care, and understand.* If someone listens, cares, and understands by talking a blue streak, it obviously presents a conflict and places the behavior in a context that provides more information than merely listing Gemini traits.

2. *The motivation behind the behavior should be explicit.* There is a common assumption among astrologers, which is then perpetrated by non-astrologers that the cause of behavior resides in the planets. It is typical to read, for example, that Saturn *causes* depression, or Mars *makes* people angry. Any interpretation of a planet that does not make explicit that the causes of behavior originate in psychological drives—that human beings are intrinsically motivated and that every sign symbolizes a motive—is perpetrating a myth that damages astrology's credibility as a personality theory.

3. *The core action should be differentiated from the way the action is expressed.* Perhaps the most obvious feature of a good interpretation is its behavioral dimension. Planets symbolize actions; ways of being that are modified by their sign positions. While signs provide a plethora of adverbs and adjectives to qualify the behavior of planets, the sign is always an adjunct to the action itself. Someone with Sun in Virgo, for example, may behave in a manner that is superficially similar to Moon in Virgo, yet the underlying action is critically different. The Sun *expresses* in an analytical, precise manner; the Moon *cares* in an analytical, precise manner. Again, any listing of

Virgo traits must be supplemented by a proper understanding of the fundamental action symbolized by the planet.

4. *A planetary affect state should be related to the domain of its sign position.* While planets symbolize psychological functions, are motivated by specific needs, and manifest in particular types of behavior, they also express themselves *affectively*, i.e., through distinct feelings and mental states. In fact, one way of determining a planet's relative integration is by monitoring how it feels to the individual. If someone with Sun in Scorpio derives a sense of pride from his ability to transform corrupt conditions, this constitutes evidence that his Sun is well integrated. If, however, this same person feels shame and disempowerment in relation to impure conditions, this suggests that his Sun is not well functioning. The goal, of course, is for the planet to attain its target state by expressing itself through the domain of the sign it occupies.

5. *The empirical consequences of a planet's actions should be related to a theme of its sign position.* Every sign rules over its own area of experience, which constitutes the primary theme of that sign. These are the actual concrete experiences through which the need of the sign seeks satisfaction. Planetary actions take place within the domain of signs; that is, the intention of the planet is fulfilled through specific activities that are ruled over by the sign it occupies. Signs, therefore, not only show *how* and *why* the planet is doing its thing; it shows *what* that thing is. The interests, conditions, and outcomes of the sign complement the planet's intentions.

SUMMARY AND DISCUSSION

In this chapter, we have explored the various ways that planets and signs interact. When planets are referred to as psychological functions, they are signified by nouns that can be modified by complements—nouns and adjectives—that relate to their sign position. When a planet is referred to as an archetypal character, it again performs a noun function and can be qualified by its sign adjectives.

Perhaps the most fundamental and telling description of a planet, however, is when it is referred to as a psychological process—a verb—that is motivated by the need/noun of the sign it rules. If a planet is described as a verb that is qualified by its sign position, then the occupied sign functions as an adverb or adverbial clause; i.e., the sign answers the question, *how, why, or in what manner does the planet verb (act)?*

The archetypal relationship between the sign a planet rules and the sign that planet is *in* provides important information about the ease of that sign position. Planets also symbolize specific states of mind that manifest in the domain of the sign the planet occupies; the sign's domain tends to be saturated with the planetary affect. Finally, a sign functions as a complement to the planetary verb in that it signifies the concrete, external circumstances through which the planetary action is expressed.

By deconstructing typical meaning statements of planets in signs, and showing how they relate to parts of speech, an implicit astrological grammar is revealed. This has the further advantage of clarifying the rules of chart synthesis and establishing criteria for what constitutes a good interpretation.

A caveat is in order here. The first criterion in the previous section stressed that the psychological function of a planet needs to be clarified when making statements about a person's behavior; for to do otherwise implies that one is talking about the whole person rather than merely a particular function. In other words, one should not generalize from the part to the whole. But there is another reason why this is important. Invariably, those qualities that are most salient in an individual's personality are emergent properties that derive from how the chart functions as a totality. While inner planet sign positions constitute observable themes within the personality; the further out the planet, the less relevant its sign position becomes to empirical traits and life themes.

To say that sign positions of planets from Saturn outwards are not descriptive of dominant personality traits is not to say that these planets *per se* are insignificant. I am not talking about outer planet functions in themselves, for their qualities can be very noticeable when forming aspects to inner planets or when highlighted in other ways, such as being on the Ascendant or Midheaven. I am merely saying *their sign position alone should not be interpreted as explanatory of a dominant trait within the person.*

Outer planet sign positions have great relevance when considered as generational significators or when in aspect to inner planets; however, their contribution to observable character traits and life themes is relatively minor. Too often one hears, for example, that a person is highly organized, efficient, and analytical simply because his Saturn is in Virgo. If, in fact, a person does evidence Virgo traits in a pronounced manner, it will not be due merely to the fact that his Saturn is in Virgo—a position he shares with everyone born over a two year period and not all of whom, assuredly, are highly organized, efficient, and analytical. Rather, those traits are likely to be emergent properties of aspects, signs, and house positions of other relevant planets.

Chapter Eight

Interpretive Rules for Planets in Houses

CONTEXTS FOR ACTION AND TYPES OF OUTCOME

J ust as rules of grammar can be applied to interpreting planets in signs, so they can be applied to interpreting planets in houses, too. In this chapter, we will explore ways of relating standard rules of planetary sign interpretation to situational contexts symbolized by houses. In effect, there is a progressive layering of meaning, beginning with the planet; then adding its sign position; and then its house position. In subsequent chapters, we will add in the significance of planetary aspects and dispositorships. In so doing, it will become increasingly evident that the chart as a whole symbolizes a complex story replete with main characters, primary motivations, background information, core conflicts, overall plot, and a central theme.

GROWTH AND DEVELOPMENT

An important connection between signs and houses has to do with the growth aspect involved. As stated in Chapter Five, every sign of the zodiac corresponds to a specific house, which is the situational or contextual expression of the sign via specific circumstances and characters. If sign-planet systems signify types of human potential, houses are the actual experiences, the fertile ground, through which human potentials are nourished and developed. They provide the concrete events necessary for the unfoldment of innate capacities.

In an example of the 5th house given in Chapter Five, we saw how events indigenous to its environment served to satisfy the need of Leo.

Not only do houses satisfy, however, they also demand; every house has its own set of requirements to fulfill if experiences within that house are to be fully satisfying. The requirements have to do with the attributes associated with the sign to which that house corresponds. A 5th house experience of romance, for instance, would best be met by being romantic—a quality of Leo. Just so for every other experience of that house: the Leonine attributes of creativity, dramatic flair, spontaneity, playfulness and dynamic self-confidence are all ideally suited to meeting the requirements of 5th house experiences.

Knowing this helps in assessing the ease or difficulty of signs and planets that actually tenant the 5th house. For example, if Uranus in Scorpio is in the 5th, this could be challenging. Uranus rules Aquarius, the sign naturally opposed to Leo; moreover, Scorpio is square Leo. Accordingly, Uranus in Scorpio constitutes a planet and sign naturally antithetical to the requirements of the 5th house. This immediately clues the astrologer to the nature of the challenge that is implicit in this planet-sign-house combination.

Regardless of what planets and signs tenant a given house, the requirements of that house have to be met. In striving to do so, the native is stimulated to develop those qualities in ways that are indicated by the occupants of that house. If a man with Uranus in Scorpio in the 5th meets a woman whom he finds attractive, his romantic proclivities are activated. For better or worse, he makes the effort to be charming and romantic, drawing upon his Uranus in Scorpio as a primary resource. He may, for example, take her to a bizarre, experimental film with shocking sexual content. If she is offended, he is forced to re-evaluate and consider alternative, more suitable ways of utilizing his Uranus in Scorpio if he expects to win her over.

This example illustrates how houses are actually psychological environments that make for the fuller development and expression of personality potentials. As stated, the aspect of personality being developed is indicated by the natural sign ruler of that house, e.g., Leo rules the 5th house; therefore, 5th house experiences are specifically designed to activate/develop those attributes and qualities associated with the sign Leo. Ways of meeting houses challenges are suggested by the signs and planets that actually occupy the house.

Depending upon the time of birth, any sign can be on the cusp of any house. For example, someone may have Cancer on the cusp of the 1st house, which constitutes their Ascendant, or Rising Sign. For a person with Cancer Rising, the need and style of Cancer would be evident in the way 1st house situations are handled. Again, the ease or difficulty of negotiating the challenges of a house will be reflected in the sign that marks the cusp of that house. Since Aries is the archetypal ruler of the 1st, the timid, sensitive, and shy nature of Cancer is ill suited for 1st house experiences that require strength, assertion, and boldness. This is indicated by the fact that Cancer is naturally square to Aries. Tackling Aries situations in a Cancerian way is inherently problematic, like going into battle with an intention to nurture the enemy and extend sympathy for their distress. More important than signs on house cusps, however, are the planets that occupy houses, a subject to which we now turn.

PLACING NEED AND STYLE IN CONTEXT

Just as with signs, any planet can be in any house. When a planet occupies a house it simply means that the psychological faculty symbolized by that planet will express itself through the circumstances symbolized by that house. Thus, planets in houses show what faculty is associated with what circumstances. Houses, in turn, show the context within which these faculties and their derivatives are to be experienced. Planets in houses manifest in three distinct ways: (1) as actions; (2) as states; and (3) as events, i.e., a relationship with a person or a situation. We will consider each of these in turn and explore how one derives from the other.

Recall that a planet's behavior is always motivated by a basic, psychological need. Accordingly, the planet's house position shows *where* the native attempts to satisfy that need. If Pluto is in the 6th, the need for transformation must get satisfied in relation to one's work and health. In striving to meet its motivating need, each planet represents a particular type of action e.g., the Sun expresses, the Moon listens, Mars asserts, Venus attracts, Jupiter teaches, and so on. Of course, there is more than one verb related to each of the planets, but each verb is self-consistent with every other verb that belongs to that planet. A planet's range of action is going to be most apparent in that department of life symbolized by the house it occupies. Saturn in the 7th, for instance, is going to control, regulate, and perfect human relationships, working hard to make sure that things are balanced, fair, and equitable.

A planet approaches the challenge of a house in its own characteristic way, for better or worse. For example, success in a career (10th house) generally requires disciplined focus and painstaking hard work. Any planet in the 10th must dedicate itself to this task. But how easily can it do so? Jupiter in the 10th house is going to feel restrained by such demands, for Jupiter is happy-go-lucky, full of faith and hope, and content to talk about the possibilities of what might be accomplished. But actually *work?* Well, Jupiter might work as long as things don't get too boring. It would actually prefer to *teach* about work, establishing sure fire principles for achieving success.

SITUATIONAL SPECIFICITY OF PROCESSES

From a process perspective, we can assume the following: (1) the need that a planet is pledged to fulfill will be satisfied through the circumstances of the house that planet occupies; and (2) the requirements of a house will be met in a manner symbolized by the planets that tenant it. As an example, consider Saturn in Virgo in the 5th house. Recall that Saturn rules Capricorn, meaning that Saturn is the faculty that satisfies the Capricorn drive for perfection in material form. Since Virgo represents the need for efficiency and productive service to others, Saturn in Virgo would mean structuring (perfecting) in an efficient, detailed manner toward pragmatic ends.

Taking one aspect of the 5th house—that of creativity—and relating it to the process symbolized by Saturn in Virgo, we come up with a person who has a very structured, perfectionistic and analytical approach to creative projects. This is a person who may be short on spontaneity, but quite successful when given the time to complete his project in the slow, laborious and highly technical manner that Saturn in Virgo requires. In turn, the creative endeavor would probably serve a useful purpose; e.g., it might help the native accomplish some kind of task (Virgo).

Summing up the process, we find the Capricorn need is satisfied by the Saturn *faculty* in a Virgo *manner* in a 5th house *context*. Or, to be more specific: (1) the need for perfection is satisfied through creativity;

(2) the manner it is expressed is Virgonian, i.e., in an analytical, utilitarian framework; and (3) 5th house requirements of spontaneity and creativity are met in a Saturn in Virgo manner—serious, disciplined, precise, and systematic. If this person were to describe the process, he might say: "My need for order (Capricorn) is satisfied by organizing (Saturn) a creative project (5th house) in such a way that it is efficient, practical and utilitarian (Virgo)." The point here is that the behavioral activity that Saturn in Virgo symbolizes will be most evident in 5th house situations. This suggests that many personality traits are situationally specific, i.e., they will be evidenced most clearly in a certain situational context (house).

SITUATIONAL SPECIFICITY OF STATES

A planet is not only a behavioral pattern, but also symbolizes an attitude, mood, or feeling. The affects that characterize a planet generally derive from underlying *beliefs* that reflect the degree to which that planet is functional or dysfunctional. These beliefs will be oriented around the target states that the planet strives to attain, e.g., does a person believe s/he is capable of success (Saturn), of intimacy (Venus), or of belonging (Moon)? If the planet is fully functional, its corresponding beliefs will be constructive and will produce positive attitudes, moods, and feeling states. If the planet is not well integrated, then the resultant beliefs will produce dysfunctional behaviors and negative states.

Just as a behavioral pattern can be situationally specific, so psychological states can be triggered by specific situations. Because a house represents a specific kind of situation, planets in houses suggest that affect states are situational as much as they are characterological. With the exception of the Sun, Moon, and Ascendant, which tend to be fairly dominant features of a personality, the personality traits that accrue to various planets are more or less situationally specific.

Recall, for example, that an unintegrated Saturn symbolizes an anxious, fearful state of mind. *Where* and *how* this fear manifests will be fairly consistent over the range of activities that characterize its house position. An unintegrated Saturn in the 5th may result in creative paralysis or a "creative block." If Saturn in the 5th suggests there are emotional blockages to overcome in regard to creativity, what of romance? How would this person feel at a party? What kind of attitude might he have toward competitive sports? Saturn would describe all these 5th house experiences. Romance, for instance, may be experienced as difficult and frightening. Seeing a girl to whom he is attracted may cause a boy to be immediately plagued with doubts concerning his own worth. Swallowing his fear, he approaches her anyway, yet he feels tight, nervous, inhibited. The girl, sensing he is uncomfortable, feels uncomfortable in return and thus rejects him. After numerous such experiences, he is reluctant to keep trying; his suspicion that he is not good enough is confirmed. If Saturn is projected, just the opposite may occur: no one is good enough for him. Wanting to have the perfect romance, he is frustrated when no one seems to measure up. This boy may price himself out of the market. In either event, the result is the same: no romance.

At parties, the same process takes over. Needing to be perfectly popular, yet falling short of his own high standards, he may relentlessly find fault with himself. Because of his insecurity, others shun him thus confirming once again what he already fears; that he is drab, boring and a dull individual. If this process continues, he may eventually avoid parties altogether. Socially he might feel lonely as a consequence of not allowing himself to engage in activities that are recreational and "fun." When it comes to sports, this individual could feel that he must be the best. If he has any talent, he would probably hone it to perfection through long hours of disciplined practice. However, if he is only average, he may be so overwhelmed by what seems to him to be inexcusable failure, that he gives up sports in the same manner that he avoids parties and romance.

All of the above suggests that there are a variety of possible outcomes for a given planetary position, and no one outcome is exclusive of any other. Outcomes are a flow, a constantly transitioning and evolving process that proceeds from more simple, less satisfying outcomes to more complex, gratifying ones. Saturn in the 5th may initially be experienced as performance anxiety, yet over time it could evolve into a masterful, authoritative performance that succeeds precisely because it is practiced and perfected.

When delineating planetary states in the context of a specific house, one must determine how these states logically relate to the affairs associated with the house the planet occupies. For example, if Neptune is in the 2nd house and Neptune's target state is "oneness with all sentient beings," how might this relate to the 2nd house? Perhaps the individual feels a sense of unconscious guilt in relation to what s/he owns and is compelled, therefore, to sacrifice personal savings for the greater good—e.g., by giving excessively to charities. Or, the person may seek transcendence through communion with nature, perhaps by engaging in a communal farming project.

Once it is understood that planetary states will be logically related to the entire range of affairs symbolized by the occupied house, the astrologer can look for evidence to this effect. She might notice, for example, that a client with Mars in the 8th house feels impatient and impulsive in matters pertaining to sexuality, shared finances, taxation, investments, and in situations requiring a sensitive attunement to human vulnerability. Jupiter in the 12th house might feel optimistic that the larger system (God, the church, the legal system) will care for victims of poverty, illness, oppression, or discrimination. Saturn in the 7th house might feel pessimistic about whether contractual agreements will be honored or whether one's partner will be fair. Each planet is going to achieve a state of mind within the context of the house it tenants, and that state will pervade the entire range of phenomena associated with that house.

OUTCOMES VARY OVER TIME

Again, these outcomes or "contents" are only possibilities. There are a variety of possible outcomes for a planet in a house. Since in an actual chart everything affects everything else, the way a planet actually manifests is based on: (1) the sign and aspects of that planet; and (2) the degree to which the planet is integrated. What was true at one stage of a person's life may not be true at a later stage. Saturn, for example, has a tendency to mature the individual in precisely those areas it is located. The need for perfection can result in pessimism and control issues, or be a spur to great achievements. Accordingly, if Saturn is in the 5th, the native could eventually become a professional athlete, creative artist, or even a *Don Juan*.

How Saturn in the 5th actually manifests will vary from individual to individual as well as at different points in the life. At twenty-five a man may be so fearful of failure that he experiences a paralyzing creative block. Nothing flows. After experiencing success in other areas of his life, however, this same individual may be ready to tackle the challenge that Saturn in the 5th represents. Once started, he pursues his goal with unwavering determination and persistence, ultimately becoming an authority in the specialized 5th house area of his choice, e.g., he becomes a theatrical director, the coach of a professional sports team, or an expert in the field of creative writing. Such an unfoldment of events would typify the Saturn process.

Because people tend to evolve over time, and because the outcome of a planetary house position is affected by a complex host of astrological factors that extend beyond that house, it is impossible to know how people are actually living their charts until you talk to them.

Just as a gradual maturation of talent is characteristic of Saturn's sign and house placement, similar types of development are true for other planets as well. Ideally, no planetary function remains the same. All evolve. As planets become integrated with one another, and as each becomes more fully conscious and actualized within the psyche, the person progresses along a continuum from relatively distressing states to more satisfying ones. The Sun becomes less arrogant and more genuinely confident; the Moon becomes less clinging and more caring; Mars becomes less angry and more dynamic, Venus less possessive and more secure, Jupiter less dogmatic and more faithful, Uranus less unstable and more resilient, Neptune less tragic and more compassionate, and Pluto less paranoid and more powerful.

PLANETS AS PROJECTIONS

Projections occur when an individual attributes an aspect of his own nature to someone or something outside of himself. Since houses represent environmental circumstances, and planets psychological faculties, planets in houses provide a key to projections. The specifics of the projection are revealed by the house-planet interaction; that is, we project the part of ourselves represented by the planet onto the people and circumstances associated with the house it occupies. Accordingly, a planet may show up in the guise of a *person* with whom the subject is relating or as a *situation* in which the person is engaged.

To return to our previous example of Saturn in the 5th, the individual may typically feel that it is others who are judging and controlling him rather than himself. If he were an actor, he would expect his audience to be highly demanding and critical; women (in romantic situations) may appear to be cold and denying; as a member of a team his coach would seem harsh and authoritarian; he might imagine that his teammates expect him to be perfect. Feeling pressured and overwhelmed by forces that appear to be outside of him, it would be easy for this individual to project responsibility for the sense of failure he feels inside. It probably would not occur to him that his experiences are self-created and his expectations self-fulfilling.

Projections are not always illusory. What a person thinks he sees and experiences may actually be so; his coach may be the stern taskmaster he appears. The important thing to realize, however, is that not only does the individual experience his coach through the subjective filter of his own attitudes; he experiences him as a consequence of those attitudes. That is, the coach is the material manifestation of a psychic process.

This can be described in terms of a psychological concept called "projective identification," which is the tendency to think, feel, and act in ways that cause others to respond in a manner that conforms to one's expectations. Projective identification is similar to what we mean by "self-fulfilling prophecy." If our hypothetical athlete expects his coach to be stern and harsh, then he may become defensive whenever the coach corrects a mistake. The coach, frustrated at how "difficult" his young charge is, presses harder to get his message across. A process of action and reaction is set up that eventually culminates in the young athlete feeling pressured, disliked, and inadequate.

Note how the young man has brought about the very thing he feared. If he were different, his coach, too, would be different. The coach may be a stern taskmaster to him and a gentle, paternal guide to someone else. Why? *Because the coach is an embodiment of that aspect of the athlete's psyche.* He can be no other. Though he may have a thousand faces, he will show but one, the one that most clearly conforms to the boy's expectations—Saturn.

ARCHETYPAL RELATIONSHIP OF PLANET TO HOUSE

In order to determine how a planet approaches the affairs of a house, one must first determine the natural relationship between that planet and house. Since Saturn rules Capricorn, and the 7th house corresponds to the sign of Libra, and Capricorn and Libra are square one another, then Saturn in the 7th constitutes a natural square relationship. Recall that square means stress and conflict; thus, Saturn in the 7th is a difficult placement because Saturn wants to dominate in an area of life that requires fairness and compromise.

Likewise, Jupiter is archetypally semi-sextile the 10th house since Sagittarius and Capricorn are semi-sextile. The 10th house constricts Jupiter, like taking a cloud of hot steam and condensing it into ice. Jupiter won't expand, but at least it becomes *real*. The 10th says to Jupiter, "Put your money where your mouth is; prove your point." What Jupiter represents, therefore, has to become grounded, substantiated, and manifest in some tangible form. Perhaps the person teaches or advises people as part of his career, but the particular content of what he teaches/advises—his philosophy—must be made manifest; it must be organized, published, and disseminated in some concrete fashion that furthers his success. A typical example would be for the person to write a course that says, in effect, "This is how to be successful in this field."

Saturn in the 3rd also represents a difficult situation. This is partially due to the fact that Saturn is itself a difficult planet. No matter where its location, circumstances that result are likely to be trying. In this case, however, the difficulty is compounded due to the archetypal relationship between Saturn and the 3rd as indicated by the signs to which they correspond. The 3rd house corresponds to Gemini, and Saturn to Capricorn. In the natural zodiac, these signs are 150 degrees apart, symbolizing the quincunx relationship. The situation is one of paradox, incompatibility, stress and conflict. The 3rd house, serving Gemini, represents an area of lightness, open learning, and facile communication. Saturn, serving Capricorn, represents a heavy, serious process that emphasizes duty, responsibility, and achievement. The relationship is one of contraries. Just as Capricorn is the antithesis of Gemini, so Saturn would be antithetical to the 3rd house. How this situation is to be resolved presents a challenge to the psyche. At least initially, the native is apt to feel tremendous pressure to master a particular subject and measure up to an unrelenting standard that impedes the joy of learning.

According to Ziporah Dobyns, one of the main sources of problems in life involves looking for satisfaction in the wrong places. "Placement of planets in...houses which are square, opposite, or quincunx their own... houses (the houses they rule) may show this misplaced aim."[5] Calling it a "misplaced aim" may be overstating the matter somewhat, but awareness of these archetypal relationships certainly provides important clues to the psychic process of the individual concerned.

The principle involved can be summarized accordingly: the quality of experience within a certain house is affected by (1) planets in that house, and (2) the natural (archetypal) relationship of the signs that rule that house and planet. In other words, a planet's archetypal relationship to the house it tenants indicates how readily it satisfies its motivational need and how effectively it meets the challenge of that house.

What happens if we place Saturn in the 6th house? Since Virgo rules the 6th house, and Virgo (being an earth sign) is trine Capricorn (harmonious relationship), we can expect that Saturn in the 6th will be quite comfortable. The 6th house represents an area of problem solving and the mundane day-to-day responsibilities that must be attended to on a regular basis. Work applies here, the emphasis being on the Virgonian principle of useful and productive service to others. Saturn in the 6th would suggest a disciplined, systematic and highly organized approach to such matters. Here, we have the perfect worker always in control of the situation (at least he would experience the need to be in control).

One can easily see how Saturn is more compatible with the requirements of the 6th house than with the 3rd. A disciplined, systematic and highly organized approach to learning may ultimately be conducive to success, but the individual will likely have to overcome some obstacle—either psychological or circumstantial—that impedes learning and that generates fears of intellectual inadequacy.

Regardless of how easy or difficult a planet's house position, the planet must be made to serve the master of the house it tenants. Like it or not, the house is going to appropriate the planet for its own ends. The planet can go willingly or unwillingly, but either way it must be consecrated to the requirements of its house. In my opinion, there is no planetary placement that cannot be made to work.

PLANETS IN SIGNS IN HOUSES

Thus far we have been talking mainly about planets in houses. Recall, however, that a planet is going to manifest *through* the sign it occupies *in* the house it tenants. In other words, a comprehensive interpretation of a planet entails a layering of meanings. The first level is the planetary sign position. To simplify, the planet can manifest as a behavior, a psychological state, or an event (complement), all of which are qualified by the sign. The second level is the planetary house position wherein the behavior, state, or event is made manifest. This constitutes a blending of three different factors—planet, sign, and house.

Carl Jung had Jupiter in Libra in the 8th house. Behaviorally he expressed his faith (♃) in an objective, rational manner with a willingness to look at both sides (♎) of a philosophical issue. Jung was optimistic (♃) about human relationship (♎), believing that love itself was a psycho-spiritual path. He wrote, taught, and published materials on the principle of balance (♎) in regard to the organization of the psyche. For example, he formulated the *law of opposites* which held that the processes of the psyche depend on a tension and interplay between opposite poles, and that if one side of a pair of opposites becomes excessively predominant in the personality—out of balance— it is likely to turn into its contrary, a process he called *enantiodromia*. He theorized (♃) that conscious and unconscious were related in a compensatory way, and that a one-sided conscious attitude will constellate its opposite in the unconscious. The imprint of Jupiter in Libra is clearly evident in these theoretical formulations.

However, Jung's Jupiter was also in the 8th house. We can hypothesize, therefore, that all of the above—behavior, state, and event—will in some way relate to the situational context of the 8th. In fact, Jung's theory about marriage as a psychological relationship emphasized how each person's unconscious image of the opposite sex is projected onto the partner for purposes of bringing the unconscious into view. Once these inner contents—anima and animus—were made visible in the partner, the real work of integration began. Jung theorized (♃) that marriage (♎) was a vehicle for healing and transformation (8th house).

Recall that the 8th house is an area of wounding and trauma. Whatever planets and signs are in the 8th house, therefore, point to that which is injured and must be healed. Often, these planetary functions are buried in the unconscious and regarded with dread. In his autobiography, Jung recounts his first trauma as one involving his relationship (☖) to "Lord Jesus," a religious figure (♃) whom he perceived as a dark and dangerous god who lived underground (8th) and devoured young children. In one particularly telling passage, Jung writes:

> Lord Jesus seemed to me in some ways a god of death, helpful
> it is true, in that he scared away the terrors of the night, but
> himself uncanny, a crucified and bloody corpse. Secretly, his love
> and kindness, which I always heard praised, appeared doubtful
> to me, chiefly because the people who talked most about "dear
> Lord Jesus" wore black frock coats and shiny black boots which
> reminded me of burials.... For many years they inspired fear—not
> to speak of occasional Catholic priests who reminded me of the
> terrifying Jesuit who had irritated and even alarmed my father.
> In later years and until my confirmation, I made every effort to
> force myself to take the required positive attitude to Christ. But I
> could never succeed in overcoming my secret distrust[6]

In the previous paragraph we can see all the elements of Jupiter in Libra in the 8th. There is a religious figure (Lord Jesus) of alleged love and kindness and with whom Jung is invited to have a personal relationship (Libra); yet, he associates Christ with death, bloody corpses, terror, uncanniness, alarm, and secret distrust—in other words, Jung's "Lord Jesus" is an 8th house figure.

Of course, there are countless other ways that Jung's Jupiter in Libra in the 8th can and did manifest. Suffice to say that a planet's sign will be subtly interwoven with the meaning of its house position. The sign, in effect, is interposed between the planet and the house. To return to our narrative metaphor, a planet (actor) is always itself, but can assume different roles in different contexts, e.g., if John Wayne were a planet, we could put him in different signs and houses. He is always John Wayne the actor, but in one film he is a soldier (Aries) fighting in a foreign land (9th house), while in another he is a private detective (Scorpio) who falls in love with a high society dame (7th house). In a good interpretation, a planet, sign, and house are inextricably related. For a thorough outline of precise rules on how to do this, be sure to see Appendix II.

Summary & Discussion

Houses represent psychological environments that present certain requirements and challenges to the individual. These challenges may be met in any number of ways, but the easiest manner of meeting them is represented by the nature of the sign and planet that are the natural rulers of that house. These planets and signs symbolize the abilities and attributes that are best suited for meeting the requirements of the house they rule. It follows that Mars and Aries are the planet and sign best suited to meeting first house requirements.

The archetypal relationship between the *natural* ruler of a house and the sign and planets that *actually* tenant it will provide information as to the ease or difficulty of that house placement. Moon in the 7th can be understood in terms of the square relationship between the sign the Moon rules (Cancer) and the natural sign ruler of the 7th (Libra). In effect, the Moon is naturally "square" the 7th house; as such, there is an inherent conflict with this placement. Knowing the archetypal relationship of planet to house provides immediate insight into the nature of the fit between them, and guides the practitioner in formulating hypotheses and interpretations that are appropriate to the client.

A sign on a house cusp symbolizes the psychological need that is associated with the circumstances of that house. The challenge of a house will be partially met in a manner symbolized by the nature of the sign on the house cusp. Likewise, the content of a house will take on the quality of the sign on the house cusp; i.e., the sign will color or qualify the natural content of the house.

Planets in a house mean the area of life represented by that house is going to be a source of some interest to the native, and the nature of the interest will be indicated by the function of the planet. If Uranus is in the 12th, the individual may be interested in people victimized by progress in some way, e.g., a man loses his job as a freehand illustrator due to technological innovations that led to computer animation. The more planets in a house, the more emphasis will be put on that department of life. The native will tend to be experienced in matters pertaining to that house.

Subjectively, planets in a house represent the psychological faculty that is associated with the circumstances of that house. The planet symbolizes the style or manner of approach to house requirements, and the planetary sign position further qualifies the nature and focus of the approach. This process can be expressed actively, i.e., as some sort of action, or it can be expressed passively as a state of mind. Pluto in Leo in the 9th house, for example, can symbolize the act of investigating, uncovering, and exposing (Pluto) ethical infractions (9th) by sports celebrities (Leo), such as taking performance enhancing drugs. At the same time, it can represent an attitude of distrust and suspicion toward athletes whose enhanced performance suggests they might be engaged in illegal steroid use. Both the action and the attitude/state of mind are equally symbolized by the configuration.

A planet in a sign in a house will also manifest objectively as a quality or condition of that house. This condition may manifest as a person, place, thing, or event. Again, the manifestation will invariably be a mixture of planet, sign, and house. Jupiter in Scorpio in the 7th may manifest as a partner (*person*) who does fundraising for a University. Or, the partner might be a lawyer with an office at a federal courthouse (*place*) where crimes are tried. Another possibility is that the native enjoys a fortunate marriage (*thing*) characterized by emotional depth, abundant sex, and financial prosperity. The native may have to contend with an *event* that requires her partner to do extensive traveling, which arouses jealousy and distrust. Note in the examples above how Jupiter in Scorpio in the 7th manifested as a person, place, thing, and event, all in the context of partnership and marriage.

The simplest way to understand how planetary signs qualify the content of a house is to think of the planet-sign combo as a *character* that one meets in that house, and as an *activity* that one experiences as occurring in that house. For example, Mars in Scorpio in the 11th may manifest as an aggressive-do-gooder (character) who, along with others of like mind, is engaged in a furious war against sociopathic drug dealers that are corrupting the streets of local communities (activity).

All of these examples illustrate how a planet in a house can be experienced in projected form. The native projects the self-part represented by the planet/sign onto the people and circumstances associated with the house that planet/sign occupies. In effect, there is a blending or superimposition of the planet-sign over the usual characters one meets in a given house. A character that embodies the process of that planet-sign will be encountered in the circumstances of its house position.

For example, Uranus in Cancer in the 10th might manifest as a father (10th house) who is very aloof, eccentric, and unpredictable (Uranus). He is also emotionally unstable and frequently uproots the family with sudden moves (Cancer) necessitated by his constantly shifting career. Here we see how Uranus in Cancer suggests one type of character (an erratic, emotionally unstable person), which is then merged with the general characters that belong to the 10th house—fathers, bosses, and authority figures.

Although a planet might manifest as an unwanted predicament in a house, astrologers should keep in mind that house content invariably symbolizes the psychological process of the planet(s) that tenant it. As always, content mirrors process; what happens *in* a house reflects the planetary functions operative within that house. As an example, Uranus in Cancer in the 10th might mean one's career (10th house) is subject to upheavals resulting from unexpected changes (Uranus) in the real estate field (Cancer). A collapsing housing market brought about by a sudden recession makes one's work as a realtor no longer viable. However, it is also likely that the native regards settled careers with a certain disdain and tends to operate as a catalyst for fomenting change in her profession. For example, as a realtor working within an agency she lobbied management for women's rights to fully paid paternity leaves.

This example illustrates how her general attitude and behavior (fomenting change in her profession) is synchronistically reflected in events that appear to happen *to* her, e.g., unexpected changes in the real estate field. However, such events and the context in which they occur merely serve as a vehicle for the development of resilience, openness, perspective, non-attachment, and humanitarianism—all Uranian attributes. These attributes, in turn, are utilized in the service of developing those skills that are required for meeting the demands of the 10th house, such as perseverance, organization, and discipline. Given that the archetypal relationship of Uranus to the 10th is compensatory (semi-sextile), this makes for an interesting challenge. As the ruler of Aquarius, Uranus is a reaction *against* the Capricornian requirements of the 10th. This is a topic that will be taken up again in Chapter 9. Suffice to say here that adjacent (semi-sextile) signs have a compensatory relationship. Aquarius is pushing Capricorn away and has moved beyond Capricornian values. It has succeeded Capricorn and is leaving it behind, so to speak; therefore, Aquarius is a reaction against everything Capricorn symbolizes. If a planet occupies a house to which it is naturally semi-sextile, e.g., Uranus in the 10th, then it is antithetical to the requisite attributes and values that define that domain. This is like placing a revolutionary in the office of the president and saddling him with responsibility for maintaining the status quo.

It bears repeating that any planet can be made to work in any house by finding a way to comply with the demands of that house. The nearly infinite ways this is accomplished is testament to the boundless creativity of the human condition. That individuals persistently come up with ingenious solutions to life's challenges reminds us that there are no good or bad planetary positions; only positions of greater and lesser difficulty, which, depending upon how they are handled, may produce good or bad outcomes.

Chapter Nine

Aspects as Personal Myths

CENTRAL THEMES AND CORE CONFLICTS

I n the previous chapter, we explored how planets in houses constitute types of action in specific context, like actors upon a stage. As
the action unfolds, there are invariably conflicts and allegiances that
form between the various characters that make up the narrative. As
archetypal characters, planets symbolize specific types of action, and
every action has the potential for harmonizing or conflicting with
other types of action. In other words, planetary characters have relations with one another for good or ill. The challenge of any story is to
resolve conflicts and pull all the characters together into a harmonious
whole. To the extent this is accomplished, one becomes a person of
good *character*, i.e. one attains integrity.

Conflict is essential to stories. This is as true for the average person
as it is for the protagonists of myth and literature. Conflict is what
drives a story forward. No conflict, no story. In external conflict, characters struggle against the environment or with each other. In internal
conflict, one part of the psyche struggles against another part; motives
clash and ideas vie for dominance. In most stories, a strong element of
inner conflict balances the outer conflict. To understand a story it is
crucial to determine the nature of the conflict and the pattern that the
opposing forces assume. Toward this end the astrological chart is an
invaluable aid, for almost invariably there is a central conflict clearly
revealed in the horoscope. Often, there is more than one.

In this chapter, we will explore how planetary aspects symbolize the various types of relations—some conflictual, some harmonizing—that exist between parts of psychological structure. Aspects not only signify the organization of the internal world, they also describe how the external world is structured. Planetary archetypes are non-local entities that manifest simultaneously in both inner and outer events. Just as in stories, inner conflicts tend to be balanced by outer conflicts.

In the beginning of a story, there is generally some situation that entails a lack of wholeness—in other words, a conflict between characters, within a character, or both. Stories can be thought of in terms of problem and solution, conflict and repose, tension and resolution. Whether and how the conflict is resolved constitutes the main question of the drama. This is what creates suspense. A story is a movement through disunity to unity, complication to simplicity, mystery to revelation.

Again, a story can be seen as a metaphor for a person. Just as stories denote conflicts between characters, so every human being experiences internal conflict between various parts of his nature. The planetary archetypes make up our inner cast of characters. They are the gods and goddesses within that constitute the ongoing unfoldment of our psychic life. Whereas one part of our nature may be quite compatible with another part, e.g., our maternal instinct (Moon) may form an alliance with our inner warrior (Mars) so that we become fierce in our capacity to care and protect, other parts of the psyche may be at war, e.g., our impulse for pleasure (Venus) may be at odds with the drive for perfection (Saturn) so that we feel undeserving of pleasure. This may show up in the outer world as an interpersonal conflict. One person craves the pleasures of physical intimacy, the other withholds. The outer conflict reflects the inner one while also providing a vehicle for its resolution.

Purely physical conflict does not denote a story. A story requires characterization. There has to be characters that arouse sympathy or antipathy. We have to evaluate the ideas or motives that underlay the external conflict. We may sympathize with one character's perspective, and feel hostile toward another. Sympathy and antipathy, a conflict of ideas, is what makes up the story.

In astrology, too, the horoscope reveals how the native may be more sympathetic toward some planets than others. Conflicting emotions and motivations can easily be portrayed by planetary aspects, e.g., the antagonism between family ties and personal inclination (Moon-Mars), friction between the individual and society (Mars-Venus), disharmony between the aesthetic and the practical sides of life (Venus-Saturn), dissonance between work and play (Saturn-Sun), and strife between career and family (Saturn-Moon).

Conflicts of motive are displayed as hard angles between planets, which often emerge as pathogenic beliefs—negative ideas—that express pessimism or fear about the relative likelihood of meeting basic needs. Negative ideas generate self-defeating behaviors that result in external conflicts and frustration of needs, and so the story goes.

The relation between character and events is a fundamental principle of organization in astrology, just as it is in stories. In story, plot is the unfolding of character; in astrology, character is destiny. Just as in every story there is an obvious external conflict and a less obvious internal conflict in the hero's mind, so each planetary aspect has an objective and subjective meaning. An aspect symbolizes a facet of character and a characteristic event. If an individual believes that he can never truly belong (Moon) unless he achieves distinction in his profession (Saturn), while also fearing that too much work will jeopardize his relations with his family, this internal conflict of Moon-Saturn ideas may emerge externally, for example, as a situation in which his wife accuses him of neglecting the children in favor of his career.

Often these conflicts appear as impossible predicaments for which there is no solution. Yet, it is the challenge of the life to integrate the respective planetary functions and, in so doing, bring into being a unique talent or accomplishment that resolves the conflict. Perhaps our Moon-Saturn man builds a company (Saturn) that provides a protective service (Moon) to the community, an accomplishment that ultimately allows him to spend more time with his family.

In every story, there is a key moment that brings into focus all previous events and suddenly reveals their meaning. It is the moment of **illumination** for the whole story, the instant in which the underlying unity is perceived as inherent in the complexity. All the relationships between the elements become clear and the story is seen to have a meaning as a whole. This meaning constitutes the story's key **theme**, which is the principle topic of the story.

The moment of illumination also reveals the story's message or **moral**. Generally, this involves some lesson that the main character has to learn. A story's moral is revealed only after there has been a clear resolution or outcome of the main conflict. Likewise in an astrological chart, there is a potential unity that is inherent in the complexity of the various parts and relations. If the chart is properly interpreted, this wholeness can be illumined. Suddenly the native sees his life as all of a piece; there is an "ah ha!" recognition. Most importantly, the native realizes that the main conflict of his life provides an opportunity for learning a lesson and for actualizing a potential that can only be achieved by working *through* complexity, complication, and confusion—just as in any good story. Pointing the way toward such a "happy ending" is one of the main values of interpreting a chart.

CONFLICT IN STAR WARS

By way of example, George Lucas, the creator and author of the Star Wars Trilogy, has his Moon in Aquarius in the 10th opposing Pluto in Leo in the 4th (see chart on p. 300). While it is not possible here to give a full interpretation of the aspect, suffice to say it represents one of the key themes in the Star Wars movies.* The Moon, of course, symbolizes one's feelings, dependency needs, and capacity for tender, loving relations. As the feminine component of the male psyche, it also symbolizes home and family. Pluto, on the other hand, symbolizes one's capacity for transformation through encounters with the shadow, evil, and death. The archetype of the wounded healer is Pluto's role.

When these two planets are in opposition, there is a conflict between the functions they symbolize. This can mean that the Moon, the feminine, is "killed off" by Pluto, at least initially. One's capacity to love is wounded; feelings and dependency needs are repressed. Ultimately, this is what needs to be healed. To the extent that healing occurs, the

---

* One might argue that Star Wars is just fiction, just a story. But the point is that every life is a story, including the life of George Lucas. His Moon-Pluto opposition not only shows up in his fantasy life, it is alive and well in his "real" life, too. If everything is a metaphor of deeper, archetypal forces, it doesn't matter if we analyze Lucas' films or his own, personal experiences. The same archetypal patterns will be there. Suffice to say that "Luke" is an equivalent for "Lucas." Symbolically speaking, the film is auto-biographical. For more on Lucas, see Perry, G. (2012), "An Examination of Star Wars and George Lucas," in the book *Finding the Shadow in the Horoscope*.

individual's capacity to love is powerful indeed. Feelings are potent and deep, and one is able to penetrate others emotionally in a manner that is transformative.

Since the Moon is in the 10th, and the 10th house signifies father, we can assume that the injury is to the feminine component of the father's psyche, i.e., *father is wounded in his feeling function.* Since Pluto darkens the 4th house, which represents home and family, we can also assume that the problem originated in some crisis, or wounding, to the family. The Moon-Pluto opposition between the 4th and 10th suggests that the native's career (10th) requires him to regenerate a sense of family by healing his capacity to love. Also, he must attain mastery of his emotions and become a protector of the public. This, in effect, is his destiny.

In *Star Wars*, we immediately see evidence of a lunar wound in Luke Skywalker, who is introduced as an orphan living with his aunt and uncle on a dry, inhospitable planet infested with dangerous, dark creatures—sand people—lurking in shadows. By the end of the first act, his aunt and uncle are roasted by the Imperial storm troopers. We eventually learn that Luke's father has been transformed into the evil Darth Vader, his mother is dead, and his sister, Leia, is a princess yet unknown to him. The family, in short, has been destroyed. Throughout most of this first film, Luke is emotionally upset, angry, and impatient with people around him. He is warned not to give in to the dark side, which feeds off negative feelings—fear, hatred, anger, revenge. At this point in the story, Luke embodies an unintegrated Moon-Pluto opposition. The message is clear: certain kinds of feelings are dangerous; you must learn to integrate and control them or they will possess you and turn you into an evil thing, as they did Darth Vader.

In each of the three Star Wars films, there is a key moment when the Moon-Pluto theme is revealed. Near the end of *Star Wars,* Luke is encouraged by the discarnate voice of his mentor, Obi-wan Kenobi, to *trust his feelings* precisely when he is required to shoot the lethal rocket into the interior of the Death Star. But, to trust his feelings he has to *depend on* the force, which is the supreme intelligence and power of the Universe. "Let go, Luke," says Obi Wan. "Trust the force." Luke turns off his computerized targeter, closes his eyes, turns inward and shoots his missal. It penetrates the one vulnerable spot on the Death Star and blows it to bits.

In the sequel, *The Empire Strikes Back,* the key moment is when Luke is told by Darth Vader, "*I* am your father. Search your feelings. You know it to be true. Join with me and together we can rule the galaxy as father and son." Again he is required to trust his feelings in a dangerous situation; he could be seduced by his paternal longings into the dark side. Again Luke has to "let go," this time to tumble head over foot into the empty abyss of the reactor shaft in a desperate attempt to escape Vader's hypnotic power. When the Moon opposes Pluto, trusting one's feelings can literally feel like falling into a deep, black hole—a motif that occurs again and again in Lucas' films.

Finally, in *Return of The Jedi,* the key moment occurs when Vader "turns" and rescues Luke from the evil Emperor. Earlier, Luke told Vader, "I will not turn—you will be forced to destroy me. Search your feelings, Father. You can't do this. I feel the conflict within you. Let go of your hate." This time it is Vader who must "let go." Vader emerges as the film's ultimate hero when he realizes that Luke is right; love *is* stronger than hate. And with this realization he forthwith dispatches the Emperor by throwing him into the reactor shaft where he is annihilated in a fitting, plutonic explosion. Although this heroic act ultimately kills Vader, he has already been healed and transformed by his son's love. When Luke cries out to his father, "I've got to save you," Vader replies, "You already have, Luke." And in his final moment, he whispers: "Luke, you were right...you were right about me...Tell your sister...you were right."

In each of these three key moments, the Moon-Pluto theme is fully revealed. Both Luke and Vader had to open to their feelings, let go of control, and face the possibility of death. In so doing, there was healing, transformation, and empowerment. One could argue that evil is born out of a failure to transform, to suffer pain, to die to one's old self and be reborn. The film hints that this was Vader's original sin; it was *why* he became Vader. He could not tolerate —"let go"— to the pain (Pluto) of his emotions (Moon) when he lost his wife as a younger man. He did not trust that the way of healing is *through* death, i.e., through enduring the pain of mortality.

In *Star Wars*, Luke faced death when he trusted his feelings and attacked the menacing Death Star without his targeter; in *The Empire*

Strikes Back he faced death when he resisted Vader's seductive appeals and jumped into the reactor shaft; in *Return of the Jedi* it was Vader who faced death when his feelings "turned" and he threw the Emperor into the reactor shaft. While this act of love proved fatal, it was also self-redemptive, enabling Vader to be reborn as his true self—Anakin (and again) Skywalker, a play on words that tells us Vader was meant to be a Pluto symbol of death and rebirth.

The Star Wars trilogy is also about a conflict of Moon-Pluto ideas. The pathogenic version of the aspect is: "You should not trust your tender feelings, nor should you depend on anyone, for love makes you weak and dark forces will exploit your emotional vulnerability. Therefore repress your pain; give in to your hatred, anger, and revenge, for these pave the way to true power." Clearly, this idea is embodied in the character of Darth Vader, who literally masks his feelings under an ominous black mask and cloak. The healthy, integrated version is taught by Yoda and Obi-wan, and ultimately comes to be embodied in Luke: "Trust your feelings, open to your capacity to love even at great emotional risk, for the force will then be with you." Here, the force is the ultimate Moon-Pluto symbol, for it binds the Universe together, permeates and unifies all things, and can only be accessed by "letting go" of one's thoughts and intentions. This, of course, is how one accesses the Moon, by letting oneself be vulnerable, by turning inward and *feeling*.

The Moon-Pluto theme also contains the moral of the story. For Luke, the lesson he had to learn was to control his angry, bitter, and vindictive feelings and transform them into love, a love so powerful that it can penetrate the darkest evil, eliminate hatred, and heal a soul—that of his father. The moral of the story is "don't give up on the goodness in people; relate to the higher man, good and evil can be reconciled through love."

When Luke surrenders himself to Vader near the end of *Return of the Jedi*, his Moon-Pluto opposition is fully integrated. He addresses Vader as "Father" for the first time, and reminds him: "you were once Anakin Skywalker, my father. It is the name of your true self." Vader resists, but Luke's emotional power has already penetrated his father's defenses. "I know there is good [love] in you," he says, "That's why you could not destroy me." Vader acknowledges his son's ability—which is really the power of his love—when he responds, "Indeed, you *are* as powerful as the Emperor has foreseen." Although the Dark Lord tries to resist, his emotions are moved. That Luke has touched his father's feelings is evidenced by Vader's final statement in the scene, "It is too late for me, Son." One senses Vader's anguish when he has to steady himself against the railing as Luke is taken away. He has resisted Luke for the moment, but it is only a matter of time before he turns completely, i.e., transforms.

In the beginning of the film, the Moon-Pluto theme is at its most disintegrated state. Luke's family (Moon) has been destroyed and evil (Pluto) reigns. Significantly, it was a woman (Moon) in danger (Pluto) that ignites Luke's healing journey, for it was his familial love for Leia, his sister, which inspires him to seek out Obi-wan. Again, the main conflict revolves around Moon and Pluto. Will Luke's family/Moon be reunited, or completely annihilated? Will Luke be turned by the Emperor to the dark side of the Force, or will he succeed in killing or perhaps even turning Vader to the light side—healing Vader's feminine wound? Luke's willingness to complete his training, a kind of martial arts therapy with Yoda, readies him for the final confrontation with Vader and his own dark side. He does *not* turn; he would rather die (Pluto) than give in to hatred, kill his father, and become the Emperor's pawn.

This is the moment of illumination in the film. Luke foils the Emperor's plans, and darkness is transformed into light when Vader throws the Emperor into the reactor shaft where he explodes in a brilliant flash. In that moment, father and son are reunited. Shortly after, when the missile penetrates the Death Star's main reactor, there is again a brilliant explosion, like a fulminant supernova. These are all metaphors of lunar transformation. The Death Star was a dark, evil womb (another Moon-Pluto image) that contained at its atomic core the heart of evil itself, the Emperor.

Whereas in *Star Wars* we witnessed the Death Star shatter Leia's home planet into a billion pieces, by the end of *Return of the Jedi* it is the Death Star that is annihilated. Disunity has been reconciled into a new Moon-Pluto unity. By working through complexity, complication, and confusion, Luke fulfilled his destiny as an emotional master; he transformed hate into love, healed his father, and regenerated his family, newly composed of Han, Leia, Chewbacca, the children (Ewoks and Droids) and the ancestors—Yoda, Obi Wan, and Anakin Sky-walker. Wholeness has returned. Order again prevails in the Universe.

Lucas' Star Wars trilogy exemplifies how an aspect can be a powerful thematic element in a life story. The psychological conflict within Luke, which was mirrored by an interpersonal conflict with his father, was clearly symbolized by the Moon-Pluto opposition. This same aspect also represented the story's primary theme, the core conflict of ideas, the key moment of illumination, and the moral lesson imparted.

OPENING AND CLOSING ASPECTS

Technically speaking, an 'aspect' denotes two or more planets that form a specific angular relationship to one another. This angle is measured in degrees of longitude along the ecliptic. There are seven major categories (angles) of relationship based on a division of the circle into twelve phases.

Aspect	Degree	Symbol
Conjunction	0°	☌
Semisextile	30°	⚺
Sextile	60°	✶
Square	90°	□
Trine	120°	△
Quincunx	150°	⚻
Opposition	180°	☍

An aspect is actually a phase of relationship between two planets within a more encompassing 360° cycle. The synodic cycle between two planets is the period of time it takes for the faster moving of the two planets to separate from its slower moving counterpart, progress all the way around the ecliptic, and arrive back again at the conjunction point of the two planets. Different planetary pairs are going to have different synodic cycles, depending upon the relative speeds the planets move. With Mars and Saturn, the synodic cycle is just over two years. With Saturn and Neptune, it is approximately thirty-six years.

Whatever the actual length of the cycle, different angles are going to form at different phases. When the faster moving planet achieves a 60° separation, we have the first (opening or lower) sextile. When it has moved 300° away from the slower planet, we have the second (closing or upper) sextile, because now the planet is only 60° away from the conjunction again. In between, we have the opening square, trine, and quincunx, and the closing quincunx, trine, and square. Conjunctions and oppositions are neither closing nor opening as they only occur once a cycle, at the beginning (conjunction) and halfway point (opposition).

To determine whether an aspect is opening or closing, first note which planet is the faster moving planet, e.g., the Moon is the fastest, then Mercury, Venus, Sun, Mars, Jupiter, and so on. Then consider whether the faster moving planet is approaching the opposition point or the conjunction point of the two planets. For example, if Venus in Pisces were 120° ahead of Pluto in Scorpio, this would be an opening trine. But if Venus in Cancer were 120° away from Pluto in Scorpio, this would be a closing trine.

Astrologically speaking, all meaning is an angle. Each phase of relationship within the 360° cycle has a particular significance. Just as there are twelve signs of the zodiac, so there are twelve phases in any 360-degree cycle. In actuality, however, there are only seven angles because the semi-sextile, sextile, square, trine, and quincunx all occur twice (opening and closing).

An aspect derives its meaning from the nature of the sign to which it corresponds. This means that opening and closing angles have slightly different meanings, e.g., an opening square has a Cancerian quality, whereas a closing square is Capricornian. This is because the first 90° of the zodiac marks the beginning of Cancer. Accordingly, when two planets form the first 90° angle of their synodic cycle, it is called an opening (or lower) square and has a Cancer quality. Likewise, the last 90° of the zodiac marks the beginning of Capricorn. Thus when two planets reach the last 90° angle of their cycle, it is called a closing (or upper) square and has a Capricorn quality. For purposes of convenience, however, the differences between opening and closing aspects are generally not recognized.

For two planets to be in aspect they have to be "in orb." Orbs are a measure of the degree of separation from an exact angle (exactitude). For example, if Mars is at 5° Cancer and Saturn is at 8° Libra, then Mars and Saturn are 93° apart and thus three degrees from an exact square. The general rule is that if planets are within six to eight degrees of exactitude they are in aspect. Hence, most astrologers allow six to eight degree orbs for major aspects of conjunction, sextile, square, trine, and opposition. The quincunx and semi-sextile are a special case and usually given orbs of one to four degrees.*

A further consideration has to do with the terms 'applying' and 'separating'. An aspect is applying if the faster moving planet is moving towards exactitude with the slower moving planet; it is, in other words, approaching the same degree as the planet it aspects. If, however, the faster moving planet is already past exactitude, then the aspect is separating. The general rule is that applying aspects are stronger than separating because the energy is still building toward a climax. Once the aspect passes exactitude and begins to separate, the energy begins to wane.

THE PSYCHOLOGICAL MEANING OF ASPECTS

An aspect can be understood as two parts of the psyche engaged in dialogue, which the native may literally experience as a form of self-talk. Any exchange of information between two functions is an internal dialogue. Each aspect, or angle, constitutes a different type of internal dialogue.

While dispositors also connote an exchange of information between planetary functions (see Chapter Nine), the difference between dispositorships and aspects is that dispositorships show a process of sequential unfoldment—one part of the personality triggers the expression of another part—whereas with aspects the relationship is one of simultaneity; both parts of the personality express themselves concurrently.

With planets in aspect, the compounding of their separate natures results in each planet being affected by the other. In a sense, each borrows or takes on the qualities of the planet to which it is in aspect. Thus, we find that planets that are constant in the quality of their energies may release by their relationships qualities foreign to them as separate bodies. If Mars is in aspect to Jupiter, for example, then the

---

* The difference is that the semi-sextile and quincunx (both of which are also called the 'inconjunct') is that they cannot be derived from division of the circle by a simple number (1-9), whereas the other aspects can, i.e., dividing a circle by 1,2,3,4, or 6 gives the conjunction, opposition, trine, square, and sextile respectively.

natural aggression of Mars is tempered by ethical principles, whereas the ethics of Jupiter are emboldened. The result may be an aggressive morality.

In the Chapter on the zodiac, we talked about aspects as signifying the angular relationships between signs. Depending upon the angle, which involves possible differences in polarity, modality, element and perspective, these relationships can be exciting (0°), mentally stimulating (60°), stressful (90°), harmonious (120°), problematic (150°), or complementary (180°). In an actual chart with planets involved (and since planets are always *in* signs), aspects depict relationships between these planets and signs. The quality of the relationship is partly determined by the signs involved (that is, their angular relationship), and partly by the essential natures of the planets themselves. In other words, planets may be either sympathetic or antithetical to each other by nature or by aspect. Astrologers term *essential* the qualities intrinsic to the planets, and term those qualities arising from aspect as *accidental*.

Let us examine these terms more closely. The essential angle between two planets is determined by the natural relationship between the signs they rule. Since the Moon rules Cancer, and Saturn rules Capricorn, their essential angle (or relationship) is an opposition. Sometimes I refer to this as the *archetypal* or natural relationship. The *accidental* relationship between two planets in a birthchart is determined by the signs those planets occupy. Accordingly, if the Moon was in Leo and Saturn was in Sagittarius, the accidental angle is a trine even if the essential angle is an opposition. It is very important to know the difference between the sign a planet rules and the sign it occupies, for this is the basis of determining that planet's compatibility with its sign and house position and any planets it might aspect.

Generally speaking, the accidental angle between two planets trumps in importance its essential angle. So, while the Moon and Cancer are essentially (or naturally, or archetypally) opposed, the actual trine they form in the birthchart indicates that their differences have been creatively reconciled; thus, they are sympathetic to one another *in that chart*.

Planets that are essentially sympathetic are those which rule signs that are either sextile or trine one another. As we recall from Chapter One, the nature of the sextile and trine is one of relative accord. Just as the signs involved in these relationships are mutually enhancing, so the planets that rule these signs are sympathetic to one another. Conversely, just as signs in square, quincunx or opposition are by nature conflictual, so the essential natures of their ruling planets would be antithetical. This does not mean they cannot get along; it means they can grow strong through the challenge posed by their relationship. Gemini and Pisces are square one another in the natural zodiac. Since Mercury rules Gemini, and Neptune rules Pisces, if Mercury forms a square to Neptune, then the individual's capacity to learn and communicate (Mercury) may be challenged by a tendency to lose focus and become confused (Neptune). After much work, there could an emergent talent for discerning order within complexity, for articulating one's intuition, or for a skillful use of metaphor and image in one's manipulation of language.

Again, the *accidental* quality of relationship between two planets derives from the actual aspect involved in the horoscope. Planets that sextile or trine one another are going to be in relative harmony regardless of the intrinsic natures of the planets themselves. These aspects are called "soft" because the planets accept and encourage one another. By contrast, the square and quincunx are called "hard" because the planets tend to resist one another. Conjunctions and oppositions are neither hard nor soft, though the opposition can certainly be difficult to integrate.

Although the essential quality of the planets involved will flavor an aspect, this is incidental to the aspect itself. Thus, we can conclude that qualities arising from aspects predominate over the qualities intrinsic to the planets themselves. An example should make this point more clear. Let us say, for instance, that we have a chart in which Mars is trine Saturn. These planets are intrinsically antithetical because the signs they rule, Aries and Capricorn, are square one another in the natural zodiac. Yet, the trine in the actual horoscope suggests that for this individual the archetypal conflict between Mars and Saturn has been resolved and thus transformed into one of harmony. Saturn, by nature slow and orderly, will be energized and stimulated by the feisty and assertive quality of Mars. Similarly Mars, by nature reckless and impulsive, will be disciplined and directed toward specific ends by the focused and methodical quality of Saturn. The two planets therefore complement one another to their mutual benefit. Each has something of value it provides to the other.

What would happen if these two planets were in square aspect? Since they would now be antithetical both by nature and by aspect, the result would be relatively clear-cut: the individual would be in conflict with himself. One part of his nature wants instant and immediate gratification of instinctual impulses; the other wants to set limits, make plans and progress forward in a disciplined, orderly fashion towards the achievement of some tangible future goal. Since each planet affects the other, we can expect that Mars would feel blocked and frustrated by the inhibiting nature of Saturn, and Saturn, in turn, would feel challenged and undermined by the combative and spontaneous nature of Mars. As a result, neither planet could fulfill smoothly nor efficiently its proper function within the psychic compound.

Behaviorally this could manifest as poor impulse control, difficulty in accepting limits, and a sullen anger that might periodically explode when frustration builds to intolerable limits. Desires might feel continually blocked, leading to resentment and consequent negative attitudes. Since actions would not likely be well regulated or directed, many projects and goals could be abandoned for lack of sustained effort.

This internal conflict would, in turn, reflect itself in outer circumstances. There may be hostility toward authority figures that are seen as rigid and controlling; or, conversely, authority figures could be seen as inconsistent and incapable of maintaining clear limits. In either case, authority is likely to be challenged and conflict result. Generally speaking, then, this is probably a person who harbors a deep-seated belief that nothing can be gotten without a struggle.

Yet, we should beware of labeling this aspect as "bad." Such an assessment is always relative. Despite the internal disharmony and external struggle that accompanies this aspect, much accomplishment can result. We have all met people who thrive on adversity. History books are full of them—Joe Louis, Evander Holyfield, T.E. Lawrence (of Arabia), Martin Luther King, J. Edgar Hoover, Earnest Hemingway, Harry Houdini, Sigmund Freud, and Charles Dickens all had Mars in hard aspect to Saturn.

Often it is the chafing of particular energies within the psyche that spurs the individual to great achievements. Mars square Saturn can manifest as the need to test oneself against overwhelming odds, giving the fortitude and strength to endure hardships and loss, and then the courage to work upwards again and climb higher than before. There is similarly a toughness, stubbornness, and defiance against those in power combined with a hearty willingness to be in the thick of the fight. When Saturn gains the upper hand, there can be devotion to a life of deprivation, asceticism and self-sacrifice. Such people can turn tragedy to their credit and hang on through punishment that would take the heart out of most people. The Bruce Willis character in the "Die Hard" films exemplifies these traits. Not surprisingly, Willis has Mars opposed Saturn.

Our point is simply this: if achievement and contribution to one's society are considered good, and the struggle of Martian and Saturnian energies contributes to this, might not the aspect itself be considered desirable? Similarly, the psychological growth that derives from this aspect might also be considered in a positive light. One cannot help but grow and change from the problems such a conflict engenders.

GENERAL PRINCIPLES

When interpreting an aspect, keep in mind that the two planets are having a relationship, yet each planet has a primary task: *to fulfill the need of the sign it rules.* This task will be aided or impeded by the nature of the planet making the aspect and by the nature of the angle involved. Ultimately, the two planets will combine to create an emergent belief that pertains to the needs that the two planets are dedicated to fulfill.

After discerning the essential and accidental nature of the aspect, the next step is to determine how the planets affect one another. This is easiest if you consider one planet at a time. A general rule here is that the faster moving planet will tend to be more affected by the slower moving planet than *vice versa*, so it makes sense to consider how the faster moving planet is being affected first. What is the nature of the stimulus from the aspecting planet? Recall that a planet is a verb, an active process, a *doing*. Thus the slower moving planet will *do something* to the faster moving planet (the faster moving planet will affect the slower one, too, but not as much). Each planet, in other words, will act upon the other; each will infuse the other with its essence.

The Sun will encourage expression of a planet by identifying (or dis-identifying) with it; the Moon will tenderize the planet and involve it with nurturing; Mercury will stimulate the planet intellectually; Venus will appropriate the planet for purposes of pleasure or intimacy—thus soothing, harmonizing, and beautifying that planet's energy; Mars will energize, vitalize, and render the planet more aggressive; Jupiter will inflate, enthuse, and make the planet more optimistic; Saturn will constrict, deepen, and ultimately perfect the function of planets it aspects; Uranus will destabilize, detach, and awaken the planet to a more enlightened perspective; Neptune will confuse, diffuse, and/or inspire a planet; and Pluto will darken, wound, and transform whatever it touches.

Of course, each planet is more complicated in its effects than the simple keywords chosen here, but this should give you a sense of how to consider the nature and influence of the aspecting planet. Think of the planet in its verb form, i.e., as a quality of action. It may be invigorating, expanding, suppressing, destabilizing, mystifying, or shaming. Like a planetary transfusion process, the slower-moving planet infuses the faster planet with its energy. Thus, the faster-moving planet must orient itself to the demands imposed upon it by the nature of the slower-moving planet. If Saturn is squaring Mercury, then Mercury must slow down and think deeply and seriously about how to achieve a long-term goal. Saturn, in other words, appropriates Mercury for its own ends. In effect, planets in aspect are both interpenetrating and interacting; each planet transfuses the other with its nature. The general principles can be summarized accordingly:

- Each planet is striving to fulfill a need.

- Each planet must fulfill its need through its interactions with the other planet.

- The ease of the task will be affected by the nature of the planets involved and the nature of the angle itself.

- A belief will emerge out of the interaction.

As an example, consider Jupiter conjunct the Moon. Jupiter is striving to meet the need for expansion and meaning, whereas the Moon is concerned with nurturance and emotional connection. The fact they are in aspect dictates that each need necessarily involves the other and thus the two functions must find a way to collaborate. Because Jupiter rules Sagittarius, and the Moon rules Cancer (quincunx relationship), Jupiter and the Moon pose a problem for one another as they have little in common. Yet, the accidental angle between them is a conjunction, thus we can expect that despite their differences the two planets will embolden one another and encourage mutual spontaneous expression. A positive belief is likely to emerge that pertains to the need for meaning (♐) and nurturance (♋).

Jupiter will tend to *increase* the Moon's natural emotionality and capacity for care, thus creating a supermom, someone who loves everyone she meets. The Moon, in turn, may *emotionalize* Jupiter, creating a belief system (a personal philosophy) that makes caring for and protecting others a central value. The quincunxial connection between the two planets suggests a problem, e.g., a tendency to intellectualize feelings or overextend emotionally. Yet, the conjunction suggests an optimistic attitude toward caretaking that manifests behaviorally as a *direct and forceful* style in expressing positive, expansive feelings of tenderness and maternal warmth. Finally, the person may *believe* that "love is the answer" and that the more one gives the more one receives.

What Are The Needs Involved?

The first step in interpreting an aspect is to discern the psychological needs that the two planets are striving to fulfill. What signs do the aspecting planets rule and what is the archetypal relationship between those signs?

If we are considering a Venus-Neptune aspect, then we are talking about two sign-needs that are quincunx one another—the Libran need for intimacy and the Pisces need for transcendence. The function of Venus is to engage an "equal other" in intimate rapport, whereas the function of Neptune is to transcend duality altogether. Thus we can immediately see that the *essential* natures of these planets contradict one another, for they produce a quincunxial dilemma not easily solved. To have a Venus/Libra relationship requires separation so the two partners can see each other objectively. Compromises and adjustments are made in order to assure a balanced and fair exchange. Neptune, however, is not interested in objective reality, but in what can be imagined.

Neptune pursues the highest ideal—a fantasy of sorts. It does not want relationship; it wants to collapse boundaries so separateness can be resolved and all things can merge in ecstatic union with the divine. One can see how this presents a problem.

At the same time, Venus also rules Taurus, which is sextile Pisces. This implies that Venus and Neptune also have an archetypally sextile relationship. Taurus and Pisces are both yin signs; instincts to pleasure the body and merge in ecstatic oneness can coordinate in disciplines like yoga or communing with nature. Concern for material security and an impulse for selfless charity might combine in efforts to feed the poor. From this angle, Venus and Neptune can be mutually supportive. This does not necessarily contradict the Libra-Pisces quincunxial dynamic between the two planets. One simply needs to consider the essential relationship of Venus-Neptune from two different perspectives.

WHAT IS THE ACCIDENTAL ASPECT?

The second consideration needs to be the *accidental* nature of the relationship. Are Venus and Neptune conjunct, sextile, square, trine, quincunx, or opposed to one another? Each one of these angles qualifies the relationship in its own specific way. As stated, an aspect derives its meaning from the nature of the sign that constitutes that angle in the natural zodiac. An actual angle, or aspect, is a particular quality of dialogue—a *dialect* of the zodiac—with a vocabulary and style and feeling tone all its own. For example, if it is a closing trine, the planets are speaking Sagittarian. They are pumping one another up, telling each other all is well, giving encouraging advice and promoting hope, faith, and optimism relative to the affairs of the two planets. If it is a closing square, they are speaking Capricornese. They are telling each other that all is not well, there is work to be done, goals to attain, plans to make, and that control and discipline is needed. There can be anxious, stressed feeling.

Aspects provide information as to the ease or dis-ease of the expression of the planet's involved. The nature of the dialogue can either enhance or obstruct the functionality of the respective planets. In effect, an aspect constitutes a sharing of knowledge between two functions that may help or hinder those functions. The key factor is the accidental angle, which determines the nature of the dialogue.

Imagine a dialogue between two sub-personalities that inhabit a single person. One personality may say to the other, "Hey, let's you and I resolve our differences, stop competing, and form a partnership!" (opposition), or it may silently convey the message: "Don't even think about intruding on my operation here, because I will fight you" (square). If the planets are trine, one may say to the other, "let's have fun and do something creative together!" In short, each angle constitutes a distinct type of dialogue, or relationship, and determines whether the sub-personalities will be partners or opponents, allies or enemies.

Aspects can be divided into two general categories: yang and yin. Yang aspects correlate to yang signs (fire and air). These angles include the conjunction, sextile, trine, and opposition. Yin angles correlate to yin signs (earth and water), which include the semi-sextile, the square, and the quincunx.

By definition, yang aspects tend to be expressive, outgoing, and life affirming. Yin aspects, by contrast, are more suppressive, introverted, and doubting. Whereas yang angles encourage the respective planets to express themselves through some form of spontaneous action, yin angles caution restraint and require reticence, control, reserve, and discipline. Yin angles, in other words, have an inhibiting, suppressive effect on planets. They constitute the so-called "hard aspects" in astrology. Because hard aspects indicate conflict and because conflict is what drives the life story forward, these aspects are deserving of further comment.

Recall that yin signs are concerned with mastery and responsibility. They ground the psyche in the body (earth) and the emotions (water). Because they signify attachment needs on a physical and emotional level, yin signs are vulnerable to loss and pain. In an attempt to avoid suffering, yin is particularly responsive to the demands of the environment; in other words, yin signs are related to the development of conscience. Failure to adequately control and direct one's impulses makes one susceptible to guilt, shame, anxiety, and depression. On the other hand, it is precisely the introspective quality of yin signs that enables human beings to tolerate frustration, regulate drives, and hold intrapsychic contents in awareness.

Everything we have said about yin signs also pertains to yin aspects.

Just as yin signs function as an inhibiting, restraining, counterforce to yang energy, so yin aspects check and constrain the functioning of the planets that comprise these angles. Poor resolution of intrapsychic conflict is usually accompanied by a negative belief which predicts that unchecked expression of the respective functions will lead to suffering. These negative ideas have their roots in early childhood experiences. In striving to meet the needs of the respective planets, the child had some kind of negative experience—e.g., censure, loss, criticism, humiliation, rejection, abandonment, or neglect. This might have stimulated feelings of rejection, incompetence, shame, or inferiority. Not only do these feelings tend to be repressed, but the accompanying belief that predicts suffering from expression of the planetary functions is also pushed out of awareness.

In other words, the entire structure of needs, impulses, memories, feelings, and belief constitutes a *complex*—a dynamic nuclei of affectively charged psychic contents that operate outside of conscious awareness and control. The complex is, in effect, the monster in the basement.

THE ASPECT REFLECTS THE SIGN

As stated, an aspect derives its meaning from the nature of the sign that corresponds to that angle. Conjunctions have a quality of Aries; thus, they tend to invigorate and strengthen the expression of the planets involved.

Sextiles have a quality of Gemini and Aquarius; thus they enable the planets to function in a more conscious and enlightened manner. Sextiles constitute planetary functions that are aware of and learn from one another. Accordingly, the have an airy quality and confer mental abilities, especially pertaining to the affairs of the planets that constitute the aspect.

Squares have a quality of Cancer and Capricorn; thus there is an inhibited, stressful quality about the relationship, with possible suppression of the functions signified by the two planets. Planets in square may overcompensate, leading to eventual accomplishment and success.

Leo and Sagittarius both signify the nature of the trine, which infuses the relationship with faith, confidence, and ease of expression. The two planets do not challenge one another as in the square, but instead encourage one another to express themselves spontaneously and creatively.

With the quincunx there is again conflict, for this angle corresponds to Virgo and Scorpio. Here the two planets have a problem seeing one another. Mistakes and mutual wounding occur; there is a sense of crisis, error, fear, and possible repression pertaining to the planets involved.

The opposition derives from Libra; thus there is a possibility of complementation and mutual understanding. Yet, the two planets must find a way of resolving their differences, i.e., forming a partnership, without one attempting to dominate the other.

I want to especially stress that the quality associated with an aspect pertains to the dynamic *between* the two planets, not the personality in total. If I say the Moon is 'wounded' by virtue of its closing quincunx to Uranus, this should not imply that the Moon is wounded in general. It may be quite functional in relation to other planets. Likewise, if an opening square between two planets has a Cancerian quality of containment, sensitivity, and caring, this meaning applies to the relationship between those two planets, not to the person as a whole. It may be a contributing factor to character, but does not have the same power to produce traits as the Sun, Moon or Ascendant in a particular sign.*

This can be confusing to students who are just beginning their study. To say that a closing square between Mars and Pluto requires discipline and control to actualize the potential of the aspect should not imply that "discipline and control" are general features of the personality, as they would be, for instance, if the Sun were in Capricorn, or Saturn was on the Ascendant. The quality that ties the aspected planets together may not be a predominant trait within the personality as a whole, but it is essential to the functionality of that *part* of the person.

THE ANGLE IS THE SOLUTION

If hard aspects are to be rendered functional, then the solution to the challenge is symbolized by the angle itself. The planets must come

---

* The sign positions of Mercury, Venus, and Mars can also produce noticeable traits. Other characteristics might derive from core aspects to inner planets, or from the way the chart is configured as a whole. The sign positions of the Sun, Moon, and Ascendant, however, along with aspects to them, are the primary components of what we call personality.

together in a way that both honors and reflects the angle involved. Earlier I mentioned that planets are active and that each planet infuses the other with its energy. It is the nature of the angle between the planets, however, which symbolizes *how* that energy will be received. There is always mutual influence regardless of the angle; yet, the angle determines the relational context of the exchange. By this I mean the theme that undergirds the circumstances which result from interaction between the two planets.

Imagine two people who have a great deal in common and may, under favorable circumstances, become fast friends. This would be analogous to two planets that have an essential trine dynamic, such as Jupiter and the Sun. Regrettably, these two people become involved in a court battle wherein one, a lawyer, seeks a guilty verdict against the other, the defendant. In this context, we might say Jupiter and the Sun are in square. While there is an underlying attraction and natural compatibility, the circumstances of the meeting bring out the worst in one another. Jupiter is highly judgmental and condemning, the Sun defensive and belligerent.

In effect, there are three primary factors involved in an aspect that are all occurring simultaneously: the two planets and the angle between them. Added to these factors is another layer of information, which is the signs the two planets occupy. This provides a greater degree of specificity to the relational context. For example, if Jupiter is in Scorpio and the Sun is in Aquarius, the conflict between them will involve experiences that pertain to the domains symbolized by those signs. This might entail the lawyer (Jupiter) prosecuting the defendant (Sun) for sexual misconduct (Scorpio) involving young boys at a community organization (Aquarius) where the defendant worked. As an opening square, the issue at hand is the sexual exploitation of children, which reflects Cancerian themes of care and protection. Assuming this is the chart of the defendant (it could be the chart of the lawyer, too), the aspect is clearly not integrated for it is precisely the failure "to care for and protect" that is at issue.

A yet additional layer of information would include the house positions involved. If the Sun was in the 12th and Jupiter in the 9th, the situational context might involve a scandalous court case involving a large University (♃ ♏ 9th) that is under scrutiny for hiding the guilt of the defendant (☉ ♒ 12th), a former coach at the University. Sun in the 12th often correlates to someone who has a secret life and engages in unconsciously motivated behavior that brings about his own undoing.

Again, either the lawyer or the coach might have the aspect. What is important to recognize is how the multiplicity of factors involved coalesce to form a single pattern of experience. The dynamics between the two planets are naturally going to manifest in an event that involves people and circumstances that embody the various parts of the aspect—planets, angle, signs, and houses.

Given the number of variables involved (7), it is unrealistic to expect that such an event could have been predicted. In fact, there will be a variety of different manifestations that reflect the same aspect over the course of the person's life. Underlying all of them, however, would be the archetypal patterning reflected by the configuration. The challenge of this aspect is to bring all the variables together such that the Cancerian angle operates in a *functional* way, allowing planets, signs and houses to collaborate in a joint project that serves a theme of caring, protection, and belonging.

Let us take the opposite view, for instance, and imagine that this is actually the chart of the lawyer prosecuting the case. He conceives himself (☉) as a humanitarian and liberator (♒) who awakens the community to the plight of victims (12th house) unable to afford legal representation (♃). Seeing them as legally *unprotected* (♋ theme), he volunteers his services for a small stipend provided by a legal charity (12th) that he created. For reasons involving his own experience as a child, he is particularly concerned with cases involving physical and sexual abuse (♏).

From this perspective, the same aspect manifests in an integrated way. Cancerian themes of caring, protection, and belonging are implicit in his role as a lawyer who cares for the legally unprotected heretofore abandoned by the legal system. Note how the solution to the opening square *is* the angle itself. The planets, signs, and houses are knitted together in a functionally Cancerian way to serve a joint mission.

This same principle is reflected in all hard aspects between two planets. The angle not only depicts the potential conflict involved, but also points the way to its resolution. Planets in an opening square (Cancer angle) generate feelings that must be contained rather than repressed or acted out in destructive ways. The planetary functions, in turn, must be utilized in the service of caring.

Planets in opening quincunx (Virgo angle) need to work together to develop a serviceable skill that enhances competence in tasks related to those functions. Often this entails working through some kind of problem that impedes satisfaction of the needs these planets are designed to fulfill.

With planets in a closing quincunx (Scorpio angle), there is usually fear, shame, and pain that impair these functions; each planet tends to be wounded with respect to the other. If and when the wound is healed, transformation follows; the individual is able to integrate those planetary skills in a deep, powerful way, and there is potency in the way the functions combine.

In the closing square (Capricorn angle), the individual may initially feel inadequate with respect to the functions involved. Eventually, however, the planets are able to work together in a manner that achieves some tangible goal or fulfills a public responsibility. Where the individual once felt inferior, s/he develops a sense of mastery and control.

With the neutral aspects—the opposition and conjunction—the angle is again implicit in the manner that the planets combine their respective skills. While these aspects can also be challenging, they are not repressive in the manner of yin aspects. We will have more to say about these aspects later.

WHAT IS THE EMERGENT BELIEF?

Synthesis truly begins when you consider how the individual will subjectively experience the aspect in terms of beliefs, thoughts, feelings, and behavior. Given that an aspect signifies the combining of two psychological functions, the most important consideration is *what are the likely beliefs that can result?* In other words, the aspect is going to reflect the nature of the individual's beliefs about those functions. Since a planetary function is always in the service of a psychological need, beliefs that emerge from the aspect will be about the perceived likelihood of meeting the respective needs of the planets involved.

If the aspect is between Mercury and Uranus, the belief will pertain to the need for information (Mercury) and change (Uranus). A trine between these planets suggests the person will probably feel confident that he can acquire the necessary information to bring about desired changes. In fact, it will be fun! The signs and houses involved will provide hints as to *what* these changes will be. If Mercury and Uranus are in quincunx, the person might worry that a critically important change can only be brought about by acquiring information that is difficult to access and understand. This aspect will have more of an obsessional, passionate quality to it. The individual assumes as a matter of course that there is some sort of problem or crisis that must be overcome. With the conjunction, the person will strongly believe he *knows* something radical. Communications are characterized by certainty, decisiveness, and unquestioning conviction.

In each instance, the belief will reflect the nature of the planets involved as well as the angle between them. If we are talking about the Venus function, i.e., the capacity to establish meaningful relationships, then it is the individual's beliefs about love and her capacity to attain it that is affected. If Neptune is square Venus, then the individual may believe that her capacity to love (Venus) has no bounds (Neptune). She may have unrealistic expectations about the ecstatic joys of marriage, only to be disillusioned later in life when she realizes that no human being can match her ideal. Because she associates love with an unattainable fantasy, she may compulsively fall in love with individuals who are unavailable to her—i.e., unreal, dream lovers who, because she never really knows them, remain unblemished by the flaws and limitations of ordinary mortals. Such behavior, again, is a product of her beliefs.

The native's spiritual beliefs (Neptune) will have something to do with Venus as well. Perhaps she will conceptualize relationship and the pleasures of the flesh as something that needs to be sacrificed in order to attain godliness—as exemplified by Pope John Paul II, who has the square. Or, she might conclude that relationship itself is a spiritual path—an opportunity to practice forgiveness, deepen compassion, and transcend selfish, egoic concerns.

Invariably there is a **core aspect** in a chart that constitutes a primary theme of the life story. Usually this is a hard aspect from Saturn, Uranus, Neptune, or Pluto to one of the inner planets, most notably the Sun or Moon. Often there is more than one aspect, or more than two planets involved. It is important to identify this aspect because much of the life will revolve around it. In effect, it constitutes the main conflict of the story. There will be certain problematic states, pathogenic beliefs, dysfunctional behaviors, and traumatic life experiences associated with the aspect.

ASPECTS AS OUTER EXPERIENCES

To understand how certain aspects signify core beliefs and themes, we have to discern how the individual experienced the aspect in terms of outer events, especially early formative experiences with parents and caretakers. One's core beliefs about any given matter will begin to form at an early age in response to emotionally significant childhood experiences. The quality of these experiences contributes to the nature of the beliefs that form. An aspect signifies both the quality of the childhood event-pattern and the belief that develops from it.

To give a simple example, suppose our Venus square Neptune child observes from an early age that family members do not touch one another or express affection. She further observes that occasionally her parents endure long periods of silence in which they do not even acknowledge one another. As the years pass, it becomes evident that father has affairs and that mother suffers through them, not having the courage to end the marriage out of concern for her children. Eventually the mother has an affair too, and involves the daughter by telling her about it. By the time the daughter is old enough to go out with boys she has had years of training in the art of intimacy. She has learned that absence of affection is to be expected, that men lie and cheat, that woman suffer in silence, feel unloved and martyr themselves, and that deception is an acceptable practice on both sides. Her beliefs—personal myths—about love and marriage have already been shaped by her experiences; she now has only to carry out the program by choosing to involve herself with someone who fits her personal mythology.

The beliefs that she develops will be consistent with the nature of Venus square Neptune. If she could articulate her unconscious convictions, she might say: "My need for love and happiness (Venus) will be stressed and frustrated (square) by experiences of neglect, loss, deceit, disillusionment, and sacrifice (Neptune), all of which will lead to general suffering in my relations with the opposite sex until I become aware of the unconscious programming that resulted from my childhood experiences."

Even though much of her early experience around love was observational, the model is internalized just the same. Most people have great difficulty allowing themselves to have experiences that are significantly different from those of their parents, especially when the parental experiences were negative. Children tend to identify with their parents, and experience guilt if they go beyond what the parent was able to achieve. This is referred to as "survivor guilt," meaning the child feels guilty if she allows herself to have something—love, happiness, prosperity—the lack of which she perceived as the cause of a parent's suffering.

Accordingly, these Venus-Neptune themes are likely to be acted out over and over in various guises, with the individual and her partner playing various Neptunian roles—victim, savior, martyr, deceiver, abandoner, and the like. Although her underlying beliefs about love may be completely unconscious, her conscious thoughts, feelings, and behavior will reflect her personal mythology. For example, she may think that her partner is her dream lover when actually he is merely a good actor; she may periodically feel confused and uncertain about the reality of his commitment, and she may behave toward him in a manner that avoids real discussion of the relationship, e.g., clinging, idealizing, avoiding conflict, denying her true feelings, martyring herself in his behalf, and the like.

As an adult, her experiences with men are likely to repeat the themes that she internalized from her childhood experiences. As long as the underlying beliefs that derive from these early experiences remain unconscious, she is likely to experience a range of Neptunian men and situations—victims, alcoholics, deceivers, affairs, emotional or physical illness, martyrdom, sacrifice, guilt, illusion of dream lovers, subsequent disillusionment, loss, and grief.

Hopefully, this rather grim example illustrates the various steps involved in interpreting any aspect. The situation is not unlike what was described in the Chapter on planets, except now we have to interpret two planets together. First, determine the basic needs that the planets are striving to fulfill and the psychological functions that the planets represent. Next, what is the characteristic action of each planet? What kind of *emergent* qualities of action are produced when these actions are combined?

The specific type of combining is signified by the angle of the aspect. What are the emergent beliefs that the planets combine to produce? Given the nature of these beliefs, what kind of psychological states and observable traits will manifest? Finally, the way the planets interact with one another is going to manifest in objective events, such as relationships and situations. These objective conditions will be synchronistically related to their subjective correlates. The following steps illustrate the formula in condensed form.

A FORMULA FOR INTERPRETING ASPECTS

1. Determine the *essential* nature of the planets involved in the aspect. What are the psychological needs that the planets are striving to fulfill? What is the archetypal relationship between the sign-needs that the planets rule?

   For example, if Mars is in aspect to Saturn, Mars symbolizes the need for autonomy and Saturn symbolizes the need for control. This is archetypally a square relationship since the signs these planets rule—Aries and Capricorn—are square one another.

2. What is the *accidental* relation between the two planets, i.e., what is the actual angle of the aspect—conjunction, sextile, square, trine, quincunx, or opposition? This qualifies the nature of the dialogue and creates an emergent belief that reflects the individual's perceived capacity to meet the needs of the planets involved.

   If Mars is opposed to Saturn, the individual may believe that authority figures (Saturn) must be appeased (opposition) if one's freedom (Mars) is to be gained. Or, there could be a belief that authority must be opposed for freedom's sake.

3. How does the nature of the slower moving planet affect the nature of the planet it aspects? How does the aspected planet incorporate the other into its functioning? This will further help to clarify the nature of the emergent belief.

   Saturn will tend to restrict, limit, and discipline the spontaneity and aggression of Mars. Mars, in turn, must learn to harness its aggressive energies in the service of Saturnian long-term goals.

4. What kind of early experiences are likely to reflect the aspect? Try to determine the relevant emotionally significant childhood

experiences. How did the individual interpret these experiences? How was the person affected? What were the likely beliefs that resulted? These form the core of the personal myth that surrounds that planetary function.

With Mars opposed Saturn, the individual's father might have been overly punitive and restrictive. The person might have learned to regard Martian impulses with fear and caution. He could believe that aggression must be controlled and directed towards constructive ends that defend the prevailing order.

5. What are the thoughts, feelings, and behavior that emerge out of the underlying belief? What are the emergent traits and characteristics that reflect this part of the personality?

   Mars-Saturn thoughts might be: "I have to fight to achieve my career ambitions." There could be feelings of suppressed rage or defiant determination. A dominant trait might be steely courage in the face of formidable obstacles.

6. What is the nature of the recurrent events, circumstances, and relationships that reflect the aspect? How are these outer patterns synchronistically related to the psychological dimension of the aspect?

   An event that typifies Mars opposition Saturn could be recurrent encounters with unruly and reckless agents who operate in defiance of the law. This outer pattern would reflect the intrapsychic conflict between one's own aggressive impulses and the need for self-restraint.

An easy way to remember these basic steps is to memorize the formula, AICD BE. "A" stands for **angle**, both essential and accidental. "I" stands for the **influence** each planet has upon the other. "CD" signifies **childhood development**, i.e., the emotionally significant, early formative experiences that gave rise to core beliefs. "B" stands for **behavioral traits** that emerge out of these underlying beliefs, and "E" signifies the outer **events** that reflect the intrapsychic condition. The AICD BE formula can be summarized as:

A = Angle, essential and accidental.
I = Influence each planet has upon the other.
CD = Childhood development and resultant beliefs.
B = Behavioral traits, thoughts, and feelings.
E = Events, circumstances, and relationships.

CORE MEANINGS OF MAJOR ASPECTS

THE CONJUNCTION ☌ (0°)

Starting from the proposition that all meaning is an angle, the conjunction is the division of the 360° circle by 1. One is the number of unity. Corresponding to the sign Aries, the conjunction is an Aries aspect. The planets are united, merged, or blended together such that one cannot function without the other also functioning. Their respective functions are not differentiated from one another; neither planet can see or objectify the other.

The ease or difficulty of the aspect is determined more by the archetypal relationship of the planets involved than by the nature of the angle itself. Planets that rule signs which are sextile or trine one another will tend to enhance one another's expression, e.g., Mars conjunct Sun or Jupiter works easily. Planets that rule signs which are semi-sextile, square, quincunx, or opposed *may* obstruct one another. There are exceptions to this, of course. A conjunction between Mars and Venus may actually enhance the functioning of both planets. Generally speaking, the slower moving planet will have a greater influence upon the faster moving planet than *vice versa.*

Like Aries, a conjunction has a self-absorbed, subjective quality. It can be a psychological blind spot in the sense that there is limited awareness of how the conjuncted functions operate. Also, there can be the assumption that other people are more or less like oneself, whereas with the opposition there is greater objective awareness of the differences between self and other. The conjunction is forceful, potent, and somewhat impulsive. The planets combine to produce a beginning in the affairs that together they collectively rule; e.g., Jupiter conjunct Pluto may express itself as the founding of a new religion that transforms lives.

A chart with many conjunctions could indicate a driven, self-motivated individual with considerable personal power. If four or more planets are conjunct in the same sign or house, this is called a *stellium* and constitutes a very intense concentration of energy with a single-minded focus. With so much emphasis upon a single sign or house, it suggests a certain egocentricity, which in extreme cases can border on sociopathy. The personality may have a lop-sided, one dimensional quality; the individual could be a "one note Johnny" or have a "one-track mind," doing one thing very well but having little interest or aptitude for anything else. There is frequently an unmitigated aggression to this planetary configuration; the personality is animated, emboldened, and vitalized by the planets/signs involved. Images that come to mind are wild horses straining at the bit, a runaway train, a stampede of wild buffalo, or a person shot out of a cannon. Characteristics include an independence of spirit, a yearning for freedom and adventure, and a tendency to start more things than can be finished.

THE SEXTILE ✶ (60°)

The sextile results from division of the circle by six. Planets in sextile occupy signs that are of the same polarity. Although the elements will differ, they are compatible, i.e., fire and air (yang), or earth and water (yin). Also, the modality will differ, e.g., cardinal to mutable, fixed to cardinal, or mutable to fixed. The signs that correspond to the nature of the sextile are Gemini and Aquarius, two air signs, which should give some hint as to the meaning of the angle. Sextiles are aspects of mental stimulation and learning, the two planets enjoying a healthy curiosity and interest in one another. In effect, the planets excite and awaken each other's respective functions; there is a stirring and arousing of awareness. Because the planets basically like each other, they coax one another to expression, each being informed and supported by the attributes of the other.

Even though sextiles do not have the easy, natural flow of the creative trine, they are still yang in nature. The planets may operate in a cooler, more detached manner than in the trine. There is a relative absence of struggle along with an objective interest in one another's functions. Whereas planets in trine are like bosom buddies, sextiles are more like siblings, neighbors, colleagues, or group associates. Subjectively, this can simply mean mutual compatibility, perspective, and awareness. Unlike squares, sextiles are not noted for their objective manifestation, i.e., they are not productive of tangible results. However, they do correlate to opportunities, perhaps because of their airy quality and their association with communication and rational discourse.

THE SQUARE ☐ (90°)

The square results from the division of the circle by four. Four is the number of matter and form. Planets that are square one another occupy signs that are of incompatible element and polarity, though similar in modality. Squares have a Capricorn-Cancer quality, both of which are inhibited in their manner of expression.

Again, the natural relationship between the elements gives us a sense of what the aspect means. Water tends to put out fire, fire tends to scorch earth, earth can suffocate air, and air is replaced by water. Metaphorically, the same conflict exists psychologically. Sentiment (water) can douse enthusiasm (fire); zeal can overcome judicious restraint (earth); plodding conservatism (earth) can eclipse rational thought (air); and emotion (water) can overcome reason. The fundamental problem in all these combinations is the conflict between yin (water/earth) and yang (air/fire), which signifies the struggle between conscious and unconscious that is at the root of the square. With one planet trying to hold the other down, the result is a state of stress, friction, inhibition, and repression.

A square is considered an aspect of resistance in that one planet defends itself against the other, rejecting its values and challenging its right of expression. The tension and strain that results can create a state of exhaustion, or even breakdown. Just as likely, however, this same tension can result in explosive or violent action when the repressed planet overcomes the inhibiting force. Again, the slower moving planet tends to predominate, just as the unconscious is deeper and more enduring than the smaller, ephemeral conscious self. The faster moving planet tends to feel boxed in and inhibited by the slower moving planet until it has struggled to reorient itself, i.e., adjust itself to the necessary and inevitable demands imposed by the heavier planet.

Squares conjure up images of the irresistible force and the immovable object, the hammer and the anvil, the pressure cooker. Planets in square have a conflict of interests and work at cross-purposes. Subjectively, this can be experienced as a state of uncertainty, doubt, fear, anxiety, and frustration in relation to the functions the planets represent. Intrapsychic blockages may manifest outwardly as situations of stalemate, impasse, standoff, and deadlock. The person may feel backed into a corner with no way out.

Like the sign of Capricorn and its ruling planet Saturn, **closing squares** have a tendency to overcompensate. The individual may feel preoccupied or even obsessed with the area of life that the square signifies. This is where the person feels compelled to action and displays a willingness to be in the thick of the fight. This is where s/he endeavors to climb mountains, defy the odds, and achieve the impossible.

Yet, if the aspect is not integrated, the individual may try too hard in an effort to overcome an inherent sense of inadequacy specific to the functions involved. By forcing the issue, a situation could develop where the individual's efforts are blocked or frustrated by counteracting forces. If the person is able to integrate the aspect, however, there can be a sense of fulfillment and tangible achievement.

Opening squares have a Cancer quality. If unintegrated, planets in an opening square will have a tendency act out the conflict through an inappropriate display of emotion and anger. The person is more likely to be reactive, irrational, and out of control in this area. Rather than controlling the emotions, the emotions control the person. If the planets in the opening square are naturally explosive, e.g., Mars square Uranus, then the emotions are more likely to be acted out.

In general, there is a vulnerability to hurt feelings in relation to the planets that make up the opening square. The person fears that if the planetary functions are expressed wrongly, s/he could be rejected. On the other hand, an opening square between two yin planets is more likely to be repressed. For example, with Moon square Saturn the native's feelings and dependency needs tend to be pushed out of awareness. If one planet is yang and the other yin, then there can be an alternation between repression and acting out.

When an opening square is integrated, the salient feature is **caring** and **containment**. The frustration, stress, and conflict of the aspect can be held in awareness without denying the feelings and needs that the planets represent. Like "initiation cuts," it is through these planets that the individual has experiences that initiate him or her into the world of feelings. This is where the person may ultimately feel tender, protective, sympathetic, and "moved" to express care and concern for others. Feelings are expressed in an appropriate way, and the individual naturally has sympathetic rapport for the issue which that particular square represents. For example, the person may feel super-caring or be a super-provider in this area of the chart.

Underlying the behavior of planets in an opening square is the need for belonging vis-à-vis the affairs of the planets involved. For example, if Mercury forms an opening square to Neptune, the native may wish to connect emotionally, i.e., belong, by virtue of her ability to utilize imagery and symbol in her communications. Picture a screenwriter in the Disney tradition that employs fantasy in relation to themes of caring, home, and family for films that appeal mainly to children.

Whereas trines can be complacent, squares are ambitious. The natural stress of the aspect literally stretches the person in new directions. Thus no aspect is more productive of growth and concrete results than the square. Anyone who exercises with weights knows that struggling to overcome the resistance of the weight is precisely what builds muscle; yet, this building of muscle takes time. Squares are like weights that one must struggle to lift; but in the struggle there is enduring action, slow growth, and eventual accomplishment.

In the *I Ching* it is often stated, "Perseverance furthers." This captures the essence of the square. Resistance requires effort, and sustained effort (perseverance) builds strength of character. Squares help people to actualize the potentials of the planetary functions involved. Again, the two salient attributes of the square are *containment* and *control*. When the person can contain and control the energies of the representative planets, the unconscious is made conscious, and disciplined, focused action results.

THE TRINE △ (120°)

The trine results from the division of the circle by three. It corresponds to the fire signs Leo and Sagittarius. Planets in trine share the same element and polarity, though they differ in modality and perspective. When planets are in the same element and polarity they naturally augment and amplify one another's functioning. There is no resistance or stress; rather, there is an easy, effortless flow of information between the two functions that results in a creative, uninhibited expressiveness. Think of a relationship with your best friend, someone who appreciates and enjoys your company. Such a relationship naturally encourages a sense of play and creativity. This is precisely how the two planets regard one another; each enhances and makes things better for the other. Thus trines are where we feel confident and enjoy being ourselves.

Planets in trine may constitute innate talents in that they tend to function well without strain or effort. Their expression feels like second nature; they are invigorating and uplifting, like a vacation. In comparison to hard aspects, trines allow us to recharge our batteries and catch our breath. As aspects of acceptance, they have a kind of Zen quality. "Going with the flow," "bending with the wind," "the path of least resistance," and "effortless effort" are expressions that capture this quality. Because there is a sense of unquestioning acceptance with a trine, the individual is likely to accept the status quo in this area of the life. There is a sense of "being" rather than "doing." Instead of challenging a bad situation or pushing for change, the person is more likely to rationalize and excuse behavior that others might find intolerable. Trines can be a bit pollyanna and complacent. Lacking drive and ambition in respect to these functions, the individual may settle for second best, be content with mediocrity, and generally feel that "things are good enough." This tendency to take the easy path is not productive of either growth or accomplishment.

QUINCUNX ⚻ (150°)

Of all the major aspects, the quincunx is the only one that does not correlate to the division of the circle by a prime number. This is fitting when you consider the nature of the quincunx, for the aspect itself represents a problem or crisis of some sort, and this problem/crisis is a consequence of things not fitting together. The signs that correlate to the meaning of the quincunx are Virgo and Scorpio. Again, it is significant that these are the only signs that have literally nothing in common with Aries, being different in polarity, element, modality, and perspective. What this suggests is that planets in quincunx have no basis for understanding one another, for the signs they occupy have nothing in common.

The signs Virgo and Scorpio both have to do with a dilemma of some sort, and this gives us the meaning of the quincunx. The planets in question face a problem or crisis related to the affairs of those planets. Something is not working right or fitting together, and it is not immediately clear how to correct the problem. The dilemma invariably centers on a situation involving a choice between what appear to be equally unsatisfactory alternatives. The general rule here is that both the cause and the solution to the crisis will involve integrating the planets that make up the quincunx.

The challenge of the quincunx is to get the planets involved to resolve what appear to be irreconcilable differences. How can two totally unlike things work together? How can incompatibles unite? A quincunx is like trying to float a house, or put wings on an elephant. "Dumbo," Disney's flying elephant, clearly was a quincunxial creature. Subjectively the person may feel awkward and clumsy in matters that relate to the planets in quincunx. There is a state of incongruity, puzzlement, and perplexity. Yet, just as Virgo and Scorpio represent problem solving and healing mechanisms of the psyche, so the quincunx ultimately requires fixing things and resolving crises.

If unintegrated, the two planets have difficulty recognizing one another with the result that the whole aspect functions unconsciously as a complex, i.e., a state of distress and impairment pertaining to the functions involved. One planet may undermine or sabotage the other; there can be a sense of wrongness, fear, inefficiency, or worry that may erupt as a crisis or problem in some particular area, e.g., health, sexuality, work, finances, career, marriage—whatever affairs the aspecting planets rule.

The external manifestation of the aspect generally involves a predicament of some sort. The individual finds himself in an unpleasant, trying, or unfortunate position. A situation exists in which he faces a quandary that both creates and reflects an internal state of puzzlement or perplexity. When quincunxes are functioning in an integrated manner, the individual generally succeeds in coming up with a novel or creative solution to the paradoxical predicament. The situation is analyzed, fears are faced, solutions are proposed, and somehow the puzzle is "worked out" through an integration of the functions involved. Although the "working through" may entail a certain amount of pain and suffering, in the end there is a sense of relief and empowerment. Quincunxes, therefore, are aspects both of adjustment and of transformation.

THE OPPOSITION ☍ (180°)

The opposition results from a division of the circle by two. Two is the number of polarity, thus the opposition has a Libran flavor. Because it is composed of planets that are in signs of like polarity and modality, yet differing element and perspective, the planets have enough in common to get along and enough at variance to be naturally attracted. The challenge of the aspect is to reconcile differences between elements, for an opposition occurs along a fire-air axis or an earth-water axis. Even here, however, opposing elements are naturally complementary. Air is necessary to ignite fire, and water is necessary to fertilize earth. Metaphorically speaking, these same natural partnerships exist psychologically. The rational intellect (air) keeps fiery impulses from raging out of control, whereas feelings (water) soften the hard-nosed realist (earth). Oppositions also differ in perspective. Planets can be in personal-social signs (first two), personal-universal (second two), or social-universal (third two).

The goal of the opposition is to unite warring opposites and create a loving partnership between the two planetary functions. Yet, this goal is no easier to attain than a good marriage. We know that 50% of marriages end in divorce, and the percentage of integrated oppositions is probably no better. Because the two planets naturally oppose one another, the opposition is an aspect of objective awareness and potential completion, i.e., the planets can *complete* themselves through one another. By "completion" I mean a state of balance. The planetary functions have to face each other, find out how they can link up and collaborate, and adjust their natures to accommodate one another.

A key to the opposition is that each planet has to treat the other *fairly*. When working optimally, the respective functions will cooperate, collaborate, and work together in a mutually beneficial fashion. Each function will compromise somewhat in order to coordinate with the opposing function; each will balance and check the other's extremism. As with Libra, the essence of the opposition is moderation and restraint.

When not working optimally, the opposition is an aspect of indecision and conflict. The individual may vacillate between the two functions and feel caught between two sides of an issue. The inability to integrate both sides may result in a seesaw quality, with the person first expressing one planet and then the other, but not both together. Either the individual becomes indecisive and dependent, or expresses one planet at the expense of the other.

The expression of one planet at a time tends to create a pattern of symmetrical escalation as each planet vies for dominance. Whichever planet is weaker and less acceptable will tend to get projected onto someone with whom the individual is in relationship. This person is then perceived as intrusive, excessive, and unreasonable in the way that planetary quality is expressed. Ideally, the externalization of the conflict leads to increased awareness of the rejected planetary function, and the relationship becomes the vehicle through which the two functions gradually become integrated. The opposition, therefore, tends to show up as a primary theme in one's relationship patterns.

THE RASHOMON PRINCIPLE

If one had the luxury of writing a comprehensive analysis of a birthchart, each planet would ideally receive several paragraphs of interpretation encompassing the planet's sign and house position and all its major aspects to other planets.* Each planet constitutes a kind of identity and thus represents a story in itself—a subplot of the overall plot structure. Try to imagine how each character in a story experiences the story from his or her perspective. For each character, the story is slightly different. Likewise in the astrological chart, there are different characters—planets—each of which constitutes a separate identity, and each of which contributes to the story in its own way. When circumstances trigger the activation of that character, it springs to action and experiences the chart from its perspective.

The situation is not unlike the classic film, *Rashomon*, by the great Japanese filmmaker, Akira Kurosawa. Considered one of the most brilliantly constructed films of all time, the story takes place in 9th century Japan and centers about a nobleman's bride who is raped by a bandit; the nobleman is murdered, or possibly he is a suicide. This

---

* In an actual chart consultation this is seldom possible or desirable, since the typical 90 minute consultation is not sufficient to cover all the bases in one session. Moreover, the astrologer should focus on the client's presenting concern (if specified) and orient the reading to those factors in the chart that are most relevant.

double crime is acted out four times, in the versions of the three participants and in the version of a woodcutter who witnessed the episode. Each person gives an account that enhances the prestige of his conduct. Continuously reconstructing the crime, *Rashomon* asks, how can we ever know the truth?

Although the film has been described by some as being about the search for truth, it is much more than that. Kurosawa's interests lie chiefly in human nature. Because their stories clearly conflict, it is possible that each of the four testifying characters in the film is distorting the truth. It follows that *Rashomon* is not about *the* truth, but about how multiple truths can be constructed from the same incident—each version being a product of human fallibility and self-interest. The story suggests that reality is a construction that is built upon the perspective of the observer, which, in turn, is shaped by that person's predominant feelings, values, and concerns.

Rashomon is an apt metaphor for how the psyche operates as depicted by the chart Made up of different parts, each of which plays a role in the larger story, the psyche is a composite structure made up of at least ten interweaving planetary perspectives. Each part perceives the whole from its own viewpoint; each planet enacts a role that is determined by specific motivations, intentions, feelings, and goals. At the same time, that planet has a relationship with every other planet and must come to terms with the predominant concerns and values of those parts.

An example should suffice to illustrate this. If the native's Venus function is activated, then Venus' sign, house, and aspects will dominate the person's experience of his life at that moment. For all practical purposes, he *is* Venus and the rest of the planets are reduced to a supporting cast. If Venus is in Capricorn in the 5th house, the person may experience himself as a disciplined and focused artist engaged in a creative pursuit—perhaps he is an aspiring sculptor. If Mars is sextiling Venus from the 7th house, his artistic proclivities may be encouraged by the support of an active and enthusiastic partner. Each aspect that Venus receives adds a new dimension to the story which Venus is experiencing. Yet, each planet also has its *own* experience and constitutes a separate identity that may be assumed as circumstances require.

If Venus in the 5th is squaring Saturn in Libra in the 2nd, the native's creative endeavors may be frustrated by lack of adequate funding.

296 • INTRODUCTION TO ASTROPSYCHOLOGY

Perhaps he would like to make money with his art, but suffers from a fear of failure and thus tends to procrastinate. His Venus function *wishes* that money was not a problem, and justifies itself by arguing that "art is what I enjoy and so I should persist even if poverty threatens." This part of his nature resents materialistic values and resists financial pressures. So he buys more art supplies, pays another month's rent at his studio, and throws caution to the wind.

At the end of the month, however, his Saturn function is activated when he is required to examine whether he has adequate funds for basic necessities. Realizing that money is tight, he sees his artistic efforts in a different light. Saturn scolds, "All that time spent on sculpting and nothing to show for it!" Now he feels doubtful, anxious, and disillusioned with his creative efforts. Saturn worries, "my art is not practical; how will I ever succeed?" Here we see how Saturn constitutes a separate identity and experiences the story from the perspective of *its* concerns, values, and goals.

Now imagine if Saturn in the 2nd quincunxes Mars in Pisces in the 7th. Earlier I mentioned how Mars was sextiling Venus in the 5th. The native felt encouraged by his wife because she was an ardent supporter of his artistic visions. Saturn, however, does not take kindly to the partner's impulsive spending habits, which play havoc with the monthly budget. In fact, it's a big problem (quincunx). Thus, while the native may appreciate his partner's excitement in regard to art, there are frequent fights over her tendency to lie about unnecessary purchases (♂ ♓ 7th ⚻ ♄ ♎ 2nd). With regard to Mars in the 7th, his Saturn says, "She is out of control," but his Venus says, "I appreciate that you encourage my sculpting efforts." And in response to Saturn, his Pisces Mars says, "I'm going to do what I want regardless of what you say (and I'm not going to tell you about it)." Depending upon the aspect, these parts help or hinder one another, e.g., Venus and Mars help each other, but Saturn helps neither and vice versa.

This brief example illustrates how each planet plays a role, has its own voice, interacts with the other participants, and experiences the larger story from the perspective of its predominant concerns and values. At different times and circumstances, the native may feel submerged in one of these identities; he experiences the planet as if it *were* him; it is his life at that moment. Sometimes he is fiscally responsible, other times he is an impractical artist, and still other times he is (or has) a pugnaciously elusive spouse. When he is creating in his studio, he enjoys his wife; when he is balancing the budget, she infuriates him.

The Rashomon Principle also underscores how a particular aspect will be expressed and experienced differently depending upon the native's predominant activity of the moment. If the native is in a situation that pertains to a particular house, then any planet in that house will constitute his primary means of expression, whereas planets to which it forms a hard aspect will tend to be repressed, devalued, or avoided. In the foregoing example involving Venus in the 5th squaring Saturn in the 2nd, the native suppresses the voice of Saturn when he is working creatively; however, when he is focused on his savings (♄ 2nd), he tends to devalue his artistic hobby and may, for a while, avoid further creative work that would entail additional expenditures of time and money.

Astrology implies that one's identity is neither simple nor fixed; rather, people are multi-selved and multi-storied. Each planet has its role to play; each contributes to the larger story and to the emergence of a complex, multidimensional self.

A WORD ABOUT SYNTHESIS

In Joseph Campbell's landmark work, *The Hero with a Thousand Faces,* he asserts that the most persistent theme in oral tradition and recorded literature is the myth of the hero.* The hero's story, says Campbell, is essentially a symbolic journey that reflects the soul's search for wholeness. During the journey the hero encounters all manner of different archetypes—warriors, monsters, helpers, demons, servants, scapegoats, masters, seducers, tricksters, lover, friends, and foes. Yet, each archetype is a facet of the hero's own true self. Following the tradition of Carl Jung, Campbell believes that the psyche is divided into archetypal characters that symbolize different psychological functions. While each archetype has its part to play in the life story, it is the task of every human being to integrate these parts into a unified whole. The ego (hero) initially thinks it is separate from its parts, yet it must incorporate them to become the *Self*—a complete, balanced, integrated

---

* Campbell's use of the word 'Hero' describes a central character or protagonist of either sex.

human being capable of expressing *all* the archetypes. This, in effect, is the hero's journey.

At first glance, it may seem that the hero's journey is best symbolized by the Sun. The Sun is the ego, the archetype of the hero, and is on a journey toward becoming the Self—the archetype of wholeness. According to Jung, the Self incorporates within its paradoxical unity all the opposites embodied in the various archetypes. Astrologically, this means integrating the polarized sign-pairs of the zodiac and their respective ruling planets into a unified whole. However, if we apply Campbell's thesis to each planet in the chart, the implication is that not only the Sun (ego) changes, but every part of the self must integrate every other part. This means that each planet must become a bit like every other planet.

Venus, for instance, must grow beyond its central preoccupation with love, pleasure, and beauty. It must develop courage (♂), become informed (☿), and be utilized for purposes of caring (☽). One should take pride (☉) in the expression of beauty, yet also know when the pursuit of pleasure exceeds what is morally proper (♃). Love sometimes must endure privation (♄), or sudden change (♅), and pleasure temporarily give way to pain (♇). Very often love requires a willingness to sacrifice (♆). This brief example shows that while each planet possesses a primary quality, a planet can potentially become a part of every other planet by infusing its nature with the various planetary archetypes.

The ideal of wholeness is something that one approaches gradually, possibly even over a succession of lifetimes. Meanwhile, a planet's aspects show the specific opportunities and challenges one faces when integrating that function with other parts of the psyche. In effect, a planet's aspects show which facets of its character are evolving. Hard aspects especially indicate how a planet will be challenged to grow.

In every good story, the main character grows and changes over the course of the narrative. Changes in character cannot be arbitrary, however. Different kinds of action, both good and bad, must be potential in the character and thus consistent with each other. Generally there is a psychological pattern that is evident even in cases of reversal of character. When Darth Vader "turned" in the final act of the Star Wars Trilogy, it was not entirely unexpected. His potential for good was implicit from the beginning of the story when we learned that he was once Obi-wan's apprentice and a great Jedi warrior. Likewise, Luke transformed from an angry, impatient, and reckless youth into a wise and powerful Jedi capable of controlling his lower emotions. George Lucas' Moon-Pluto opposition helps us to understand how and why these characters evolved. For both Luke and Vader changed in ways that were consistent with the potential of the aspect.

A chart reveals how planets are required to interact with other planets and to integrate the characteristics of those archetypes into themselves. A planet is not a static, flat, one-dimensional figure; rather, planets have the capacity of exhibiting different facets and, more importantly, of changing and evolving over time. As Star Wars showed, a planet's aspects suggest the direction in which that psychological function will develop.

In stories, a character may be "flat" or "round". Flat characters are simple stereotypes, stock types. They can be defined quickly and easily. Round characters are complex with conflicting elements. They are more difficult to describe precisely because they are more developed. A character can also be "static" (unchanging) or "developing" and growing.

These ideas can be applied to astrology. A planet with few aspects is apt to be flat, simple, and comparatively undeveloped. The native may express this planet in an immature way. If a planet does not aspect other planets in other houses, its voice will be more or less limited to the house it occupies. An unaspected Mars, for example, could indicate someone who is petulant and immature in his expression of anger. He may be relatively unassertive, easily discouraged, and his competitive instincts limited to a specific area of life (the house Mars occupies). Likewise, if Jupiter has few aspects, the native is likely to be simple and childlike in her philosophy. Perhaps she holds to the cultural norm in spiritual values and has an unquestioning and superficial faith in orthodox religion. Her faith and optimism are confined to a small area of her life and are not salient features of her personality.

Planets with few aspects may evolve more slowly because there is relatively little psychic energy going into them. Remember, aspects denote exchanges of information; one planet transfuses the other with its energy. If a planet is not being "fed" by other planets, then it lacks the archetypal nutrients it needs to grow. Accordingly, the person may

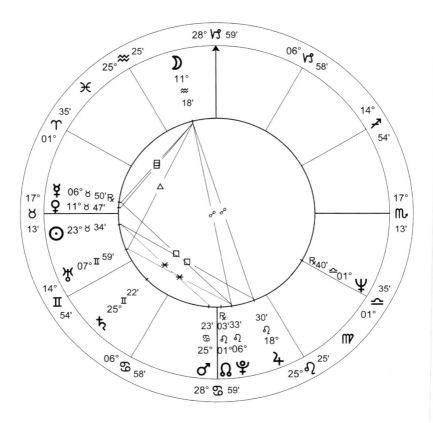

Figure 18: The Chart of George Lucas

be relatively disinterested in that function, with the result that it tends to languish or even atrophy. An unaspected Mercury, for instance, suggests someone who is not an avid learner. Planets in Gemini, Virgo, or the 3rd house may offset this tendency, of course, but Mercury's lack of aspects would still suggest an underfunctioning intellect. This does not mean the person lacks intelligence, but that it is not strongly integrated with other parts of her nature. Likewise, a weakly aspected Venus suggests someone for whom beauty, pleasure, and intimacy are not a primary concern.

Conversely, a planet with many aspects tends to be a more complex character in the horoscope. Soft aspects indicate innate talents,

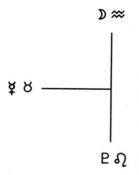

Figure 19: T-Square with Mercury as Focal Planet

whereas hard aspects indicate abilities that can develop. If the Moon *trines* the Sun, the individual's self-expression is naturally sensitized; if the Moon *squares* the Sun, the ego may struggle against its vulnerable, tender side, yet can be gradually sensitized over time. A planet's soft aspects identify characters that are perceived as friends, whereas its hard aspects indicate foes that must be converted into friends. Either way, a planet's various dimensions are reflected by its aspects.

The more aspects a planet has, the rounder, fuller, and richer that planet's character; that planetary function is multi-dimensional and tends to evolve at a faster rate than planets with fewer aspects. A well aspected planet will also be more central to the life story. Rather than limited to a specific area of life, it will spread its influence into other houses occupied by the planets it aspects. In general, the native will be captivated and compelled by the attributes of that planetary function.

By way of example, consider George Lucas' Mercury in Taurus in the 12th house (Figure 18). Although both the Moon and Pluto receive the greatest number of aspects (five), Mercury is interesting because it squares both the Moon and Pluto. When two planets in opposition both square a third, they form a configuration that looks like a T-square (Figure 19). A T-square is a highly dynamic, emotionally charged structure that corresponds to "make or break" situations. All three planets are interdependent, but it is the planet that squares the other two which receives the greatest stress.

The "focal planet," so named because it is the focus of an intense conflict, tends to overfunction by trying too hard to satisfy its motivating need. Like a referee in a prize fight, the focal planet is burdened with the responsibility of controlling the two combatants who are opposing each other. It serves both a protective function and a regulating one, having to care for the fighters but also discipline them if they break the rules. In other words, the focal planet must control and contain the planets that are in opposition. It is precisely because of this unusual stress that the focal planet tends to evolve at a rapid rate.

In addition to squaring the Moon and Pluto, Mercury conjuncts Venus and quincunxes Neptune. Because it aspects four planets *and* is under considerable stress, Mercury is challenged to function at a very high level. Additionally, it has to keep evolving if it is going to assimilate all the information beamed at it by Moon, Pluto, Venus, and Neptune. In other words, Lucas' thinking and communication (☿) is required to be sensitive (☽), deep (♇), artistic (♀), and imaginative (♆). Lucas, of course, is the author of innumerable stories that have become part of our cultural heritage. *THX 1138, American Graffiti, Star Wars, Willow,* and the *Indiana Jones* films are his more notable works. This alone is testament to a high-functioning Mercury. But what kind of stories are these and what kind of characters and conflicts? Again, we can assume that the way Mercury manifests in his stories is a metaphor for how it operates in his own life. The T-square it forms to the Moon and Pluto is clearly a core aspect of his chart, a main conflict of his story, and a theme around which his life revolves. We can expect, therefore, that Mercury characters will play a key role in his films.

Mercury symbolizes the messenger or herald archetype. Like the heralds of medieval chivalry, these characters issue challenges and inform the protagonist about changing events. In Star Wars, Mercury is embodied in the characters of R2D2 (Artoo) and See-Vee-Threepio, companion droids who perform communicative functions for Luke and the Rebel Alliance. With Mercury in the 12th, it is fitting that Luke first encounters the droids as victims—refugees—from the rebellion against the Empire.

See-Vee-Threepio is more the Gemini version of Mercury, a veritable chatterbox who is conversant in over six million languages (Vee stands for "versatility," a known Gemini trait). Like Gemini, Threepio never seems to know when to shut up! Artoo embodies the Virgo side of Mercury. Smaller in stature and thus closer to earth than Threepio, he is a competent and diligent worker-servant performing endless tasks for Luke and his friends. Whenever there is a mechanical problem, e.g., a door can't open or the *Millennium Falcon's* hyperdrive is malfunctioning, Artoo figures out the solution—like any good Virgo.

Each aspect Mercury makes to other planets reflects a different dimension of the archetype. With the conjunction to Venus, Threepio is appropriately a "protocol droid," programmed to function as a mediator, diplomat, and translator. His job is to facilitate smooth communication between the various races and cultures that exist throughout the galaxy. Clearly, Venus and Mercury have combined their talents in the character of Threepio. With his clipped British accent and shiny brass suit, Threepio epitomizes culture and refinement.

Mercury's exact square to Pluto constitutes an important element in the plot. The thinking function has to infiltrate the plutonian realm of secret intrigues, dangerous information, and hidden data. The square, however, suggests it is not going to be easy. A Mercury-Pluto closing square is a Capricorn angle, suggesting that information (☿) of critical importance (♇) must be controlled, harnessed, and directed toward specific, long term ends. With Mercury-Pluto, knowledge is power, and having the right kind of knowledge can mean the difference between life and death.

In *Star Wars*, the entire film revolves around information hidden in the memory of Artoo by Princess Leia. This information consists of intercepted data from an Imperial transmission regarding the construction of the Death Star—a huge battle station destined to become "the ultimate power in the Universe." Darth Vader is in hot pursuit of this data, and barbecues Luke's aunt and uncle in the process. True to his function as a Herald, Artoo delivers the holographic transmission of Princess Leia and the Death Star data to Luke, thus issuing the challenge that inaugurates our hero's journey.

A particularly nasty image of the Mercury-Pluto square is the Imperial mind probe, a dark metal globe with a frightful buzz that glides into Princess Leia's holding hole with the programmed intent to extract from her mind knowledge pertaining to the location of the Rebel Alliance. With a farrago of metal arms protruding from its sides, and tipped with a multitude of delicate instruments, the mind probe is designed to penetrate the brain and torture its victim with hideous images and excruciating pain until the desired information is released. Yet, Princess Leia somehow resists.

We find out later, of course, that she is Luke's sister and Darth Vader's daughter; thus she, too, is strong with the force. Leia's mental power is another expression of the Mercury-Pluto square, a power which is also demonstrated by Obi-wan Kenobi, Vader, Yoda, and later Luke. These powers include the ability to penetrate the mind of another being and control their thinking and decisions. In fact, a fully developed Jedi has an entire arsenal of psychic powers—the ability to see the future, read minds, perceive events at a distance, and even control physical matter (psychokinesis).

Mercury's square to the Moon also figures predominantly in the story. A Mercury-Moon square suggests a conflict between the rational, objective qualities of Mercury and the emotional, subjective qualities of the Moon. In effect, caring (☽) interferes with reasoning (☿), and vice versa. As a closing square, the aspect must be utilized in the service of some public responsibility. One must learn to contain one's feelings and hold them in awareness, yet not allow them to overly influence one's thinking.

To the extent that the aspect is not integrated, the individual is in danger of allowing emotional states to cloud his mind and obscure reason. This is sometimes referred to as "emotional reasoning," such as when a person feels "bad" and thus concludes that s/he must be a "bad" person. The other side of the problem occurs when feelings are denied in an effort to remain rational at all costs. If feelings are overly suppressed, the informational value of what one feels cannot be accessed by the intellect. The person appears insensitive, out of touch with feelings, overly intellectual, and "stuck in his head." Emotional rapport is lost and the person talks "over" his feelings with little awareness of how his words impact others.

An example of the latter is the character of Threepio, whose capacity *to listen* (Moon) is compromised when he is stressed. On such occasions he flies into an emotional tizzy and babbles nonstop (Mercury) until someone switches him off. Early on, Luke also evidences this quality. Eventually he learns to integrate his feelings with his thinking, but this does not fully occur until the final film. An example of an uninte-grated Moon-Mercury occurs in *The Empire Strikes Back* when Luke is practicing mental concentration during his training with Yoda. "My mind fills with so many images," he says. Yoda instructs him, "Con-trol, control you must learn control." But when Luke has a precognitive vision of Han and Leia imprisoned by Darth Vader on the cloud city of Bespin, he turns frantic. Luke feels their pain and is compelled to rescue them. "Save them you may," said Yoda, "But you would destroy all for which they have fought and suffered."

At this point in the story, Luke is Yoda's pupil and is thus playing a Mercury role. While an avid student and quick study, his biggest challenge is to control his feelings—especially his anger and fear. In effect, Mercury is stressed by the pain that is implicit in the Moon's opposition to Pluto. Recall that squares are aspects of containment and control, and Luke has yet to learn how to control his feelings so that they do not interfere with his mental concentration. He can feel the force, but cannot yet control it. Yoda and Obi-wan implore him to complete his schooling (Mercury), but Luke's feelings (Moon) for Han and Leia obscure his reason. He is so afraid to lose them, as he lost the rest of his family, that he ignores the warnings of his mentors and rushes off to confront Vader.

It is fitting that his first confrontation with Vader occurs on the "cloud" city of Bespin, for at this point in the story Luke's thinking is clouded by his darker emotions—again, Mercury square the Moon-Pluto opposition. Luke's feelings are "ungrounded" and his head is in the clouds. His concern for Han and Leia cause him to behave stupidly and irrationally. Thus, he naively falls into the trap that Vader has set for him, and it nearly destroys him.

In these scenes we see how Mercury is a central player in the Star Wars saga. This is altogether fitting for the focal planet of a T-square. It is precisely Luke's wound to his feelings (☽ ☍ ♇) that generates the emotional pain that Mercury must learn to harness and direct. In the final film, Luke completes his training with Yoda and emerges as a fully mature Jedi warrior. In actuality, what emerges is a fully inte-grated Mercury T-square. Luke is now more thoughtful, reflective, and responsive to the concerns of others. His caring (☽), potency (♇), and thinking (☿) are all working together.

Throughout *Return of the Jedi*, Luke's heroics are in large part a reflection of this integration. He remains cool and detached even under the most extraordinarily dangerous situations, always coming up with the appropriate response to solve the crisis. Not only has he become a master of his emotions, but he utilizes his mental powers (☿) in the service of his desire to protect (☽) and transform (♇) those he loves.

CONCLUDING REMARKS

In this chapter, we have explored how conflict is essential to stories. Conflict shows up in two ways: internally and externally. Likewise in astrology, certain planetary aspects depict both the internal and external conflict of the native's life. Outer circumstances and relations provide the vehicle through which internal changes can occur.

An aspect is an angular relationship between planets that constitutes an exchange of information between two functions. Each planet strives to infuse the other with its nature. The ease or disease with which the planets harmonize is reflected by the nature of the angle between them. An aspect's meaning is derived from the nature of the sign that constitutes that angle in the natural zodiac. Because each planet is striving to meet a specific need, aspects symbolize either a conformity or a clash of needs. What emerges from this interaction is a belief that reflects the individual's convictions about the relative likelihood of meeting these needs. Generally speaking, emergent beliefs originate in emotionally significant childhood conditions that provide the first and thus prototypical experiences that conform to the aspect.

The hero's journey is an apt metaphor for the process of integrating the astrological chart. Just as a hero must ultimately recognize that every archetype is but a facet of the hero's personality, so each planet must gather and incorporate the energy and traits of the other planets. Each planetary function must learn from the others, fusing them into a fully integrated function that reflects in microcosm the total integration of the psyche; that is, a completely integrated, maximally functional planet contains within its nature certain aspects of every other planet.

Like characters in a drama, a planetary archetype can be flat or round, static or evolving. The nature and number of the planet's aspects will indicate how complex the function is as well as its rate of evolution. Although analysis of the parts must always precede synthesis, we must be aware of the dangers involved in drawing final conclusions based on analysis of parts alone. The complexities of a chart can be as intricate as the circuitry of a computer. For instance, not only can Moon in the 10th be opposed Pluto in the 4th, but it can also be aspecting numerous other planets and houses, e.g., Lucas's Moon trines Uranus and opposes Jupiter. The implications of these additional aspects may sharply contradict the nature of the Moon-Pluto opposition. Also, there are sign positions and dispositorships to consider, as well as planets, signs, and houses that are not aspected, all of which make their own unique contributions to the totality of the psychic compound.

A core principle of General Systems Theory is that measuring a fragmented piece of a whole system gives misleading information. This principle applies equally to chart interpretation. One cannot isolate a given factor from the whole of the chart and expect to come up with valid statements about a person's life and character. This implies that a chart must be considered in a circular fashion. Looking at isolated components of the chart can give only a partially accurate, fragmented view of the human being it symbolizes. This approach is exemplified in the typical computerized chart interpretation that interprets no more than two variables at a time, e.g., a planet in a sign, a planet in a house, or two planets in aspect.

There is an axiom in biology: *structure determines function.* This simply means that the essential nature of an organism is determined by the formal arrangement of its parts, and not by the nature of these parts themselves. Similarly, it is an axiom of astrology that the whole is greater than the sum of its parts. Since everything is affecting everything else, it is impossible to isolate any one factor from the whole; thus, one cannot speak of astrological results in definite, concrete terms. A certain degree of ambiguity is inescapable. Like the behavior of atomic particles in quantum physics, the manifestation of chart processes can only be described in terms of tendencies or primary possibilities. The indeterminism of the whole is preeminent.

All of this underscores that the chart describes a set of relationships rather than things or facts. These relationships are not static, but constantly in a process of interaction, integration, and transformation. In the final Chapter, we will consider the chart as a whole system knitted together by dispositors, which reveal the plot structure of the life story.

Chapter Ten

Dispositors and Significators

THE PLOT STRUCTURE OF THE LIFE SCRIPT

In previous chapters, I likened the interaction of planet, sign, and house to the sentences of a story. By considering the various ways these factors combine, it is possible to further construct these sentences into paragraphs. Taking every planet in the chart and treating it in a similar manner, we would have about a dozen paragraphs all of which are in some manner descriptive of the process and probable experiences of the person involved. Each planet, however, would exist separately, isolated from every other planet. Consequently, though the paragraphs describing these planetary factors might be meaningful within themselves, the chart as a whole would remain fragmented. Conceived of in this manner, the person's life would make no more sense than a novel without a theme or plot.

Obviously, a story is not told by sentences alone. In order to be fully understood by a reader, it must be unified and coherent. Each paragraph must be logically related to the others so that, taken together, they constitute a plot structure. This plot can only be gleaned by looking at the story as a whole. It is the same with the astrological chart, which symbolically tells the story of an individual's life. The individual is not simply a conglomerate of disparate and unrelated parts, but a complex network of interlocking needs and functions. We call this approach to the chart synergistic, meaning the whole is greater than the sum of its parts.

Where signs, planets and houses provide the raw material of a chart, aspects and dispositorships give the system unity and coherence. In Chapter Eight, we explored how planetary aspects represent enduring core beliefs that can symbolize the main theme and conflict of the story. In this final Chapter, the focus will be on how dispositors and significators tie signs and planets together into a continuous and flowing whole, thus revealing the skeletal structure of the life story. The meaning of these terms—dispositors and significators—will be fully explained as we go along.

Because every chart tells a story, we can utilize a narrative metaphor in explaining the principles of chart interpretation, e.g., planets symbolize the story's characters; signs represent their underlying motives; houses depict the various settings that provide a background for the story's action; aspects signify the quality of relationships between characters; and dispositors and significators reveal the overall plot or story line of the chart.

In a good story, all the elements are functionally related to one another so that there is a discernible structure to the action. This is what gives a story unity and coherence, unity in the sense that all the parts are related, and coherence in that there is an internal consistency among the parts so that the story is intelligible as a whole. Plot constitutes the arrangement of various elements in a story and is characterized by a reoccurring sequence of events that are all related to a central question. This sequence makes up the plot's pattern; incidents keep occurring that have a similar meaning or quality.

Pattern is not simply a mechanical repetition, but a process of stages in progression. Each incident brings about a modification in awareness that leads toward resolution of the core conflict. In this sense, a plot is a pattern of logical, psychological change, logical as it relates to the theme of the story, and psychological as it relates to the motivation and development of characters within the story.

A chart has a plot, too. Just as the planets and their various relations symbolize one's character, so they also symbolize the plot of one's story. Each planetary character represents a type of action. Taken as a whole, the chart symbolizes the structure of action. An astrological chart has a pattern; incidents of the same or similar quality keep reoccurring, e.g., an individual continually experiences the same kind of outcomes in his relationships, career, or finances. Ideally, pattern is not simply repetition, but constitutes a path of evolutionary unfoldment. Each incident modifies awareness, which leads toward a progressive development and integration of character. Every new episode has the potential to alter consciousness. People learn, develop insight, and realize their potentials over time. In this sense, plot is an unfolding of character; fate is soul spread out in time. One could even say that fate is the means whereby soul unifies itself.

DISPOSITORS

Dispositorships provide the key to understanding the chart's structure of action. Simply put, a dispositor is a planet that rules the sign that another planet is in. Saturn, for example, is the dispositor of any planets in Capricorn; Mars would disposit any planets in Aries; the Sun would disposit any planets in Leo, and so on. Dispositors are like runners in a relay race; one planet hands off to the next. The relationship is one of sequential unfoldment. Just as every paragraph of a story must be logically related to the one that precedes it, so planets need their antecedents as well. We find these antecedents by tracing dispositorships.

Let us back up for a moment and consider what the word 'disposed' actually means. To be disposed is to be willing or receptive to something, e.g., "Charlie Sheen is disposed to being a winning actor." In this context, disposed means to be inclined, i.e., to be willing to experience something, like winning. To dispose also means to put something in its place, to arrange or position it for a particular purpose. We might say, "General Patton disposed his troops along the border." Finally, to dispose something is to settle the matter by putting it into its correct or definitive form. "The outcome is to be disposed by the judge."

Astrologically, 'disposed' has similar meanings. When one planet is disposed by another, it means the dispositor is receptive to that planet and is inclined to do something on its behalf. It will receive the impetus provided by the disposed planet and then apply itself in a particular way (planet and sign) in a specific place (house) and for a precise purpose related to the planet it disposes. It will settle the matter started by the disposed planet by pursuing a goal that is in the service of the originating impulse.

Imagine, for instance, that someone with Mercury in Taurus in the 5th creates a board game that requires answering questions for the sake of accumulating fake money of varying financial value. Mercury's dispositor, Venus in Cancer in the 8th, contributes to the game's success by forming partnerships (Venus) with caring others (Cancer) who perceive the game's value for teaching financial skills (8th house). They perceive that parents and children can play the game together, thus enhancing family (Cancer) relations. Here we see how the dispositor supports the purposes of the disposed planet and gives it a means and a place for further development.

Recall that a dispositor receives the impetus from the disposed planet and strives to settle the matter by putting it into a definitive form. If Pluto in Leo in the 4th symbolizes a painful wound from one's family of origin that was humiliating; then Sun in Cancer in the 3rd encourages others to discuss such wounds openly by expressing their feelings. As dispositor, Sun Cancer in the 3rd will further the matter by pursuing an objective that is in the service of Pluto in Leo in the 4th. This might, for example, entail teaching parenting classes that involve active listening skills, or writing an article that provides instruction in how to resolve painful family conflicts. Sun Cancer in the 3rd is behaving in a way that is entirely consistent with its own position; yet, the motivation for its behavior can be traced back to circumstances symbolized by Pluto Leo in the 4th. In short, the disposed planet is a contributing factor to what its dispositor subsequently does.

Note how dispositorships tie the chart together as a unified whole. The disposed planet is the back story of its dispositor, which is the back story of *its* dispositor, and so on until we reach the end of the line—at which point, the story repeats. In literature, a back story is a specific set of factors that occurs chronologically earlier than the main narrative. A planet's actions can best be understood by considering how such actions organically derive from planets earlier in the sequence.

TRACING THE STRUCTURE OF ACTION

Because each planet constitutes a type of action, the flow of dispositors symbolizes the structure of action. If Jupiter is in Capricorn, then Saturn is the dispositor of Jupiter. The process of Jupiter, therefore, both precedes and leads to the process of Saturn; similarly, the process of Saturn derives from and occurs as a consequence of the process of Jupiter. If Saturn were in Virgo, then astrologically the sentence might

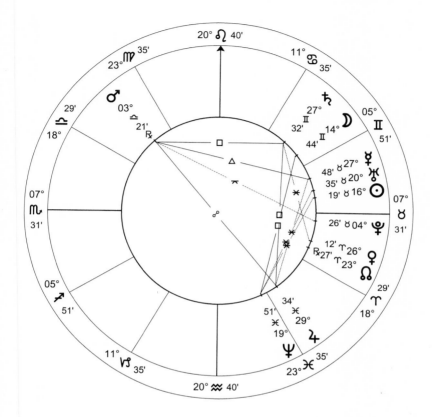

Figure 20: The Chart of Sigmund Freud

read, "My need to Jupiter in Capricorn results in my Saturning in Virgo" — or conversely, "I Saturn in Virgo as a consequence of Jupiter-ing in Capricorn." These transitional phrases connect planets together. Rather than remaining fragmented, the chart flows together into a continuous whole. In this regard, dispositors function as transitional linkages between one part of the chart and another.

Every disposed planet relies upon its dispositor to help it achieve its aims. Sigmund Freud's Moon (see Figure 20) was in Gemini; thus, every time his Moon was activated it stimulated his Mercury function. Imagine Freud **listening** (Moon) to one of his clients, and then **thinking** (Mercury), "This is very interesting, it reminds of the Oedipus myth, which reminds me of what anthropologists say about the hostility of young apes toward the primal father of their group. If I am to truly understand this patient before me, I must learn more about...," and so on.

One can see that for Freud, his capacity to listen and understand (Moon) leads him to exercise his Mercury function, i.e., studying, learning, and cataloging information that he has received from his attempt to understand others. Just so, every disposed planet stimulates and relies upon its dispositor to achieve its goal. It is a relationship of dependency, like an investor with his broker, or a playwright with a director. The investor may desire to profit from the stock market, but he lacks the specialized knowledge that his broker has for negotiating purchases and sales to achieve the envisioned end. Likewise, a playwright may be brilliant at formulating a story and writing dialogue, but lacks the practiced skill of a director to choose and manage actors, organize props, cooperate with producers, and do the myriad things that are necessary to produce the play. Dispositorships show the chain of command that is necessary for the complex, collaborative work required to actually live a life.

Below is the planetary sequence that shows the plot structure of Sigmund Freud's story. Like any biography, Freud's story begins at birth, which is signified by the sign on the Ascendant and any planets that are in that sign. It then proceeds to the ruler of the Ascendant, and from there it flows to the dispositor of that planet and so on until all the planets are accounted for. Note that Freud has four planets in Taurus and one planet in Libra. Therefore, as the ruler of Taurus and Libra, Venus occupies an especially important place in the scheme of things. This is because Venus is the dispositor of five planets. A dispositor is like a landlord who owns the land that another planet is temporarily *in.* The more occupants to a territory, the more powerful the landlord becomes. If we were going to create a flow chart to trace Freud's structure of action, it would look like this:

Scorpio Ascendant → Pluto in Taurus, Sun in Taurus, Mercury in Taurus, Uranus in Taurus →Venus in Aries →Mars in Libra →Venus in Aries (Venus goes back to Mars, which goes back to Venus in a repetitive, nonterminating sequence).

Moon in Gemini, Saturn in Gemini → Mercury in Taurus (since Mercury in Taurus is also part of the above sequence, the rest of the sequence is indicated above).

Jupiter in Pisces → Neptune in Pisces (Neptune is in its own sign, and thus has no dispositor).

While we have somewhat arbitrarily started Freud's sequence with the Ascendant, the best way of doing a flow chart is to start with any planet that is in its own sign and then trace backwards until you reach the beginning of the chain, which is the "lead" planet. In the above example, Neptune is the only planet that is in its own sign, and the only planet it disposes is Jupiter. Since Jupiter does not disposit any planets, Jupiter is the lead planet of *that* chain; i.e., the chain starts there. We could draw it like this:

A more important grouping of planets in Freud's chart begins with Saturn and the Moon, as these two "lead" planets initiate a chain that involves the remaining eight planets. Note that a **lead planet** is *any planet that is not itself the dispositor of any other planet and is not part of a group of planets all in the same sign, one of which is disposing another planet.* In Freud's chart, for example, Uranus does not disposit any planets, but is part of a group of planets in Taurus, one of which—Mercury—is the dispositor of the Moon and Saturn. Uranus, therefore, cannot be a lead planet. Since Moon and Saturn do not disposit any other planets, they are the two lead planets in the chain. The longer the chain, the more central that plot line in the story.

Although there is no final dispositor in this chain, Venus and Mars effectively end the chain because they disposit one another. In many flow charts, the end planet will "circle back" by being disposed of by a planet that occurs at an earlier point in the sequence. In that case, just draw a line from the end planet back to its dispositor. This grouping of planets would look like this:

Note how Mars disposes Venus, but then links back to Venus, which links back to Mars, and so on. This is because the two planets mutually dispose one another, i.e., Mars is in Libra, and Venus is in Aries; thus, they are locked in a closed feedback loop. We will have more to say about mutual reception later.

Sometimes, a planet can be in its own sign and stand by itself since it does not disposit any planets. If a planet is left out of the chain of command such that it disposes only of itself or perhaps one other planet, it is called an "escape" planet and may indicate a function that operates like a loose cannon or rogue function that is relatively unintegrated with the rest of the personality. It may be a very important function, yet is not easily integrated or expressed. Because the planet is in its own sign, it tends to be strong; yet, because it operates outside the main flow of action, it may feel like the "odd man out" or constitute a sub-plot in the life story. In Freud's case, this planet would be Neptune. While Freud held a lifelong interest in dreams, he also abhorred spiritual and mystical pursuits, as expressed in his disdain for this element of Jung's work. Neptune, therefore, was a bit of a shadow for Freud.

A planet that is in its own sign is potentially the final dispositor of the whole chart. I say 'potentially' because there may be more than one planet in its own sign. It is the planet in its own sign that disposes the *longest chain* that is the actual final dispositor. Once you find a planet in its own sign, trace backwards. First, determine if there are any other planets in the same sign as that planet. If so, draw a line from these planets to the final dispositor. For example, if Saturn is in Capricorn, and Venus and Neptune are also in Capricorn, it would look like this:

Next, see if any of these planets disposit other planets. For example, are there any planets in Taurus or Libra? If so, Venus would disposit these planets. Likewise, any planets in Pisces? Neptune would disposit those. Draw a line from these planets to Venus or Neptune. If Jupiter were in Libra, and Mercury in Pisces, our flow chart would look like this.

Note that Mercury (in Pisces) and Jupiter (in Libra) are not directly under one another because they are not in the same sign. Since Neptune and Venus are in the same sign (Capricorn), they are drawn one under the other. Saturn is placed by itself at the end of the chain because it is in its own sign.

If Jupiter or Mercury disposes any planets, then we would again trace backwards and show arrows pointing from those planets to Mercury and/or Jupiter. Eventually, you will get to a planet that is not itself the dispositor of any other planet. This means there are no planets occupying the sign which that planet rules. That planet becomes the first link in the chain, the lead runner so to speak. In the above example, if there were no planets in the signs of Sagittarius, Gemini, or Virgo, then Jupiter and Mercury would "co-lead" that chain.

PLANETS IN MUTUAL RECEPTION

Mutual reception involves two planets, each of which is in the sign ruled by the other. For example, in Freud's chart Venus is in the sign of Aries, which Mars rules; and Mars is in the sign of Libra, which Venus rules. Planets in mutual reception are operating on the same frequency. Like two cellular phones tuned into the same wavelength, the planets are in constant communication with one another. Whenever Venus expresses itself, it stimulates Mars, which re-stimulates Venus, and so on in a repeating cycle. The two are locked into a dialogue in which they keep repeating the same message to each other. In this regard, planets in mutual reception operate like a broken record, reciting the same refrain, singing the same old song. Ultimately, it may feel like being caught in a loop (or stuck in a rut). The person just keeps doing the same thing over and over, hopefully getting better at it with time.

318 • INTRODUCTION TO ASTROPSYCHOLOGY

Because the relationship is a self-stimulating one, it can also function like a self-escalating closed system. As each planet looks to the other to fulfill its need, the cycle keeps feeding back on itself so that the planets in question become overstimulated. This is neither good nor bad; it simply means that there is a recurring pattern in the native's behavior that these planets symbolize. It can indicate a subject, for example, with which the person is obsessively preoccupied. Like a core issue or dilemma, it is never too far from the native's thoughts. And because it constitutes a primary focus, the native may develop important skills or insights in regard to the affairs ruled by those planets. There is some kind of psychological link or open channel of communication between the two planets that weaves their respective voices together.

When planets are in mutual reception, it is important to determine if there is any aspect between the two planets. If so, then the nature of the relationship will be qualified by the aspect. If it is an opposition, then Mars and Venus will struggle against one another until they find a way of resolving their conflict, in which case something very good can be achieved. The minister of war (Mars) and the minister of peace (Venus) have to work out a compromise. If there is no aspect between them, then the relationship is more difficult to qualify. Also, when Mars and Venus are in mutual reception then the houses they occupy become linked in a closed, repeating cycle. In Freud's chart, for example, his 6th house Venus is linked to his 11th house Mars. What Freud discovered at work (6th) in his relationships with his clients (Venus) stimulated an ardent desire to initiate (Mars) a radical new movement (11th house) called psychoanalysis; Freud spearheaded a group of followers—the Vienna group that included Jung—who collectively championed Freud's theories.

FINAL DISPOSITORS

Recall that dispositorships establish a chain of transitional linkages, with each planet constituting a scene in an unfolding story. One scene leads to another as the story unfolds. A planet's action is triggered by the planet it disposes, and this action, in turn, stimulates the next planet in the chain. But every story has to end somewhere, and this somewhere is called the final dispositor. The final dispositor is, in effect, the final scene of the story (before the story repeats itself).

In Freud's chart, Neptune is in its own sign, Pisces. This means that no other planets can disposit Neptune and, therefore, Neptune is Freud's final dispositor. A final dispositor has added strength, dignity, and importance. As the final scene in Freud's life story, all action has been leading toward this planet. This is not to imply that Freud did not get to Neptune until the end of his life. An astrological chart tells an ongoing story that tends to repeat itself in various ways throughout the course of the life.

A final dispositor is like a final determinant in the decision making process. If Neptune could speak, it would say "the buck stops here." As Neptune is the final purpose, or final cause of Freud's chart, it acts like a lure that pulls the life forward toward the ideal that the final dispositor symbolizes. When a planet is in its own sign, it functions like a hand in a glove. It is a perfect fit. Therefore, the final dispositor symbolizes a psychological function that at least potentially can approach perfection. It is the ideal most realizable, thus the head of the board, the policy maker, the bottom line. If there is no final dispositor, there may be no bottom line; that is, there is no final motive around which the life circles. In fact, the person may be going in circles or lack an ultimate guiding ideal. It is certainly not unusual, however, for a chart to be without a final dispositor, so one should not make too much of it. Here is an interpretation for Neptune in Pisces as Freud's final dispositor.

> Neptune indicates that the final determinant in your decision making process is a transcendent ideal. The precise nature of this ideal will be indicated by Neptune's house placement and aspects. Suffice to say that a striving for infinite love and beauty is the bottom line for you.

> Even if other parts of your chart indicate that you struggle against your own spiritual longings, on some level you know there is more to life than can be perceived through the senses. You may seek an image of God in an artistic medium, such as film or music, or you may seek the infinite by exploring the unconscious and the world of dreams and fantasy. Perhaps you embody a spiritual ideal by helping the less fortunate in some way.

Of course, the tried and true path is a spiritual practice that involves prayer, meditation, and humble devotion to the divine. To the degree that you allow yourself to be the instrument of a will and consciousness higher than your own, you will fulfill your destiny.

CO-FINAL DISPOSITORS

If you have two or more planets that are in their own sign, then you have co-final dispositors. Co-final dispositors share decision making power. If each planet disposes its own chain of planets, then it is like two relay races occurring simultaneously that constitute shifting centers of action. If the co-final dispositors are in aspect, they signify conflicting or harmonizing tendencies depending upon the aspect. If they are not in aspect, the planets may act as if they are divided into two camps, each one headed by a different dispositor. The result may be a personality at odds with itself or with a tendency to follow two distinctly different lines of action.*

Dispositorships operate like a chain of command. Each planet must pass on authority to the planet that disposes it, until the final dispositor ends the chain. However, some chains are longer than others. When there is more than one planet in its own sign, the ultimate final dispositor is the planet that disposes the longer chain.

Figure 21 shows the chart of a man who exemplifies this tendency toward two distinctly separate lines of action. Note that his Neptune, Uranus, and Virgo planets lead to Mercury in the 8th as the co-final dispositor. The heavy 8th house emphasis suggests a strong involvement with 8th house issues—the underworld, sex, crisis intervention work, and financial dealings. Conversely, his Saturn and Libra planets lead to Venus in the 9th as the other co-final dispositor. The heavy Libra, 9th house emphasis of this group suggests an interest in leisure, travel, academia, and the pursuit of truth and justice. Whereas the 8th house grouping of planets is rather heavy, deep, dark, and intense, the 9th house group shows just the opposite trend—something airy, light, and elevated.

---

* This kind of situation can also occur when two or more groups of planets do not have co-final dispositors, but never-the-less constitute two separate lines of action.

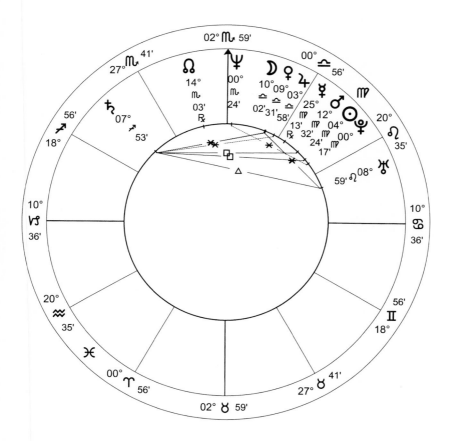

Figure 21: Chart of Prostitute

The planet that ties the two groups together is Saturn, as it both squares the Virgo group and sextiles the Libra group. This man worked as a high class male prostitute and made large amounts of money off his rich clients (up to $150,000 per/year with no taxes), which reflected his 8th house emphasis, but he also spent an enormous amount of time traveling to leisure resorts, socializing with the upper classes, and pursuing advanced academic degrees at a number of different graduate schools, which reflected the Libra/9th house emphasis.

These two distinctly different lines of action are reflected in his flow chart. On the one hand, his career involved working in the sex industry

(Saturn square Sun, Pluto, and Mars in the 8th) where he was coldly efficient in servicing his clients; on the other hand, he was equally ambitious on an academic level, studying to attain his law degree so that he could work as a defense attorney (Saturn sextile Venus, Moon, and Jupiter in the 9th). Saturn seemed to enable him to parry a rather sleazy, underworld involvement in sex and prostitution into a life of leisure, abundant travel, and higher education. His flow chart looks like this:

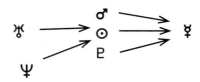

8th House Group

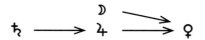

9th House Group

SIGNIFICATORS

Not only do planets disposit other planets, they signify houses as well. The key to this process lies in sign rulerships. We have already explored how planets rule particular signs. The significator of a house is simply the planet that rules the sign that is on the cusp of that house.

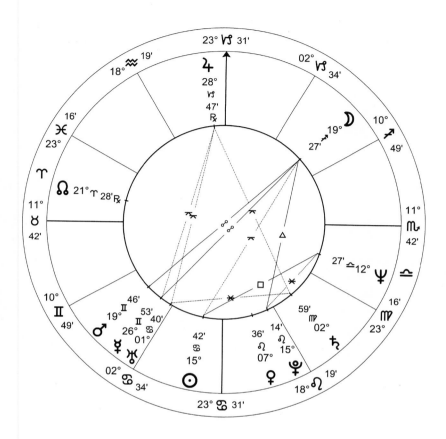

Figure 22: Example Chart

Recall that in an actual chart, any sign can be on any house cusp. The arrangement of zodiacal signs in relation to house cusps is determined by the moment of birth. Because the earth rotates on its axis, a new sign appears on the horizon every two hours. The horizon marks the cusp of the first house, or what we call the Ascendant (Rising Sign), so named because it was rising on the eastern horizon when the native was born.

In Chapter Five, it was stated that when a sign is on the cusp of a house it means that the need represented by that sign is associated with the circumstances of that house. In the example chart of Figure

22, Capricorn is on the cusp of the 9th house. Thus the Capricorn need for structure and control would, in part, be fulfilled through 9th house activities—philosophy, religion, ethics, and the like. These activities would need to be structured and organized into a system experienced in some concrete form. One's beliefs may be rigid and conservative. But where does this lead the individual? What happens next?

For this, we have to look at the sign and house placement of the planet that rules Capricorn. Since this is Saturn, and Saturn is in Virgo in the 5th house, then the 9th and the 5th would be tied together. Saturn, in effect, would be the significator of the 9th house. Therefore, the Capricorn need for perfection, associated with an ethical belief system, would somehow be fulfilled through a 5th house activity. In short, everything we earlier said about Saturn in Virgo in the 5th (in Chapter Five) would still apply, except we now have the added factor of the 9th house to consider. Hence, we know the origin of the need to structure a creative project in a highly detailed and technical (Virgo) fashion. We can now be more specific about exactly what this person needs to create.

Because Saturn comes from the 9th house, and therefore is obligated to the 9th, we can legitimately expect that our creative project will have something to do with 9th house concerns. Again, this would involve philosophy, religion, theory—in short, the pursuit and dissemination of a particular truth. The individual's creative project might involve a highly structured (Saturn in Virgo) philosophical belief system, perhaps the construction of a theoretical model of some sort (9th house).

Note in our sample chart that Capricorn is on the cusp of the 9th house *and* the 10th house. Also, Jupiter is in the sign of Capricorn. This means that Saturn, as the ruler of Capricorn, is the significator of both the 9th and 10th houses as well as being the dispositor of Jupiter.*

Let us pull back even further and see where Jupiter originates. As the ruler of Sagittarius, Jupiter would disposit all planets in Sagittarius and be the significator of the house that has Sagittarius on its cusp. In the chart we are considering, Sagittarius would be on the cusp of the

---

* Sometimes one sign is on the cusp of two adjacent houses; e.g., this chart has 3°♑ on the 9th and 24°♑ on the 10th. Thus, Saturn is the significator of both houses. Sometimes a house completely swallows one sign, which then does not appear on any house cusp. In Figure 22 [change], for example, Aries is "intercepted" in the 12th house. This means the affairs of that house have two rulers, i.e., both Neptune and Mars are the significators of the 12th house.

8th. Again, what does all this mean? Let's take an overview of the situation and consider some of the possible outcomes that might flow from the houses, planets, and signs mentioned so far. By doing so, hopefully some sort of theme will emerge that ties all these factors together.

Because we are only considering three houses (8th, 10th, and 5th) and two planets (Saturn and Jupiter), this theme will necessarily be incomplete. Nevertheless, these factors represent a significant portion of the chart and thus should provide some understanding of how dispositorships and significators combine to make "the whole greater than the sum of its parts."

A clear-cut formulation of the factors we are considering will help us get started. Remembering that signs are needs, planets verbs, and houses areas of experience, astrologically the formula reads: "As a consequence of Sagittarius on the 8th, I Jupiter in Capricorn in the 10th. This subsequently leads me to Saturn in Virgo in the 5th." Starting at the beginning, we recall that the 8th house corresponds to the sign Scorpio, which has to do with transformation and catharsis. Factors associated with the 8th generally constitute an area of risk and danger; not because they are inherently risky and dangerous, but because they are subjectively perceived in this context. Consequently, whatever signs and planets are connected to the 8th may be (1) repressed because personally taboo, or (2) expressed in defiance of the dangers that are believed to be inherent. In either case, there is likely to be risk involved.

Sagittarius represents the quest for meaning and significance. It symbolizes our religious impulse, the need to believe in something greater than ourselves. With Sagittarius on the 8th, this suggests that matters of faith are in some way associated with danger. One's capacity to believe in a higher power may be repressed, perhaps expressed as an atheistic stance, or expressed regardless of the danger felt. Because matters of faith constitute a risk, the actual doctrine chosen by this individual is likely to be consistent with the subjective association; it will, in effect, be a dangerous doctrine. Why dangerous? Because the beliefs chosen may in some way be condemned and prohibited by the established powers of society. Like the Communist manifestos of the McCarthy era, these beliefs may have a quality of the forbidden about them. Truth for this individual may have to do with occult knowledge or constitute a hidden mystery that needs to be exposed and brought to the surface. Whatever the subject, it has a quality of taboo.

As a consequence, the expression of Sagittarian energy would have the character of something erupting up out of the shadows—a forbidden truth. Further, these beliefs are likely to have a powerful and transformative effect. Convictions would be expressed with passion and intensity, not because they are truer, but because subjectively this is how truth is experienced.

As ruler of Sagittarius and significator of the 8th house, Jupiter in Capricorn in the 10th constitutes the next step of the process. If Sagittarius is the need to believe, then Jupiter is the urge to teach. Jupiter represents the verbs to theorize, to proselytize, and to proclaim as true. The 10th house has to do with career and the ultimate impact one has upon society. Because it corresponds to the sign Capricorn (the natural ruler of the 10th), it is connected with the need to attain status and distinction. Factors associated with the 10th will in some way characterize one's profession. Deriving out of the 8th and thus associated with danger, Jupiter in the 10th suggests that the forbidden belief system will be made public. It will, in effect, be the vehicle through which career is launched.

Because Jupiter is in Capricorn, the manner in which this belief system is promulgated will be conservative, structured and organized. The heavy Capricorn/10th house emphasis suggests it is very important that whatever this individual has to teach be respectable and of high quality, regardless of its questionable origin and implications (taboo quality). Quite likely, then, this individual would construct an elaborate theoretical model to house his beliefs. This model would further serve as a platform for their dissemination. As nearly as possible, he would want his model to be perfect—perfect in the sense of being the best, and perfect in the sense of having a powerful and lasting impact upon society.

JUPITER QUINCUNX MERCURY

Once Jupiter's origins are traced back to its dispositor and signified house, and Jupiter's sign and house position is fully interpreted, the next step is to interpret Jupiter's aspects. Although aspects were discussed in Chapter Eight, we will explore Jupiter's aspects here for the sake of illustrating how to tie all the factors together in a total planetary configuration—in this case, the configuration of Jupiter. The general rule is that a planet's aspects should be thoroughly delineated before moving on to its dispositor.

In effect, a planet is like a scene in which the main character (the planet being delineated) is having a dialogue with other characters in the story. Jupiter's motivation (back story) comes from the house it signifies and any planets it might disposit, while the style and context of its behavior is symbolized by its sign and house position. Aspects, however, tell us how Jupiter is getting along with other characters in the personal narrative, which are actually aspects of one self. Are they allies, friends, supporters, potential partners, antagonists, or adversaries with whom one must resolve a conflict? Again, once these relationships are delineated, the next step in the story is Jupiter's own dispositor—in this case, Saturn.

Note that Jupiter is the focal planet of a Yod, which involves four planets—an opening quincunx from Mercury in the 2nd, a closing quincunx to Uranus on the cusp of the 3rd, and an opening quincunx to Saturn in the 5th. Typically, a Yod involves three planets: two of which are in sextile, and a third that forms quincunxes to the other two. In this case, Jupiter quincunxes three planets, two of which are conjunct (Mercury and Uranus), both of which sextile Saturn.

Opening quincunxes are aspects of adjustment, whereas closing quincunxes are aspects of transformation.* Accordingly, Jupiter will be required to continuously adjust and transform itself over the course of the life. In effect, Jupiter is under considerable stress, which requires it to work harder in order to satisfy its operative need for meaning, truth, and justice. This is interesting in light of Jupiter's position at the top of the chart conjunct the Midheaven. Clearly, Jupiter is an important planet that signifies an ongoing struggle in the context of career and reputation.

With regard to its opening quincunx to Mercury, Jupiter has a dilemma. This, in effect, is the hallmark of the opening quincunx: both planets regard one another as a problem to be solved. There is a

---

* Recall that an aspect derives its meaning from the nature of the sign to which it corresponds in the natural zodiac. Thus, opening quincunxes have a Virgo quality, and closing quincunxes have a Scorpio connotation.

feeling of worry, concern, or anxiety vis-à-vis the functions that the two planets symbolize. Because Jupiter and Mercury rule signs—Sagittarius and Gemini—that oppose one another in the natural zodiac, they have a natural complementary relationship. Jupiter is about theory; Gemini is about facts. Jupiter believes; Mercury questions. Mercury learns; Jupiter teaches. It's the classic dialectic between science and religion, fact and faith.

Mercury's rulership of Virgo, however, adds a further tension to the mix, for Virgo is the Doubting Thomas of the zodiac. It naturally looks for flaws, errors, and mistakes—in this case, in Jupiter's doctrine. Jupiter's aspect to Mercury is itself a Virgo angle (opening quincunx); thus, we have a repeating theme: Jupiter aspects the planet that rules Virgo, and the angle itself is Virgonian. It cannot be too strongly emphasized that a person's life and character is defined most clearly by such repeating themes. If something is important, it will generally show up in multiple ways in the chart.

Jupiter's quincunxial problem is with Mercury's tendency to accumulate data without sufficient vision to see what the information *means*. From Jupiter's perspective, Mercury may accumulate large amounts of knowledge; yet, never arrive at a valid conclusion. Jupiter expands the thinking function and inclines Mercury toward big ideas—religions, philosophies, ideologies, and laws. It renders communication not merely informative, but persuasive. However, this does not necessarily mean that one's thinking is correct.

As with any aspect, one can view the relationship from either planet's perspective. With the quincunx, Jupiter is apt to see Mercury as scatterbrained; conversely, Mercury worries that Jupiter is dogmatic. The winged messenger insists that a theoretical claim or metaphysical belief be substantiated with empirical evidence—or, at least with sufficient anecdotal evidence to be persuasive.

Accordingly, the native may be obsessively preoccupied with whether and how data can be organized to support a theoretical claim. Mercury would be concerned with this regardless of the specific aspect to Jupiter; however, since it is an opening quincunx, Mercury's worried concern is compounded.

There are other, related problems that can stem from an unintegrated Mercury-Jupiter quincunx. For example, the native may be careless in what he claims to know, sometimes exaggerating the extent of his actual knowledge. Jupiter amplifies Mercury's thinking function and gives it a sense of certainty that may be unwarranted by the native's actual mastery of a subject. Buoyed by Jupiter's gaseous quality, the individual might be just that: full of hot air, glib and convincing, regardless of the quality of his thinking or the actual extent of his knowledge. This is the proverbial know-it-all. He may *seem* informed, but the depth of his knowledge about a given topic may be paper-thin.

In a quincunx, both planets tend to be relatively unconscious with respect to the other. Accordingly, each planet's influence operates outside of awareness. This suggests that the native may not be aware that he is exaggerating the extent of his knowledge. Since what is unconscious generally gets projected, one is apt to notice negative Mercury-Jupiter traits in others rather than in oneself. This does not mean that the thing noticed is merely illusory. What is noticed may actually be there; however, *that* it is noticed and scanned for like a missile honing in on a target is testament that the aspect is an issue for the native. Moreover, the response to the external condition is apt to be emotionally charged in a negative way *if* he is not conscious of the very same qualities in himself—or, at least the potential for them.

To the extent that such qualities are projected, there is apt to be a carping, critical quality in his response to the affairs ruled by Mercury and Jupiter. The person may be preoccupied with an external problem—unsubstantiated opinions, false beliefs, exaggerated knowledge claims—without any awareness that the same tendencies exist within him. However, as the aspect becomes integrated over time, Mercury and Jupiter will constitute a skill that enables him to solve problems that relate to the aspect in a highly competent manner. For example, he could become an expert in critical thinking skills.

JUPITER QUINCUNX URANUS

A second Jupiter aspect involves a closing quincunx to Uranus. Since the closing quincunx is an aspect of transformation, it is associated with crisis. Each planet regards the other as its shadow; there is a sense of danger, destructiveness, or evil with regard to the other planet's behavior. Together the two planets create a joint concern that combines their respective domains. Yet, each may be perceived by the other as embodying a quality that is extreme.

Whereas Jupiter symbolizes belief systems and ideologies, Uranus symbolizes a wholistic perspective that is oriented toward change and progress. To the extent that the aspect is integrated, there is an ability to assess various theories in an objective manner and abstract what is of universal significance from each. The resulting synthesis may be a totally original conception that is inclusive and integrative of diverse ideas, a multidisciplinary perspective that stresses the need for growth and change. One may formulate a theory of change, or express faith in change, or stress the importance of allowing for change in one's philosophical or political convictions.

Concurrently, there is a tendency to rebel against cultural norms and outmoded beliefs. Conventional systems of thought may be regarded as too subjective, simple, or antiquated. Jupiter-Uranus is an aspect of radical, revolutionary theories, progressive opinions, and unorthodox views, e.g., the person may study a variety of different religious systems and then write a book that provides an integrated overview.

When the closing quincunx is not integrated, some sort of crisis or danger is likely to be perceived that relates to Jupiter and Uranian domains. Two equally negative and mutually contradictory beliefs emerge. Jupiter is apt to regard Uranian perspectives as threatening, crazy, flaky, strange, or eccentric. The emotional response to such ideas may have a quality of life and death. For example, a new theory may be vehemently attacked because it is regarded as both invalid and having a high probability for destructive consequences. Uranus, on the other hand, is likely to regard Jupiter's actions as equally destructive but for different reasons, e.g., a conventional belief system is ridiculed because it is mired in the past, too narrow, provincial, one-sided, or arbitrary. Again, there is an anxious concern that adherents or recipients of such a belief-system may come to harm.

The native may tend to resist new developments in his chosen profession, seeing them as wildly speculative and dangerous. On the other hand, he may abhor conventional religion and orthodox theories in general. Ideally speaking, the closing quincunx is an aspect of healing and rebirth. To the extent the native can integrate Jupiter and Uranus, he will incorporate various perspectives from outside his field and use them to synthesize a new theory—an innovative, wholistic model that focuses on growth, development, and evolution in some way (Uranus), which is then promulgated with an emotional intensity and passion befitting the closing quincunx.

JUPITER QUINCUNX SATURN

The final aspect involving Jupiter is an opening quincunx to Saturn. Again, an opening quincunx is a Virgo angle that connotes a problem between the respective planets. For example, Saturn may regard Jupiter's faith and convictions as ungrounded and of dubious validity. Jupiter, on the other hand, may regard Saturn's conservative, traditional approach to wisdom as hopelessly narrow and limited to material reality.

This aspect symbolizes a dynamic tension between two fundamentally different principles. Jupiter represents expansion and one's capacity for faith. Saturn signifies contraction and the tendency toward doubt. Whereas Jupiter sees purpose and meaning in life, Saturn sees only limitation and duty. If Jupiter is theoretical and abstract, Saturn is realistic and concrete. Jupiter affirms; Saturn negates. Optimism versus pessimism, joy versus distress, hope versus despair—each planet will challenge the other, each will tend to overfunction within its respective sphere of activity until somehow the problem between them is resolved.

Saturn's influence is to render Jupiter's views more conservative. This does not necessarily mean that the native's philosophy will, in fact, be conservative; it only means this is Saturn's contribution to the mix. Remember, Jupiter must reconcile itself to Mercury and Uranus as well, which have a decidedly different kind of impact. In any event, Saturn has a tendency to throw cold water on the natural faith of Jupiter, creating doubt where there should be hope.

We might surmise that to some extent, at least, the native is a hardcore realist when it comes to philosophy. He might not easily believe a truth claim unless its validity can be empirically demonstrated, and that usually means within the laboratory of his own personal experience. This is all the more likely given that Jupiter is *in* Saturn's sign; thus, Jupiter is not only in Capricorn, but forms a quincunx to its own dispositor (Saturn). I call this being 'ill-disposed', which I will have more to say about later.

Perhaps on some level the native worries that there is no meaning, purpose, or higher power in the Universe. He might not be aware of this doubt consciously, but Saturn will force him to test, refine, and solidify his faith until it is an unassailable bulwark that can hold back the black tide of disbelief. In effect, the strength of his convictions may be compensatory to unconscious doubts, which must continually be refuted.

Internal conflicts generally show up via a conflict with some external situation. He could be concerned, for instance, with irresponsible truth claims in his profession (10th house). Perhaps he worries that certain practices are inherently untruthful or unethical. Saturn demands perfection; thus, when directed at Jupiterian concerns for ethics and morality, there is a tendency to work diligently toward the achievement of something that will both solve the issue and stand the test of time. A formal, legal-type document, such as an organizational code of ethics, would be fitting, for it provides a solution to a problem—e.g., fraudulent claims or unethical practices within his profession. These are just possibilities, of course, but they serve to illustrate how the conflict might play itself out.

The native might also have a tendency to get caught up in challenges to the validity of his beliefs. If Saturnian skeptics refute the truth of his convictions, or materialistic science contests the legitimacy of his faith, or when an atheist argues that life is meaningless and without any overarching purpose, he may feel compelled to enter the fray. Again, all of this would merely be the exteriorization of the intrapsychic conflict that Jupiter quincunx Saturn represents. The outer situation provides a vehicle for working out the inner struggle.

Saturn's inhibiting, depriving influence can create a craving for truth, and this craving can be felt in any Jupiter field that involves questions of right and wrong or true/false—politics, religion, philosophy, law, even advertising. Sometimes this aspect seems to block efforts to broaden the mind, or at least to delay the acquisition of wisdom. Such frustration may be the very thing that drives the native to educate himself through long hours of disciplined study.

Always, Saturn will test the native's faith in the meaning and purpose of life (or whether there *is* any purpose and meaning). Unable to accept a doctrine at face value, he will likely feel compelled to examine and define in practical terms the nature of his beliefs, for these will be central to his career (10th). In effect, he has to carve out his own truth over the long haul, slowly chipping away at doubts and polishing ideas until, finally, he has sculpted a theoretical structure that is solid and defensible. These are hard-won truths that once established are likely to be unshakable.

Once integrated, the opening quincunx represents a method or skill that enhances competencies related to Saturn and Jupiter's combined functions. The native may feel compelled to develop skills in critical thinking, theory building, ethics, research methodologies, epistemology, and other such academic disciplines. These skills would enable him to utilize his Saturn-Jupiter functions in a systematic, methodical manner in the service of his community, for that is the nature of an integrated opening quincunx.

THE FOLLOWING SCENE

Once Jupiter's signified house, disposed planets, sign and house position, and various aspects are delineated, what next? As ruler of Capricorn and dispositor of Jupiter in the 10th, Saturn holds the key to the next scene of the story. In Chapter Five, we explored how Saturn in Virgo in the 5th suggests a creative project structured in some useful form. But now we have other variables to consider. What kind of project? What purpose will it serve? Since Saturn in the 5th derives from Jupiter in the 10th, we know that creativity will in some way be in service to career; vocation will fulfill itself through the 5th house, which represents an area of performance and creative self-expression. Since career ($\mathrm{2\!\!\!+\,V\!\!3}$ 10th) involves the propagation of a taboo belief system ($\mathrm{D\,\nearrow}$ 8th), we can assume that the creative project ($\mathrm{\hbar\,\eta}$ performance) of the 5th may serve as a vehicle for the dissemination of this knowledge.

How, specifically, will this knowledge be presented? Virgo is concerned with efficiency and is characterized by a need to dissect, analyze, and break a system down into minute detail to see how all the parts work. Further, Virgo is pragmatic; it is chiefly concerned with how something can be used to provide a service to others. Consequently, Saturn in Virgo suggests that the theoretical model will be broken down into component parts, analyzed for potential flaws, and reconstituted to be utilized in a serviceable fashion. Virgo also suggests that our model will be detailed and precise. Taking all the preceding factors into consideration, we come up with the following summary statement:

> As a consequence of my need to experience truth in a context that involves risk and danger, my career involves promoting a theoretical model of the human condition whose implications are bizarre and threatening to the established powers of society (academia). At the same time, this belief system will be structured and organized to attain maximum respectability. As a consequence of my need to attain status through the propagation of my beliefs, I am led to construct a creative project that will present my system in a highly technical, orderly and pragmatic fashion.

By now, the reader will probably have guessed that the chart we have been considering is my own. Hopefully, the foregoing not only explains what these factors mean, but is itself evidence of how they work. Astrology is my forbidden belief system and outlaw profession; writing is my creative self-expression; and the book you are reading is my creative project that explains the use of astrology as a diagnostic tool.

With regard to Jupiter's aspects, Jupiter's quincunx to Mercury reflects my concern as to whether scientific evidence supports or refutes the metaphysical implications of astrology. Science tends to overemphasize facts at the expense of meaning, whereas religion too often ignores facts in defense of faith. Astrology can provide a middle ground, correlating the empirical data of planetary cycles with archetypal patterns in human affairs. Such correlations provide the basis for a wider, more comprehensive theory of our relationship with the divine.

Jupiter's closing quincunx to Uranus is evident in my efforts to regenerate and reform the traditional, archaic theory of astrology by assimilating new ideas that derive from postmodern science and psychology. Whereas traditional astrology tends to be static and fatalistic, a Uranian emphasis on progressive change is implicit in AstroPsychology. My emphasis on how ideas—personal myths—can be empowering or disempowering also reflects the closing quincunx to Uranus. By using astrology as a diagnostic tool, individuals can be liberated from pathogenic ideas that impede their growth and development.

Finally, the quincunx to Saturn is evident in my focus on problems pertaining to research and ethics that compromise our profession. For example, I wrote a book on research methodologies that addresses how to make responsible knowledge claims in astrology that meet reasonable academic standards.[7] This same aspect also inclines me to examine ethical issues in astrology, which is the subject of yet another book.*

All of the above, I submit, are expressive of the aspect. Although the astrological factors involved in my Jupiter configuration will not always manifest themselves in exactly the same way, the details presented here are consistent with the meaning of the symbols involved. Although I wrote the foregoing analysis nearly thirty years ago for my Master's thesis, the situation has not appreciably changed. Content continues to mirror process, as this book should attest. Circumstances may be different to a degree, yet qualitatively they reflect the same needs and drives that dominated my life in 1977.

THE BACK STORY

While Jupiter is always expressing a theory, theory can relate to many things—a theory of relationships, a theory of creativity, a theory of religion, a theory of language, and so on. In my case, the origin of Jupiter's theoretical model is Moon in Sagittarius in the 8th house. The fact that Jupiter comes from the 8th suggests that my theory is going to be motivated by 8th house concerns of healing and transformation. More importantly, its impetus derives from a very personal wound that afflicted my family of origin (Moon). To be specific, the theory is a consequence of a need to heal a religious (Sagittarius) wound (8th) that afflicted my mother, who was both atheistic and alcoholic.

The important thing to remember about dispositorships is that a planet's behavior is, in part, motivated by the planet it disposes. In my chart, Jupiter's behavior is an extension of what the Moon was doing in the 8th. Jupiter is not simply motivated to build a theoretical structure, but to redress a grievance symbolized by Moon in the 8th—namely that my need to belong and to be loved was injured by a moral and religious crisis that occurred in my family of origin (☽ ♐ 8th).

---

* See Perry, G. (2012). *Issues & Ethics in the Profession of Astrology*, which contains an ethics code that I developed for the International Society for Astrological Research (ISAR).

A partial factor underlying my mother's alcoholism was her inability to resolve her religious doubts. Disinclination to believe in God is often symptomatic of a more general problem with Sagittarius-Jupiter—lack of faith that life is unfolding in a purposeful way and governed by a supreme intelligence. It is precisely such faith that enables one to stay positive in the face of life's myriad challenges and disappointments; while adhering to a moral code based on trust that the Universe is just and lawful. Had she a stronger faith, I suspect she could have found a way to manage her emotional pain without alcohol, and to deal with her feelings in a more honest manner. As it was, her atheism left her with no moral compass.*

My forbidden truth was acknowledgment of my mother's alcoholism and the devastating impact it had on our family. Because her emotional pain was denied, and with it the truth of her alcoholism, it was not permissible for anyone to talk about feelings (Moon), though I certainly did my share of acting out. However, there was so much shame and embarrassment associated with her condition that the rest of my family simply buried it. But like any planet in the 8th, it does not go away; it simply festers and gathers steam, looking for a way out of the underworld. That, in effect, is the back story that motivates Jupiter's actions in the 10th.

Since the Moon is in Sagittarius, the way out is Jupiter. Jupiter in the 10th inherited the legacy of a distraught Moon. As Jupiter must *do* something for the Moon, it appropriates a forbidden truth—astrology—and promotes it with an intensity fueled by the affective charge that accumulated around the denial of truth in my family. On a psychological and emotional level, they are inseparably linked. I feel passionate about astrology precisely because I identify with its suppression. Just as the truth and pain of my mother's alcoholism had to be denied, so as a member of modern culture I am invited to deny the truth of astrology. Yet, if the wound to my Moon is to be healed, I cannot condone by silence the suppression of something that I know and *feel* to be true. This is the true motivation behind what Jupiter in the 10th is endeavoring to accomplish.

In effect, my family's unwillingness to confront my mother's

---

* The first and primary tenet of Alcoholics Anonymous is to admit that one is powerless over the effects of alcoholism, and to turn one's life and will over to a higher power.

alcoholism, along with the dishonesty and moral bankruptcy that underlay her condition (☽ ♐ 8th), is the motivation behind my desire to construct a theory of healing that involves a forbidden truth. Whether disclosing the naked truth of my mother's alcoholism or arguing the validity of astrology, the feeling and meaning is analogous.

Once the theoretical model is constructed (♃ ♑ 10th), this, in turn, leads me to write/teach in a creative context (♄ ♍ 5th ✶ ☿ ♊). The product of my 5th house creativity is a diagnostic (Virgonian) tool designed to support the applied use of astrology in a counseling setting. In each instance, one can see how the function of the dispositor logically follows the activities of the planet it disposes.

FROM PROTOTYPE TO ANALOGUE

One of the keys to finding the life script in the chart is to realize that the whole chart is childhood. Right from birth the individual begins to experience the objective conditions that the chart symbolizes. At any point in time, his lived experience can be seen as a microcosm of his entire life story. Childhood will encapsulate and activate the major themes that the individual will be reliving and working out over the course of adulthood.

Planets symbolize various characters and roles that are embodied in key childhood relationships. There will be a *part* of father that embodies the Sun, a part of him that is Saturnian, another part Martian, and so on. Likewise, the mother will fulfill various roles, too, some of which will overlap with the father's roles, e.g., the mother will fulfill a Saturnian role as well as a Lunar and Venusian one. Siblings will embody Mercury functions, grandparents Jupiter, and so on.

No one planet or aspect captures the whole of a major character in the life. Relationships with important figures are too complex to be reduced to a single dimension of the chart. Key individuals like father or mother perform certain roles that embody some archetypes more than others; however, they can be characterized by other planets, too, e.g., a father can be a Jupiter figure if and when he expresses his philosophical convictions. Moreover, a child's total experience of a planetary archetype will involve multiple relationships with different figures over the course of the life. The Sun can be reflected in an aspect of the father, mother, an older sibling, a sports hero, one's best friend, a romantic interest, a coach, and so on.

As the child experiences planetary archetypes embodied in key figures, he or she attributes meaning to these experiences. If experiences and subsequent meanings vis-à-vis a particular archetype are consistently negative, this becomes the basis for later recapitulations of the original pattern. By re-casting the story with new people that stand in for old—like a play that changes actors but retains the same plot—there is an opportunity to remythologize, i.e., to become conscious of the story one is living. This enables one to intentionally experiment with alternative behaviors in a kind of trial and error learning process. In so doing, the native is empowered to redirect the personal narrative toward more satisfying outcomes.

Perhaps the main value of astrology is that it enables one to objectify his or her story. Patterns can be recognized and negative beliefs can be questioned and eventually disconfirmed. In the process, the individual is slowly liberated from a pattern in which his or her life was previously mired.

THE STORY AS A WHOLE

In previous sections, I've tried to demonstrate how to delineate a single planet in the context of the chart as a whole. The first step in my own chart was to determine the house Jupiter signifies and what planet(s) it disposes. The next step was to interpret Jupiter's house and sign position, and then its aspects. Finally, Jupiter's dispositor (Saturn) is considered. This leads to the full delineation of that planet, and so on until one reaches the final dispositor. In short, the chart represents a sequence of action, like scenes in a film.

The purpose of tracing dispositors is to reveal the plot or story line of the chart. In effect, the flow of dispositors reveals the structure of action and chain of command; each planet commands its dispositor to carry on the mission. Dispositorships and significators help us to see that a chart has coherence as a whole. There should be an interconnectedness and internal consistency among the parts that makes the story intelligible. Otherwise, one is apt to interpret the chart as a series of paragraphs that have no discernible relation to one another. This would be like seeing a movie wherein each scene has no logical relationship to scenes that cover before or after.

The ultimate goal is to delineate the entire structure of action, from the lead planet to the final dispositor. In the flow chart below, one can see that Saturn is disposed by Mercury, which is the final dispositor. Mars, too, is in the sign of Gemini; thus, Mercury also disposes Mars. To complete the interpretation of my chart, I would need to consider all of Mercury and Mars' aspects, especially the conjunction of Mercury to Uranus and their sextiles to Saturn, as these make up the bottom portion of the yod to Jupiter. Below is a depiction of my flow chart and a brief summation of my story as a whole.

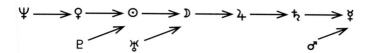

I work (6th) with the unconscious (Neptune) of my clients as it is expressed through dreams and synchronicities. As a symbolic language, astrology helps me gain access to the spiritual realm (Neptune). Relationships with my clients (Libra) lead me to explore their childhood memories involving early experiences of love and attachment (Venus in 4th). My job as a marriage and family therapist entails the healing (Pluto) of relationships (Venus) that are expressions of old wounds that originate in my client's families of origin (Pluto in 4th house). My work (6th house) also requires that I explore my own family of origin issues.

These experiences, in turn, lead me to communicate what I have learned about families. I hope to earn recognition and validation for this knowledge (Sun in Cancer in 3rd). Such efforts to express myself, however, stimulate deep feelings and personal memories of my own childhood traumas, which involved growing up with an alcoholic mother who was in great pain (Moon in 8th). There is a part of me that feels quite radical about the need to impart information (3rd) that liberates people (Uranus) from unfamiliarity with dysfunctional family systems (Uranus in Cancer conjunct 3rd house cusp).

Because no one in my family was willing to acknowledge the truth of my mother's illness and its destructive impact on the family, I have strong feelings about the denial of truth in general

(Moon in Sagittarius in 8ᵗʰ), but especially as it relates to an immoral situation of childhood abuse. Often, I have to help my clients in precisely the area that I was wounded myself—that is, to heal their capacity for self-care and honest, direct expression of emotional needs (Moon in Sag in 8ᵗʰ). In other words, I labor to help them open to the truth of their own feelings and their personal past.

Suppression of the truth is something I have strong feelings about. In my career, therefore, I endeavor to build a highly organized, theoretical model (Jupiter in Capricorn in 10ᵗʰ) that confronts the denial of another truth—the truth of astrology— and of its capacity to reveal what lies hidden in the psyche. Sometimes this can be kind of fun, as it provides me opportunities for lecturing and teaching, which I experience as a kind of performance that allows me to be creative in the service of my career (Saturn in 5ᵗʰ).

While I used to become quite anxious and fearful (Saturn) that I would be an incompetent (Virgo) performer (5ᵗʰ), I gradually overcame these fears and now feel more in control when in performance situations. The highly detailed, precise nature of my (Saturn in Virgo) lecture notes comes in handy when I sit down to write articles. My final goal (final dispositor) is to make money (2ⁿᵈ house) as a writer (Mercury in Gemini). Sometimes this requires willingness to fight (Mars) with words (Gemini) in battling prejudices that critics have against astrology. If I have the courage of my convictions, however, perhaps I will eventually turn adversity to advantage and gain the economic security that I seek (Mars in Gemini in 2ⁿᵈ).

As a general rule, when there are two or more planets in the same sign, interpret the dispositor of the preceding planets first and *then* the other planets in that group, one by one. For example, I have two planets in Leo (Venus and Pluto), but Venus is the dispositor of Neptune (the preceding planet); thus, I would interpret Venus first since Pluto does not disposit any planets in my chart. Once I finish interpreting Venus' sign, house, and aspects, I would move on to Pluto. Next would be the Sun, which disposes Pluto and Venus, and so on.

In reality, a chart does not need to be interpreted in quite so formal a way, as most consultations entail focusing on that part of the chart which is most relevant to the client's presenting problem. However, it's useful to know how to do the sequence in the event that one is trying to discern the overall plot structure of the story. Or perhaps the astrologer simply wishes to know the origin (signified house) of a planet that appears central to the client's concern.

TRANSITIONAL PHRASES

What follows is a series of incomplete sentences composed of connecting phrases that tie houses and house significators together. As illustrated, these transitional phrases link the processes represented by the associated signs, planets and houses. When interpreting a chart, it helps to utilize connecting phrases. Starting with the signified sign-house combination, e.g., Sagittarius on the cusp of the 8th, and then moving on to the signifying planet (Jupiter), the structure of the sentence would be one or another version of the following:

- As a result of my need to (sign-house), this leads me to... then...I subsequently (planet-sign-house).
- As a consequence of (sign-house), I am led to (planet-sign-house).
- My need to (sign-house), results in my (planet-sign-house).
- In order to (sign-house), I then ...I must (planet-sign-house).

Of course, the same rules apply when tracing the linkages that occur between planets. For example, I could say: "As a result of my Moon in Sagittarius in the 8th, I am led to Jupiter Capricorn in the 10th." Although the reasoning is the same, an alternative would be to start the sentence with the dispositor and then trace backwards to the planet it disposes and the house it signifies (the back story). I could then say: "I Jupiter in Capricorn in the 10th because I Moon in Sagittarius in the 8th." The structure of our astrological sentence would take the following form(s):

- I (planet-sign-house). This stems from my need to (planet-sign) in a context of (house).
- The fact that I (planet-sign-house) is due to my need to (planet-sign) in (house).

With Moon in Sagittarius on the 8th and Jupiter in the 10th, we could say the following.

> My career involves teaching and promoting, in a highly orga-
> nized manner, a theoretical model of the human condition
> (Jupiter in Capricorn in 10th) whose implications are bizarre
> and threatening to the established powers of the academic
> world. This stems from the fact that truth, for me, is subjec-
> tively associated with risk and danger (Sagittarius on the 8th).
> Because there was an emotional wound in my family that
> involved denial of my mother's alcoholism, I have deep and
> intense feelings about the immorality of such denial (Moon in
> Sagittarius in 8th). These feelings fuel my desire to advocate a
> truth—astrology—no matter how unpopular or threatening it
> might be.

THE MAIN POINTS

The sign on a house cusp shows (1) the need that is satisfied through the activities of that house; (2) the manner in which the activities of that house are approached; and (3) the actual content (psychological states, events) of that house. For example, if Capricorn were on the cusp of the 3rd house, then one's need for structure and perfection would be satisfied through communications, writing, language, and learning; the acquisition and communication of information would be approached in a methodical, disciplined manner; and the outcome may be fears of inadequacy around learning, learning blocks, sense of pressure to perform, and overcompensation leading to achievements and distinction within some field of communication. In regard to the third point (content), the process of a sign in a house is always weaker than the process of a planet. Specific, concrete results in a house are seldom apparent from sign alone.

The *significator* of a given house is the planet that rules the sign on the cusp of that house, e.g., if Capricorn were on the cusp of the third, then Saturn would be the significator of the 3rd house. Another way of saying the same thing is that Saturn is the "actual" ruler of the 3rd house for that chart. The actual ruler of a house needs to be distinguished from the "natural" or "archetypal" ruler of a house. Mercury is the natural ruler of the 3rd.

The sign on a house cusp shows the "why" or the *origin* of the process expressed by the significator of that house. The relationship is one of sequential unfoldment; the need of the sign on the cusp of the signified house both precedes and leads to the process of the signifying planet. Similarly, the process of the signifying planet derives from and occurs as a consequence of the need of the sign on the signified house cusp. The signifying planet shows *where* and *how* the process represented by that sign/house will manifest. If Jupiter is in the 10th, for example, and Sagittarius is on the cusp of the 8th, then Jupiter shows where and how the process of Sagittarius in the 8th will manifest.

The process of dispositors is essentially the same as significators, the only difference being that a dispositor rules the sign that the disposed planet occupies, whereas a significator signifies the house that begins with the sign that the signifying planet rules. In my chart, Saturn is the dispositor of Jupiter, just as Jupiter is the dispositor of the Moon. The Moon, therefore, shows the "why" or the origin of the process expressed by Jupiter in the 10th house. Jupiter shows the origin of the process expressed by Saturn in the 5th house, and Saturn shows the origin of the process expressed by Mercury in Gemini in the 2nd house. Because Mercury is in its own sign, it is the "final dispositor," which means that Mercury has the final say. It is the terminal point, the bottom line, the final cause of the whole chart.

Again, my flow chart would look like this:

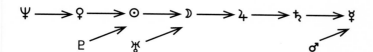

A FLOW CHART

A flow chart can be further analyzed by listing the sign and house position of each planet in their proper order. Follow these steps: (1) list the sign and house position of the "lead" planet; (2) list the house which that planet signifies (Mercury and Venus will signify two houses each); and (3) list the dispositor of the lead planet. Recall that a lead planet is a planet that does not dispose of any other planets;

also, it is not part of a group of planets in the same sign, one of which is a dispositor of another planet(s). If a planet meets these criteria, it can be a lead planet.

Let us suppose, for example, that the Moon is in Pisces in the 10th and there are no planets in Cancer. Also, the Moon is not part of a group of planets in Pisces, one of which could be a dispositor of another planet. The Moon, therefore, can be the lead planet of the chain. Here is a fictional example of a chain that begins with the Moon in Pisces.

Moon in Pisces in 10th

Significator of 2nd

Disposed by Neptune in Libra in 5th

Now, repeat the process by listing the next planet to be delineated (Neptune), but include in this group the planet (Moon) that Neptune disposes.

Neptune in Libra in 5th

Significator of 10th

Dispositor of Moon in Pisces in 10th

Disposed by Venus in Capricorn in 8th

Again, note that this group includes any planets that Neptune disposes—in this case, Moon in Pisces. In the first example, the lead planet by definition does not disposit any other planets.

The next planet to be listed would be Venus in Capricorn *unless* there are additional planets in the sign of Libra. If so, we would need to list those planets first. In other words, the next group after Neptune in Libra would be any other planet also in the sign of Libra. For example, if Mars were in Libra, it would look like this:

Mars in Libra in 5th

Significator of 11th

Disposed by Venus in Capricorn in 8th

Since Mars is not the dispositor of any planets in Aries, one might think that Mars could be a lead planet. Remember, however, Mars is part of a group of planets in the same sign, one of which (Neptune) *is* the dispositor of another planet. Thus, Mars cannot be a lead planet.

If there are no other planets in Libra, we can move on to Venus in

Capricorn. First, list its sign and house position (Capricorn in 8th), then the house it signifies (the 5th), the planets it disposes (Neptune and Mars), and the planet that is its dispositor (Saturn). This group should look like this:

Venus in Capricorn in 8th
Significator of 5th
Dispositor of Neptune in Libra in 5th
Dispositor of Mars in Libra in 5th
Disposed by Saturn in Gemini in 1st

Saturn then becomes the next planet to be listed. Each planet constitutes a separate grouping, e.g., Neptune is one group; Venus will be the next, Saturn the next, and so on until all ten planetary bodies are listed in their proper order. Technically, these groupings of planetary factors constitute a *configuration*—the arrangement of all factors that pertain to a particular planet. An interpretation of any one planet, e.g., Neptune, should strive to:

- Delineate the signified house and the disposed planet (Moon in Pisces in 10th).
- Connect the above to the significator and dispositor of that house and planet (Neptune in Libra in 5th). This statement should incorporate Neptune's sign and house position.
- Relate the above to the dispositor of *that* planet. Again, this statement should incorporate the dispositor's sign and house position (Venus in Capricorn in 8th).

Just like transitional linkages in a good script relate one scene to the next, so an astrological interpretation should establish a sequential connection between planetary actions. In the example above, the Moon should be followed by Neptune; Neptune should lead to Venus, and so on. Here is one possible interpretation of this group of planets.

In my career (10th house), I seek infinite love and beauty (Pisces) and work toward creating an ideal society. This involves caring (Moon) for people whom I perceive as less fortunate than myself—e.g., victims, the poor, the homeless, or the disadvantaged (Pisces).

This, in turn, leads me to involve myself in a creative project (5th house) that expresses my most sublime longings for a better world. I utilize my imagination and artistic talents (Neptune) to inspire others to share my vision—a vision that focuses on fairness, beauty, and cooperation (Libra) between all people. I am particularly drawn to creative performances that give expression to ideals that elevate the feelings of the audience and move us to be more compassionate human beings. This is especially meaningful when such creative expression can further my career (10th house).

My artistic self-expression stimulates a need for intimacy and social relations in general (Venus). When it comes to relationships, I can be very ambitious and practical (Venus in Capricorn). I want a partner (Venus) who is successful and mature (Capricorn). Ideally, such a relationship will increase my sense of power (8th house) in the world, especially financial power. Possibly my creative self-expression (5th) will result in a cooperative financial venture that will enrich my life (Venus in 8th). On the other hand, I am wary of people who may exploit or abuse me in the name of love. Thus I must be careful that my ambitions don't draw me into relationships that are destructive (Venus in 8th). These fears must be resolved before I can give myself fully to another.

Note how in the above example the interpretation starts with the 10th house, moves to the 5th, and then to the 8th. It goes back and forth between these houses in an effort to tie the factors together in a way that makes sense. Keep in mind that the chart tells a story; thus a good interpretation will relate the motivations of a planet to the house it signifies and the planet(s) it disposes.

Like signs on house cusps, planets in houses show (1) the process that is expressed within the context of that house, (2) the manner in which the activities of that house are approached, and (3) the actual content (events) of that house. In the previous example of Neptune in Libra in the 5th, the process was to imagine something beautiful and then inspire others by expressing one's imagination through a creative project (♆ ♎ 5th). The manner in which the creative activity of the 5th is approached is again Neptunian, e.g., an imaginative, inspirational, and idealistic expression of Libran beauty. This way of behaving occurs in the context of creative self-expression—a creative project of some sort.

The actual content of the action can vary enormously and thus is difficult to predict. One can only say that it will be consistent with the range of possibilities indicated by the planets, signs, and houses involved. The philosopher-astrologer Richard Tarnas has Neptune in Libra in the 5th. He uses multi-media presentations combining music and image to reveal the creative styles of famous musicians and artists whose astrological charts he is seeking to explain. By combining music, image, and spirituality (Neptune), artistic beauty (Libra), and creative performance (5th house), Tarnas' multi-media presentation is a summary product of Neptune in Libra in the 5th. As his Neptune also disposes his Sun in Pisces in the 10th, this imaginative use of music and image is in the service of his career (10th house) and his need for self-esteem and creativity (Sun).

Another example is Martin Luther King who has Neptune in Virgo in the 5th. His famous "I have a dream" speech expressed a spiritual vision (Neptune) as a solution to a social problem (Virgo) in a dramatic, emotional style that was as entertaining (5th house) as it was uplifting. King's Neptune was the significator of his 12th house and the dispositor of Moon in Pisces in the 12th. This obligates whatever Neptune does creatively (5th house) to a spiritual vision of an ideal society—a kind of heaven on earth (12th house)—wherein all people care for and protect each other (Moon) in an all-inclusive, undifferentiated love (Pisces). In so doing, a spiritual and emotional unity is achieved, i.e., hatred, discrimination, and oppression are transcended. This vision, of course, is what his dramatic speech portrayed.

When a planet is the significator or "ruler" of one of more houses in a chart, those houses will form a kind of background motivation (back-story) for the process of that planet. A planet that signifies a house is *obligated* to that house. Like an ambassador for a foreign country, the significator is beholden to the affairs of the house it signifies; the business of that house will be an integral part of what the signifying planet attempts to accomplish in its current locale. One house, in effect, gets superimposed over the other; they become fused together (associated) in the psyche, the signified house forming a kind of backdrop to the activities of the house the significator occupies.

An example would be Capricorn on the cusp of the 3rd house, with Saturn in Pisces in the 5th house. This could be described in the following way.

> One's need for perfection in communication (Capricorn in 3rd) is expressed through creative works (5th house). These creative works may involve an ambitious, highly organized project expressed in an imaginative manner with possible spiritual overtones (Saturn in Pisces).

Although we could speculate further about this planetary placement, and perhaps write several paragraphs on possible outcomes, the above statement captures the essence of the process. In looking at a chart, there are many possible expressions that would be consistent with the meaning of planetary placements. It follows that it is impossible to know exactly how a person will be living their chart. As always, this underscores a major point of psychological astrology: we can know the process of a planet, i.e., the psychological drives and goals, but its manifest content is a matter of speculation.

In the above example, a person might write an instructional manual for children that has lots of pictures and imaginative stories; or she could be a music teacher in an elementary school who organizes children in the performance of musicals—staged productions that involve children singing and dancing for their parents; or the person might be the head of an English Department at a local college who organizes a curriculum for the teaching of poetry. He could be interested in the tradition of poetry as a means of communication, perhaps even write a book on the subject or organize a forum for aspiring poets to read their works.

Again, the possibilities are endless, yet all of the elements of Capricorn on the 3rd with Saturn in Pisces in the 5th are implicit in the above descriptions. In each example, the ambition (Capricorn) to teach or communicate information (3rd house) is implicit within the creative work of Saturn in the 5th. The creative project in each instance is an expression of the Saturnian principle of authority, organization, and achievement. And each expression of the Saturnian project involves Pisces—a picture book with imaginative stories, a musical production with dancing and singing, and a curriculum designed for the teaching and performing of poetry.

BEING WELL OR ILL DISPOSED

In the previous section, we examined how to list the sequence of dispositorships by grouping planetary factors into a configuration, beginning with the lead planet's sign and house, the house it signifies, and then its dispositor. Subsequent groups in the chain would begin with the dispositor's sign and house, the house it signifies, the planet(s) it disposes, and finally its dispositor. Each group of planetary factors is analogous to a scene in a movie. However, to complete the picture, we would also need to list the aspects each planet forms. These flesh out the scene by adding the relationship dynamics between the pertinent characters.

Recall in my own chart that Jupiter in Capricorn in the 10th not only disposes Moon in Sagittarius in the 8th, it also forms multiple aspects to other planets. To formulate a complete interpretation of Jupiter, all these aspects would need to be delineated before moving on to Jupiter's dispositor. As a planetary group, therefore, I would write out Jupiter accordingly:

> Jupiter in Capricorn in the 10th
> Significator of 8th
> Dispositor of Moon in Sagittarius in 8th
> Quincunx Mercury in Gemini in 2nd
> Quincunx Uranus in Cancer in 2nd
> Quincunx Saturn in Virgo in 5th
> Disposed by Saturn in Virgo in 5th

Note from the above list that Jupiter has several different types of relationship with Saturn: 1) it is in Saturn's house (the 10th); 2) it is in Saturn's sign (Capricorn); and 3) it is quincunx Saturn. Again, the more ways that two astrological archetypes are entangled in the chart, the more significant that theme becomes in the life story of the individual.

It is especially important when a planet forms an aspect to its dispositor. In such cases, the dispositor is not only required to help the disposed planet; it also has a personal relationship with that planet and thus a particular attitude toward it. Drawing from the example of Jupiter in Capricorn quincunx Saturn, imagine that a person aspires to a higher standard in his profession and seeks the help of a mentor to further develop certain skills. The only mentor that is available, however, knows the aspirant personally and has a problem with him. He feels that the aspirant utilizes certain methods in his work that are unethical and invalid; thus, he is predisposed to feel critical toward the aspirant and is disinclined to help him. In fact, the feelings are mutual; the aspirant is similarly critical toward the mentor from whom he is requesting help, but he has no other options. How can such a conundrum be resolved?

This is precisely the situation in my own chart. Jupiter in Capricorn in the 10th signifies my wish to aspire to a higher standard (Capricorn) as a theorist (Jupiter) in my profession (10th). To succeed, however, I must utilize the gifts of Jupiter's dispositor—Saturn in Virgo in the 5th. Ideally, Saturn's gifts will improve my capacity to think critically and develop techniques (Virgo) that can be utilized in a creative project (5th) that advances my career (10th). If all goes well, this project—a lecture, book, or academic program—will earn me a certain amount of validation and recognition from my peers. Saturn, however, makes an opening quincunx to Jupiter, which is a Virgo angle that connotes a problem to be analyzed, critiqued, and hopefully resolved. Over the years, this problem has taken a number of different forms.

As a young astrologer aspiring to become a psychotherapist, my mentors in the field of psychology could not help me because they did not understand astrology, and in fact were threatened by it; thus, they were critical of my efforts to utilize astrology as a diagnostic tool in psychotherapy. Some even felt that my use of astrology was ethically questionable and lacking validity. The feeling was mutual; I was critical of their simplistic theoretical models and inadequate therapeutic tools. Orthodox psychotherapy was too limiting, I thought. As an intern seeking licensure, however, I had no other options but to accept whatever help they had to offer.

Ironically, the reverse situation developed in my relationship to the astrological community. My training as a psychotherapist often compelled me to criticize traditional ideas and practices that I perceived as unhelpful and ethically questionable. Because the majority of my astrological colleagues do not have a similar background in psychology, my critiques were often not appreciated or supported. This rebounded upon my 10th house reputation in a problematic way.

Note in the above examples how the configuration in question signifies both a characterological predisposition and a pattern of experience that conforms to it. With regard to the outer pattern, it can be experienced in either of two ways: Sometimes it is my beliefs and practices that are criticized; other times the situation is reversed and I am the critic of other's practices and beliefs. In either case, the external condition provides a vehicle for the working through of what is essentially an intrapsychic conflict. To return to my earlier question, how *can* such a quincunxial conundrum be resolved?

As a Virgo angle, an opening quincunx not only signifies a problem, it also represents a potential solution to the problem. This generally takes the form of a method, technique, or tool that applies to the affairs of the participating planets and utilizes their respective strengths. I have already detailed some of the ways this manifested in the previous section on Jupiter quincunx Saturn, so I will not repeat them here. Suffice to say that my career reflects a concern for building a theoretical model and academic program (♃ ♑ 10th) that provides clear, cogent techniques (⚻) for utilizing astrology in a grounded, practical and efficient manner (♄ ♍). If this, in turn, provides an outlet for creative self-expression (5th house), all the better. Ideally, all of this contributes to solving a problem (⚻) that pertains to astrology's reputation within the academic community.

The central point is that when a planet forms a hard aspect to its dispositor, the nature of the conflict is compounded. In effect, the disposed planet is *ill-disposed* by virtue of being in conflict with the function that will fulfill it. To say that a planet is ill-disposed has a dual meaning. The disposed planet is ill-disposed because its dispositor is disinclined to help it—or, stated in the reverse, the dispositor is ill-disposed to help the planet it disposes. Recall that the relationship between a planet and its dispositor is one of dependency. The disposed planet relies upon its dispositor to help in the fulfillment of its need. However, if it is in conflict with that planet, it may reject the very help it requires. This is analogous to biting the hand that feeds you. The disposed planet needs its dispositor's help—yet, is resisting that help.

At the same time, consider that there are *two* types of influence occurring vis-à-vis the disposed planet. The first occurs by virtue of

349 • INTRODUCTION TO ASTROPSYCHOLOGY

the disposed planet's sign position; the occupied sign modifies and qualifies the expression of that planet. The second type of influence is received from its aspect to its dispositor. Since the dispositor shares a kinship with the sign the disposed planet occupies, there is a compounding of that sign-planet archetype on the disposed planet; thus, its influence is likely to be extreme.

This might not be a problem with a soft aspect, but a hard aspect connotes reciprocal influence with mutual resistance; thus, the dispositor's influence tends to operate unconsciously, upsetting and thwarting the aims of the planet it disposes. Since unconscious influence by definition is not consciously regulated, this can result in a problematic excess of that sign-planet archetype vis-à-vis the disposed planet. My Jupiter, for example, could be negatively impacted by *too much* Capricorn-Saturn influence. Jupiter's resultant behavior and experience is apt to reflect Capricorn-Saturn traits and themes in their more extreme, dysfunctional versions, at least initially.

An ill-disposed planet can result in backlash or *blowback*. Blowback is a negative reaction to a preceding action or cause. As a metaphor, it derives from an actual technical problem: the reverse flow of gases in a malfunctioning mechanical system. When gases travel in a direction opposite to the usual one, there is 'blowback'. In a generic sense, of course, blowback simply refers to the unintended adverse results of an action or situation. The astrological parallel is exact. The disposed planet signifies a preceding action or situation that stimulates its dispositor to respond in an adverse way that rebounds negatively on the disposed planet. Again, however, it is precisely the excess of that sign-planet archetype on the disposed planet that creates blowback, which we can understand as an attempt to redress a situation that has become too one-sided.

For example, a Fox news journalist, Chris Wallace, has Mercury in Scorpio square Pluto in Leo. Mercury in Scorpio can ask penetrating questions, but when squaring its own dispositor it can be intensely, disturbingly provocative—again, too much of a good thing. When interviewing guests, Wallace has a penchant for asking so called 'gotcha questions' – exposing where his guests are most vulnerable, watching them squirm and become defensive, and then going in for the kill. Various sources have described Wallace as an "equal opportunity inquisitor…an aggressive journalist…sharp edged, and an equal-opportunity ravager."[8] In 2006, he was in the news for his explosive interview with former President Bill Clinton. Wallace asked Clinton why, during his presidency, he did not do more to get Osama Bin Laden. An infuriated Clinton responded by shaking his finger in Wallace's face and accusing him of engaging in a right-wing hit job. One might surmise that Clinton's anger was an attempt to redress a Scorpio-Pluto imbalance in Wallace's questioning. This is blowback.

Another example is the investigative journalist John Stossel, who's Moon in Virgo opposes its dispositor, Mercury in Pisces. Stossel is famous for his contrarian views, which itself is testament to the opposition. Stossel, however, takes the concept of 'opposing view' to another level. The titles of his two books speak for themselves. *Give Me a Break: How I Exposed Hucksters, Cheats, and Scam Artists and Became the Scourge of the Liberal Media* documents his philosophical transition from liberalism to libertarianism. The book describes his opposition to government regulation and his advocacy for shifting social services from the government to private charities. His second book, *Myths, Lies, and Downright Stupidity: Get Out the Shovel — Why Everything You Know Is Wrong* dismantles conventional wisdoms while, again, exposing the ineffectiveness of government programs that purport to help victims.

Astrologically, this all makes sense when one considers that Moon Virgo symbolizes an impulse to express caring (Moon) by helping (Virgo), especially with regard to analyzing and solving problems. In so doing, however, the Moon relies upon Mercury in Pisces, which responds by implementing idealistic solutions that ultimately prove muddled and ineffective (Pisces). The primary source of such solutions, of course, is well-intentioned but misguided government policies that attempt to eliminate suffering. In Stossel's own words:

> I started out by viewing the marketplace as a cruel place, where you need intervention by government and lawyers to protect people. But after watching the regulators work, I have come to believe that markets are magical and the best protectors of the consumer. I'm a little embarrassed about how long it took me to see the folly of most government intervention. It was probably 15 years before I really woke up to the fact that almost everything government attempts to do, it makes worse.[9]

Note how the last sentence captures the essence of blowback. Moon Virgo notes the problem and asks Mercury in Pisces to intervene; yet, in doing so, Mercury actually makes the problem worse. The problem, in effect, is too much Virgo-Mercury to the point that it becomes meddlesome and ineffective. Early in his career, Stossel was complicit in perpetuating the very problems he was attempting to solve; however, as he learned from observing the consequences of his mistakes, he began expressing his Moon-Mercury opposition in a more integrated way. The very nature of his work and writings elucidate a higher, more conscious synthesis of the polarity. Stossel has won 19 Emmy Awards and was honored five times for excellence in consumer reporting by the National Press Club. About Stossel, best-selling author P.J. O'Rourke writes:

> He seeks the truths that destroy truisms, wields reason against all that's unreasonable, and ... puncture(s) sanctimonious idealism.... He makes the maddening mad. And Stossel's tales of the outrageous are outrageously amusing.[10]

O'Rourke's description captures how the aspect in question transcends its own contradiction. Stossel "wields reason against all that is unreasonable...and punctures sanctimonious idealism," an apt phrasing that perfectly expresses an integrated Moon Virgo-Mercury Pisces opposition.

Another useful example of an ill-disposed configuration is the famous comedian from the 1980's, Sam Kinison, who had Sun in Sagittarius opposed Jupiter in Gemini. As the son of an itinerant preacher, Kinison was pressured to follow in his father's footsteps. After a few years on the stump, Kinison rebelled and tried his hand at stand-up comedy. His rebellion against the role (solar identity) in which he had been cast by his father reflects the opposition between his Sun and its dispositor, Jupiter. In effect, Kinison was saying, "I have been cast in a role (preacher/Jupiter) against my will (Sun), and I oppose it!"

Utilizing to full advantage the bellowing, fire-and-brimstone style that he developed as a Pentecostal preacher, his humor largely consisted of declaring a conventional truth, then opposing it by adopting a common sense but actually juvenile position that betrayed a lack of wisdom to comedic effect. His comedic style, in other words, again reflected the nature of his opposition. His Sun expresses a higher truth (Sagittarius); then looks to Jupiter for follow-through, but Jupiter responds with a lower-level understanding (Gemini) that blows-up in his face.

In one famous rant, he began by declaring the immorality of world hunger and how people are starving in Africa. He then immediately reverses course by blaming the victim and screaming out his solution: *"It occurred to me that there wouldn't be world hunger, if you people would MOVE WHERE THE FOOD IS!!!"* as if he does not understand the larger economic, geographic, and cultural circumstances that make such a solution inane. His uninformed stupidity (Gemini) in the face of larger, more complex truths (Sagittarius) was the basis of his humor. Righteous indignation and moral outrage were exaggerated to the point of inspired lunacy.

Obviously, Kinison got the joke, which betrays a greater integration of the aspect than his comedic persona might suggest. Even so, his life was apparently one of never-ending, out-of-control excess including a prodigious appetite for drugs and alcohol. This in itself is a testament to *too much* Sagittarius-Jupiter.

More eerily, his premature death at age 38 might be a synchronistic metaphor of the aspect in question. Traveling down the highway on his way to a gig, Kinison's Pontiac Trans Am was struck head-on by a truck driven by a 17-year old male who had been drinking alcohol; however, an autopsy revealed that Kinison had cocaine and other illicit substances in his system at the time of his death. A head-on collision of two drivers both under the influence, one significantly younger than the other, mimics Kinison's comedic style and encapsulates the blow-back of his Sagittarius-Gemini opposition—the latter with chilling finality. Though I suspect if anyone could laugh at his own demise, it would be Kinison. What are the odds of a substance abusing, out-of-control comic on the fast track being killed by a substance abusing, out-of-control adolescent driving too fast?

Astrological blowback can be especially evident when two planets in mutual reception are also in hard aspect to one another. In this case, both planets dispose one another, while also being in conflict. This is the equivalent of a double-bind—or, in systems terms: a self-escalating closed system that goes into runaway mode. The latter refers to a situation in which a system becomes increasingly unstable as it attempts to correct for its instability; the more it tries to solve the problem, the worse the problem becomes.

A good example of this is Terry Ryan's Moon in Capricorn opposed Saturn in Cancer. Ryan is the author of *The Prize Winner of Defiance, Ohio*, a true story that recounts her mother's attempt to raise ten children and contend with an alcoholic, ne'er-do-well, screw-up husband. After the husband's latest binge, a priest pays the family a visit. The mother explains: "He drinks because he feels inadequate to provide for his family. But he can't provide for his family because he wastes his money on alcohol." The fact that the priest also turns out to be alcoholic only underscores the futility of the mother's situation, which is perfectly reflected in the Moon-Saturn mutual reception/ opposition.

Moon in Capricorn reflects a grim, distressing situation in which the family has limited resources but extensive needs (10 children). The Moon reaches out to Saturn for help, but Saturn can only respond in the form of an infantile, dependent father who nurses himself at the bottle like a baby sucking on his mother's tit (Cancer). His inadequacy to deal with his family's dependency on him only makes him feel worse, and drink more. The situation escalates until the family teeters on the brink of homelessness.

Terry Ryan's chart reflects the double-bind of her predicament. As a child (Moon) growing up in the 1950's, she looks to the breadwinner (Saturn/father) for a solution to their poverty, but her father's solution to the problem *is* the problem. There is no escape, just as there is no escape from her Moon Capricorn–Saturn Cancer mutual reception, which goes round and round in a closed system that periodically escalates out-of-control. Terry's mother, Evelyn Ryan, actually *does* find a solution to the problem, which expresses the same aspect at a higher level of integration. Evelyn's loving perseverance, disciplined caring, and unwavering focus on her family's needs somehow saves them, over and over.

The reverse situation applies when planets form soft aspects to their dispositors, in which case they are "well-disposed." Again, this has a dual meaning. The disposed planet is well-disposed because its dispositor is inclined to help it; and, the dispositor is well-disposed to help the planet it disposes.

An example is the American novelist, John Ehle, who wrote *The Journey of August King*. Ehle has Neptune in Leo trine the Sun in Sagittarius. In his novel, which was later made into a movie, the protagonist, August King, willingly loses everything in his efforts to save Annalees, a young runaway slave. *Publisher's Weekly* described the work as "Like a classic folk tale...full of poetry and beauty."

Set against the lush landscape of North Carolina's Appalachian mountains in the summer of 1817, August is journeying home after traveling down the mountain to purchase supplies for the winter—a steer, a boar, three geese, and sundry items. On his way home, Annalees emerges from the waters of a creek as if directly out of his unconscious. Cold, weak, and frightened, she asks for help. To rescue Annalees from the pursuing dogs and a cruel master, August must sacrifice everything he owns—including his reputation. His journey is ultimately a spiritual one that helps to heal his tragic past. The last line of the novel speaks volumes:

> *"But I tell you," he said to the graves and the wind, "I've never been so proud."*

As always, a work of fiction expresses the birthchart of its author. Note how the name 'August King' symbolizes the Leo-Sun archetype, both by virtue of August being the month of Leo, and King being a solar character. While I am sure this was not intentional, it fits. Consistent with the directional flow of energy symbolized by Neptune's dispositor, the story is essentially a journey from Neptune Leo *to* the Sun. Moreover, the opening trine is a Leo angle. So clearly the Leo-Sun archetype is central.

The story begins with August still grieving the loss of his wife, an apparent suicide for which he harbors guilt. He could not save her, nor prevent the death of their baby. Neptune, of course, has to do with tragedy, loss, guilt, sacrifice, and the impulse to relieve suffering. In saving Annalees, he was able to atone for his guilt and restore his self-esteem (Sun), which was rooted in his sense of morality (Sagittarius).

That August was *willing* (Sun) to do Neptune's bidding exemplifies how the Sun-Neptune trine is well-disposed. As a victim of slavery, Annalees embodies Neptune; August symbolizes the Sun; and the trine reflects the complete lack of resistance that August feels toward

Neptune's imperative: humiliating loss in which all his attachments are forfeited and his home burned to the ground. Rather than mourn, there is a sense of solar triumph; hence, the last line: "I've never been so proud."

SUMMARY

When doing interpretations for each planet, keep in mind that every planet triggers the function of its dispositor, which triggers its dispositor, and so on around the wheel like a relay race in which each planet hands the baton to the next. In an actual chart, however, the sequence is constantly reoccurring and forms an interminable pattern; thus, a relay race that never ends. While it may be repetitive, it is also purposive. How the native adjusts to this chronology, i.e., the level at which s/he expresses and experiences the planetary functions, reflects that person's psychological development at any given point in time.

In short, an astrological chart tells an ongoing story that tends to repeat itself in various ways throughout the course of the life. Again, one is reminded of the movie *Groundhog Day* where every morning Bill Murray wakes up to the same day, and has to relive the events of that day, until he actualizes the day's potential and eventually realizes his full capacity to love. Just so, we keep reliving the same pattern of our natal chart until we realize the full potential of our life, a process that does not stop until we take our last breath. As we evolve, so the pattern evolves, manifesting more satisfying outcomes in accordance with the growth attained.

APPENDIX I

KEYWORDS FOR SIGNS, PLANETS & HOUSES

ARIES ♈

Planetary Ruler:	Mars
Corollary House:	First
Corollary Aspect:	Conjunction
Polarity:	Yang
Element:	Fire
Modality:	Cardinal
Perspective:	Personal

Psychological Need: Survival, Being, Freedom, Independence, Immediate Gratification.

Archetype: Warrior, Pioneer, Noble Savage, Adventurer, Explorer.

Developmental Stage: Birth to 18 months. Need for basic trust. Primary Narcissism. Undifferentiated Self. Sense of omnipotence.

Behavioral Traits: Assertive, egocentric, primitive, innocent, independent, direct, energetic, decisive, initiating, impulsive, fearless, impatient.

MARS ♂

Psychological Faculty: Survival Instinct, Assertion, Aggression, Initiative, Id.

Psychological Process: To assert, to initiate, to vitalize, to act, to do, to endeavor.

Psychological States: Aliveness, *joi de vivre,* vitality, energy, impetuousness, decisiveness, omnipotence, impulsiveness, recklessness, impatience, selfishness, aggression, irritability, anger.

Environmental Events: New enterprises or projects (starts with no finish), fights, competitions, accidents, headaches, high blood pressure, mechanical ability, engineering skill, "do it yourself" type work.

FIRST HOUSE (ASCENDANT)

Surface personality, how we initiate and assert, how others see us initially (first impression), instinctual expression, spontaneous action, initial impulse, first step forward, body language, what we need and what we do to survive as a separate entity. Focus on adventure, freedom, autonomy.

TAURUS ♉

Planetary Ruler: Venus
Corollary House: Second
Corollary Aspect: Opening Semi-sextile
Polarity: Yin
Element: Earth
Modality: Fixed
Perspective: Personal

Psychological Need: Safety, Security, Stability, Sensual Gratification, Pleasure.

Archetype: Earth Mother, Fertility Goddess, Settler, Sensualist, Glutton.

Developmental Stage:18 months to 4 years. Focus on self and object constancy.

Behavioral Traits: Sensuous, attractive, materialistic, concrete, calm, stable, placid, steadfast, plodding, patient, enduring, conservative, possessive, retentive, attached, resistive to change, stubborn.

VENUS ♀

Psychological Faculty: Self and Object Constancy, Personal Security, Stability.

Psychological Process: To acquire (things), to have, to secure, to accumulate, to soothe, to comfort, to pleasure oneself, to gratify.

Psychological States: Safety, security, comfort, pleasure, serenity, equanimity, self-indulgence, laziness, lethargy, resistance, gluttony, greed.

Environmental Events: Accumulation of goods and money; experiences that provide for security, pleasure and comfort.

SECOND HOUSE

Approach to money, physical resources, possessions. That which gives pleasure, comfort and security. One's attitude toward the physical body and bodily needs (sensual gratification). Focus on attachment and ownership. Issues around safety and stability. The *way* one acquires physical security and possessions, and *what* one acquires.

GEMINI ♊

Planetary Ruler: Mercury
Corollary House: Third
Corollary Aspect: Opening Sextile
Polarity: Yang
Element: Air
Modality: Mutable
Perspective: Personal

Psychological Need: Information, Data, Factual Knowledge, Learning, Mental Stimulation, Communication, Language.

Archetype: Messenger, Herald, Reporter, Student, Amateur, Puer Aeternus.

Developmental Stage: 4 to 7 years. Learning to read & write. Stage of curiosity and language development. Explosion of learning.

Behavioral Traits: Curious, communicative, bright, precocious, restless, witty, hyperactive, knowledgeable (about factual matters), versatile, adroit, superficial, chatty, glib, fickle, light, flighty, scattered.

MERCURY ☿

Psychological Faculty: Cognition, Thinking, Intellect, Reason, Mentation, Wit.

Psychological Process: To learn, to inquire, to study, to define, to label & classify, to communicate, to report, to inform (get the message out).

Psychological States: Curiosity, interest, attentiveness, verbosity, restlessness, nervousness, hyperactivity, scatteredness.

Environmental Events: Any learning situation. Involvement in communications media — writing, reporting, journalism, research. Classifying and filing of information. Being an amateur, dilettante, or jack-of-all-trades (master of none).

THIRD HOUSE

Focus on acquiring and communicating information. Day-to-day thinking. Rote learning and early school experiences. Data gathering, writing, and reporting. Getting the message out. Short distance travel. Sibling relationships. Neighbors.

CANCER ♋

Planetary Ruler: Moon
Corollary House: Fourth
Corollary Aspect: Opening Square
Polarity: Yin
Element: Water
Modality: Cardinal
Perspective: Personal

Psychological Need: Nurturing, Care, Tenderness, Unconditional Love, Belonging, Sympathetic Understanding, Closeness, Emotional Support.

Archetype: Mother, Caretaker, Dependents, Wombs, Containers.

Developmental Stage: 8 to 12 years. Period of introspection. Consolidation of super-ego (self-inhibition). Capacity to contain & reflect on feelings.

Behavioral Traits: Nurturing, caring, protective, tender, soft, sensitive, gentle, receptive, mirroring, reactive, impressionable, indirect, shy, timid, introverted, sentimental, vulnerable, dependent.

MOON ☽

Psychological Faculty: Receptive Function, Listening Response, Nurturing Faculty, Memory, Personal Unconscious.

Psychological Process: To nurture and protect, to listen and understand, to reflect, to sympathize, and love unconditionally.

Psychological States: Loving feelings, belonging, closeness, warmth and tenderness. Vulnerability to rejection, dependency, self-protectiveness.

Environmental Events: Relations with mother/women. Restaurant work, caretaking work, any activity that involves nurturing & protecting (feeding, housing, or providing emotional support).

FOURTH HOUSE

Mother, personal past, nesting experience, family, roots, foundations, early childhood experiences of nurturing, home, domestic conditions (past and present). Sense of belonging. Real estate and other activities having to do with the land, or homeland (patriotism).

LEO ♌

Planetary Ruler: Sun
Corollary House: Fifth
Corollary Aspect: Opening Trine
Polarity: Yang
Element: Fire
Modality: Fixed
Perspective: Social

Psychological Need: Validation of Identity, Self-esteem, Approval, Attention, Creative Self-expression, Enjoyment of Self and Others.

Archetype: Hero, Star Performer, Romantic, Peacock, Playmate.

Developmental Stage: 12 to 18 years. Consolidation of identity. Separation from family matrix. Emphasis on peer relations.

Behavioral Traits: Proud, confident, playful, affable, magnanimous, creative, expressive, dramatic, positive, overbearing, showy, boastful, naive (uncritical), egocentric, defensive, prideful.

SUN ☉

Psychological Faculty: Ego, Identity, Self-Concept, Creativity, Intention, Will, Volition.

Psychological Process: To create, to express, to intend, to choose, to play, to validate (others), to impress (seek approval), to defend (self), to romance.

Psychological States: Pride and Self-esteem (vs. Shame), Confidence (vs. Self-doubt), Playfulness, Willfulness, Vitality, Creativity, Huberis.

Environmental Events: Father/Men, Play and Playmates, Fun and Games, Romance & Courtship, Good Times, Sports, Hedonism, Extravagance.

FIFTH HOUSE

Creative self-expression or performance via theater, teaching, or the arts. Subjective perception of "audience," e.g., fans, spectators, supporters, detractors. Experiences of validation or invalidation, especially through romance and courtship. One's romantic interest. All forms of play and recreation—parties, vacation, fun & games, entertainment, sports, gambling, and speculation. Playmates, bosom buddies. The results of creativity, including one's children.

VIRGO ♍

Planetary Ruler: Mercury
Corollary House: Sixth
Corollary Aspect: Opening Quincunx
Polarity: Yin
Element: Earth
Modality: Mutable
Perspective: Social

Psychological Need: Efficiency, Competency, Service, Improvement.

Archetype: Efficiency Expert, Troubleshooter, Fix-it Man, Apprentice/ Novice, Doubting Thomas, Analyst, Critic, Worry Wart, Spinster.

Developmental Stage: 19 to 26 years. Novice stage of adulthood. Period of apprenticeship. Developing a skill and entering work force.

Behavioral Traits: Efficient, competent, pragmatic, conscientious, helpful, technical, precise, systematic, orderly, humble, modest, skeptical, restrained, analytical, discriminating, critical, picky, fastidious, meticulous.

MERCURY ☿

Psychological Faculty: Cognition, Intellect. Discrimination. Analysis. Problem Solving.

Psychological Process: To analyze and criticize, to reduce (to parts), to correct or fix, to problem solve, to improve, to serve, to discriminate.

Psychological States: Feeling useful/productive. State of efficiency/ competence. Negative, critical mind-set. Worrying, analyzing, obsessing.

Environmental Events: Problems that need solving. Things that need fixing. Mistakes that need correcting. Any kind of work or service, especially crafts, trades, merchandising, and the health field, e.g., diet and nutrition.

SIXTH HOUSE

Mundane, day-to-day responsibilities—chores, tasks, attending to details. Health and hygiene. Repair and maintenance department. Work and relations with co-workers/employees. Being of service to the community. Focus on tasks and getting the job done. Employment.

LIBRA ♎

Planetary Ruler: Venus
Corollary House: Seventh
Corollary Aspect: Opposition
Polarity: Yang
Element: Air
Modality: Cardinal
Perspective: Social

Psychological Need: Harmony, Beauty, Intimacy, Companionship, Relatedness, Fairness.

Archetype: Love Goddess, Beloved, Peacemaker, Mediator, Diplomat, Public Relations Person, Networker, Social Butterfly, Artist.

Developmental Stage: 26 to 35 years. Emergence into full adult status as "social equal." Increased ethical sense. Partnership. Networking.

Behavioral Traits: Engaging, charming, nice, sociable, polite, tactful, graceful, aesthetic, appealing, kind, fair, just, impartial, considerate, cooperative, placating, superficial, compliant, indecisive, equivocating.

VENUS ♀

Psychological Faculty: Aesthetic Function ("taste"), Artistic Sense, Social Ability.

Psychological Process: To beautify, to harmonize; to cooperate, to consider; to mediate, to negotiate; to attract and engage; to socialize.

Psychological States: Love and affection; intimacy, harmony, cooperation; grace and charm; aesthetic appreciation, love of beauty; serenity, equanimity; overdependency on others for love and connection.

Environmental Events: All relationships of partnership or cooperation with "equal others." Contracts, agreements (or conflicts, lawsuits); social connections and networking; pursuit of beauty, artistic endeavors.

SEVENTH HOUSE

Partner or open enemy. The "not-self," i.e., qualities we project, attract, and evoke in other people. Contracts and agreements. Marriage/divorce. Public relations and networking in general. Ability to socialize and conform to social amenities. Social contract. Art, beauty, aesthetics.

SCORPIO ♏

Planetary Ruler: Pluto
Corollary House: Eighth
Corollary Aspect: Closing Quincunx
Polarity: Yin
Element: Water
Modality: Fixed
Perspective: Social

Psychological Need: Transformation, Healing, Reform, Catharsis, Elimination, Sex. Power through union with the unknown. Integrity.

Archetype: Wounded Healer, Shaman, Shadow Figures, Monsters & Villains, Underworld Figures, Erotic Types, Tyrants, The Stranger.

Developmental Stage: 35 to 45. Mid-life crisis. Facing one's mortality and unlived self. Self-renewal. Becoming authentic. Owning one's power.

Behavioral Traits: Erotic, provocative, penetrating, suspicious, guarded, intense, deep, passionate, powerful, controlling, dangerous, covert, tactical, manipulative, vindictive, extreme, exposing, regenerative.

PLUTO ♇

Psychological Faculty: Sexuality, Eros, Power, Healing Function.

Psychological Process: To penetrate, to integrate; to transform, to heal, to regenerate; to purify, to cleanse, to eliminate; to distrust; to control, to coerce, to dominate; to scheme, to sabotage, to destroy.

Psychological States: Crisis, Fear, Paranoia. Trauma, Pain & Suffering. Aroused, Passion, Possessed. Intensity, Focus, Power, Integrity.

Environmental Events: Dealing with crises, facing one's fears. Power struggles, control issues. Tyranny, crime, subversion, evil. Descent to the underworld and confronting the shadow. Healing or reforming work.

EIGHTH HOUSE

Sexuality. Crisis intervention work (paramedics, firemen, police). Healing relationships (doctors, therapists). Shared financial relationships (investments, taxes, debts). Personal taboos, shadows, and wounds. Interest in matters pertaining to danger, death, the occult, or simply the unknown.

SAGITTARIUS ♐

Planetary Ruler: Jupiter
Corollary House: Ninth
Corollary Aspect: Closing Trine
Polarity: Yang
Element: Fire
Modality: Mutable
Perspective: Universal

Psychological Need: Truth, Meaning, Purpose, Justice, Virtue, Morality, Expansion, Hope, Faith, Belief in a Higher Power

Archetype: Teacher, Guru, Demagogue, Moralist, Pollyanna, Promoter.

Developmental Stage: 45 to 56 years. Age of wisdom and influence, insightfulness and philosophic concern. True integrity. Grandparent.

Behavioral Traits: Jovial, enthusiastic, optimistic, philosophical, opinionated, truthful, frank, moralistic, righteous, persuasive, expansive, travel-loving, benevolent, philanthropic, excessive, grandiose, manic.

JUPITER ♃

Psychological Faculty: Judgment, Morality, Faith, Hope.

Psychological Process: To judge, to theorize, to interpret (explain); to teach, to preach, to affirm as right or true; to predict; to trust, to hope, to have faith; to expand or broaden; to overextend and exaggerate.

Psychological States: Hope, optimism, faith, enthusiasm, great expectations (fairy godmother complex), trust in the Universe; wisdom, foresight; grandiosity, dogmatism, extravagance, blind optimism, mania.

Environmental Events: Luck, philanthropic activities, acts of influencing or persuading, religious or philosophical practices, encounters with teachers, consequences of excess or extravagance.

NINTH HOUSE

Experiences in higher education, philosophy, or religion. Approach to matters of faith, ideology, ethics, and values. Encounters with teachers. Truth seeking. Scholarship. Concerns about justice and legality. Dissemination of knowledge through teaching, publishing, promotion, or advertising. Travel, sacred journeys.

CAPRICORN ♑

Planetary Ruler: Saturn
Corollary House: Tenth
Corollary Aspect: Closing Square
Polarity: Yin
Element: Earth
Modality: Cardinal
Perspective: Universal

Psychological Need: Perfection, Success, Structure, Order, Control.

Archetype: Senex, Authority Figure, Control Freak, Scrooge.

Developmental Stage: 56 to 68. Highest career achievement. Zenith of one's life. Antithesis of success is despair and regret. Final reckoning.

Behavioral Traits: Serious, reserved, formal, ambitious, persevering, perfectionistic, exacting, focused, fastidious, orderly, organized, disciplined, planful, practical, realistic, traditional, conservative, prudent, callous, grim.

SATURN ♄

Psychological Faculty: Sense of Duty. Ambition, Self-Discipline, Self-Control, Limits.

Psychological Process: To achieve, to succeed, to persevere; to structure, to order, to manage; to plan, to control; to perfect, to master; to fear, to inhibit, to restrict, to contract; to deprive, to crave, to overcompensate.

Psychological States: Successful, mission accomplished, patient, in control, determined, dutiful, obligated, pressured, driven, inferior, inadequate, deficient, negative, pessimistic, gloomy, lonely, despairing.

Environmental Events: Experiences of limitation, delay, deficiency, obstacles, blocks, and restrictions. Responsibilities, duties; Success through perseverance, or failure through procrastination and fear.

TENTH HOUSE

Career, vocation, dominant goal. Potential for success. Ultimate impact one has upon society. Reputation, public image, honors, status, distinctions. Dominant other, attitudes toward authority and limits. Father, bosses, superiors. Capacity for and the way one handles authority.

AQUARIUS ♒

Planetary Ruler: Uranus
Corollary House: Eleventh
Corollary Aspect: Closing Sextile
Polarity: Yang
Element: Air
Modality: Fixed
Perspective: Universal

Psychological Need: Awakening, Revelation, Perspective, Liberation, Change, Progress.

Archetype: Trickster, Objective Witness, Prometheus, Revolutionary, Radical, Humanitarian, Utopian Visionary, Mad Scientist, Eccentric.

Developmental Stage: 68 to 80 years. Seeing one's life as a whole. Radical objectivity. Eccentricity of old age. Outspokenness. Detachment.

Behavioral Traits: Detached, objective, cool, whimsical, broadminded, non-judgmental, impersonal, eccentric, original, innovative, progressive, humanitarian, altruistic, rebellious, outspoken, enlightening, shocking.

URANUS ♅

Psychological Faculty: Observing Ego, Objective Witness, Universal Mind, Altruism, Wholistic Thinking, Radical Insight, Capacity for Change.

Psychological Process: To awaken, to enlighten, to liberate, to change, to progress, to advance, to rebel, to agitate, to disrupt.

Psychological States: Altruistic love (agape), sudden flash of insight, realization, detached overview, choiceless awareness, liberation, dissent, agitation, upset, startled, shock, instability, schizoid detachment.

Environmental Events: Sudden change, instability, the unexpected. Something bizarre, strange, extraordinary. Anything involving advanced technology. A revolution or breakthrough or breakdown.

ELEVENTH HOUSE

Ideals and aspirations for humanity as a whole. Friends of like mind bound together for acommon cause. Movements, humanitarian concerns, group associations. Activities on the cutting edge of change. Colleagues and associates. Progressive ideas, hopes, altruistic acts.

PISCES ♓

Planetary Ruler:	Neptune
Corollary House:	Twelfth
Corollary Aspect:	Closing Semi-Sextile
Polarity:	Yin
Element:	Water
Modality:	Mutable
Perspective:	Universal

Psychological Need: Transcendence, Unity, Infinite Love & Beauty, Oneness with nature.

Archetype: Mystic, Rescuer, Martyr, Victim, Poet, Dreamer, Fraud.

Developmental Stage: 80 to end of life. Diffuse awareness. Confusion, deterioration, loss, senility, infirmity, decay.

Behavioral Traits: Passive, submissive, delicate, dreamy, yielding, compassionate, empathic, forgiving, sensitive, vague, confused, vacillating, imaginative, idealistic, escapist, spiritual, intuitive.

NEPTUNE ♆

Psychological Faculty: Imagination, Empathy, Dreams, Intuition.

Psychological Process: To transcend, to surrender, to sacrifice; to empathize, to rescue; to imagine, to dream, to inspire; to escape, to deny; to vacillate, to sabotage, to confuse, to mystify, to deceive.

Psychological States: Selfless love, unitive awareness, empathy, compassion, forgiveness, guilt (often unconscious), passivity, confusion, delusion, weakness, grief, victimization, helplessness.

Environmental Events: Spiritual pursuits, aspiring to an ideal; rescuing victims; victim of fraud or deceit; losses, endings, working with grief; use of the imagination, imagistic art forms (film, painting).

TWELFTH HOUSE

The collective unconscious, mysticism. Service of a selfless or spiritual nature. Charity work. Places of solitude & escape—retreats, the wilderness. Places of incarceration—hospitals, shelters, prisons. Sacrifice, victimization, self-undoing. Transcendent creativity—poetry, film, music, dance. Working with the unconscious, dream analysis, intuition training, psi phenomena.

REFERENCES

Averill, J.R. (1980). The emotions. In E. Staub (Ed.) *Personality: Basic aspects and current research* (pp. 133-199). Englewood Cliffs, NJ: Prentice Hall

Deci, E.L. (1980). Intrinsic motivation and personality. In E. Staub (Ed.) *Personality:*

Basic aspects and current research (pp. 35-80). Englewood Cliffs, NJ: Prentice Hall

Dobyns, Zipporah (1973). *Finding the person in the horoscope.* Los Angeles: T.I.A. Publications

Campbell, J. (1949). *The hero with a thousand faces.* New York: Bollingen Foundation

Erikson, E.H. (1968). *Identity, youth and crisis.* New York: W.W. Norton & Company

Goleman, D. (1995). *Emotional intelligence.* New York: Bantam

Grasse, R. (1996). *The waking dream.* Wheaton, IL: Quest Books

Hall, C., & Lindzey, G. (1978). *Theories of personality.* New York: John Wiley & Sons

Hall, M.P. (1954). *The essential nature of consciousness.* Los Angeles: Philosophical-Research Society

Horowitz, M.J. (1987). *States of mind: Configurational analysis of individual psychology.* New York: Plenum Medical Book Company

Idemon, Richard. (1988). "Astrology and the Quest for a Universal Psychological

Model," *The Astrotherapy Newsletter,* Vol. 1, No. 1, January, 1988, p. 6

Jones, J. (1995). *Affects as process.* Hillsdale, NJ: The Analytic Press

Jung, C.G. (1926). *The development of personality. Collected Works,* Vol 17, pp. 324-345

Jung, C.G. (1955). Synchronicity: An acausal connecting principle. In C. Jung & W. Pauli, *The interpretation of nature and psyche* (pp. 1-146). New York: Pantheon

Jung, C.G. (1960). *The structure and dynamics of the psyche.* Collected Works, Vol. 8, Bollingen Series 20. New York: Pantheon

Jung, C.G. (1961). *Memories, Dreams, Reflections.* New York: Vintage Books

Lichtenberg, J. *Psychoanalysis and motivation.* Hillsdale, NJ: The Analytic Press

Maslow, A. (1968). *Toward a psychology of being.* Princeton, NJ: Van Nostrand

Miller, G.A., Galanter, E., & Pribram, K.A. (1960). *Plans and the structure of behavior.* NY: Holt.

Perry, G. (2012). *Stealing fire from the gods: myth and method in astrological research.* East Hampton, CT: AAP Press

Perry, G. (2012a). *Depth analysis of the natal chart: advanced therapeutic astrology.* East Hampton, CT: AAP Press

Perry, G. (2012b). *Issues & ethics in the profession of astrology.* East Hampton, CT: AAP Press

Perry, G. (2012c). *Mapping the Landscape of the Soul: Essays in Psychological Astrology.* East Hampton, CT: AAP Press

Sakoian, F., Acker, L. (1973). *The Astrologer's Handbook.* New York: Harper & Row

Pike, D.K. (1997). *Life is a waking dream.* New York: Riverhead Books

Whitehead, A. (1925). *Science and the modern world.* New York: Free Press

Wilber, K. (1981). *Up from Eden.* Garden City, NY: Doubleday

ENDNOTES

1   Dobyns, 1973, p. 21

2   Jung, 1961, p. 13-14

3   Perry, 2012. Stealing Fire from the Gods

4   See Chris Wallace Bio on the Fox News website: http://www.foxnews.com/on-air/personalities/chris-wallace/bio/#s=r-z

5   Sigall, Ed (2006-06-03). "John Stossel: Not Afraid to Tell the Truth". NewsMax. Retrieved 2007-09-24

6   "John Stossel – Libertarian". Advocates for Self-Government. Archived from the original on July 2, 2007. Retrieved 2007-07-10

7   Perry, 2012. Stealing Fire from the Gods

8   See Chris Wallace Bio on the Fox News website: http://www.foxnews.com/on-air/personalities/chris-wallace/bio/#s=r-z

9   Sigall, Ed (2006-06-03). "John Stossel: Not Afraid to Tell the Truth". NewsMax. Retrieved 2007-09-24

10   "John Stossel - Libertarian". Advocates for Self-Government. Archived from the original on July 2, 2007. Retrieved 2007-07-10

Made in United States
North Haven, CT
12 February 2025

65735947R00231